A Beginner's Guide to the Later Philosophy of Wittgenstein

ANTHEM STUDIES IN WITTGENSTEIN

Anthem Studies in Wittgenstein publishes new and classic works on Wittgenstein and Wittgensteinian philosophy. This book series aims to bring Wittgenstein's thought into the mainstream by highlighting its relevance to 21st-century concerns. Titles include original monographs, themed edited volumes, forgotten classics, biographical works and books intended to introduce Wittgenstein to the general public. The series is published in association with the British Wittgenstein Society.

Anthem Studies in Wittgenstein sets out to put in place whatever measures may emerge as necessary in order to carry out the editorial selection process purely on merit and to counter bias on the basis of gender, race, ethnicity, religion, sexual orientation and other characteristics protected by law. These measures include subscribing to the British Philosophical Association/Society for Women in Philosophy (UK) Good Practice Scheme.

Series Editor

Constantine Sandis – University of Hertfordshire, UK

Forthcoming Titles in the Series

Political Authority: Contract and Critique

Kripke's Wittgenstein: Meaning, Rules, and Scepticism

Wittgenstein on Other Minds: Strangers in a Strange Land

Wittgenstein and Popular Culture

Nightmariners and Wideawakes: The Philosophy of Dreams

A Beginner's Guide to the Later Philosophy of Wittgenstein

Seventeen Lectures and Dialogues on the *Philosophical Investigations*

P. M. S. Hacker

ANTHEM PRESS

Anthem Press
An imprint of Wimbledon Publishing Company
www.anthempress.com

This edition first published in UK and USA 2024
by ANTHEM PRESS
75–76 Blackfriars Road, London SE1 8HA, UK
or PO Box 9779, London SW19 7ZG, UK
and
244 Madison Ave #116, New York, NY 10016, USA

© 2024 Peter Hacker

The author asserts the moral right to be identified as the author of this work.
All rights reserved. Without limiting the rights under copyright reserved above,
no part of this publication may be reproduced, stored or introduced into
a retrieval system, or transmitted, in any form or by any means
(electronic, mechanical, photocopying, recording or otherwise),
without the prior written permission of both the copyright
owner and the above publisher of this book.

British Library Cataloguing-in-Publication Data
A catalogue record for this book is available from the British Library.

Library of Congress Cataloging-in-Publication Data: 2023948892
A catalog record for this book has been requested.

ISBN-13: 978-1-83999-113-4 (Hbk)
ISBN-10: 1-83999-113-5 (Hbk)

ISBN-13: 978-1-83999-114-1 (Pbk)
ISBN-10: 1-83999-114-3 (Pbk)

Cover Credit: Labyrinth Calligraphy Maze, public domain

This title is also available as an e-book.

For
Peter Lawlor
and
Constantine Sandis

But for whom not

CONTENTS

Preface		ix
1	Introduction	1
2	Augustine's Picture of Language and the Referential Conception of Linguistic Meaning	17
3	Names and Their Meaning, Sentences and Descriptions	35
4	Meaning and Use, Understanding and Interpreting	53
5	Ostensive Definition and Family Resemblance: Undermining the Foundations and Destroying the Essences	75
6	Metaphysics, Necessity and Grammar	91
7	Thought and Language	111
8	The Private Language Arguments	127
9	Private Ownership of Experience	143
10	Epistemic Privacy of Experience	159
11	Private Ostensive Definition	177
12	My Mind and Other Minds	197
13	The Inner and the Outer – Behaviour and Behaviourism	215
14	'Only of a Human Being and What Behaves like a Human Being …': The Mereological Fallacy and Cognitive Neuroscience	233
15	Wittgenstein's Conception of Philosophy - I	253
16	Wittgenstein's Conception of Philosophy - II	271

17 Wittgenstein's Conception of Philosophy - III	291
Abbreviations	309
Further Reading	311
Index	313

PREFACE

The *Philosophical Investigations* (1953) is one of the most revolutionary philosophical works ever written. It ploughs up the fields of philosophical thought on the nature of language and linguistic meaning, on the relation between language and reality, on metaphysics, on the relation between language and thinking, on the nature of the mind, on self-knowledge and knowledge of others, and on the nature of philosophy itself. On each subject, Wittgenstein dug down to the roots of our reflections, exposing our tacit, often mistaken, presuppositions.

Wittgenstein wrote the *Investigations* in a laid-back colloquial style. It is easy to see what he says. On the other hand, it is difficult to understand why he says what he says. It is also easy to misinterpret what he wrote and to ascribe to him views that he did not hold. It is not surprising that misinterpretations of Wittgenstein's ideas are common among twenty-first century philosophers, who are more eager to dismiss his views than to understand what they are.

Having spent more than 25 years working intensively on Wittgenstein's philosophy in general, and on the *Investigations* in particular, and reaching the end of my long career of teaching and writing philosophy, it seemed to me that I was at long last ready to publish a beginner's guide to some of the central themes in his masterpiece. What I present here is not a textbook. It does not examine the multitudinous interpretations of Wittgenstein (I have done that in great detail in a dozen other books), although widespread criticisms of Wittgenstein are examined and refuted. It does not attempt to examine all the major themes in the *Investigations* – but only those that, in my judgement, are the most likely to interest beginners. So, for example, I have not discussed Wittgenstein's important scrutiny of the concept of following a rule, for that is too difficult and unlikely to excite the imaginations of those I wish to guide around select landmarks in his book. What I have written is directed at open-minded readers, who know no philosophy but who are willing to grapple with Wittgenstein's radical arguments in order to gain insight into subjects that are of concern to any thinking person. Undergraduates taking a course on the philosophy of the later Wittgenstein would likewise benefit from this volume as background reading, as would anyone taking an A-level course in philosophy. It is also directed at those who are prepared to begin again, to approach the book afresh – to entertain the thought that maybe their preconceptions and prejudices on language and meaning, on human nature and the nature of thinking, on the mind and the body, need comprehensive revision. Such readers need a guide to find pathways through the jungle, to help them over the crevices and crevasses, and to provide pitons on the rock face. I hope that when my readers emerge from this intellectual journey with me, high up the mountain, they will find a sunlit view of the landscape of language, thought and the mind.

P. M. S. H.
St John's College,
Oxford, 2023

PREFACE

The *Philosophical Investigations* (1953) is one of the most revolutionary philosophical works ever written. It ploughs up the fields of philosophical thought on the nature of language and linguistic meaning, on the relation between language and reality, on metaphysics, on the relation between language and thinking, on the nature of the mind, on self-knowledge and knowledge of others, and on the nature of philosophy itself. On each subject, Wittgenstein dug down to the roots of our reflections, exposing our tacit, often mistaken, presuppositions.

Wittgenstein wrote the *Investigations* in a laid-back colloquial style. It is easy to see what he says. On the other hand, it is difficult to understand why he says what he says. It is also easy to misinterpret what he wrote and to ascribe to him views that he did not hold. It is not surprising that misinterpretations of Wittgenstein's ideas are common among twenty-first century philosophers, who are more eager to dismiss his views than to understand what they are.

Having spent more than 25 years working intensively on Wittgenstein's philosophy in general, and on the *Investigations* in particular, and reaching the end of my long career of teaching and writing philosophy, it seemed to me that I was at long last ready to publish a beginner's guide to some of the central themes in his masterpiece. What I present here is not a textbook. It does not examine the multitudinous interpretations of Wittgenstein (I have done that in great detail in a dozen other books), although widespread criticisms of Wittgenstein are examined and refuted. It does not attempt to examine all the major themes in the *Investigations* – but only those that, in my judgement, are the most likely to interest beginners. So, for example, I have not discussed Wittgenstein's important scrutiny of the concept of following a rule, for that is too difficult and unlikely to excite the imaginations of those I wish to guide around select landmarks in his book. What I have written is directed at open-minded readers, who know no philosophy but who are willing to grapple with Wittgenstein's radical arguments in order to gain insight into subjects that are of concern to any thinking person. Undergraduates taking a course on the philosophy of the later Wittgenstein would likewise benefit from this volume as background reading, as would anyone taking an A-level course in philosophy. It is also directed at those who are prepared to begin again, to approach the book afresh – to entertain the thought that maybe their preconceptions and prejudices on language and meaning, on human nature and the nature of thinking, on the mind and the body, need comprehensive revision. Such readers need a guide to find pathways through the jungle, to help them over the crevices and crevasses, and to provide pitons on the rock face. I hope that when my readers emerge from this intellectual journey with me, high up the mountain, they will find a sunlit view of the landscape of language, thought and the mind.

P. M. S. H.
St John's College,
Oxford, 2023

Chapter 1

INTRODUCTION

Wittgenstein – Life and Works

Ludwig Wittgenstein was born in 1889 in Vienna, the eighth child of Karl and Leopoldine Wittgenstein. The family was of Jewish descent, although they had converted to Catholicism a generation earlier. Karl Wittgenstein was the leading Austrian steel baron – the Carnegie of the Austrian steel industry – and one of the wealthiest men in the Austro-Hungarian Empire. He was a great patron of the arts, and the family's palatial home in Vienna was the leading music salon there at the turn of the century. Brahms was a friend of the family, Mahler frequented the house, and Bruno Walter, Joseph Joachim and young Pablo Casals all played at the Wittgenstein musical evenings. Young Ludwig was brought up in an *haute-bourgeois* family of great cultivation and refined sensibility, wide intellectual and artistic interests, and a powerful sense of social and moral obligation.

Wittgenstein was taught at home by private tutors until the age of 14, after which he went to school in Linz. After graduating from high school, he went to study for a diploma in engineering at a technical college in Berlin. He completed the diploma course in 1908. Having become interested in the budding science of aeronautics, he went to Manchester University to do research on flight and subsequently on a jet reaction propeller. It was while doing this that he came across, and became fascinated by, the writings of Gottlob Frege and of Bertrand Russell on the philosophy of logic and mathematics. The upshot was that he went to Trinity College, Cambridge in 1911 to read for an advanced degree under the supervision of Russell. Russell later described him at this period as being 'perhaps the most perfect example I have known of genius as traditionally conceived, passionate, profound, intense and dominating'.[1] Within six months, the two men were discussing philosophy as equals, and Russell looked upon Wittgenstein as his successor

---

1 Russell, *Autobiography* (George Allen and Unwin, London, 1956), vol. 2, pp. 98f.

in philosophical research.² Between 1913 and early 1917, Wittgenstein worked on composing materials for his first philosophical masterpiece: the *Tractatus Logico-Philosophicus*. In this work, he confronted the views of his two great predecessors and mentors, the German mathematical logician Gottlob Frege and Bertrand Russell, undermining their conceptions of logic as a science with a subject matter. Both Frege and Russell thought that the mark of a logical proposition was complete generality. Frege held logic to be the science of the most general laws of truth. Hence, in his view, 'Either it is raining or it is not raining' is not a proposition of logic but an *instance* of the proposition of logic that every proposition is either true or false. Logic, he held, is the science of the most general laws of thought, laws that govern all thinking if we wish to reason truly. Russell agreed that the propositions of logic are marked by perfect generality, but he thought them to be the most general truths there are about reality. The laws of logic are general truths about the ultimate logical forms of reality. They govern relations between such entities as particulars, universals, relations, dual complexes and such like that are the ultimate constituents of the universe. By contrast, Wittgenstein argued that the mark of logical propositions is not generality but necessity. He demonstrated that the logical propositions of the propositional calculus are vacuous tautologies that say nothing about reality. They are senseless, that is, limiting cases of propositions with a sense. They describe nothing. He showed that logic is not a *science* that yields knowledge of reality in any shape or form, neither of a 'third world' of thoughts (as Frege held) nor of the actual world (as Russell believed). It is rather a calculus of propositions.

With the outbreak of the First World War, Wittgenstein volunteered for service in the Austrian army. For him, the war was a personal test, and he believed that he could only discover his true worth when confronting the danger of death. He served both on the Russian and the Italian fronts and was decorated a number of times for gallantry. His intense preoccupation with the problems of philosophy did not cease during his military service at the front. He completed writing most of the material for the *Tractatus* in 1916 and spent the next three years arranging his remarks in a highly complex numerical system that generates a hypertext which perspicuously presents the order of the thoughts expressed in the form of a logical tree.³ The *Tractatus* was published in Britain in 1922, in a bi-lingual edition with an introduction

---

2 Hermine Wittgenstein, 'My Brother Ludwig', in F. A. Flowers III and Ian Ground (eds.), *Portraits of Wittgenstein* (Bloomsbury, London), vol. 1, p. 122.
3 Set forth in Luciano Bazzocchi's centenary edition of *Tractatus Logico-Philosophicus* (Anthem Press, London, 2021).

by Russell. The book quickly established Wittgenstein's reputation as one of the leading philosophers of the age. His friend, John Maynard Keynes, the great economist, wrote to him from Cambridge:

> I still don't know what to say about your book, except that I feel certain that it is a work of extraordinary importance and genius. Right or wrong, it dominates all fundamental discussion at Cambridge since it was written.[4]

In the meantime, however, Wittgenstein had abandoned philosophy and rid himself of all his inherited wealth. After taking a teacher's training course, he became a primary school teacher. In a Tolstoyan spirit, he went to teach peasant children in small mountain villages in Lower Austria. He did this for six years, but the experience was an unhappy one. He returned to Vienna in 1926 and was persuaded to cooperate with his architect friend Paul Engelmann in designing and building a mansion for his sister Margarete. He rapidly took over the project – and the austerely beautiful house that he built can still be seen in Vienna. It was during this period that he encountered the Vienna Circle, a group of scientifically minded philosophers under the leadership of Moritz Schlick. The Vienna Circle was the source of the philosophical movement known as logical positivism or logical empiricism. Members of the Circle were greatly influenced by the *Tractatus*. Indeed, they had spent two years of their meetings, in 1924 and again in 1926, reading the book together line by line. Schlick wrote of the *Tractatus* that it was 'the most significant philosophical work of our time' and remarked that Wittgenstein was 'the greatest genius of all time in logic' (i.e. the philosophy of logic) – for he made clear, for the first time, the true nature of logic and logical propositions. Jörgensen, writing the official history of the Circle years later, observed that the ideas of the *Tractatus* 'have, on essential points determined the view of the Circle on philosophy and its relation to the special sciences' and remarked that the book 'contributed essentially to the formation of logical positivism and provoked both agreement and disagreement'.

In 1929, after having completed the architectural work for his sister, Wittgenstein decided to return to Cambridge in order to resume work on philosophy. He found this congenial. In order to obtain support for his research from Trinity College, he had to have a higher degree. Fortunately, those days were more liberal than ours and he was allowed to submit the *Tractatus* in lieu of writing a doctorate. He was examined by Russell and G. E. Moore. The oral examination for the doctorate consisted of an amicable chat with his two

---

4 J. M. Keynes, letter to Wittgenstein, 29 March 1924, repr. in B. F. McGuinness, ed., *Wittgenstein in Cambridge, Letter and Documents 1911-1951* (Blackwell, Oxford, 2008), p. 151.

old friends, who did, after a while, ask him some questions about the famous book. Wittgenstein in due course brought the viva to an end by jumping to his feet, clapping Moore and Russell on the shoulders and exclaiming 'Don't worry, I know you'll never understand it!'. In his examiner's report, Moore wrote:

> It is my personal opinion that Mr Wittgenstein's thesis is a work of genius; but be that as it may, it is certainly well up to the standard required for the Cambridge degree of Doctor of Philosophy.

In 1930, Wittgenstein was appointed to a university post. He lectured in Cambridge, with occasional breaks, from 1930 until his retirement in 1947. In 1938, he was appointed as successor to Moore in one of the two chairs in philosophy at Cambridge. C. D. Broad – the holder of the other chair and no friend of Wittgenstein – remarked at the time of the election that to refuse the chair to Wittgenstein would be like refusing a chair in physics to Einstein.

Between 1929 and 1932, Wittgenstein's ideas underwent a dramatic change, which he consolidated over the next 15 years. Reacting against his own early philosophy, he developed a quite different viewpoint. Initially communicated only through pupils who attended his legendary classes in Cambridge, these ideas revolutionized philosophy in the mid-twentieth century. Although he published nothing, his new philosophy was transmitted to others by his pupils, many of whom became leading philosophers of the next generation.

Between 1929 and 1944, more than a third of his work was on the philosophy of mathematics. This project, however, was never completed. His primary endeavour was to compose a major work that would stand in contrast to the *Tractatus* and present his new philosophy. In 1932/33, he dictated a 768-page typescript which was meant as the basis for a major book, but after having tried to redraft it twice, it was abandoned. In 1934/35, he essayed a dictation in English to a couple of his students, which he hoped would be the foundation for the presentation of his new ideas, but after translating it back into German, he rejected it as 'worthless'. In 1936/37, he managed to produce a typescript which did not altogether dissatisfy him. It became the first draft of the *Philosophical Investigations*. But over the next nine years, it underwent three more thorough-going revisions and extensions before completion in 1946. Even then he felt dissatisfied with it and refused to publish it. It was published posthumously in 1953, two years after his death, and was immediately hailed as a masterpiece. Peter Strawson, himself destined to become one of the leading philosophers of the latter half of the twentieth century, characterized the book as 'a treatment, by a philosopher of genius, of a number of intricate problems, intricately connected' and later added

> He has an extraordinary, almost unique power of dispelling philosophical illusion, of helping us to get a clear view of how our language, and hence our thought, *actually works* [...] it would be hard to mention any other twentieth-century philosopher who is likely to have such a profound and lasting influence.

And Gilbert Ryle, the leading Oxford philosopher of the day, wrote:

> I do not think that anybody could read the *Philosophical Investigations* without feeling that its author had his finger on the pulse of the activity of philosophizing.

The book dealt with great philosophical themes: the nature of language and linguistic representation, the scope and limits of philosophy, the nature of rules and of the following of rules, the existence of rules in a human practice, the critical repudiation of the idea that language has foundations in subjective experience, the relation between mental phenomena and behaviour, the nature of thought and imagination and their relation to language and mastery of language, the nature of consciousness, intention and the will. In this series of lectures, we shall dwell on some of these themes. It is striking that, by contrast with the *Tractatus*, the *Investigations* does *not* discuss the nature of logic and of the necessary truths of logic. It is clear that this was to be left for a second book on the philosophy of logic and mathematics – which, as mentioned above, was never completed. Some of his unfinished notes for it have been published under the rather misleading title *Remarks on the Foundations of Mathematics*. It is misleading in as much as the endeavour traditionally known as 'the foundation of mathematics' is repudiated by Wittgenstein.

After completing the *Investigations*, Wittgenstein concentrated largely on philosophy of psychology. He retired prematurely in 1947 in order to concentrate on his work on this subject. Alas, here too nothing was completed, but at his death he left some 1,900 pages of notes on psychology and the philosophy of psychology (since published as *Remarks on the Philosophy of Psychology*). In the last year or so of his life, he turned to themes in the theory of knowledge and wrote some exceedingly original but sadly fragmentary and inconclusive notes on doubt, certainty, knowledge of other minds and colour. He died of cancer in Cambridge on 29 April 1951 at the age of 62, leaving as his literary remains some 20,000 pages of notes, manuscripts and typescripts, mostly in German, which have since been published either in the form of books, which have been translated into English, or in electronic form.

Two Masterworks of the Twentieth Century

Wittgenstein dominates twentieth-century philosophy much as Picasso bestrides twentieth-century art. He did not create a 'school' of philosophy but rather changed the philosophical landscape. Indeed, he did this not once, but twice. His successors within the broad stream of analytic philosophy, whether they followed the paths he pioneered or not, had to orient themselves by reference to his thought. He completed two philosophical masterpieces – the *Tractatus Logico-Philosophicus* (1921) and the *Philosophical Investigations* (1953) – each of which gave rise to distinct phases in the history of the analytic movement.

The *Tractatus* was the source of Cambridge analysis in the decade after the First World War. More importantly, it greatly influenced the formation of *logical positivism*. This was the leading philosophical movement in the inter-war years. It arose in Vienna, and its influence spread from there to Germany, Scandinavia and Britain, and to the United States. Most of its leading figures had a scientific background in physics or mathematics, and the doctrines they advanced were a form of *logical empiricism*, marrying the empiricism of David Hume to the new logic invented by Frege and Russell.

The *Investigations* was a primary inspiration for the form of analytic philosophy that flourished for a quarter of a century after the end of the Second World War, with its centre at Oxford and its circumference everywhere in the English-speaking world and beyond. This movement was known as *linguistic philosophy* or, somewhat misleadingly, as *ordinary language philosophy*.

Bertrand Russell, who admired Wittgenstein's first philosophy and intensely disliked his later philosophy, wrote:

> During the period since 1914 three philosophies have successively dominated the British philosophical world. First that of Wittgenstein's *Tractatus*, second that of the logical positivists, and third that of Wittgenstein's *Philosophical Investigations*.

Each of Wittgenstein's two masterworks advanced a highly original philosophical world view – and the two are very different indeed from each other. It wasn't merely that Wittgenstein came to recognize what he called 'grave mistakes' in the *Tractatus*, but his *whole point of view* underwent fundamental reorientation in his later work.

The *Tractatus* lies firmly in the great tradition of European philosophy. It is an investigation into the essence of logic, language and the world. It is a quest for the hidden metaphysical structure of reality – which Wittgenstein thought *must*, of necessity, be *mirrored* in the hidden logical structure of language. The surface grammar of our language – what can be taken in by eye or ear – is, he held, altogether deceptive, for it does not disclose its true logical character. For example, the word 'exists' looks like any other ordinary verb, but it isn't. One can say that some tame tigers don't growl, but one can't say that some tame tigers don't exist. It is the logical analysis that reveals the underlying logical character of the different kinds of words of our language. And, according to the *Tractatus*, it is the logical analysis that shows that words *must* be connected with the world. For, although many words are definable in terms of other words, sooner or later one is going to come across simple names that are indefinable – for example, names of colours, or names of sounds or smells. And it is precisely here that the web of words is *pinned* to the world – for these simple names *mean* precisely those simple qualities in reality.

The expression 'proposition' is a quasi-technical term. In the *Tractatus*, a proposition is conceived as a declarative sentence that has a determinate sense, and that may be used to assert something true or false. For every proposition is either true or false. According to the *Tractatus*, logical analysis shows that it is of the *essence* of the proposition to *depict* a possibility in the world – a possibility that is either actualized in the world or is not actualized. If the possibility depicted by a proposition is actualized, then the proposition is true; if it is not, then it is false. For a proposition is true if things are as it depicts them as being.

Propositions consist of words or names. But they are not just *lists* of names. Rather, they are constructed according to formation rules. Such rules Wittgenstein called *the logical syntax of language*. It is they that determine *what makes sense* in language – what is a meaningful combination of words as opposed to a mere nonsensical one. *What makes sense* in language, the *Tractatus* argued, coincides with *what is possible* in reality. So, the limits of language and the *metaphysical* limits of the world coincide. The propositions of our language can depict *any* possibility. What they *cannot* depict is *their own pictorial relationship to reality* – just as a map cannot represent its own relation to what it is a map of, and a painting cannot depict its own relation to what it depicts.

It is an appealingly paradoxical consequence of this conception that the very sentences of the *Tractatus* itself are attempts to say something that cannot, by its very nature, be said. For the sentences of the *Tractatus* attempt to delineate the essential relation between language and the world. And *that*, according to the *Tractatus* account of the nature of language, *cannot be represented in language*. It is *shown* – made *manifest* – by the well-formed sentences of language, but it cannot be *said* – cannot be *described*. It is *ineffable*. Hence the bewildering penultimate remark of the book:

> My propositions serve as elucidations in the following way: anyone who understands me eventually recognizes them as nonsensical, when he has used them – as steps – to climb up beyond them. (He must, so to speak, throw away the ladder after he has climbed up it.)
>
> He must transcend these propositions, and then he will see the world aright. (TLP 6.54)

The *Tractatus* was characterized by a striving for sublime philosophical insight into the ultimate nature of things. The *Investigations*, by contrast, is the fruit of disillusionment. What had seemed to be an insight into the essences of things was no more than a glimpse of shadows dancing on the walls of the cave we inhabit. What is needed, Wittgenstein now thought, is a 'quiet weighing of linguistic facts' (Z §447). This, when done with the subtlety and imagination that Wittgenstein everywhere displays, will disabuse us of the illusion of metaphysical insight and illuminate the cave with clear light that chases away the shadows.

The problems concerning logic, linguistic representation, the relation between thought and language, and the nature of linguistic meaning, with which the *Tractatus* had struggled, *can* be resolved. But they cannot be resolved in the way Wittgenstein had earlier thought – by logical analysis into depth grammar. For, he now thought, it is an *illusion* that language has a hidden depth grammar that awaits discovery. Nor can the problems be *solved* by ineffable metaphysical *theories*. For it is an *illusion* that there is any such thing – there are only metaphysical *confusions*. But the problems can be *dissolved* by a quiet weighing of linguistic facts familiar to us all. They can be made to waft away – to disappear, like morning mist in sunshine. And that, as I shall show you in the course of these lectures, is precisely what the *Investigations* does. Philosophical problems and philosophical puzzlement are rooted in conceptual unclarity – and they can be resolved by achieving clarity.

In 1930, when he began undermining his first philosophy, Wittgenstein wrote that for him clarity and perspicuity were valuable in themselves. 'I am not interested in constructing a building', he wrote, 'so much as in having a clear view of the foundations of possible buildings'.[5] And he continued, with a deliberate back-reference to *Tractatus* 6.54 that was just mentioned:

> I might say: if the place I want to get to could only be reached by way of a ladder, I would give up trying to get there. For where I really have to get to is where I must already be.
>
> Anything that I might reach by climbing a ladder does not interest me.

For, of course, 'where I now am' is *having the conceptual scheme I have,* and 'where I have to get to' is having that conceptual scheme *and knowing my way around it,* so that I am no longer beset by conceptual puzzlement. To achieve that clarity regarding the conceptual structures with which we operate, we do not need a ladder in order to reach *metaphysical theories* or *ineffable truths*. Such theories are chimeras. And there are no ineffable truths. We need a perspicuous *description* – an *overview* – of whatever part of our conceptual scheme that gives rise to confusion and bewilderment.

---

5 Wittgenstein, *Culture and Value* (Blackwell, Oxford, 1980), p. 7.

T. S. Eliot, in a quite different context, put the matter well:

> We shall not cease from exploration
> And the end of all our exploring
> Will be to arrive where we started
> And know the place for the first time. (*Four Quartets* IV, ll. 239–43)

Two Styles of Writing

Not only are the ideas of the *Tractatus* and of the *Investigations* in fundamental opposition on many crucial subjects, but the styles of the two books are totally different. Both are great and remarkable contributions to the Republic of Letters. The *Tractatus* is written in austere marmoreal sentences, in which remarks on logic, the world and the soul are delivered with the authority of a prophet. The book opens with the terse remarks

> The world is all that is the case.
> The world is the totality of facts, not of things.
> The world is determined by the facts, and by their being *all* the facts.
> For the totality of facts determines what is the case and also what is not the case. (TLP 1–1.12)

As the book approaches its climactic conclusion, we hear the Sibylline pronouncements:

> Death is not an event in life: we do not live to experience death.
> If we take eternity to mean not infinite duration but timelessness, then eternal life belongs to those who live in the present.
> Our life has no end in just the way in which our visual field has no limits. (TLP 6.4311)

And just a little later,

> We feel that even when *all possible* scientific questions have been answered, the problems of life remain completely untouched. Of course there are then no questions left, and this itself is the answer.
> The solution of the problem of life is seen in the vanishing of the problem.
> (Is not this the reason why those who have found after a long period of doubt that the sense of life became clear to them have then been unable to say what constituted that sense?)
> There are, indeed, things that cannot be put into words. They *make themselves manifest*. They are what is mystical. (TLP 6.52–6.522)

The book then ends with the famous remark.

> What we cannot speak about, we must pass over in silence. (TLP 7)

The *Tractatus* is written with great compression of ideas, virtually no illustrative examples, and minimal explicit argument. Everywhere there is a striving for the highest degree of generality and abstraction. It is laden with recondite technical terminology and the symbolism of formal logic. It is exceedingly difficult to follow.

By contrast, the *Philosophical Investigations* is written in a down-to-earth colloquial style, with virtually no technical terminology. It consists of 693 numbered remarks, some only a sentence long, many a paragraph or two and some four or five paragraphs long. Many of the remarks consist of fragments of imaginary dialogues between an interlocutor and respondent. In one sense, there is no difficulty at all in understanding the author's words – there is no technical vocabulary, no symbolism of formal logic, and the sentences are crisp and simple. But there is immense difficulty in understanding what he means. Let me give you a couple of examples:

> 'Thinking must be something unique.' When we say, *mean*, that such-and-such is the case, then, with what we mean, we do not stop anywhere short of the fact, but mean: *such-and-such – is – thus-and-so*. – But this paradox (which indeed has the form of a truism) can also be expressed in this way: one can *think* what is not the case. (PI §95)

And similarly,

> The agreement, the harmony, between thought and reality consists in this: that if I say falsely that something is [coloured] *red*, then all the same, it is *red* that it isn't. And in this: that if I want to explain the word 'red' to someone, in the sentence 'That is not red'', I do so by pointing to something that *is* red. (PI 429)

Here one can see vividly that, in one sense, what he says is perfectly clear, but in another sense, very unclear – for it is difficult to apprehend what he is driving at. To discern *that* needs much careful thought. Wittgenstein wrote in the Preface to the book, 'I should not like my writing to spare other people the trouble of thinking' – and it certainly does not. What is written is often akin to the tip of an iceberg – what lies beneath the surface is left to the reader to discover by his or her own endeavours. This course of introductory lectures is designed to help the reader make those discoveries.

Wittgenstein's remarks in the *Investigations* are illustrated with numerous lively and sometimes comical examples, and everywhere, by contrast with the *Tractatus*, the concrete is preferred to the abstract, the instance to the generalization, the question to the answer. To provide an answer to a philosophical question often fails to do justice to the question in as much as it does not disclose its depth. But to question the question has no such flaw.

His later style of writing is no less distinctive and idiosyncratic than his earlier *Tractatus* style. It is replete with wonderful similes and metaphors. Writing about the destructive nature of his *Philosophical Investigations*, he remarks:

> Where does this investigation get its importance from, given that it seems only to destroy everything interesting: that is, all that is great and important? (As it were, all the buildings, leaving behind only bits of stone and rubble.) But what we are destroying are only houses of cards, and we are clearing up the ground of language on which they stood. (PI §118)

And again:

> The results of philosophy are the discovery of some piece of plain nonsense and the bumps that the understanding has got by running up against the limits of language. They – the bumps – make us see the value of that discovery. (PI §119)

There are likewise many wonderful aphoristic remarks, for example:

> What is your aim in philosophy? – To show the fly the way out of the fly-bottle. (PI §309)

Or

> The philosopher treats a question; like an illness. (PI §255)

And

> A main cause of philosophical diseases – a one-sided diet: one nourishes one's thinking with only one kind of example. (PI §593)

One has to read Wittgenstein *very* slowly and to reflect on each paragraph. One has to ask constantly why he is saying what he is saying, and to work out what its implications are.

Studying Wittgenstein

So, in studying Wittgenstein, one will be studying one of the greatest thinkers of the past century, and thereby be learning something about the history of twentieth-century philosophy. But the following lectures are not only lectures in the history of ideas. We shall not merely be learning what Wittgenstein said, but *doing what he did*. We shall be doing philosophy in the manner of Wittgenstein himself and following his footsteps through the landscape he traversed. For that is the only way to come to understand his writings. What Wittgenstein said that he had discovered in 1929/30, when he began to dismantle his first philosophy, was *a new method* – and the only way to learn his method of philosophical or conceptual analysis is to practice it.

In learning this method, one will learn to distinguish conceptual claims from factual ones. Factual (i.e. empirical) claims are established by experience, by experiment and by empirical theories and their confirmation. Philosophy and philosophical analysis are not concerned with factual claims; for the latter is the province of observation and empirical science. Philosophy is concerned with describing the conceptual forms and structures that we employ *in making factual claims*. It is not always easy to distinguish factual from conceptual claims. One great source of *scientistic metaphysics* – that is, metaphysics that misguidedly emulates the explanatory methods of science – is failure to distinguish the two. But if one fails to differentiate between the empirical and the conceptual, one will try to resolve conceptual problems – such as what thinking is, or what consciousness is, or how the mind is related to the body – by means of hypotheses and theories. And what one will produce will be nonsense. We shall discuss this powerful, contentious claim in detail in later lectures.

One of the merits of doing philosophy in the wake of Wittgenstein is that one must make what he called 'the transition from the method of truth to the method of sense'. Metaphysics strives to discover *non-empirical truths* concerning the objective, language-independent essences of all things. But, Wittgenstein argued, that is an *illusory quest* and a *chimerical goal*. The natural sciences are concerned with empirical truths – with factual claims about the world. By contrast, philosophy is concerned only with *conceptual* claims concerning the ways in which we think of the world. Conceptual investigations are investigations into *what makes sense* and *what does not*. And, of course, questions of sense *antecede* questions of empirical truth – for if something *makes no sense*, it can be *neither* true nor false. It is just *nonsense* – and I don't mean *silly*, but rather that it transgresses the bounds of sense. Let me give you a simple example or two.

When psychologists and cognitive scientists say that it is your brain that thinks, then, rather than nodding your head and saying 'How interesting! What an important discovery!', you should pause to wonder what this means. What, you might then ask, is a thoughtful brain, and what is a thoughtless one? Can my brain concentrate on what I am doing – or does it just concentrate on what it is doing? Does my brain hold political opinions? Is it, as Gilbert and Sullivan might ask, a little Conservative or a little Liberal? Can it be opinionated? Or narrow-minded? – What on earth would an opinionated and narrow-minded *brain* be? Just ask yourself: if it is your brain that thinks, how does your brain *tell you* what it thinks? And can you *disagree* with it? And if you do, *how do you tell it* that it is mistaken – that what it thinks is false? And can your brain understand what you say to it? Can it speak English? – If you continue this line of questioning, you will come to realize that the very idea that the brain thinks *makes no sense*. But, of course, to show *why* it makes no sense requires a great deal of more work – which we shall undertake in Lecture 14.

Let me give you another example. You may have come across mention of a letter attributed to Mozart in which he is said to have written that sometimes, when in the fever of creativity, he could hear the whole concerto that he was composing *in a flash* – all he then had to do was to write it down. On hearing this tale, you may nod your head wisely and think: what an amazing genius! How could he possibly do such a thing? Roger Penrose, a distinguished scientist and mathematician, reflecting on the same letter, thought that we shall only be able to understand this remarkable phenomenon when we have an adequate theory of quantum gravity and a better understanding of time. – Ah, you may think, how true! How amazing! But you should pause, not to wonder whether what Mozart allegedly said is true, nor to wonder how he could do something so amazing – but to wonder *whether this form of words means anything at all*. After all, if he could hear the whole concerto in his imagination in a flash, all he would have imagined hearing was a crashing chord, not a concerto! – In fact, the famous letter is a forgery. But that doesn't matter. What matters is that the only sense that can be given to the phrase *hearing the concerto in one's imagination in a flash* is that it means that he suddenly realized that he knew how to complete the concerto he was writing, not that he had already completed it in his imagination. The sudden dawning of an ability is not the same as its high-speed exercise and to have a *Eureka* experience is not to rehearse the whole solution to a problem in a flash, but to know that one *can* rehearse the whole solution – on request, at normal speed.

Pursuing the method of sense in the manner of Wittgenstein will teach you not only to *raise questions about assertions* that are conceptually suspect, but equally importantly to *raise questions about questions*. If biological scientists pose what seems to them to be a deep question, for example: *What is consciousness for?* you will not hasten to think of a true answer, nor pause to think that you are confronted by a great mystery to which science has not yet discovered the answer. What you will do is wonder about this seemingly innocuous question and think of some questions with which to confront it. For example: Is consciousness the sort of thing that might be *for* something? Perhaps the question of what consciousness is for is akin to the question of what *life* is for. What precisely is *meant* by consciousness? Is being conscious the same as being awake? If so, does the allegedly deep question amount to: What is *being awake* for? – That seems a silly question. Or is being conscious the same as being conscious *of* something or other – for example, of the ticking of the clock or the smell of fried onions? – in which case, the question: *What is consciousness for?* amounts to the same as *What is peripheral attention for?* – and although that is an intelligible question, it is neither deep nor difficult to answer.

Even more strikingly, if one pursues the question of sense, one may not only reduce some apparently deep questions to altogether straightforward ones, one will also challenge the very sense of some apparently deep questions. For some questions *look* as if they make sense and *appear* to be exceedingly difficult to answer – whereas they are *impossible* to answer, since *they make no sense*.

Let me hint at an example, which we shall examine in due course. We are very commonly confronted with the question: How is the mind related to the body? – and we are baffled. We may initially think of the mind as something immaterial and wonder how something immaterial could possibly interact with something material like the body. So we may then wonder whether the mind is not after all a material thing, namely: the brain, and whether the answer to the question of how the mind interacts with the body does not boil down to the question of how the brain interacts with the body. But then we may have qualms, since if the mind just is the brain, then our mind weighs three pounds and is seven inches tall – which seems nonsense. And by now our mind – but not our brain – is in a whirl. But what we ought to do is to start to wonder whether it makes any sense to talk of the mind as being *related* to the body. Maybe the mind is not a kind of entity at all – neither a material nor an immaterial one. We all have minds, to be sure, but the mind, like health, is not *a kind of thing*. If so, then the question of how the mind is *related* to the body is thoroughly confused. Maybe it is like the question of how my sake is related to me – or like the question of how your sake is related to my sake. And that should give us pause. We shall examine the issue in detail in Lecture 12.

You must bear in mind that in studying the later ideas of Wittgenstein you will be studying a radical thinker in the true sense of the term, namely someone who digs down to the very roots of our thought. Wittgenstein was a master of the art of disclosing the fundamental presuppositions of our thought, presuppositions of which we are barely aware, since they are constantly in place – like the glasses upon our nose. He was a genius at exposing the roots of conceptual error and confusion. And the philosophy he advanced in his later work had no precedent in the history of the subject. The radicalism of his later philosophy can be characterized by reference to four distinct domains. First, and above all, he advanced a wholly novel conception of philosophy itself. For, in stark contrast with the whole philosophical tradition, he denied that philosophy was a discipline that adds to human knowledge in the manner of the sciences. It is not, he argued, a quest for new knowledge, but a quest for a certain form of understanding. Secondly, he gave a wholly novel and radical account of the necessary truths of metaphysics, logic and mathematics, holding them to be not descriptions of necessary facts of super-physics, or of the domains of number, but as rules of representation in the misleading guise of descriptions. Thirdly, he argued for a radical conception of linguistic meaning and representation. The meanings of words, he argued, are not entities that we assign to words, associate with words, or link with words. They are neither in the mind nor objects, properties or relations in the world – rather, the meaning of a word is its use in the language. Fourthly, his philosophy of psychology is revolutionary – demanding a fundamental reorientation in the way in which we think about the mind, consciousness and self-consciousness. He endeavoured to displace the Cartesian conception of the mind and of the mental that has dominated European thought since the mid-seventeenth century. If he is right then much of current psychology, so-called cognitive science, and cognitive neuroscience is misconceived.

All of this gives you a foretaste of what lies ahead in these lectures.

The Plan of the Course

The course of lectures which I shall present to you is divided into three parts. The first part, which runs from Lectures 2 to 7, elaborates on Wittgenstein's mature reflections on language and linguistic representation, and on the nature of linguistic meaning. Here we shall also investigate the question of whether language is connected to reality and whether language has foundations. We shall go on to discuss Wittgenstein's critical deconstruction of metaphysics, and his account of what appear to be objective metaphysical necessities, for example, that red is *necessarily* darker than pink, or that causes *cannot* follow their effects. The final lecture of this set will investigate the questions of whether one needs language in order to be able to think, whether animals can be said to think and whether one thinks *in* a language, or in *images*, or in *anything*.

The second part of the course runs from Lectures 8 to 14. It commences with an examination of Wittgenstein's famous *Private Language Arguments*, in which he argues against the idea that our common public language rests on foundations constituted by our own subjective, private experiences. According to that conception, the words of our language stand for the ideas in our minds, ideas which we get from experience – from the interaction of our nerve endings with the environment. I shall go on to examine Wittgenstein's account of the nature of *our own* mental states and of our knowledge of *other people's* mental states, the relationship between the mental and behaviour, the vexed question of the relation of mind to body and the bearing of his analysis upon current cognitive neuroscience.

The final three lectures of the course are on Wittgenstein's *later conception of philosophy*. For having followed Wittgenstein's footsteps over a part of the conceptual landscape that he traversed, you will be in a position to reflect on his methodology – for you will be able to measure it against his clarificatory achievements with which you will by then be well acquainted. And you will be in a position to try to attain an overview of his revolutionary conception of philosophy – for you will have seen it in action. In the last of these three lectures, some of the objections to Wittgenstein's methods and to his radical conception of philosophy will be rehearsed, and I will try to show you how they can be rebutted.

Some of these lectures will be difficult. Philosophy is not an easy subject, and it cannot be made easy, any more than mountain climbing can be made easy. It demands effort and perseverance. I shall guide you over the crevasses and up the rock faces. Sometimes you will wonder why you have to ascend some particularly difficult ridge – and you will have to have faith that it leads somewhere exciting. I shall try not to disappoint you. It is worth persevering. The satisfaction of reaching the mountain peaks is great, and the views are wonderful.

Wittgenstein said that his aim in philosophy was not to teach his readers any doctrines – but to teach them to fend for themselves when they come across conceptual problems and become entangled in conceptual confusion. Conceptual problems and confusions are not unique to philosophy – as I shall illustrate from the domains of cognitive neuroscience, experimental psychology and theoretical linguistics. The temptation to transgress the bounds of sense is part of the human condition and a corollary of being a language user.

As will become clear in the course of these lectures, conceptual confusions are not only exceedingly difficult to detect – they are usually *very appealing*. For we have an almost irresistible *taste* for the weird and the wonderful – for the idea of *time-travel*, for the thought that *we are our brains,* for the supposition that *the mind interacts with the body*, for the assumption that we *cannot really know what other people experience* but only what we ourselves experience. But all these ideas and suppositions *make no sense* – and can be *shown* to make no sense. They are merely enticing and intriguing forms of well-concealed nonsense. Similarly, we are charmed by the latest scientific news – that genes can be selfish, for example, or that the brain makes decisions for us before we even know, or – as some economists have tried to persuade us – that greed can be perfectly virtuous. But it *makes no sense* to ascribe selfishness *or* selflessness to a gene, it is an egregious blunder to suppose that there is any such thing as a brain making or failing to make decisions, and it is absurd to suppose that greed – or gluttony – might be praiseworthy and morally meritorious. To be able to detect when the bounds of sense are being transgressed, to be able to identify the manner of their transgression and to be able to resist the temptations of transgressing them are goals worthy of pursuit. If these lectures succeed in giving you *a nose*, rather than *a taste*, for nonsense, they will have succeeded in their mission.

Chapter 2

AUGUSTINE'S PICTURE OF LANGUAGE AND THE REFERENTIAL CONCEPTION OF LINGUISTIC MEANING

Representation by Means of Language

When Wittgenstein turned to writing what became the *Philosophical Investigations*, he thought hard about how to begin the book. His primary theme was to be the nature of language and linguistic representation. In 1931, he wrote that he should begin his book with an analysis of an ordinary sentence such as 'A lamp is standing on my table' since everything should be derivable from this. What did he have in mind?

His concern was with how sentences manage to represent. Such a humdrum sentence as 'A lamp is standing on my table' is meaningful – it has a meaning. By using such a meaningful sentence, one *describes* a certain state of affairs. One says *that there is a lamp on one's table*, and *what* one says may be either *true* or *false*. How does a sentence in use, a sequence of sounds one utters, manage to do all this – to represent a situation, to describe how things are, to be true or false? – The question is odd, and it may well engender a feeling of bafflement. You may well feel that you can't *really* see a problem. You may be inclined to say that this is just what sentences in use do! — Let me try to show you that there is more that is puzzling about linguistic representation that comes immediately to the eye. I shall do so by means of a little dialogue between myself and an interlocutor, who I imagine as a thoughtful member of my audience given to asking good questions. I'll set the ball rolling:

> **PMSH.** When one says 'A lamp is standing on my table', one produces a sequence of sounds. A parrot may do that no less than you or I. But if a parrot squawks 'A lamp is standing on my table', these are just empty sounds. The parrot is not describing anything, and it understands nothing. It is just mimicking the sounds it hears. But if you or I utter the sentence in an appropriate context, it has a meaning – it signifies something, describes something. So how is this effected? How is a sequence

of sounds transformed into a meaningful utterance that represents how things are? We are tempted to ask, 'What does a human speaker *do* that a parrot cannot do? And how does what he does transform the sounds he makes into a meaningful description or representation of how things are?'

Int. Well, surely, he *means something* by the sounds he makes. When one speaks, one means, *by the words one utters*, that very thing that one has in mind. Isn't it this which gives one's words their meaning, that makes them signify whatever they signify?

PMSH. I agree with you that when we speak, we mean something by the words we utter. But *what is it* to *mean* something by a sound? How does one *do* this meaning? And how can this *act of meaning* that one *does* give the sounds one emits a meaning – which they patently lack in the parrot's case? How does it *make them mean something*?

Int. Clearly, the individual words one utters have a meaning. The word 'lamp' means or signifies an artefact made for the purpose of illumination; the phrase 'standing on' means or signifies a spatial relation; and so forth. That is what *the speaker* means by those words in that sentence. That's what those words *mean*.

PMSH. But how are we to characterize *the meaning of a word* such as 'lamp' or 'on'? When I say 'There is a lamp on my table', is the meaning of the word 'lamp' the lamp about which I am speaking?

Int. Well, it is certainly that lamp *that I mean*.

PMSH. And is the meaning of the word 'on' the relation of *being on*?

Int. Well, that was certainly what I had in mind when I said, '*on* the table'.

PMSH. So are the meanings of words then the things, properties and relations which the words represent or stand for?

Int. Yes, that's exactly what I had in mind.

PMSH. All right. But now stop to reflect. If the meanings of words are the objects, properties and relations that the words stand for or represent, then it seems to follow that the world is not only full of meaning – which, to be sure, it is – but it must also be full of meanings, that is: of meanings of words. But surely, no one would want to say that some meanings of words are brown – like the sofa I am sitting on – and others are red – like the red rose in the vase. But if the sofa is the meaning of the word 'sofa' and the rose is the meaning of the word 'rose', that is what we would have to say.

Int. All right, let's drop that line and try a different one. Perhaps we should say that the meanings of words are *ideas in one's mind*? Surely, whenever I think, I have certain ideas in my mind. For isn't *thinking* precisely putting ideas together to form a thought? Then, when I speak,

I am trying to convey to others the thought that I have. So don't I use words to stand for ideas in my mind and order the words into a well-formed sentence that represents the thought in my mind which I want to communicate? Of course, I assume that these words will stimulate the same ideas in the mind of my hearer, and so he will understand what thought I was trying to convey to him.

PMSH. Well, I agree that this is a line of reasoning which many philosophers have explored for many centuries. And indeed there are some reasons for thinking so.

Int. There are *lots* of reasons for thinking that what words mean are ideas in one's mind. After all, don't we say 'I have no idea what you mean by that word'? Doesn't that show that the meaning of a word is the idea with which it is linked? And what about words like 'dragon', 'unicorn' or 'ghost'? They have a meaning, despite the fact that there are no dragons, unicorns or ghosts for them to stand for. So surely it suffices for the words to have a meaning that we have ideas corresponding to them! And these ideas are *what the words mean*. Surely, to know what one means by a word one uses is precisely to know what idea in one's mind it stands for.

PMSH. Well, I agree that you might be tempted to think so.

Int. Well, let me try to persuade you that I've got it right. Scientists, at least since the seventeenth century, have been telling us that things are not really coloured, but merely emit light waves of varying wave lengths which *produce* ideas of colour *in our minds*. So too, they have explained, there are no sounds in the external world, only sound waves that affect our eardrums, and so produce ideas of sounds in our minds. So colour names *must* mean ideas in our mind, since there is nothing else for them to mean! And sound names must mean auditory ideas, for there are no objective sounds. The *meanings* of colour names and sound names *are* ideas. What applies to colour names must apply likewise to names of tastes and smells, to names of sensations of hot or cold, and so forth.

PMSH. Well, that's exactly wrong! I agree that it can be made *very tempting* to suppose that the meanings of names are ideas in the mind. If that were not so, then some of the greatest intellects in Europe would not have been led to embrace this conception. But I urge you to resist the temptation. For if you succumb to it, you will be led into incoherence and confusion. For the moment, you will have to take this warning on trust – later I shall redeem the promissory note.

Let me bring our little dialogue to a close. I want to take you back to our parrot. The questions we must confront are these: In view of the thought that meaning something by a word is *doing something*, is the vacuity of the parrot's squawk due to its not *doing* something – namely, not performing *an act of meaning*. Or, in view of the supposition that words stand for ideas in the mind, is the vacuity of the parrot's squawks due to its not *having* something – namely, not having *ideas in its mind*? A realist philosopher who thinks that words stand directly for real objects, properties and relations in the world – that such real items are the meanings of words – will attribute the emptiness of the parrot's noises to its failure to mean by its squawks anything whatsoever. An idealist philosopher, who takes words to stand for ideas in the mind – that ideas in the mind are the meanings of words – will explain the lifelessness of the parrot's squawks by reference to the fact that parrots don't have any ideas. And some philosophers may wish to amalgamate both lines of thought, arguing that parrots have no ideas in their minds – since they have no ideas and no minds either (as indeed Descartes held) *and* that they can perform no acts of meaning. So it is precisely because they can't perform acts of meaning and have no ideas that they can't make words stand for ideas in their minds.

These are possibilities to be investigated. But don't close your mind to a further possibility, namely: *that we are barking up the wrong tree altogether*. This is something we will explore in a later lecture.

So much, for the moment, for words and word-meaning. Although we have mentioned sentence-meaning, we have glossed over it. But let me point out to you that sentence-meaning raises a further set of questions. Of course, a sentence one utters *has* a meaning. But how are the meanings of words related to the meanings of the sentences in which the words occur? Is the meaning of a sentence *made up* of the meanings of its constituent words? So do the meanings, as it were, fit together to form an intelligible unity? Certainly, a string of words such as 'Lamp the on is table my' is sheer nonsense. Is that because when thus combined, the meanings of the words *don't* fit together to form an intelligible whole – a sentence with a sense – whereas they do in the combination 'The lamp is on my table'? In short, what makes one combination of meaningful words into an intelligible proposition, and what makes another combination a nonsense?

As we've noted, a parrot may squawk the sounds of the *sentence* 'A lamp is on my table'. But, as we have emphasized, the parrot *means nothing by those sounds*. It does not, so to say, *think* anything in making these sounds. The sentence is, as it were, *dead*. But when *we* utter a sentence sincerely and mean something by it, *the sentence is an expression of our thought*. So, is it our thinking that lies behind the words we utter and gives them *life*? Are there concurrent processes of thinking that infuse sentences in use with meaning? So, does speaking presuppose thinking? It is very tempting to say that this is right. After all, we distinguish between saying something with thought and saying something without thinking, between speaking thoughtlessly and speaking thoughtfully. These turns of phrase suggest that to speak with thought is to accompany one's speech with an inner process of thinking. And that is a very tempting conception. Only remember that all that glitters is not gold!

Now *if* (and it is a big IF), *if* thought is an inner accompaniment of thoughtful speech, the question naturally arises: What does one think in? Does one think in language? And if not, does one then think in mental images or ideas? Language is surely used to communicate our thoughts to others. If so, does it mean that our thoughts, in and of themselves, require *no* language? – that we *translate* the thoughts we have into words for the benefit of others? Or are we just barking up the wrong tree?

It is, I hope, clear that not much reflection is needed to engender considerable puzzlement and to raise *very* fundamental questions about the relationship between words and world, words and sentences, sentences and what they describe, and thought and language. This is what Wittgenstein had in mind when he wrote that he should begin his book with a sentence such as 'A lamp is standing on my table'. For, as you have just seen, this very simple and mundane sentence already raises the most fundamental problems about language and linguistic meaning.

Augustine's Picture

As it turned out, Wittgenstein decided *not* to begin his book with a humdrum sentence containing in it all the materials for reflecting on the nature of language. Rather, he chose to begin his book with a quotation from the autobiography of St Augustine – *The Confessions* – in which Augustine reflected on how he must have learnt language as a child. Why did Wittgenstein do this? Certainly, Augustine's implicit conception of language can be found equally well expressed elsewhere. It was, Wittgenstein explained, because Augustine was a singularly clear-thinking man, and if so great a mind as his, in a very different culture from ours, had this unreflective preconception of language, then *it must be important*. Wittgenstein chose this autobiographical fragment from Augustine precisely because it is *not* a piece of philosophizing. It represents not *a theory* of any kind, but a *natural, pre-theoretical* notion of language and its acquisition, its function and nature. Indeed, Wittgenstein thought that it contains the tacit presuppositions of much European thought on linguistic representation.

Let's turn to what Augustine actually wrote:

> When grown-ups named some object and at the same time turned towards it, I perceived this and I grasped that the thing was signified by the sound they uttered, since they meant to point *it* out. This, however, I gathered from their gestures, the

> natural language of all peoples, the language that by means of facial expression and the play of eyes, of the movements of the limbs and the tone of voice, indicates the affections of the soul when it desires, or clings to, or rejects, or recoils from, something. In this way, little by little, I learnt to understand what things the words, which I heard uttered in their respective places in various sentences, signified. And once I got my tongue around these signs, I used them to express my wishes.

In this quotation, Wittgenstein detected what he called a *picture*, an unreflective conception of language. Augustine presupposes:

- First, that naming is of the essence of language.
- Secondly, that sentences are essentially combinations of names.

And does this not seem very plausible? Are you not inclined to agree that these two presuppositions are perfectly cogent? 'Surely', you may agree, 'words are essentially names of things'. And equally, you may concede, we combine such names into sentences. What could be more platitudinous? – Well, if that is your initial response, slow down! For you have already made some very deep mistakes. Do you really want to say that 'goodbye', 'hello', 'perhaps', 'certain', 'doubtful', 'really', 'actually', 'if', 'not', 'never', 'all', 'some' are names of things? This is surely not a path you wish to go down! And I assure you that this is not the worst of it! So, hold your horses, and I shall, in due course, show you how deeply mistaken is the idea that words are essentially names. Or rather, it is either deeply mistaken or deeply misleading, for it is either false or vacuous.

It is against the seemingly anodyne background of Augustine's two presuppositions that Wittgenstein proceeds to extract something more than a mere picture. He extracts a set of self-conscious doctrines about linguistic representation. Many of these doctrines are shared by almost anyone who has reflected on language. It may be called *the Referential* – or *Correlational – Conception of Meaning*. This conception can be summarized in seven theses:

(i) that every word has a meaning
(ii) that the meaning of a word is correlated with the word
(iii) that the meaning of a word is the object it stands for
(iv) that the ostensive (or *pointing*) form of explanation '*This* ☞ is red' or '*This* ☞ is a table' determines the foundations of language, linking words to the world. It correlates words with their meanings by *pointing* at what the words signify
(v) that a child can think, that is: talk to itself – in a language of thought, as it were – before it has learnt to speak.

This is implicit in the passage Wittgenstein quoted from Augustine, inasmuch as Augustine conceived of himself as 'grasping that the thing was signified by the sound the adults uttered, since they meant to point it out', that he 'gathered from their gestures' what the adults meant by their words, and that he used those words to express his own wishes. If he could do all these things before he had even learnt to speak, he must obviously already have learnt to *think* even before he could speak!

Finally, two theses about sentences. First:

> Thesis (vi) sentences are essentially complex – an ordered combination of names

Secondly:

> Thesis (vii) the essential function of sentences is to describe how things are

This final thesis is a corollary of the previous one that sentences are essentially *a combination* – not a mere list – of names. The elementary idea is that names stand for things, and a grammatically correct combination of words in a sentence depicts a state of affairs in the world. So the sentence 'a lamp is on the table' is a grammatically correct combination of names. The words 'lamp' and 'table' and the relation name 'on' are so combined that they describe the state of affairs that consists in the lamp being on the table. Or, to put a similar point in terms of subject/predicate grammar: a sentence consists of a subject term that picks out what one is speaking of – in this case, a particular lamp – and a predicate term that *describes* what the subject term denotes – describes it as being *on the table*.

The seven theses that Wittgenstein extracted from Augustine's picture are not a 'straw man' that he artificially constructed just to knock down. Rather, they constitute the essential core of a wide range of *different* but related conceptions of language and linguistic meaning. It is, as it were, a field of force within which much speculation on this subject has been, and often still is, trapped. Wittgenstein thought that each and every thesis that contributes to the referential or correlational conception of meaning is misconceived.

Augustine's picture is *natural* – it is *the* most natural way to think about language and linguistic meaning. But by and large, the *natural* way to think in philosophy is the *wrong* way to think. When struggling through the jungles of grammar, what is natural is to take the wrong route. Referential or correlational theories of meaning are, in their different ways, immensely persuasive. But they are no more than a set of mutually reinforcing illusions. These illusions are anything but trivial or inconsequential – for they affect how one thinks and speaks about such deep matters as the nature of the mind and the extent to which we can know the mind of another person. These illusions concerning language and linguistic meaning infiltrate our reflections on the nature of necessity – for example, on why it is not *just a matter of fact* that red is darker than pink or that nothing can simultaneously be both red all over and green all over. They distort our reflections on the relation between thought and language – and since the power of thought is part of our nature, these misconceptions ultimately play havoc with our endeavours to grasp our own nature as rational, language-using beings.

The Augustinian conception of language is immensely powerful. It has seduced most of those who have reflected on language throughout history. So, if you find yourself agreeing with it, then you are in good company. But, I shall try to show you that, despite the good company, the ideas are bad ideas. They are weeds in the gardens of thought. They need to be extirpated. But, to extirpate them, we need to find their roots.

Names and Their Fascination

Augustine's picture that naming is of the essence of language and that sentences are combinations of names *appears* anodyne. It is *meant* to appear anodyne. But it is *not*. It presupposes that language *has* an essence, which is something Wittgenstein challenged. It presupposes that the concept of *naming* is perspicuous and readily characterizable: a word is a name if it stands for something. Equally, it presupposes that there is *one relation* – namely: *standing for* – that can be conceived as *the name relation*. But that too is mistaken. And it presupposes that sentences *are essentially complex*, that the very possibility of fulfilling whatever roles are fundamental to sentences turns on their consisting of a number of different names appropriately combined. This too is questionable.

Let's have a preliminary glance at naming. Wittgenstein was fascinated by the ideas of names, naming and the name relation. This should be unsurprising. Not only had these notions played a prominent and mistaken role in his first book, the *Tractatus*, as it had in the writings of his predecessors Frege and Russell, but, more importantly, there is an *aura* and *magic* surrounding the ideas of naming and of names. Reflect that, according to the book of *Genesis*, the first thing Adam did after his creation was to *name* all the beasts of the field:

> And out of the ground the LORD God formed every beast of the field, and every fowl of the air; and brought them unto Adam to see what he would call them: and whatsoever Adam called every living creature, that was the name thereof.
>
> And Adam gave names to all cattle, and to the fowl of the air and to every beast of the field.

Reflect too on the magical significance of baptismal naming in Christian practices to this very day. And think what it would be like if we were all deprived of our names and were given numbers instead. Think how demeaning it is for prisoners to be given numbers and then called by a number. And how injurious puns on one's name are.

It is equally noteworthy that there is a long tradition in both philosophy and mythology according to which all things have both a *conventional* name and a *true* name. So, Socrates, in Plato's dialogue *Cratylus*, remarks:

> I should say that this giving of names can be no such light matter as you fancy, or the work of light or chance persons. And Cratylus is right in saying that things have names by nature, and that not every man is an artificer of names, but he only who looks to the name which each thing by nature has and is able to express the true forms of things in letters and syllables. (390d–e)

To know the true name of a thing, it was supposed, is to know the essence or nature of the thing, and is that not in itself to possess power over the thing? This idea is a mythologizing of the simple truth that mastery of the use of words, including names of things, enables us to *think* about things, both things that exist and things that do not, about things that are present and things that are absent, real things and ideal things – and *that* is a power that no non-language using animal possesses.

A modern residue *in philosophy* of this distinction between the common name and the true name of a thing lies in the idea that some names are names of *natural kinds* – and that these are the 'true names' of things. The common-or-garden name 'a drink', one might say, is not the *real name* of anything, but the expression 'water' or better 'H_2O' *is* the real name of *a natural kind*, a name which discloses the essential form of water and which occurs in statements of general laws of chemistry. For names of natural kinds are precisely those names in terms of which true generalizations and statements of laws of nature can be cast.

We not only mythologize names, but we also associate names with magic. The association of knowledge of names with magical power over what is named is reflected in fairy tales, for example in Grimm's 'Rumpelstiltskin' story in which the maiden's knowledge of the dwarf's real name enables her to deprive him of his power over her. The attraction of this association does not belong merely to past folklore. The magical power of names is a living presence with immense appeal and resonance in fantasy fiction such as Tolkien's *Lord of the Rings* and Ursula Le Guin's *Earthsea* novels. And, to abandon fictionalized magic, just think of the power of proper names in the politics of the street and mob, and in the mass rally. Think how the name of a hero, politician or pop-star, military leader or footballer – chanted by thousands – intoxicates and unifies a mob, crowd, audience or army. Is that not part of the magic of a proper name?

The idea that words are essentially names, the role of which is to stand for things, and the idea that what they stand for are their meanings is no straw man. Let me give you a few examples from the history of philosophy. Many philosophers have thought that words are basically names. John Stuart Mill, for example, wrote:

> It seems proper to consider a word as the *name* of that which we intend to be understood by it when we use it.

The idea that words *stand for* things is equally common. For example, Bertrand Russell held that:

> Words all have meanings, in the simple sense that they are symbols which stand for something other than themselves.

The supposition that the meaning of a word *is* the thing it stands for is also common. It may, of course, occur in one of two forms, depending on whether words are held to stand for *ideas* in the mind, or for *things* in the world. So John Locke wrote:

> Words in their primary signification, stand for nothing but the ideas in the mind of him that uses them [...] nor can anyone apply them as marks immediately to anything else but the ideas that he himself hath.

By contrast with Locke's *idealist* conception of word meaning, the young Wittgenstein in the *Tractatus* adopted a *realist* conception. He held that:

> A name means an object. The object is its meaning. [Names] link the propositional form with quite definite objects.

He held that properties and relations were to be counted as 'objects' too. On this realist view, names stand for things, properties and relations in the world, not for ideas of them.

So, there is no lack of examples of great thinkers operating within the field of force of Augustine's picture. Now, let us move on to a further stage.

Linking Language to Reality

If one is caught within the force-field of the Augustinian conception of language, it is immensely tempting to suppose that words are linked to the entities that are their meanings. Let me bring back our interlocutor in order to explain these temptations.

> **Int.** Look, surely *language must be linked to reality*! *Words must be hooked on to things*. Or at least, the *elementary*, *indefinable*, words of our languages must be – even if the complex words are definable in terms of the simple indefinables. After all, how could the elementary words in a language, such as 'red' or 'hot' or 'noise' mean the things they do unless they were

somehow linked to the world? How could words like 'cat' or 'car' or 'river' be fit instruments for describing how things are unless they were connected to things?

PMSH. I agree that the picture is very tempting. I shall in due course try to show you that the idea is wholly misconceived. That task must be postponed until the 5th lecture, for other things must first be clarified. But, without begging any questions, let's reflect on one of the sources of this temptation.

The most common instrument to explain what a certain word means is *pointing at* an exemplar and saying, for example, 'That's a poplar tree' (explaining what the noun 'poplar' means), 'That's magenta' (explaining the colour adjective 'magenta') or 'That's walking' (explaining what the verb 'to walk' means). This form of explanation of word meaning is known as *ostensive explanation* or *definition*. When we give such explanations, we point at items in the world. So it is small wonder that on reflection it should seem that ostensive definition is the *instrument that links words to world*, and, more generally, *language to reality*. And it seems to you, does it not, that it is in virtue of these word/world connections that words have meaning?

Int. Yes, yes! That's right! Language *must* be connected to reality. Otherwise, we would be caught in a circle of words. For when we define words by means of explicit verbal definitions, we explain a word in terms of other words. We explain that 'bachelor' means the same as 'an unmarried man'. The words 'man' and 'unmarried' are simpler than the 'bachelor', we *analyse* the meaning of the word 'bachelor' by giving it in simpler terms. We give *an analytic definition*. This specifies the necessary and sufficient conditions for something to be, for example, a bachelor. For it is necessary that anyone who is a bachelor be a man, and it is also necessary that he be unmarried. These two necessary conditions are jointly sufficient for being a bachelor – that is, nothing *else* is necessary. Analytic definitions specify necessary and sufficient conditions that anything *must* satisfy in order to fall under the concept that is thus defined. Now, if the words in such an analytic definition also need defining, we can do that too. So 'man', for example, means the same as 'adult male human being'. And so on. But unless we are to go round in circles within this web of words, sometime or other we must *exit from language* and *make contact with reality*.

Now, are there not many *indefinable* words in a language, such as 'red' or 'green', 'sour' or 'sweet', 'hot' or 'cold'? You can't give an analytic definition of the word 'red'! Or of 'sweet'! These are *obviously* names of simple, indefinable qualities! Indeed, according to British empiricists such as Locke, Berkeley and Hume, they are names of simple indefinable ideas. It is *here* that language is *attached to reality*. Here we *exit from language* by attaching words to the world — or to our experiences of it.

PMSH. You have spelt all this out very nicely. If we think as you do, it will seem that language consists of a vast *network* of definable and indefinable expressions. Most expressions are definable by means of intra-linguistic connections within the web of words. But that gives them no content – merely an array of inter-definables. But the simple indefinables of language are the points at which this web is connected to the world or to our experiences of it. It is at these points that *content* is extra-linguistically *injected* into the web of language – by connecting the indefinables with qualities and relations in the world, or – according to linguistic idealists – with ideas in the mind. Ostensive definitions, on your view, constitute the foundations of language. That is a very tempting, although altogether mistaken, idea.

Int. But why? Surely, understanding an indefinable word requires immediate acquaintance with the entity that is its meaning. One cannot understand what the word 'red', for example, means, if one has never seen anything red. One cannot understand what the word 'pain' means if one has never experienced a sensation of pain. So, the foundations of language *must* lie in the simple indefinable entities for which simple names stand, for it is upon *these foundations* that all other words can be given meanings by explicit definitions. And the foundations of linguistic understanding lie in acquaintance with the simple things, qualities, and relations, or alternatively, with the simple ideas, which are the meanings of the simple indefinable names.

PMSH. Of course, I agree with you that this is a venerable conception of the sources of linguistic meaning, and of the essential links between language and reality that are presupposed by the very possibility of representing in language how things are in reality. It *seems* that this is how things *must* be. If we are to use language as we do, namely to describe how things stand in reality – which is certainly something we do, even if it is not all we do with words – it *seems* that words must *derive their meanings* from things. Or, more accurately, from the very things of which they are the names. That is how it *seems*.

With this conciliatory but *non-concessive* remark, let me halt the dialogue. The path to intellectual perdition is paved with *seeming stones*! In the next lectures, I shall show you how to avoid this road that leads to quagmires of confusion. I shall show you that these seeming stones are mere illusions – that the ways in which you are naturally inclined to think are the wrong ways.

Sentences and Sentence Meanings

Now let's turn to the theses about sentences and sentential meaning that Wittgenstein extracted from Augustine's picture. You remember the two theses: first, that sentences are essentially complex, that is: ordered combinations of names; second, that the essential function of sentences is to describe how things are.

The idea that sentences are essentially combinations of names is almost as old as philosophy itself. It is, like so much else, already to be found in Plato. It was vividly expressed in the famous seventeenth-century treatise on language, the *Port Royal Logic*:

> Judgements are propositions expressed by sentences [...] sentences themselves are composed of words [...] The product of judging is expressed by a sentence which must contain two terms – the one term is the subject, which expresses the idea of which one may affirm or deny another idea; the second term is the predicate, which expresses the idea which is affirmed or denied of the idea expressed by the subject.[1]

Much the same thought was expressed two centuries later by John Stuart Mill, who wrote in his book *System of Logic*:

> Now the first glance at a proposition shows that it is formed by putting together two names. A proposition [...] is discourse in which something is affirmed or denied of something [...] every proposition consists of two names; and every proposition affirms or denies one of these names of the other. (I – i – sections 1–3)

So, sentences seem to be essentially complex – the role of a sentence, it seems, can be fulfilled only by a *complex* symbol. For there must be one symbol that identifies what one is speaking of, and another that specifies what one is saying about it. So, every sentence must contain at least two parts. Classical logicians thought that every sentence must contain a *subject expression* and *predicate expression*. Modern function-theoretic logicians disagree. They conceive of the parts of a sentence as *argument name* and *function name*. But at any rate, all logicians agree that sentences *must* be complex. The internal complexity of a sentence is, it seems, required, if the sentence is to fulfil its essential role. Why is this such a tempting thought?

Well, what is the essential role of a sentence? You just heard Mill specify it. It is to affirm or deny some property or feature of something. So, the essential role of sentences seems to be *to describe how things are*. And only a complex expression – a sentence, not a name – can do that. Only a sentence can affirm or deny something of a subject.

---

1 Antoine Arnauld, *The Art of Thinking*, Part II, chapters 1–3.

Why is it so tempting to suppose that the essential role of sentences is to describe how things are? One powerful reason, which may indeed tempt you, is to assume that the essential function of sentences is to *express our thoughts*. Hobbes observed:

> The general use of speech is to transfer our mental discourse into verbal; or the train of our thoughts into a train of words. (*Leviathan*, Pt 1, chap. 4)

And Locke wrote:

> The Comfort and Advantage of Society, not being to be had without Communication of Thoughts, it was necessary that Man should find out some external sensible Signs, whereby those invisible *Ideas*, which his thoughts are made up of, might be made known to others [...] Thus we may conceive how *Words*, which were by Nature so well adapted to that purpose, come to be made use of by Men, as the *Signs* of their *Ideas*. (*Essay Concerning Human Understanding*, III – i – 1)

If you are persuaded by this, then only one step further is necessary for you to reach the position that the essential function of sentences is to describe how things are. For surely, when you think a thought, you think that something is thus-and-so. Is not the question 'What are you thinking?' given by an answer of the form 'I was thinking that ...' – followed by a declarative sentence? For example: I was thinking that *rain is going to fall soon* – thus describing how the weather is going to turn out. Or: I was thinking that *the roses are looking wonderful* – describing how the roses look. Or: I was thinking that *the film we saw last night was excellent*' – describing the quality of the film. So, if sentences are essentially expressions of thought, then they are *really* descriptions, even if they do not always look as if they are. In the next lecture I shall show you that I have been leading you up the garden path. For it is altogether misguided to suppose that sentences are essentially descriptions. Sentences have vastly many different roles and describing is only one of them. Moreover, there is not just one thing called 'describing'!

Understanding and Meaning

Now let us move on to yet another step. And let me again address our interlocutor.

> **PMSH.** You are attracted to a referential or correlational conception of meaning, and to a representational or descriptive conception of language. What a language is *for*, you are inclined to say, is to represent how things are. Now it seems evident that correlational conceptions of meaning commit one to a very specific range of *psychological doctrines* about understanding.

Int. Yes. That's right. If the meaning of a name is the entity it stands for, then *to know what a word means* just is *to know what it stands for*. That's exactly what Russell explained when he wrote:

> in order to understand a name for a particular, the only thing necessary is to be acquainted with that particular. When you are acquainted with that particular, you have full, adequate, and complete understanding of the name, and no further information is required.[2]

Now, isn't that right?

PMSH. So far, so good – as the man who jumped off the Empire State Building said as he passed the thirtieth floor! But you must think this through. Note that if this is what understanding a name is, then knowing its combinatorial possibilities in grammar – that is: *what it makes sense to say* – is something that must be known by *mere acquaintance* with the thing it names. So, the combinatorial possibilities of words in our language flow not from conventions of language, but from the *essential nature of the thing* with which one is acquainted.

Int. Yes, that's right! It is just *because* a sound *can't* be red, that the word 'red' *can't* meaningfully be attached to the name of a sound. So the combination of words 'That's a red noise' makes no sense *because* noises *can't* be red. And it is *because* visible things *can* be red, that we *can* intelligibly attach the word 'red' to the name of any visible object.

PMSH. So you mean that grammar – the rules for the sensible combinations of words – is answerable to the essential, metaphysical nature of things. That is a very bold thesis!

Int. Yes. But don't you see that it *must be so*! After all, *why* can't noises be red? Why can't tastes be loud? – There must be a reason! For surely, these are not just *facts that could be otherwise*! It's not as if on Mars there might be some coloured smells, or some noisy colours. These are metaphysical impossibilities.

PMSH. Ah – you mean: this lies in the *essential, language-independent natures* of things. You think that this is the way *God* made these properties!

Int. Well – that's *very* tempting. But I could also say that metaphysical truths such as these are just those that are *true in all possible worlds*.

PMSH. Yes, you could. But would that make anything *clearer*. You want to ask *why* a sound cannot be red, and *why* a smell can't be noisy – and you tell me that this is so in *all possible worlds*. But that is just a fancy way of saying that it is necessarily true, or true no matter how things may be.

---

2 Russell, *The Philosophy of Logical Atomism and Other Essays* (Allen and Unwin, London, 1986), p. 179.

It does not *explain* anything. And even to be tempted to say that *this is the way God made properties* is to fall back on *Just So* stories, not to explain.

Enough. What we have seen is how easy it is to succumb to the magical allure of metaphysics! In Lecture 7, I shall show you that the gold of metaphysics is no more than fool's gold and that the apparent rubies and diamonds are just pebbles and glass.

Now, back to understanding. As we have seen, it is very tempting to suppose that using a word in an utterance with understanding, as opposed to mere parroting, is *meaning something* by it. What one means by a word is what it means – its meaning. Let's again give my interlocutor his say:

Int. Look, John Locke wrote as follows:

> Parrots, and several other Birds, will be taught to make articulate Sounds distinct enough, which yet, by no means, are capable of Language. Besides articulate Sounds therefore, it was farther necessary, that he should be *able to use these Sounds, as Signs of internal Conceptions*; and to make them stand as Marks for the *Ideas* within his own Mind. (*Essay* III – i – 3)

Now that is exactly what I want to say. One makes a word stand for an idea within one's mind by *meaning* or intending *by* a given word a corresponding idea. The idea is what the word that one uses means, and *what one means* by a word is *its meaning*.

PMSH. So what you have in mind is this: meaning something by a word is a mental act whereby one, as it were, *projects* the word onto the entity meant.

Int. Yes, that's right.

PMSH. Well, I see that this is what idealist philosophers such as Locke, Berkeley and Hume would wish to say. But what of realists who think that words stand directly for things in reality and not only for ideas in the mind?

Int. Of course, the realist would go down an analogous path. He would argue that it is acts of meaning that link words with things in reality. Collingwood, for example, expressed this conception of meaning something by one's words well:

> A word is not a sound or group of sounds [...] it is a sound or group of sounds having its own meaning, namely what a person using the word means by making that sound.

But we have already been through all this!

PMSH. Yes, we have indeed. And I owe you an explanation of why I think that this line of thought is completely mistaken. I shall keep my promise in the next few lectures. The reason I wanted to go over this ground again is to show you that this conception of thinking and expressing one's thoughts in speech for purposes of communicating them to others commits one to a very specific conception of understanding. Corresponding to the idea that acts of meaning breathe significance into dead signs is the idea that *understanding the words of another* is an act of *interpreting*. For on your conception, what a speaker gives one in an act of communication is *mere words* – the sounds he utters. Understanding them must amount to *linking them to their meanings*, that is: giving them a *correct interpretation*. A correct interpretation of the words of another is tantamount to taking them to mean what the speaker means by them, or to mean the very same ideas in one's own mind as the ideas in the mind of the speaker.

Int. Yes. Surely, that must be right!

PMSH. Must it? The only thing that is sure here is how easy it is to take the wrong turning in the conceptual jungle. If you choose to go down this well-worn path, then you must imagine linguistic communication on the following model: the speaker has a thought that he wishes to convey to another. So he projects the thought onto a sentence, meaning the sentence to express what he thought. He then utters the sentence. If the hearer is to understand what thought the speaker is trying to communicate, he has to interpret his words. That is, he must assign them meanings that accord exactly with what the speaker meant by his words. The meaning of the sentence must then be derived from the meanings of the words and their mode of combination in the sentence. A correct interpretation of an utterance is one in which the hearer assigns the same meaning to the sentence in use as the speaker did; then he will know what thought the speaker was trying to convey.

Int. Well, that all seems to me to be perfectly convincing. What's wrong with it?

To be sure, the interlocutor is quite right. It is evidently perfectly convincing. For this is the standard conception of linguistic communication to this day. It is common among linguists in the wake of the great Ferdinand de Saussure, common among philosophers in the wake of Donald Davidson – one of the leading philosophers of the late twentieth century – and common among psychologists and neuroscientists who study the human language faculty. It is, according to Wittgenstein, wholly misconceived. In a later lecture, I shall explain why it is misconceived.

What I have sketched out for you today does, I hope, make clear how natural Augustine's picture is and how *powerful* is the conception Wittgenstein extracts from it. It also makes clear that within the framework of this conception, one can advance a range of different substantive theories about language, its role and function. In the next five lectures, I shall demolish this house of cards.

Chapter 3

NAMES AND THEIR MEANING, SENTENCES AND DESCRIPTIONS

Names

We saw in the last lecture that the *Philosophical Investigations* begins by sketching out the widely accepted, but misguided, ideas that words are essentially names and sentences are essentially combinations of names. The function of names is to stand for things. Names have a meaning and their meaning is the thing they stand for. The function of sentences is to describe how things stand. We saw that many philosophers, both linguistic realists and linguistic idealists, have succumbed to the charms of this conception. I tried to show how very tempting these ideas are. But great though the temptation is, it must be resisted, for this syndrome of ideas is misconceived.

To *show* that it is misconceived, what needs to be done is to survey the concepts of name, description, sentence and utterance, definition and explanation, meaning and use. When these notions have been clarified, we shall turn to the psychological notions of meaning something by a word, knowing what a word or utterance means, understanding and interpreting sentences uttered. Today, I shall start by examining the concept of a name and the idea that words are essentially names, and that the essential function of words is to *stand for* the things they name.

The category of names is not sharply circumscribed. Grammarians distinguish among names, between *proper names* and *common nouns*. Proper names include names of people, pets, places, times, artefacts, names of books and other works of art. Common nouns include names of kinds of things, both natural like 'dog' and artefactual like 'car'. These are all *count nouns* – what they name are *countable*. Hence, they admit of plural form and take such quantifiers as 'many', 'most', 'a few' – as in 'many dogs', 'most trees' and 'a few cars'. Their plural form allows combination with plural indexicals, such as 'these' and 'those', and with cardinal numbers greater than one. In addition to count nouns, there is a further category of *non-count nouns*, which may be concrete or abstract. *Concrete non-count* nouns are names of stuffs. These admit quantifiers such as 'much' and 'a little', 'a good deal of' and 'a large amount of' – as in 'much silk', 'a little milk', 'a good deal of plastic' and 'a large amount of steel'. In addition to the category of concrete non-count nouns, we have the category of *abstract non-count nouns*, such as 'honesty', 'courage', 'justice' – as well as many other abstractions. So, it is evident that the category of *names* subsumes a large variety of grammatically and logically different *kinds* of expression. The differences come out in the different combinatorial possibilities with other expressions.

> **Int.** But these are just arbitrary linguistic classifications. They have no authority at all. And I don't see why this is of any importance.
>
> **PMSH.** Ah, welcome back! Can you repeat that?
>
> **Int.** Thank you. Yes. I don't see why you are bringing in such arbitrary, conventional grammatical classifications. What conceivable bearing do they have on the question of the referential conception of meaning? They seem to me to be just trivial.
>
> **PMSH.** Ah, I see. Look, we are trying to get at the roots of the Augustinian conception of meaning – in all its rich varieties. A pivotal idea in that conception is that *all words are basically names of things*, that *the function of names is to stand for things*, and *the function of sentences*, which are composed of words in licit combinations, *is to describe how things stand*. So we must be clear about the grammatical category of names.
>
> **Int.** But aren't these categories arbitrary and therefore beside the point?
>
> **PMSH.** No, not at all. For they contribute to determining the bounds of sense. It makes sense to say of what is signified by a *count*-noun such as 'dog', that there are three dogs in the field, but not that there are 2.5 dogs in the field. It makes sense to say of what is signified by a *concrete* mass noun such as 'lead' that we need 2.5 kilogrammes of lead, but not that we need 2.5 leads. And it makes no sense to say of what is signified by an *abstract* mass noun, such as 'courage' that we have 2.5 kilogrammes of courage. So these syntactical classifications are anything but trivial when what one is doing is trying to separate sense from nonsense.
>
> **Int.** But I didn't think that we *were* trying to separate sense from nonsense at all. I thought we were trying to get at the *truth*.
>
> **PMSH.** Yes, indeed. But we aren't trying to get at *empirical* truths. That is the province of science. We are trying to get at *conceptual truths*. And conceptual truths, as I shall show you in later lectures, are determinants of what does and does not make sense.
>
> **Int.** All right. So we distinguish proper names from count nouns and from mass nouns, and we distinguish concrete mass nouns from abstract mass nouns. Where are you trying to take us with all of this?

PMSH. I am trying to get you to see how fluid the notion of a name is, and how indeterminate are its boundaries. Indeed, it is clear that the notion of *a name* stretches far farther than proper names and common nouns. Wittgenstein's first response to Augustine's autobiographical fragment, which I quoted in the last lecture, is this: 'Augustine does not mention any differences between kinds of word. Someone who describes the learning of language in this way is, I believe, thinking primarily of nouns like "table", "chair", "bread" and of people's names, and only secondarily of names of certain actions and properties; and of the remaining words as something that will take care of itself (PI §1).' That is surely right. In addition to naming individual things, kinds of things and kinds of stuffs, we also name shapes, colours, sounds and smells. We name directions of the compass and ocean currents. We name days of the week and times of the day. We name numbers by number words. And, as Wittgenstein just reminded us, we also name actions such as walking, running, smiling or talking.

Int. Well, of course. But why is this relevant to the referential conception of word meaning?

PMSH. Because it is a part of the referential conception that all words (with a few exceptions that are allegedly marginal) are names, and that the function of names is to stand for – to name – entities in reality. But once your attention is drawn to the plethora of kinds of name, it should be immediately obvious to you that names do not have one single function in a language – *standing for*. Rather, they have a huge range of *different* functions – depending upon what one *does* with these expressions. Functions characteristic of one kind of name are excluded for another kind. So, for example, personal names of people are typically used to *address* a person, to *introduce* him or her, to *call* or *order* the person, to *refer* to the person, to *address letters* to the person and so forth. But one does not use names of artefacts to address things or to call them. (You may remember the amusing exchange between the six-year-old Winston Churchill and his schoolmaster teaching him Latin declensions. Having learnt that the vocative 'mensa' in Latin means 'O table' the little boy had the temerity to ask what 'O table' means – to which the teacher replied that it was the form of words one would use to address a table. Young Winston rightly answered that he never addressed tables – upon which he was told that if he carried on thus, he would come to a bad end.) Common nouns are used, among other things, to form definite descriptions, such as '*the* dog in the kennel' or '*the* table in the corner', whereas proper names don't normally take the definite article, and aren't so used. While names of things are involved in stating *how many* *things* we have, names of stuff can be used to say *how much* of some stuff we have. Names of stuffs are used to ask for ingredients, to answer such questions as 'What is it made of?' and so forth.

Int. But still, they are all names, aren't they?

PMSH. Well, we *can* stretch the concept of a name to include these and many further kinds of word. What I am trying to get you to see is, first: that the greater the diversity in the different kinds of linguistic expression that we call a 'name', the less is actually said by characterizing an expression as a name. And second: huge though the category of names may be, and elastic as the concept of a name is, there are many expressions that you would surely *not* naturally call 'names' – for example, prepositions such as 'to', 'by', 'of', connectives such as 'and', 'but', 'or', not to mention qualifiers such as 'perhaps' or 'maybe', quantifiers such as 'some', 'many', 'all' and indexicals such as 'this' and 'that', 'here' and 'there', 'now' and 'then'. Would you be willing to say that 'now' is the name of a time? Or that 'this' is the name of an entity?

Int. Well, I'll grant you that would be going overboard. To say that these are names would be no more than a kind of dogmatism.

Well, I hope that clarifies Wittgenstein's manoeuvre. The heart and core of the Augustinian conception of language is that naming and describing are the *essential functions of language*, that *all words are names, the essence of which is to stand for things*. It is with words that we construct well-formed sentences, and *the essence of the sentence in use is to describe*. Wittgenstein's response is, in effect, threefold:

First, as I've just explained, if one thinks that words are essentially names, one is thinking primarily of proper names and common nouns, perhaps also of some adjectives and verbs. Wittgenstein is even willing to concede that one *can* call the word 'three' the name of a number, the preposition 'on' the name of a relation, the word 'or' the name of a truth function, and even the quantifiers 'some', and 'all' can be said to be *names of second-level functions*, as the logician Frege called them. But the more one stretches the concept of a name, *the less one says in calling a word 'a name'*. And in the end, the claim becomes completely empty.

Second, it is evident from brief scrutiny of the kinds of expressions that we *can* comfortably call *names*, that names have a multiplicity of functions. So even if it were true that words are essentially names, that claim would not elucidate the nature and function of words. Just reflect on the manifold uses of name tags and name notices. We put a name tag on our lapel and stick a name tag on a bottle. But the tags signify differently, for the former indicates

NAMES AND THEIR MEANING, SENTENCES AND DESCRIPTIONS

the name by which to address us, and the latter signifies the name of the contents of the bottle. We write names of houses above the door, names of shops above the shops, names of railway stations above the station and names of paper currency on the currency. But the functions of these names are as diverse as the functions of the things to which they are attached or on which they are written.

Third, in calling all kinds of expression 'names', one obscures the logical roles of different kinds of words. What we need to do is to draw attention to *differences*. Wittgenstein makes this clear in the following passage:

> think of the following use of language: I send someone shopping. I give him a slip of paper marked 'five red apples'. He takes the slip to the shopkeeper, who opens the drawer marked 'apples'; then he looks up the word 'red' in a chart and finds a colour sample opposite it; then he says the series of elementary number-words – I assume that he knows them by heart – up to the word 'five', and for each number-word he takes an apple of the same colour as the sample out of the drawer. — It is in this and similar ways that one operates with words. — 'But how does he know where and how he is to look up the word "red" and what he is to do with the word "five"?' — Well, I assume that he *acts* as I have described. Explanations come to an end somewhere. (PI §1)

What Wittgenstein is suggesting is that we replace the naming conception of the essence of language with a quite different *operational* conception of language and *functional* conception of the words of language. Words are comparable to *objects in a tool box*, and the logical diversity of words is comparable to the diversity of objects in a toolbox – for example, a hammer, a screwdriver, an awl, a saw, a clamp, a spirit level, a pair of pliers, a ruler, a tape measure and so on. Objects in a toolbox, like words, have a wide range of diverse functions. To say that all words are names is as misleading as saying that all objects in a toolbox *serve to modify something*. What does a clamp or a tape measure modify? Or a spirit level? Or a pair of pliers? By parity of reasoning, we must look to the *uses* of words – not to their forms and surface-grammatical categories. We must look to what we *do* with them and to their *role* in human life – not to what they *name*.

Standing for Things

As we saw, it is a part of Augustine's picture of language and part of the correlational conception of linguistic meaning that the essential function of words is *to stand for* or *signify* things. Is this not an altogether natural idea?

> **Int.** Absolutely! The proper name 'Jack' stands for Jack. The common noun 'cat' signifies a kind of animal. The adjective 'red' stands for a colour. The adverb 'quickly' stands for a way of doing things. – So obviously

words *stand for things*, they *signify* things. And isn't that the essence of the *name relation*? Isn't that what it is to *be* a name?

PMSH. Can't you see that to characterize *standing for* as the essential function of names is as empty, and as misleading, as characterizing all words as names? Indeed, the one doctrine is the complement of the other. Naming something by itself contributes nothing to determining *the use* of the word in question.

Let me give you an analogy Wittgenstein drew between words and chess pieces, and between knowing what a given chess piece is and knowing what a given word means. If all I know about the chess king is that this piece of wood is called the 'king', then so far I know virtually nothing about the chess king and have learnt nothing about how to play chess. I don't know what I *can do* with the piece.

Int. Ah, yes. I see. You have to learn the moves of the king.

PMSH. That's right. But not just that – also the moves of the other pieces; and what counts as winning and losing; not to mention what the point of the game is – and what its role is in human life. We don't fight battles and kill people in playing chess – it is *a game*. So to understand *what a chess king is* requires vastly more than knowing that this piece of wood is named 'king'. So too with the words of language. To know what a word means is to know what one can do with it. A word – it has been said with some justice – has a meaning only in the context of a sentence in use. For only then does it make a contribution to what is said. And only then is it being used in saying something.

Int. But still, don't you first name the pieces and then go on to refer to them? And isn't it so with language too. We give names to things – and then we use the names to refer to these things.

PMSH. *No! That is not the point at all.* Just to have named a piece in a game does not even enable you to go on to refer to it unless you know much more. After all, what would you be referring to? To a curiously carved piece of wood? To talk about the chess king, you must know its powers. Otherwise, you quite literally don't know what you are talking about! The analogy between a chess piece and a word is that you don't know what the word means until you know what you can do with it – what combinatorial possibilities it has, what kind of word it is and how it is used in sentences.

So, to conceive of words as names standing for things is to confuse *preparation* for *performance*. Naming things is preparatory to the use of language. It is akin to placing the chessmen on the chess board in preparation for a game – not to making a chess move. But naming the pieces on the board gets you nowhere until you know what can be done with

NAMES AND THEIR MEANING, SENTENCES AND DESCRIPTIONS 41

them, what moves they can make and what the point of making the various moves is in a given position in a game.

Wittgenstein does indeed compare using language to playing a game. Now, naming is not *making a move* in language-game but is *preparatory* to making a move. To learn a language is not merely to learn the names of things or to give names to things; it is to learn to *do* things with words – for which learning names is merely a preparation.

Int. But surely, we learn the names of things, and *then* we can *refer* to those things in speech and *talk about* them. So I still can't see what is wrong with characterizing the essence of language as referring to things, talking about things and describing how things stand.

PMSH. That is deeply misleading. First of all, there is no one thing called 'referring', and there is no one thing called 'talking about'. Second, we do indefinitely many *other* things with language than referring and talking about things.

If we say that 'Jill' is used to refer to a woman of that name, as in the utterance 'Jill is at home', then we must remember that the name 'Jill' can occur non-referentially in other statements ('Who is that woman?' – 'That's Jill!'; or 'What is Jack thinking?' – 'He is wondering who Jill is'), in introductions ('This is Jill'), in asking questions ('Where is Jill?'), in issuing orders ('Jill, be quiet'), in writing name tags or addressing envelopes and so forth. *If* these are all conceived as referential uses of the name 'Jill', then of course, there is no one thing called 'referring'.

Int. But why does it matter that there are lots of things called *referring*?

PMSH. Because, among other things, the referential conception of meaning was trying to pin down the essence of language. But just as the more the notion of name is stretched, the less is said by claiming that all words are names, so too, the more we stretch the diversity of speech activities that can be called *referring*, the less is said by saying that the essential function of words is to refer to entities.

Int. But still, isn't it important that we use words *to talk about things*? Can't I say that?

PMSH. Well, of course you can say it. The question is what it amounts to – how much light it sheds on our conception of language and linguistic communication, on words and their manifold roles and on sentences and their indefinitely many uses. There are countless things we do with words that are not *talking about things* – we give orders and make requests, we ask questions and express puzzlement, we tell stories and make jokes, we sing songs, we volunteer, we agree or disagree, we curse, pray and greet – and so on and so forth through myriad acts and activities with words. What a child learns when he learns to speak is not *a list* *of names*, but *how to perform a range of acts and activities*. Words, Wittgenstein remarked, are deeds. The speech activities the child learns are partly constitutive of the form of life into which the child is being acculturated.

Let me give you a further analogy. Knowing that this piece of metal is called a 'ten-penny coin' is to know nothing unless one has grasped the rudiments of the idea of a means of exchange and has understood what to do with coins. Mastery of a language does not consist in knowing the names of things, and then going on to refer to things and talk about them. It consists in engaging in, and being able to engage in, the variety of speech acts and activities that make up a large part of human life. For this, naming is merely preparatory, and referring is merely one function of words among indefinitely many others.

The Meaning of a Word

All right. Now let's move on to the concept of the *meaning of a word*. As we have seen, it is part of the referential conception of language that the meaning of a word is the thing it means. So, the British empiricists held that the meaning of a word is the idea in the mind for which it stands. Other philosophers, less tempted by linguistic idealism, held that the meanings of words were not ideas in the mind, but the things *in reality* for which they stand, to wit: substances, properties, relations and so forth. Many linguists and psychologists, following de Saussure, the founder of structuralist linguistics, hold that the meaning of a word is *the concept* for which it stands. In short, there has been a wide consensus that there are such things called *meanings* that are attached to, associated with, named by words. So we need to probe this idea.

We commonly ask what a given word means. If we want to know what 'prestidigitation' means, we look it up in the dictionary. Words, we say, *have a meaning*. Furthermore, we *mean something* by the words we utter. And we are inclined to suppose that what we mean by a word in a sentence is what the word means, signifies, stands for or represents. From here it is but one short step to the thought that the meaning of the word *is* the item it stands for. We would naturally say that by the proper name 'Jack' I meant the fellow standing over there. We might explain that by the word 'ultramarine' what we meant was *that* colour [and we point at the ultramarine curtains] – *that's* ultramarine. And we slide readily from saying that *that* is ultramarine, to saying that *that* [and we point at *the colour* of the curtains] is what the word 'ultramarine' *means*. And from there it is but one short step to the supposition that *that* is *the meaning of the word 'ultramarine'*. This slippery slope is *one reason* why we might come to think that the meanings of words are the things they mean, stand for or signify.

But this is a muddle. We confuse the relative pronoun 'what' (as in 'What you have in your hand is valuable') with the interrogative pronoun 'what' (as in 'What's your opinion?'). Someone may ask 'What does "ultramarine mean"?' So we point at the ultramarine curtains, saying 'That colour is ultramarine'. But this does not imply that what one points at in *giving the meaning* of the word 'ultramarine' is *the meaning of the word* – as if the curtains were dyed with the meaning of 'ultramarine'. Rather, the utterance 'That colour is ultramarine' amounts to giving *the answer to the question* 'What does "ultramarine" mean?' In response to this question, we point at a sample. But to point at a sample of ultramarine is not to point *at* the meaning of the word 'ultramarine'. To *point out* what a word means, is not to *point at* what it means.

We slide readily into supposing that when we mean something by a word, then what the word means, and what we mean by it, is its meaning. But if the thing we meant by a word were its meaning, then if it ceased to exist, the word would cease to have a meaning. But that is absurd. The *bearer of a name* is not the same as the *meaning of a name*. You can be friends with the bearer of the name 'Jack', but not with its meaning! The proper name 'Jack' does not cease to signify Jack when Jack dies. The noun 'dodo' did not cease to have a meaning when the last dodo was slaughtered, and the word 'unicorn' is not meaningless just because there have never been any unicorns.

All right. So, the phrase 'the meaning of a word' does not signify *a kind of thing* but, roughly speaking, a *kind of answer* to a question of the form 'What does the word "W" mean?'. *The meaning of a word is what is given by an explanation of what it means.* That is a platitude – but it is a platitude of considerable importance and non-trivial ramifications. If you are puzzled at the idea of the meaning of a word, you should look at what are called 'explanations of meaning' and at what counts as explaining what a given word means.

Explanations of Meaning

Why is this important? Well, as we've seen, it enables us to sidestep talk about *meanings* – with all the confusions which that noun invites. Focussing upon humdrum explanations of what an expression means will free us of the illusion that the question 'What does it mean?' is akin to the question 'Whom do you mean?' and help us to see its kinship with the question 'What is its colour?' or 'What is its weight?'. It will also help to liberate us from the idea that *having a meaning* is a *relation* between a word and a meaning. For we need to free ourselves from the idea that meanings are kinds of things and that we *attach* meanings to words – as if meanings were *attachments*.

But there is another reason for the importance of linking the notion of meaning with that of explanation of meaning. Reminding us of our *humdrum, home-baked* explanations of word meaning prevents us from distorting the concept of explanation. There is a long tradition in philosophy, going back to Socrates, according to which the *only* adequate explanation of what a word means is an *analytic definition* – to wit: one that specifies the necessary and sufficient conditions for the word to apply to a thing. Wittgenstein thought that wrong. There are *many* different ways of explaining what words mean, and analytic definition is only one of them. It is not superior to the others, nor, indeed, is it the most common way of explaining what a word means. A far more common form of explanation is *ostensive explanation* or *definition* – as when we explain that *this* ☞ [and here we point] is a cauliflower, that *this* ☞ is a circle, that *this* ☞ is magenta, that *this* ☞ is marble and so on. And there are other kinds of explanation too, such as *contextual definition, explanation by examples together with a similarity rider, explanation by phrasal or sentential paraphrase, explanation by contrastive paraphrase* and so forth. We have well-established *practices* of explaining what words mean to children – and these practices do not consist in giving arcane and complex definitions. And they are none the worse for that. We teach children to use number words, but not by telling them that numbers are classes of classes, nor by giving them the kind of definitions that the great mathematical logician Frege offered, for example: 'One is the number which belongs to the concept "identical with zero"'. No one untrained in logic would understand that sort of definition, and no one has ever learnt the use, and therefore the meaning, of number words from such definitions. Rather we hold up one finger and say 'This is one finger', and then hold up two and say 'Here are two fingers – look: *this* is one, and *this* is two' and so on. For an explanation is satisfactory if it enables the hearer to go on to use the word correctly, and teaching the first few cardinal number words thus does indeed enable children to begin to engage in the practice of counting things and of saying how many such-and-such things they have.

An explanation of what a word means is itself *a standard of correct use*. Indeed, an explanation of meaning is a *rule* for the use of a word. For a learner, having been given an explanation of what a word means goes on to use the word correctly if he goes on to use the word *in accordance* with the explanation he was given. So, for example, an ostensive explanation of a colour word such as 'magenta' is a rule which specifies that anything which is *that* ☞ colour [and here one points at a sample of magenta] is correctly called *magenta*. An ostensive explanation of what an elephant is is given by pointing at an elephant (or at a picture of an elephant) and saying 'That's ☞ an elephant', and this is a rule that specifies that any animal that is what *this* animal is may correctly be called an 'elephant'. An analytic definition of a word such as 'A vixen is a female fox' states that any animal that is both a fox and female is correctly called a 'vixen'. That is obviously a rule for the use of the word 'vixen'. And so on.

So, explanations of meaning are rules for the use of words. They are not descriptions of *habits* of word use – but *norms for the correct use of words*. They state how words *are to be used*. But of course, the way words *are to be* used determines the way they *are in fact used* – for in a rule-governed practice most people comply with the rules. Chess players by and large play chess *as it is to be played*, and tennis players for the most part play tennis *in accordance with the rules of tennis*. So too, competent speakers of a language generally use words as they are to be used.

There is nothing theoretical about the rules for the use of words thus conceived. Explanations of meaning are patent in teaching children what words mean, in correcting their mistakes, in explaining to foreigners what words mean, in clarifying what exactly we mean, in ensuring, in a discussion, that we are not talking at cross purposes and so forth. Explanations of meaning are given in response to requests for an explanation of what a word means, and they are typically tailored to specific misunderstandings or failures of understanding. Wittgenstein's conception of explanations of meaning is humdrum, common-or-garden – for explanations of meaning must engage with the practices of speakers of the language. It is no coincidence that one criterion for whether someone knows what a given word means is that he gives a correct and acceptable explanation of what it means in a given context when asked – or at least acknowledges a correct explanation *as* correct when he is offered one.

A corollary of this is that it makes no sense to suppose that we might master the use of a word but have no idea what it means. For that would amount to claiming that we can use words in accordance with the rules for their use, holding our uses to be correct but having no idea what the rules are. But to use a word thus in accordance with the rules for its use *is* to follow the rules. And you can't follow a rule without being able to say, *in some form or other*, what rule you are following. You cannot use a word in an utterance and mean something by it, and not be able to explain *in some humdrum form or other*, what you mean by the words you uttered. If you can't even recognize a correct explanation of the use of the word you yourself used *as correct* when it is suggested to you, then it becomes doubtful whether you knew what it meant in the first place.

> **Int.** Oh come now! That can't be right. We all know how to use the word 'Amen' in church, but very few people know what it means. So one can know the use of a word without having the faintest idea of its meaning.
>
> **PMSH.** You are rushing the fences. According to the *Oxford English Dictionary* 'Amen' in ancient Hebrew meant *certainty* or *truth* and had an adverbial use to signify *certainly* or *verily*. *Something* of this may remain in

religious services today in the congregation's use of the exclamation to signify consent. But few people know this paraphrase.

Int. That's exactly what I was saying! So, knowing how to use a word is something quite different from knowing what it means.

PMSH. No, not at all. You are much too hasty. One may safely say that in modern English 'amen' is used as an expression of consent at the end of a formal recitation of a prayer. *And that says all there is to say about its meaning.* You can't say that 'amen' means the same as 'consent', since it patently doesn't. One can't say 'I give you my amen', let alone 'I amen to your going'. One may indeed say that in contemporary English 'amen' *has meaning*, that is, it is a meaningful expression; but it does not have *a meaning*. For if you were asked 'What does "amen" mean?', you would not begin your answer by saying 'It means the same as …'.

Int. Well, yes, I can see that.

PMSH Let me give you another example: What does 'Tally-ho' mean?

Int. It is a cry used by fox hunters when they sight a fox.

PMSH. If you know that, you know the use of 'Tally-ho' – and *there is nothing further to know about its meaning*. The rest consists of conjectures about its etymology. Again, does 'Good-by', let alone 'By-by', mean 'God be wi' ye'? Clearly not anymore. These are expressions used to bid someone farewell – and their origin has no more bearing on their current meaning than 'God blind me' has on 'Cor blimey!'.

So, the idea that we might all be using words, but that among these words there might be some that *no one* knows how to explain, is incoherent.

Int. But surely, the kinds of case that we have been examining *demonstrate* that it is perfectly coherent. The fact is that 'Good-by' is a transform of 'God be wi' ye' – and that because people's speech habits are sloppy, the words got run together. Pretty soon no one will know what 'Good-by' means, but they will still know how to use it. So mastery of the use of a word is not the same as knowing its meaning.

PMSH. Not at all. 'Good-by' no longer means the same as 'God be wi' ye'. And the meaning of 'By-by' *is* exhausted by explaining that it is used on parting, to bid farewell. Do you really mean to say that you don't know what 'Hullo' means if you are ignorant of the fact that it is derived from the Old High German imperative 'holon', which meant 'Fetch!'?

Int. Ah, yes. I see what you mean.

PMSH. Good. So don't forget that the function of an explanation of meaning is to provide guidance in the use of the expression explained. You must not confuse what an expression meant with what it now means. And you must not confuse and conflate an expression's being meaningful (i.e. having meaning) with an expression's having *a* specific meaning, such that one can answer the question 'What does it mean?' with the form of words 'It means ...'.

I trust that clears some things up. But let me continue the same train of thought. An explanation of meaning is in effect a rule for the use of the word explained. The function of a rule is to guide practice and to constitute a standard of correctness – *but an unknown rule can neither guide practice nor serve as a standard of correctness.* So Plato's idea that we all know the use of the word 'justice', but none of us knows what it really means is, to say the least, suspect. Frege remarked:

> Often it is only after immense intellectual effort, which may have continued over centuries, that humanity at last succeeds in achieving knowledge of a concept in its pure form, in stripping off the irrelevant accretions which veil it from the eye of the mind.

But this is more than a little questionable. For, we surely can't have been using number words since time immemorial without anyone knowing what they mean until Frege defined them in terms of classes of classes. There are many words that are not *defined* by analytic definition – but there are not any words the use of which cannot be taught and explained in some way or other. The use of words is rule-governed no less than the moves in a game. The rules for the use of words cannot be hidden from their proficient users – they must be transparent. And so indeed they are – they are exhibited in common-or-garden explanations of meaning.

Wittgenstein emphasized that explaining the meaning of words to children presupposes *antecedent linguistic training*. One cannot teach a child how to speak by means of explanations of meaning, since explanations of meaning take elementary linguistic skills for granted. These elementary skills are acquired through *training* and *drill* that inculcate habits of repetition and reactive dispositions to uses of words by others. This in turn presupposes a wide range of natural human discriminatory abilities, recognitional capacities, imitative propensities and behavioural patterns. Were these substantially different in specifiable ways, we would have a very different language – or indeed no language at all. Such *training*, with us, is the essential background for *teaching* a language to a child by means of explanations of meaning. Only when the child is in a position to ask, for example, 'What's a giraffe?' or 'What is that animal called?', and 'What does "giraffe" mean?' do explanations of word meaning get a firm grip. For explanations of meaning explain only *within language* – we explain a word in terms of other words, or in terms of other symbols, such as gestures and samples. Explanations of meaning give an array of *intra-linguistic* articulations and connections – they do not, as we shall see, *exit* from language – not even in the case of ostensive definitions. That is one reason why Wittgenstein treats explanations of meaning as belonging to what he calls 'grammar'.

We must pause here a moment, for we must be clear what he meant by 'grammar' – since he stretched the ordinary use of the term. It is customary to associate *grammar* with the *syntactical rules* of language. These are rules concerning different parts of speech and their combination into well-formed sentences. Explanations of word *meaning*, according to linguists, belong to what they call the 'lexicon' and are *not* part of grammar. Wittgenstein held that for his purposes, there is no deep difference between syntactical rules and meaning rules – both are rules for the use of words. Indeed, he said, there is no *sharp* divide between them. The grammarian will say that the phrase 'north-east of' must be followed by a noun or pronoun in the accusative or objective case. But he won't specify what *sort* of noun must follow 'north-east of', for example, a place name or the name of an object or person at a place. And he would certainly not specify that one cannot insert the phrases 'North-Pole' and 'South-Pole' after the phrase 'north-east of'. But it is precisely *that* kind of rule that interests a philosopher, whose business it is to examine the bounds of sense. The grammarian and the philosopher both have an interest in rules for the use of words, but their interests are different, and the kinds of rule that are of especial interest to philosophers are unlikely to be of any interest to the grammarian.

In the 1930s, when Wittgenstein had just arrived at his new method in philosophy, he often said in his lectures that philosophical problems are grammatical. Indeed, in one lecture he went so far as to say that 'In philosophy, all that isn't gas is grammar'. At one of these lectures, his older colleague in Cambridge, G. E. Moore, was present in the audience, and was obviously very uneasy with Wittgenstein's claim that the roots of philosophical problems lie in the grammar of our language. At last Moore ventured a question:

> Wittgenstein, how can you say that philosophy is concerned with grammar? Grammar is the kind of thing we teach children at school. We teach them that the sentence 'Three men were in the field' is grammatical, whereas 'Three men was in the field' is not. – That's grammar! And what has that got to do with philosophy?

Wittgenstein stumped up and down for a bit and then replied

> That is because your example is too smooth and unproblematic. But what about 'God the Father, God the Son, and God the Holy Ghost *were* in the field or *was* in the field'?

So, we shall follow Wittgenstein's harmless usage and accept the idea that rules for the use of words, syntactical and lexicographical alike, belong to grammar. Hence, you should not be surprised when Wittgenstein insists that explanations of meaning are part of grammar. For explanations of meaning are rules for the use of words.

Sentences and Descriptions

We noted that Augustine's picture of language takes sentences to be ordered combinations of names. So sentences are conceived to be necessarily complex. One reason for thinking this is that one is inclined to suppose that sentences are descriptions and that single names do not describe things – they name them. One needs a name to pick out a subject of discourse and another name to assert or deny something of that subject. Or, according to modern logic, one needs the name of an argument conjoined with the name of a function to assert anything that is either true or false.

Wittgenstein came to think that this was quite wrong. It is the product of imposing preconceptions upon language, rather than looking to see how it functions. After all, he said, it is easy to imagine a language in which the only sentences were one-word sentences. So, a builder might say 'Slab!' or 'Pillar!' – whereupon his assistant would be required to bring him a slab or a pillar. You may be tempted to say that this is just an elliptical way of saying 'Bring me a slab!' or 'Bring me a pillar!', but in this imagined language, there is no such sentential form of words. It is in our own language that we can make this distinction – not in the imagined one. 'Slab' in the imagined language is not elliptical for anything. It is not as if the speakers of this imagined language are to be conceived as *adding* something further to the order 'Slab!' *in thought* – any more than Russian speakers are to be imagined as adding the copula to Russian sentences in thought or as adding definite or indefinite articles.

To be sure, we ourselves use one-word sentences. Think of the diversity of exclamations:
Water!
Away!
Ow!
Help!
Splendid!
No!
These are all single-word sentences. It would be an unwarranted distortion to suggest that they are all elliptical, *because sentences must be complex.* That is mere dogma derived from failure to focus on the fact that a sentence is *the minimal unit by which we perform an act of speech – make a move in the language-game.* And one can make a move in a language-game not only with combinations of words but also with one-word sentences.

You might think that this is trivial. All right, you may respond, so there are one-word sentences. But still, most sentences are complex and consist of ordered combinations of names. Of course, that is correct. But the point is not at all trivial. For it serves to break the hold that a picture has over our imagination – the picture that a sentence essentially depicts a state of affairs, that it represents how things are by an ordered array of names that stand for things. It sharpens our awareness of the need to focus upon the manifold *different uses* of sentences – and not to be mesmerized by the idea of *descriptive* or *pictorial* role.

In this way, the reminder of one-word sentences may have served the function which a simple example had in breaking the hold the idea of logical form had on the young Wittgenstein. Sometime in 1929, Wittgenstein was travelling by train with the eminent Cambridge economist Piero Sraffa and explaining to him the notion of logical form as presented in the *Tractatus*. Sraffa was sceptical. Making a rude Neapolitan gesture of contempt with his hand, he said to Wittgenstein 'What is the logical form of *that*?' – and this broke the magic of the idea of depth-grammatical logical form. It is, of course, not an argument, let alone a conclusive one. It is a redeeming word that stops one in one's tracks at the brink of nonsense.

Not only is it mistaken to suppose that the essential function of sentences can only be performed by complex ordered combinations of words, but it is equally mistaken to suppose that sentences have a single essential function. Sentences have endlessly varied functions – and it would be wholly misguided to suppose that *they are all descriptions*. Of course, one might claim that the exclamation 'Water!' describes what the speaker wants to be given, that 'Away!' describes what the speaker wants the hearer to do, that 'Ow!' describes how much his leg hurts – But that is getting more than a little far fetched!

Moreover, we should bear in mind the obvious fact that interrogative sentences and imperative sentences are not used to describe things. Their form is indicative of their typical function – to ask a question or make a request, to give an order or entreat. And it would be perverse to characterize questions and orders as descriptions. Of course, you can, if you wish, say that the order 'Stop at the red traffic lights' describes what you ought to do, or that the question 'Is it raining?' describes what I want to know. But this does not make sentences used to give an order or to ask a question any more similar to declarative sentences that may be used to describe how things are.

Similarly, the arithmetical equation '20 and 5 make 25' may look like a description of numerical relations, but it is in effect an inference rule. It entitles you to infer from the fact that you have 20 marbles and the fact that you have just won another 5 that now you have 25 – *without counting them all up again*. To insist that this arithmetical equation is a description of a relationship between numbers would merely exhibit to view the fact that you are the victim of a deep-rooted illusion. The role and function of arithmetical equations is altogether *unlike* that of empirical descriptions.

But even if I were to concede, perhaps for the sake of argument, that you may, if you wish, say that the role of sentences is to describe how things are, you would not have achieved the essentialist goal you are craving. For to say this completely obscures the diversity of what *are* legitimately called 'descriptions'. Just as there is no one thing called 'referring', so too there is no one thing called 'describing'. Compare the following:

a description of a house one is looking at
a description of a house one remembers
a description of a house one wants one's builder to build
a description of a house in a story
an architectural drawing of the elevations of a house
an architectural ground plan of a house

The logical diversity of these kinds of description can be brought out by reflecting on how one can improve each of them: in the first case, by more careful observation, in the second by trying to call further features to mind – perhaps by trying to recollect things one did in the vicinity of the remembered house or by looking at old photographs, in the third by giving more detailed and accurate descriptions of how the house should be in order to satisfy one's needs and desires or to match current fashions, in the fourth by using one's imagination, in the fifth by further architectural inventiveness, in the sixth by a more convenient layout and relationship between the rooms. Each of these involves, in Wittgenstein's jargon, quite different language games, and also quite different skills.

So, the idea that the essential function of a sentence as such is to describe something truly or falsely is as misconceived as the idea that all words are names of things.

In the next lecture, I shall explain what Wittgenstein put in place of Augustine's picture of language and of the referential or correlational conception of linguistic meaning – namely, his constructive account of meaning as use.

Chapter 4

MEANING AND USE, UNDERSTANDING AND INTERPRETING

Meaning and Use

We saw, in the last lecture, how Wittgenstein criticized the Augustinian picture and the complex referential conceptions of linguistic meaning that elaborate it. He demonstrated the vacuity of labelling all words as *names* and refuted the claim that sentences are combinations of names, the essential function of which is to describe how things are.

Int. But all that was purely destructive! Didn't he have anything constructive to say about what it is for words or sentences to have a meaning?

PMSH. Oh, come now! It wasn't *purely* destructive. After all, you learnt a great deal about naming and reference, about explanations of meaning and about what counts as description.

Int. All right – that's fair enough. But nevertheless, Wittgenstein surely owes us an explanation of what it is for a word to have a meaning, and what *meaning* is?

PMSH. Yes, he does. And as we shall see in a moment, he discharges his obligation with much subtlety. But before I explain this to you, I want to draw your attention to something. You talk comfortably about a word *having* a meaning and about words *having* meanings. Be careful. The very form of words inclines one to think that meanings are things words have – that words and meanings stand in some mutual relationship: here the word, there the meaning. Wittgenstein compared this thought with the thought: here's the money, and there's the cow that one can buy with it. But that is altogether misconceived. The right comparison is with this: Here is the money, and this is its purchasing power.

All right. The first thing we must do is to examine the conception of word meaning that Wittgenstein advanced in place of the variations on the Augustinian, referential conception.

In *Investigations* §43, Wittgenstein wrote:

> For a *large* class of cases of the employment of the word 'meaning' – though not for *all* – this word can be explained in this way: the meaning of a word is its use in the language.

This remark has sometimes been said to express Wittgenstein's theory of meaning as use. That is a misdescription. For his brief observation is neither a theory nor any part of a theory. Wittgenstein did not think that there could *be* any such thing as a *philosophical theory* of meaning – only a clarification of the meaning of the word 'meaning'. In his lectures, he said

> I have suggested substituting for [the phrase] 'the meaning of a word', [the phrase] 'the use of a word', because *use of a word* comprises a large part of what is meant by 'the meaning of a word'.

This clearly demonstrates that what he is doing here is giving a rough paraphrase. That is no more a *theory* of anything than the assertion that for most uses of the word 'bachelor' (but not for the phrases 'bachelor of arts' or 'knight-bachelor'), it can be explained as *an unmarried man*. Still, a-theoretic as his observation is meant to be, it stands in need of clarification in three respects.

First, what exactly did he mean by 'use in the language'? There are, after all, many different things that may be meant, and not all of them can be equated with meaning. We say that the use of a certain word is popular or fashionable – but we don't say that the meaning of the word is popular or fashionable; we say that a word such as 'good' is used to commend – but we don't say that the word 'good' means the same as the verb 'to commend'; and we say that the use of a certain word on some occasion was uncalled for – but not that its meaning was uncalled for. So, it is important to pinpoint what Wittgenstein had in mind.

Second, why does Wittgenstein qualify his remark with the phrases 'for a large class of cases' and 'a large part of what is meant' – what are the exceptions he has in mind? There is no doubt that he did not mean the kinds of cases just cited, but we do need to determine what he did mean.

Finally, if his remark that the meaning of a word is its use in the language is not a theory, what is its status?

Let's start with the last question – and postpone the first two until the next lecture. The remark that *the meaning of a word is its use* is *an explanation* of the phrase 'the meaning of a word'. The concept of *the meaning of a word* is no more a theoretical one than is the concept of *the use of a tool*. The word 'meaning' has a use in such remarks as 'This word means the same as that' and 'That word has a different meaning'. These are not theoretical remarks belonging to a science of language, but common-or-garden remarks that antecede any theorizing. The word 'meaning' has a use in such questions as 'What does this word mean?' and 'Could you explain what this word means?' So, in saying that the meaning of a word, by and large, amounts to its use, Wittgenstein is making what he called a *grammatical remark*. He is pointing out a rule for the use of the phrase 'the meaning of a word', namely that in many contexts it may be replaced, or roughly paraphrased, by the expression 'the use of a word'. To ask what a word means is to ask how it is used. To know what a word means is to know the way it is used. And to wonder what a word means is to wonder how to use it. Further, to give the meaning of a word is to explain how it is used, and to stipulate a meaning for a word is to stipulate a use for it.

> **Int.** I don't really see what you are driving at. After all, I know how to use the phrase 'the meaning of a word'. I don't need Wittgenstein to tell me that I can ask 'What does this word mean?' or 'Does this word mean the same as that one?' So what are you trying to do when you tell me that you are *clarifying* the meaning of the word 'meaning'? After all, what you are telling me is news from nowhere!
>
> **PMSH.** Of course. If it were news, then it would be inappropriate. To clarify the meaning of an expression, including the expression 'the meaning of a word', is to *remind* you of something you already know full well. It is to remind you of the rules for the correct use of the phrase 'the meaning of a word'. If you weren't familiar with these standards of correct use of the word, you *wouldn't know* what the word means. Since you speak English, you already know how the phrase is used. You know that one can ask 'What does this word mean?' and that when one does so, one expects an explanation of what it means, an explanation that may be given by a synonym, by a definition, by a contextual paraphrase, by a series of examples and so forth. So you know the grammatical reticulations of the word in the network of our language.
>
> **Int.** So if it's news from nowhere, what is the point of reminding me of what I already know?
>
> **PMSH.** Because in order to dissolve the puzzles about linguistic meaning that plague philosophers, and some of which are already puzzling you, you have to marshall such features of usage in such a manner as will solve, resolve or dissolve the puzzles and problems. And that is *not* something that you know how to do. Of course, you know what the word 'meaning' means – you know how to use it correctly in ordinary discourse. But mastery of usage does not imply that you possess an overview of the rules for the use of a word. So, if I ask you how the meaning of a word is related to what a person means by a word, that may give you pause. If I press you with the question of what the relationship is between the meaning of a word and the concept that is expressed by

the word, you will not find it easy to answer, even though you know perfectly well how to use the word 'meaning' and the word 'concept'. Conceptual clarification consists in *putting order* into familiar rules for the use of a word – not any old order, but such an order as will shed light upon the conceptual problems at hand.

Int. I am beginning to see. But it is all rather strange.

PMSH. Of course it is. It will take time for you to see what Wittgenstein is doing, and why what he is doing solves or dissolves philosophical, that is – conceptual – problems. But be patient. For the moment, all I want you to do is to examine the matter before us.

We were concerned with the concept of the meaning of a word. We saw in the previous two lectures how much trouble and puzzlement this concept can and has generated. Wittgenstein has reminded us of the proximity of the phrase 'the meaning of a word' and the phrase 'the use of a word'. In most contexts, these two phrases are interchangeable. This is indeed news from nowhere. But once Wittgenstein has reminded you of this familiar grammatical point, look at the light it sheds upon the murky scene of centuries of confused reflection on meaning. Wittgenstein's grammatical clarification gets us away from speculations about meanings – for example, that meanings are kinds of things – ideas in the mind, or objects in the world, or abstract entities *attached* to words, or *associated* with words. For *the way a word is used* is neither an idea in the mind nor an abstract object or even an object in the world – since it is neither an idea nor an object of any kind. *The use of a word* is no more something *attached* to a word than *the use of a tool* is something that one might attach to a tool. Don't think that this is trivial: a very distinguished Oxford professor of philosophy used to tell the students in his lectures that we 'attach senses to words'. One wondered how – with mental glue? And one wondered how something as abstract as *a sense* or *a meaning* could be *attached* to *anything*.

So, saying that the meaning of a word is its use gives us a *dynamic* conception of word meaning – for it links the notion of meaning with that of *activity*, rather than with the static idea of *standing for* something. And linking it thus to activities, it integrates the idea of the meaning of words with *speaking* and with the *activities* into which speech is interwoven. To learn to speak is not to learn a nomenclature – it is to learn to *act*, to engage in the endless variety of language games that are aspects of the form of life of a culture.

What Wittgenstein gives us, in place of a theory of meaning, is a *description* of the web of concepts surrounding the concept of word meaning. Describing that network and the links between its various nodes will dissolve puzzlements about the concept of meaning and the nature of language which theories of meaning were misguidedly constructed to do.

MEANING AND USE, UNDERSTANDING AND INTERPRETING 57

So, in most contexts, the phrase 'the meaning of a word' signifies the use of a word. Using a word in speech is a *rule-governed activity* – one can use a word correctly or incorrectly. There are right and wrong ways of using a word – ways that accord with its meaning and ways that do not.

Int. Well, yes. I can see that in a very humdrum sense of 'rule', there are rules for the use of words – I mean: standards of correct use, just as there are rules for spelling. But you have not told us where these rules come from. Nor have you told us why just these rules and not others? After all, isn't it just an arbitrary matter?

PMSH. Your question is a little misleading – rather like 'Where do the principles of morality *come from*?' or 'Where do the rules of arithmetic – the multiplication rules, for example – *come from*?'. We learn these rules, these standards of usage, in learning to speak (and write) our language. Usage is forged by the practices of a linguistic community. Are the rules for the use of words *arbitrary*? In a sense, yes. That is, the rules are not answerable for correctness to any extra-linguistic reality. In a sense, no. That is, usage proves itself in utility. Moreover, new uses have to be carefully dovetailed into existing usage. For in accepting the uses of the words we learn to use, we are also accepting a host of logical and conceptual connections. To learn the use of the word 'father' we accept that if someone is a father, then it follows (barring sex-change operations) that he is a sexually mature male, that he has a child or children, that he is older than his children, that his children have or had a mother and so on and so forth.

So, if we look at the ordinary use of ordinary familiar words, we shall notice that certain combinations of words are licit and make sense, while others are not – they make no sense. It makes sense to say that a cushion is orange, but not to say that a pain is orange. It makes sense to claim that one remembers what one did yesteryear, but not that one remembers what one did before one was born. Utterances such as 'My backache is orange' or 'I remember that before I was born I met Julius Caesar' cannot be said to be false, for then we should have to be able to say how things would have to be for them to be true – and of course, we can't. Rather, such forms of words are nonsense – that is, they make no sense.

Int. Yes, of course. But it makes no sense to say 'My backache is orange' precisely because my backache *can't* be orange. The sentence "I remember that before I was born I met Julius Caesar' is nonsense because it is *impossible* to remember meeting Julius Caesar before I was born. So what makes sense, what combinations of words are grammatically licit, is, contrary to what you said previously, answerable to reality for their correctness. Isn't that obvious?

PMSH. Well, actually, no! It *looks* obvious, but when something *looks obvious* in philosophy, it is time to *look out*! You are jumping the gun again. We shall discuss the matter in a later lecture, I promise. But try to shelve what seems obvious to you for the moment and contemplate an alternative. These sentences are nonsense because *these combinations of words have no meaning*. And they have no meaning because they have no use – we do not know what to do with them – they say nothing. If someone were to utter the sentence: 'My backache is orange' or say: 'My backache tastes of walnuts', we simply would not understand him. That is why there are nonsense jokes in comedy, even though there is little comedy in philosophy.

Int. But you haven't really answered me. The sentence 'My backache is orange' is nonsense *precisely because* backaches can't be orange!

PMSH. No! You are presenting a logical or conceptual impossibility as if it were a possibility that is impossible. You present the matter as if *we knew* what it *would be* for a backache to be orange, or for me to talk to Julius Caesar before I was born, but as things are, these are not things that can happen. Whereas the truth of the matter is not that these things can't happen, it is that these forms of words make no sense, that they do not describe a possible state of affairs at all. But let us let the matter rest here for the moment. Think about the option Wittgenstein is proposing, and we'll examine it in greater detail later.

So, there are *rules* for the use of words, rules that determine what does and what does not make sense. These rules are given by common or-garden *explanations of meaning*, such as 'That colour is red' [pointing at something red], '"to perambulate" means the same as "to walk"', 'a vixen is a female fox'. An explanation of meaning is a rule for the use of the word explained. The rules belong to the grammar of the word, for, in Wittgenstein's extended use of the term 'grammar', everything that determines the meaning of a word *is* part of its grammar. Grammar determines not only the syntax but also which combinations of words *make sense* and which do *not*, which are semantically *licit* and which are *illicit*.

Since the rules for the use of a word are themselves part of the totality of rules of the grammar of the language, one can also say – as Wittgenstein does – that the meaning of a word is *its place in grammar*. The meaning of a word is akin to a node in the web of words. And the threads that connect one node with another are, as it were, the rules determining the logical connections

MEANING AND USE, UNDERSTANDING AND INTERPRETING   59

between uses of words in sentences – connections of implication, exclusion, compatibility, and incompatibility. For example, if something is blue all over, that implies that it has a colour, that it is not red (or any other colour), that it could be square or round (or any other shape) but could not be a smell or sound. It is the rules for the use of a word that determine which 'part of speech' it is – what its logico-grammatical character is.

Note that what Wittgenstein understands by 'part of speech' is, on the whole, more fine-grained than what grammarians take this phrase to mean. The grammarian, concerned only with syntax, rests satisfied with classifying expressions into nouns, verbs, adjectives, etc., of different syntactical kinds. Whereas a philosopher is concerned with more refined distinctions that illuminate conceptual problems. A grammarian takes adjectives to signify properties – both words like 'is blue' and words like 'is true'. But these two adjectives in fact belong to quite different categories. Whereas 'blue' attached to a noun signifies a visible property, 'true' predicated of a proposition does not signify *a property* at all, but rather signifies that things are as the proposition says they are – and that is no property. 'Walking', 'understanding', and 'sleeping' are verbs in the continuous tense – but only 'walking' signifies an activity. The grammarian will treat 'I', 'you', 'he' and 'she' as referring expressions, whereas Wittgenstein notes that the word 'I' functions quite differently from the other pronouns and is not really a referring expression that selects – picks out – one person from among other persons. It is an *index* by means of which *other people* can use a referring expression, such as 'he', when *they* identify that person and say something of him.

Int. Wait a moment – that's too quick. Surely 'I' is an ordinary personal pronoun, just like any other personal pronoun.

PMSH. Well, it is a perfectly *ordinary* personal pronoun, but it is *not* just like the other personal pronouns. You might say, as Wittgenstein does, that the personal pronouns are like points on a graph. But 'I' is like the point of origin, and other pronouns are like other points on the graph with positive coordinates. And it is by reference to their distance from the point of origin that the other points are identified – and referred to.

Int. But surely 'I' refers to the speaker, just as 'he' and 'she' refer to others.

PMSH. No – or at any rate, not 'just as'. 'He' and 'she' are like arrows shot at targets – they may hit or miss, for both misidentification and reference failure are possible. But 'I', if it is a referring expression, is a *super* referring expression, since both reference failure and misidentification of reference are excluded. So 'I' is not like an arrow shot at a target, it is like an arrow stuck in the wall, around which you now draw a circle to make the arrow look as if it has scored a bull. In this respect, the pronoun 'I' is like 'now', as opposed to 'then'. Reflect that when one gives someone the order: 'Shoot NOW!', one has not *referred* to a time – but given the hearer a temporal *cue* on which to act. For purposes of conceptual clarification, we must not allow ourselves to be taken in by grammatical form – we must focus on use and function. We must look to see how an expression is used and what it is for – what purposes are served by having the word.

Int. Yes, that's very ingenious. I see – or, at least, I think I do.

PMSH. Good. So let me proceed.

Grammar, Wittgenstein said, *describes* the use of words in a language. But this observation may be misleading. He did not mean that a statement of the grammar of an expression is a description of speech behaviour – as it were, a part of the natural history of a language. Giving the rules for the use of words is giving a *normative* description. It is like describing the laws of a legal system, as opposed to describing the actual behaviour, both legally permissible and criminal, of the people living under that legal system. To describe the use of a word does not include describing its misuses – it is to describe how the word *is to be used*, to describe the *correct* use of the word.

Int. Does that mean that one has to make extensive investigations into people's speech habits in order to make grammatical observations in philosophy? Is a grammatical investigation then a sociological one?

PMSH. No – investigating accents and dialects is a sociological investigation. But a grammatical investigation of the kind Wittgenstein engaged in is not. It is an investigation into the norms and the interrelationships of the norms of a language, *where these give rise to conceptual confusions and puzzlement.* Since any competent speaker is by definition *a master of the use of the language he speaks*, he can say how an ordinary, non-technical word is used. For a competent user of a language is precisely one who *knows how the ordinary, non-technical words of the language are used.* He needs no more to hand out sociological questionnaires than the master chess player needs to hand out questionnaires in order to be able to point out when a player has made an illicit move. A philosopher, to be sure is not a lexicographer. He is interested in the rules for the use of words *only where those words cause conceptual troubles.* The word 'meaning' gives rise to a multitude of misunderstandings and confusions – and that is why Wittgenstein sketches out its logical geography. To do this, it is not necessary to make any social surveys about the use of the phrase 'the meaning of a word' among English speakers – only to draw our attention to things that, as competent speakers, we already know, and to put them into a surveyable order.

So, to recapitulate: the meaning of a word is its use. Its meaning is given by an explanation of its meaning. An explanation of the meaning of a word is a rule for its use.

Understanding

Another node in the network, adjacent to that of *the meaning of a word*, is that of *understanding* or *knowing* the meaning of a word. For obviously the meaning of a word is what one knows when one has mastered the technique of the use of the word. The meaning of a sentence and what is meant by the utterance of a sentence on an occasion are what is understood when one understands the sentence and understands what was said by its use on an occasion. Hence too, if what the hearer understands is not what the speaker meant, then he misunderstands the speaker's utterance. And if what he understands by the sentence is not what the sentence means, then he misunderstands it or fails to understand it.

Let me make that a little clearer. We must distinguish between sentence-meaning and utterance-meaning. The sentence 'He will be there then' has a constant meaning. But on one occasion the sentence may be used to say that Jack will be in Oxford on Tuesday, and on another that Tom will be in London on Friday – so we distinguish between *knowing the meaning of a sentence* and *knowing what was said by using that sentence on some occasion*. Note that it is not the meaning of a sentence that can be said to be true or false, but rather what is said by the utterance of the sentence on a given occasion.

> **Int.** What *shows* that a person understands a word or sentence, or understands what is said by the use of a sentence on an occasion?
> **PMSH.** There are three general ways in which we judge this.
> i. A person satisfies one kind of criterion for understanding a word, sentence or utterance if he correctly explains what it means or what was said by using it – or immediately acknowledges *as* correct an explanation of what it means. But, of course, it is crucial here to take the notion of explanation of meaning in a low key. The ordinary speaker is not required to be a professional lexicographer – he is merely required to be able to say what a word, or a word in a sentence that he understands, means and to be able to explain what was said by an utterance that he understood. And his explaining this correctly is a criterion of his understanding. If he can't explain this in some acceptable form or other, we shall have good reason for thinking that he doesn't actually understand the sentence or grasp what was said or doesn't know what a given word in the sentence means.

ii. Second, a person satisfies another kind of criterion for understanding a word or sentence if he uses it correctly. That is: his correct use of the word *shows* that he knows what it means. And the correct use of a word in a sentence is use that *accords* with the rules for its use, with *received explanations* of what it means.

iii. Third, a person satisfies a criterion for understanding an utterance if he responds with understanding to its use, that is, if he responds *intelligently*. Of course, such responses may be very diverse – their propriety and intelligibility are context-dependent. What it amounts to is perhaps best captured by this formulation: that we can take his behaviour – whatever it may be (including in some contexts his saying nothing at all) – to be done *for the reason* that such-and-such was said. That is, if *what* was said is *part of his reason* for his response, then his behaviour, other things being equal, exhibits his understanding.

Because the concept of meaning is linked with that of understanding, we need to examine the concept of understanding, for it is all too easy to misconstrue it. Ask yourself, for example, whether understanding is *an act* or *activity*, *a process*, or *a mental state*?

Int. I don't see why that matters.

PMSH. Oh, it matters greatly. The expressions 'act', 'activity', 'process' and 'mental state' are categorial terms that determine the logical category to which the item under consideration belongs. To identify something as being an act or activity, a process or a mental state is to determine *what it makes sense to say of it*. Acts are done or performed, but one cannot do or perform a mental state. Processes and activities take time; one engages in activities and undergoes processes. Mental states don't take time, and one does not engage in them, but they obtain for a time, and one may be *in* a mental state for a time. And so on.

Int. Ah, yes. I see.

PMSH. Good. So what about understanding? What category do you think it belongs to?

Int. At first glance, it seems to be *an act* – for we normally understand what someone says at a stroke – we grasp what he meant. So understanding must surely be an act we perform instantaneously.

PMSH. Yes, that is one of the temptations. If we think thus, we may go on to argue that it is from this *act of understanding* that the manifestations of understanding in our behaviour flow. Gottlob Frege held that understanding an utterance is a special mental act or process of *grasping* the sense expressed by the utterance. This grasping, Frege held, 'is perhaps the most mysterious [thing] of all'. But – like all mysteries in philosophy – this is fishy. To understand what an expression means

MEANING AND USE, UNDERSTANDING AND INTERPRETING 63

is not to stand in any *relationship* to something called 'the meaning (or sense)' of that expression. It is *to be able* to use the expression, *to be able* to say what it means and *to be able* to respond cogently to its use – and that is not *grasping* anything. The metaphor of *grasping the meaning or sense* of an expression misleads us here – it looks like a relation between a speaker and a meaning or sense, but in fact *grasping the meaning of an expression* amounts to no more than *understanding the expression* and does not explain what understanding consists in.

Int. But surely, it is *because* I understand what someone has said that I respond to it intelligently. If I didn't understand what they said, then I *wouldn't* know how to respond. After all, had I not understood your query 'Where is Piccadilly Circus?' I should not have replied with the correct directions. Surely I replied cogently *because* I understood what you asked. So understanding seems to be the *result of whatever mechanism produces understanding* – the unconscious mind or the brain. The upshot of these hidden processes is that one understands, which is *a state* from which one's subsequent actions then flow. For it is *because we understood* that we did whatever we did.

PMSH. That seems very plausible, and many philosophers have found the idea irresistible. Wittgenstein, however, rejected it. He referred to this idea as the 'reservoir' model of understanding. He wrote:

> There is a kind of general disease of thinking which always looks for (and finds) what would be called a mental state from which all our acts spring as from a reservoir. Thus one says, 'The fashion changes because the taste of people changes'. The taste is the mental reservoir. But if a tailor today designs a cut of dress different from that which he designed a year ago, can't what is called his change of taste have consisted, partly or wholly, in doing just this? (BB 143)

So understanding is not a mental state from which performances manifesting understanding flow.

Int. All right. I can see that. But why not argue that understanding the words of another is a process, the successful upshot of which is a steady state from which one's subsequent performances flow? After all, understanding what someone says often *takes time*. One may understand something only *partly*, which suggests that one has not completed a task. And one may come to understand *more* of something. So surely understanding must be *a process*, which may be prolonged and may not be completed. But if it is completed, then one is in a state of understanding, and it is from this that performances manifesting understanding flow.

Well, you are disregarding Wittgenstein's criticisms of the reservoir model of understanding as a mental state. I'll return to it in a moment. But you are right in thinking that it is tempting to suppose that there are two senses of 'understanding the words of another', one of which signifies a process, and the other of which signifies the state that is the upshot of that process. Now that *is* a very appealing idea.

The British empiricists, for example, Locke and Hume, held that understanding is *a process of association*. Since, in their view, the meaning of an expression is the idea associated with it, then understanding the words of another must amount to *associating the same ideas with his words as he does* and so apprehending the judgement that he expressed by his utterance. So all understanding of the speech of others is *associative interpretation*. We noted in a previous lecture that modern linguists and philosophers are likewise inclined to think of understanding as a process or activity of *interpreting* the words heard. But they think of it as *computational* rather than *associative*. They hold that when we hear an utterance, we derive its meaning from the meanings of its constituent words and the way they are combined. That is done in accordance with our tacit, non-conscious, knowledge of a theory of meaning for a language. This theory allegedly consists in a multitude of rules and principles 'deeply buried in the unconscious mind' – as Noam Chomsky puts it. So all understanding of the speech of others is a computational process performed, as quick as a flash, in the unconscious mind or brain. Chomsky explains it thus:

> the computations involved may be fairly intricate [...] But since they rely on principles of universal grammar that are part of the fixed structure of the mind/brain, it is fair to suppose that they take place virtually instantaneously and of course with no conscious awareness and beyond the level of possible introspection.[1]

Note that little is said by modern theorists about understanding *one's own words*. If understanding the words of others is a complex computational process of derivation, *what is it to understand one's own speech – to know what one is saying*? How does a person understand what he himself says? Does he have to wait to see what he says before he can know what he means? How does a person use the 'system of knowledge in his mind/brain', as Chomsky puts it, in order to ask for a glass of water, or tell someone the time, or report on the state of the nation? It is striking that Chomsky himself asserted that all attempts to solve this problem have been futile. This is what he wrote:

> One possible reason for the lack of success in solving it or even presenting sensible ideas about it is that it is not within the range of human intellectual capacities, it is either 'too difficult', given the nature of our capacities, or beyond their limits altogether. There is some reason to suspect that this may be so, though we do not know enough about human intelligence or the properties of the problem to be sure.

---

1 N. Chomsky, *Language and Problems of Knowledge* (MIT Press, Cambridge, MA, 1988), p. 90.

Still, perhaps this dramatic declaration of the limits of human understanding is premature – maybe it is just that *Chomsky* did not understand something. After all, a navigator who declares that one cannot in principle find the coast is indeed at sea! Perhaps Chomsky did not understand that the question he was asking actually made no sense. Perhaps he had a poor grip on the very concept of understanding.

Now, back to the categorial classification of understanding. Wittgenstein argued that the customary classifications of understanding as an act or activity, a mental state or a mental process, a neural state or process in the brain were all confused. Understanding, he held, belongs to the category of *ability*. The exclamation 'Now I understand!' is not a report on the performance of a special act or activity of understanding, but *a signal* that the penny has dropped – that now one *can do* various things – such as explain, respond to questions and assertions in certain ways, act for the reason that things are as they have been understood as being. To understand is *a cluster of abilities*, it is *to be able to do* various things.

Sudden understanding is not an act one has performed, but the *heralding* of an ability or abilities. Like beginning to move or ceasing to move, suddenly understanding something marks a change, but not a change from one state to another. Rather, it is a change from being unable to do various things to being able to do those things. Of course, we say that it took us ages to understand something. But that does not mean that understanding was a prolonged process; it means that it took one a long time *to become able* to do those things in which understanding consists.

> **Int.** Wait a moment. I am worried. Surely, there are often degrees of understanding – one can understand something partly or completely, vaguely or fully. To have half understood something means that one got halfway through a process, doesn't it?
> **PMSH.** No! It means that one can do, poorly and inadequately, some of the things in which understanding consists. That is characteristic of abilities – which admit of degrees.
> **Int.** Ah, I see. Partly understanding something that was said amounts to being able to do *some* of the things that exhibit understanding, or to be able to do them only defectively. So if one partly understood what you just said, one could explain what you said only in part, or only unclearly.
> **PMSH.** Precisely. Now let me continue.

No doubt there are various neural conditions and processes that underlie understanding something and make the acquisition of the abilities possible. But the understanding is distinct from them, just as being able to ride a bicycle is something quite distinct from the neural conditions that make it possible to acquire and exercise the ability to cycle.

Understanding a word or utterance is not *a mental process*, since mental processes may be broken off or interrupted. But one cannot interrupt someone's understanding of something; one can only interrupt his *attempt* to understand. One cannot be in the middle of understanding, only in the middle of the process of *trying* to understand – trying to acquire an ability. One can therefore ask someone how long it took him to understand something, but one *cannot* ask whether he is understanding something, let alone whether he is understanding something quickly or slowly – only whether he *came* to understand it quickly or slowly. If understanding were a process, it would make sense to ask someone whether he had *finished understanding*. And when he had finished, he would have *stopped understanding* – but that is nonsense.

Understanding is not *a mental state*, since mental states, like feeling excited or depressed, or being in a state of concentration or having a headache, do not persist through loss of consciousness. One stops feeling depressed or excited when one falls asleep. But one does not cease to understand whatever one understands when one is asleep, any more than one ceases to know the things one knows when one is asleep. One may be in a certain mental state continuously, without a break – as when one has a headache all afternoon. But one cannot be said to understand an utterance continuously, without a break. We speak of being in a state of depression or in a state of anxiety – but not of being in a state of understanding. One can ask when someone was in pain or was concentrating, but not when they were understanding – only when they understood, that is, came to understand.

> **Int.** Could you stop for a moment? I am getting confused. You say that understanding is not a mental act, that it is not a mental process and that it is not a mental state either. These seem to me to be substantive conclusions. They are really important. But you have derived these conclusions from nothing more than the conventions for the use of words. And you have also admitted that these conventions are, in a sense, arbitrary. But, assuming that you are right, it is surely *anything but arbitrary* that understanding is not a mental act, activity, process or state.
>
> **PMSH.** Good. You have rightly sensed that we are here on the brink of the deepest methodological matters in philosophy.

We are constantly tempted to confuse the shadows cast upon the world by the forms and structure of grammar for substantive insights into the metaphysical structure of the world. But the world has no metaphysical structure. This will be examined in some detail in Lecture 7. But to ease any bafflement, let me drop a few hints.

The grammatical rules that determine the use, and so the meaning, of words, really *do* determine their meaning. So if one *changes* the rules for the use of a word, one *changes its meaning*. Then one is no longer talking about the same thing. It is, in one sense, an arbitrary matter that a word has the use it has. But given that it has the use it has, the logical consequences of its use are anything but arbitrary – they are constitutive of the meaning of the word. It is an arbitrary matter that 'red' is the name of the colour Red and that 'pink' is the name of the colour Pink. But given that these two words have the meaning they do and given the meaning of the relation expression 'darker than', it is anything but arbitrary that red is darker than pink. The proposition that red is darker than pink is not a description of a *necessary fact in the world* – facts aren't 'in the world', and there is no such thing as a necessary fact. 'Red is darker than pink' is not a description of *anything*. It is the expression of an inference rule, partly constitutive of the meanings of the words 'red', 'pink', 'darker than'. This inference rule allows us to infer from 'A is red' and 'B is pink' the conclusion that A is darker in colour than B. So what looks like a necessary truth in the world is no more than an inference rule in our grammar. Could we not change it? Yes, of course we could. But then we would change the meaning of the word 'red'. Or of the word 'pink'. Or of the expression 'darker than'. Reflect on the proposition 'In chess, with a king and knight, one cannot checkmate one's opponent'. Could this not be different? Yes, it could. But then it wouldn't be a king. Or it wouldn't be a knight. Or it wouldn't be chess. If we are playing chess, then nothing *counts* as checkmating one's opponent with a king and a knight. So too, nothing *counts* as being red which is at the same time not darker than anything that is pink. These are conventions of language, not the scaffolding of the world.

All right. That is as much as can be said for now. Let's return to our main theme, namely: the nature of linguistic understanding. While it is surely correct to characterize understanding as an ability or akin to an ability, note, first, that it is not an ability to do a *specific* kind of act – hence it is unlike the ability to ride a bicycle or to read. It is, rather, *a diffuse set of abilities*. Second, although one can make an effort to understand, one cannot understand or refuse to understand an utterance *at will*. If someone asks me to pass the salt, it is not within my power not to understand the utterance, only to comply or to refuse to comply with it. One cannot *but* understand the typical utterances one hears, just as one cannot but hear them. This makes understanding akin, *in this respect*, to powers of perception. For one can look or listen for something at will, but not see or hear something at will.

Characterizing understanding as akin to an ability is of capital importance. Among other things, it helps one to grapple with a point that has been at the centre of late twentieth-century discussions by linguists and philosophers alike, namely: 'How can one understand sentences one has never heard before?'

> **Int.** Yes. I have heard people say that this is one of the deepest questions there is in the theory of language – both in theoretical linguistics and in the philosophy of language. Certainly many of the linguists and psychologists of language that I have read argue that understanding is a high-speed computational process of interpretation, by which one computes the meaning of an utterance from the meanings of the words and the way they are combined, in accordance with tacitly known principles of a theory of meaning for the language.
>
> **PMSH.** Yes, you're quite right. But you must stop and reflect. After all, this is a bizarre idea: as if understanding the sentence 'The teddy bear is in the fridge' – which I venture to say you have never heard before – involves a calculation. That bizarre idea rests on the assumption that understanding a sentence or the utterance of a sentence is something one *does* – an act or activity that one performs as quickly as a flash.

This far-reaching confusion nicely exemplifies Wittgenstein's remark.

> The first mistake we encounter in a philosophical investigation is […] always the question itself. (MS 165, 55)

It is the question 'How can one understand sentences one has never heard before?' that is awry. It sounds like 'How can one start a car without the starting key?' that is, it sounds like a question about how one *does* something – but that is precisely why *the question itself* is mistaken. As we have seen, understanding is neither an act nor an activity – it is an ability. And it makes no sense to ask *how one does* an ability. So too, it makes no sense to suppose that to understand an utterance involves a process of computation that one *carries out* – as if understanding an utterance were like *doing a calculation*, and as if the upshot of one's understanding were akin to the result of a computation. But understanding the utterance 'The roses are beautiful' is not at all like computing the result of 25×25; it is much more like understanding the equation '$25 \times 25 = 625$'.

To be sure, this observation does no more than point in the direction one must move in order not *to answer* this misguided question that Chomsky thought was an impenetrable mystery but *to dissolve* it. What is important is precisely that it indicates that the question *is no mystery* and needs no answer. The question is a muddle, and what it needs is patience and careful disentangling.

Speaker's Meaning

We must turn now to a further node in the web that lies in the vicinity of the expressions 'the meaning of a word' and 'the meaning of an utterance'. This is the concept of the speaker's meaning. There is an intimate relation between what a word, phrase or sentence means and what a speaker means by using that word, phrase or sentence in an utterance. The matter is delicate and needs careful scrutiny.

Notice first that it is a peculiarity of English, and a misleading one at that, that we use the same word both in the phrase 'the meaning of a word' and in the phrase 'meaning something by the word'. In German, for example, different words are used – the noun 'Bedeutung' signifies the meaning of a word, whereas the verb 'meinen' signifies the speaker's *meaning something*. So English speakers are liable to confusions that need not arise at all for German speakers. The differences between the meaning of a word or sentence and what the speaker means by a word or utterance can be highlighted by talking of the speaker's *intention* rather than of the speaker's *meaning*. We can ask not what he *meant* by a word he used, but what he intended to signify by using it.

Note also that *to mean what one says* is different again. It is to be serious about what one says – not to be joking or acting. Furthermore, the act of saying something may itself be said *to mean something*, as when we observe that Jack's saying what he said means that he was hurt or that he was pleased. *This* use of the verb 'to mean' is akin to the sense in which we say that clouds mean rain and smoke means fire – namely that there is a good inductive correlation between two events, so that the occurrence of the first enables one to predict the second. Neither of these two different uses of 'to mean' concern us now, but we should bear them in mind simply to avoid confusing quite different meanings of the word 'meaning'.

Now back to the speaker's meaning. For a speaker to mean something by the words he uses in his utterance is not for him to perform an act or activity of any kind.

> **Int.** Yes, we talked about that before. And I must admit that I still find it very tempting to think that what gives life to words, what transforms empty sounds into words that mean something, what differentiates the parrot's imitative squawk from the human utterance, is *that the speaker means by the words he utters a certain state of affairs*. The sentence he utters, it seems, *represents* the state of affairs it depicts because the speaker *means by* the sentence *that very state of affairs*. So it seems that the speaker's *act of meaning* projects the utterance onto reality.

PMSH. Well, I agree that this is a very tempting picture. After all, if it weren't very tempting, it would be puzzling why so many great thinkers succumbed to its allure. Still, it is time to dismantle this illusion of reason.

Of course, if someone says 'Shut the door please' what he means by his utterance is *that you should shut the door*. If he says 'The door is shut', what he means by his words is *that the door is shut*. That much is trivially true. Note further that what the speaker means by the sentence he utters is *not* what the sentence he utters means. For the uttered sentence 'The door is shut' does *not* mean that the door is shut – the door may well be open and the speaker mistaken. The fact that no one is at home, on the other hand, may indeed mean that the door is shut and locked – just as smoke may indicate fire.

Meaning something by one's words is neither an act nor an activity the speaker performs when he speaks. Of course, the *surface grammar* of the verb 'to mean' misleadingly suggests that it is a verb of action or an activity verb.

Int. But why do you say that this is misleading? After all, the assertion 'I said "Jack" and I meant my old friend Jack' suggests that I performed two actions, saying and meaning. The sentences 'I remember having meant Jack by my gesture of beckoning' and 'I remember that when I said "Come here!", I meant Jack and not Jill' suggest that over and above saying what I said and beckoning as I beckoned, I did something further – I performed an act of meaning. After all, 'I remember that I *pointed at* Jack when I said "Come here!"' seems just like 'I remember that I *meant* Jack when I said "Come here!"'.

PMSH. Well, I agree. But these surface-grammatical similarities are altogether misleading. And it is easy to show this through a grammatical investigation.

If a verb is a verb of action, like 'to say', or an activity verb, like 'to discuss', then it makes sense to attach 'I intend' or 'I decided' to it – for example, to say: 'I intend to say something' or 'I decided to discuss something'. One can be asked or ordered to say something, and one may agree or refuse to discuss something. One may start to say something, be engaged in discussing something, be interrupted in the middle, and then later resume and finish discussing the matter. One may remember to say something, and one may forget to do so. It makes sense to ask whether one knows how to discuss a given matter, to find it easy or difficult to do, to enjoy doing it or to find it tedious. There may be different ways of discussing a matter, and one can do so quickly or slowly. But it is striking that *none* of this makes sense with regard to *meaning*, irrespective of whether it is meaning something or someone by a word one uttered in a sentence, meaning such-and-such by the sentence one uttered, or, quite differently, meaning what one said. One cannot *decide* to mean something by what one says, or to mean Jack by the pronoun 'he' in a sentence one utters. One can be ordered to say something or to converse about something, but one cannot be ordered to mean something by what one says. There is no such thing as beginning to mean something by what one is saying, nor can one be interrupted in the middle of meaning it and then resume and finish meaning it. One may forget to mention someone, but one cannot forget to mean someone. One does not learn to mean something by the words one utters, and one cannot be ignorant of how to mean something. There is no such thing as meaning someone slowly or quickly – and one cannot succeed or fail to mean someone. In short, the surface grammar of the verb 'to mean' is altogether deceptive.

Meaning something by a word one uses and meaning a certain state of affairs or situation by a sentence one utters are not acts or activities that are concurrent with speaking.

> **Int.** Well, I agree that nothing is meant by sentences uttered in a parrot-like fashion. When we say something, we want our hearer to understand what we mean, and if he understands our utterance, he *will* know what we mean. Furthermore, when we issue an order like 'Come here!', we know and can say *whom we meant*. And when we utter a sentence with understanding, we can say *what we meant by it*.
>
> **PMSH.** Of course. But none of this implies that meaning is an act or activity that accompanies speech, or that meaning is the method of projection, or that it is acts of meaning that breathe life into otherwise dead words.

To say that when one said, 'Come here!' one meant Jack is to say, for example, that if one had been asked whom one meant, then other things being equal, one would have replied 'Jack'. Or that if Jill had come, one would have told her that it was Jack one wanted to speak to. In short, what is coupled with the words one utters and by which one means whatever one means are not mental acts or processes, but *other words or sentences* that explain or paraphrase what one said. An answer to the question 'What did you mean?' or 'How is that meant?' is given by *another* sentence, which exhibits the relationship between *two linguistic expressions*.

If anything gives life to words, it is their use – not any mental accompaniments, let alone acts of meaning – for there is no such thing as *an act of meaning*. And it is only because words have established uses in the practices of language users that one *can* mean something by them. Of course, there are constraints on what one can mean by a word. 'There's glory for you', despite what Lewis Carroll's Humpty Dumpty says, does not mean 'That's a nice knock-down argument'. And contrary to what Humpty Dumpty says, it is not just a matter of *who's master.* Just try, when you are next in a restaurant, to mean by the words 'hot water' cold water! And just think – HOW would you try? Words are alive in practice, in the rule-governed activities of using them – and they live for those who have mastered the techniques of using them. Words are woven into the tapestry of human life, and it is there that they sparkle and flash, lending colour and shade to the patterns.

> **Int.** Aah. I am beginning to see. So, the idea that it is acts of meaning that make words meaningful is a myth. For, there is no such thing as *an act of meaning.* And, so too, the idea that words have a meaning because speakers project them onto reality by their intentions is just a mythology of symbolism. It is human communicative practices in the hurly-burly of life that endow words with meaning!
> **PMSH** Good – light is beginning to dawn!

Interpreting

So much, then, for meaning something by what one says. Complementary to the misconceptions about speaker's meaning is a correlative misconception concerning understanding what a speaker said. As we have seen, there is a venerable tradition in both philosophy and linguistic theory that someone who hears what is said must interpret it in order to understand it.

> **Int.** Yes, obviously. If the hearer's interpretation coincides with the speaker's meaning, then the hearer will have understood what the speaker said.

Indeed, so it seems. *This* conception of communication by means of language was integral to the *Port Royal Logic* in the seventeenth century and to the hugely influential Lockean idealist conception of linguistic communication that persisted until the end of the nineteenth century. It is equally integral to contemporary computational conceptions of language as advanced by such philosophers as Davidson and by linguists such as Chomsky. According to this conception, *all understanding is or involves interpreting.*

But this, Wittgenstein argued, is confused. One cannot *interpret* a sequence of signs that is opaque to one. Faced with a sequence of signs such as 'Abo oglo tiftu ineas', one can only ask for it to be translated or deciphered. When its translation is before one, *then* one can interpret the now intelligible sentence – *if it needs an interpretation*. For interpreting, in this context, means: clarifying by a paraphrase *what was said*. Now, it is absurd to suppose that what we hear in discourse is mere sounds, to which we must then *attach an interpretation*. For there is no such thing as *interpreting* mere sounds – one can interpret only intelligible speech that one understands. Interpreting an utterance in one's own language *presupposes* understanding it. The need for an interpretation arises when an utterance can be understood *in more ways than one*. A good interpretation offers the best way of understanding what was meant. So understanding cannot in general be interpreting.

Indeed, it is incoherent to suppose that all understanding even *involves* interpretation. For each sentence – on this account – requires an interpretation. But each interpretation is itself given by a sentence – which again requires an interpretation. So we would be launched on an infinite regress, and would never reach the stage of understanding at all. Clearly, the normal understanding of the speech of others no more requires an interpretation than understanding their gestures, smiles and frowns. If someone at the breakfast table asks 'Would you pass the butter, please?' – one does not interpret their words, any more than if someone whips out a knife and threatens one, one interprets his or her action.

Chapter 5

OSTENSIVE DEFINITION AND FAMILY RESEMBLANCE: UNDERMINING THE FOUNDATIONS AND DESTROYING THE ESSENCES

Unfinished Business: What *Use* Is Not and When *Meaning* Isn't *Use*

In the last lecture, the logical geography of the concept of *the meaning of a word* was sketched. Wittgenstein linked the concept of *word meaning* to the concept of *the use of a word* and to the concept of *a rule* for the use of a word. The concept of *a rule for the use of a word* is in turn linked to the concept of *an explanation of the meaning of a word* – since an explanation of meaning is, in effect, a rule – a *standard of correct use*. Moreover, the notions of meaning, use, rule and explanation are all connected with the concept of *a practice of regular use of a word* – and that is linked with the idea of a *recognized uniformity* that is viewed as *standard setting*. This network of interwoven concepts ramifies further. The concept of word meaning was also connected with the concept of *meaning something by a word*, and with the concepts of *understanding what a word means* and *understanding what someone meant* in saying what he said. The concept of understanding is in turn linked with *using a word correctly, explaining what it means* and *responding appropriately to its use by others* – which are severally *criteria* for understanding what a word or expression means. We determine whether someone understands an expression by reference to whether he *uses it correctly, explains correctly* what it means in a given context and *responds appropriately* to its use by others. One might think of this large array of interwoven concepts as a network or web of ideas, each of which is directly or indirectly connected to all the others and all of which conjunctively determine the concept of meaning.

> **Int.** Yes, I have grasped at least part of this network, and I can see that many difficulties can be resolved by attending to the place of the various concepts within this web. Nevertheless, I still have qualms about

Wittgenstein's identifying the meaning of a word with its use. I mean, he did say that *for a large class of cases* the meaning of a word is its use in the language. What worries me is that there are far too many kinds of cases in which the meaning of a word is *not* its use. And if I'm right, then we can't accept Wittgenstein's claim.

PMSH. What kind of case do you have in mind?

Int. Well, we speak of a word or phrase, for example 'elevator', as being used in the United States but not in Britain, and conversely the word 'pavement' is used in Britain but not in the United States. But despite this difference in use, 'elevator' *does* mean the same as 'lift', and 'pavement' means the same as 'sidewalk'. So surely the meaning of a word can't be the same as its use, for here we have a difference in use without any difference in meaning!

PMSH. Come now! This is actually no objection at all. Difference in *location* of use or in the *society in which the word is used* does not imply a difference *in the way in which the word is used*. It is obvious that when Wittgenstein equates meaning and use, he does not mean: location of use or sociolect. 'Elevator' and 'lift' are used *in exactly the same way* – albeit by different societies – and so they have *exactly the same meaning*.

Int. All right. But what about differences in use between one social class and another – as in the case of 'policeman' and 'copper'. Or differences in the use of words by one age group in contrast with another – as in the case of 'wireless' and 'radio'. Or differences in the use of words between professionals and laymen – as in the case of 'infarct' and 'heart attack'. Surely, in each of these cases the pairs of words have exactly the same meaning, even though they are used differently. So the meaning of a word can't be its use!

PMSH. No – again you are misinterpreting what Wittgenstein *meant* by 'use'. He did not mean 'use' by different social classes, or generational differences of the kind you have in mind or differences between laymen and professionals. The user is irrelevant to the use. The pairs of words 'wireless' and 'radio', 'infarct' and 'heart attack' do severally mean the same precisely insofar as they are used in the same way – never mind who uses them. In the case of 'policeman' and 'copper', you have a point, not so much because of difference in social class but because of the difference in 'colouring' and hence too in politeness.

Int. Mmmm. All right. I'll go along with that. But what about the following objection: many philosophers in the middle of the last century, such as J. L. Austin, made much of the idea of using words to do something. Austin wrote a book entitled *How to Do Things with Words*. Now, on this conception of use, we use words to perform certain acts of speech. For example, 'please' is used to request, 'hello' is used to greet and 'goodbye' is used to bid farewell. So too, many verbs have what Austin called 'a performative use'. For example, the sentence 'I accuse you' is used to accuse the person addressed; 'I apologize' is used to apologize; and 'I promise' is used to make a promise. And the Oxford moral philosopher Richard Hare argued that the meaning of the word 'good', which is so central to all reflections in moral philosophy, is fully explained by saying that it is the most general adjective of commendation. So 'This is good' means much the same as 'I commend this'. Now: was this what Wittgenstein had in mind? Because if he did, it is open to fatal objections.

PMSH. Very interesting. I'm glad you have raised this point, because it was raised by the American philosopher John Searle as an objection against Wittgenstein's linking meaning and use. So do go on and explain what the objection is.

Int. Well, it's obvious once you think about it. Maybe saying of something 'This is good' is to use the sentence, and so to use the word in the sentence, to commend. But the word 'good' *does not* mean the same as the verb 'to commend', and the sentence 'This is good' does not mean the same as the sentence 'I commend this'.

PMSH. Why not?

Int. Well just think of the sentence 'If these apples are good, I'll buy some'. That does not mean the same as 'If I commend these apples then I'll buy some'. And 'a good cricketer' isn't a cricketer I commend, even if I do commend some good cricketers. It is a cricketer who is skilful at playing cricket', just as a good doctor is a doctor who is good at curing people of illnesses. So the meaning of a word is obviously not the same as its use!

PMSH. You're doing splendidly. I agree with everything you have said. But, to be sure, so would Wittgenstein. What he meant by 'the use of a word' was not its use in the performance of a specific act of speech. It is indeed clear that such verbs as 'to accuse', 'to apologize' and 'to promise' are *performative verbs* which are commonly used in the first-person present tense to perform the very act they signify, namely to accuse, apologize and to promise. But, of course, the meaning of such a verb is not *exhausted* by describing its performative use. After all it can be used descriptively in the past tense – as when we say 'I apologized', or in the third-person – as when we say 'He apologized', or imperatively, as when we order someone to apologize, as well as interrogatively when we ask whether someone has promised and so on. It should be obvious that when Wittgenstein equated meaning and use, he did *not* mean by 'use': *use in the performance of a specific act of speech* – even though the fittingness of certain *rather special* verbs for the performance of certain very specific speech acts is clearly an aspect of their meaning. Remember his example at the beginning of the *Investigations* of going to the grocer with a slip of paper on which is written the order 'Five red apples!' – it was no part of Wittgenstein's argument that the word 'five' is used to make requests. The difference in meaning between the three words *all used in the same request* was brought out by the different *operations* associated with each word: of selecting apples – as opposed to pears or oranges – of selecting a colour by reference to a sample and then matching the apples to the sample and of counting up to five and taking an apple with each number counted. So the notion of use that Wittgenstein is invoking is much wider than, and distinct from, the notion of 'use to perform a specific speech act'.

Int. Yes, I see ... Let me try one last move. Surely, the use of a word may be tactless, fashionable or common, infelicitous or uncalled for. But the meaning of a word can be none of these things. One cannot speak of the meaning a word as being tactless or fashionable. So surely the use of a word cannot be the same as its meaning.

PMSH. That is too swift. What is tactless, fashionable or uncalled for is not *the way in which a given word is to be used*, but the use of that word on a given occasion or occasions. One cannot say that the way in which the word 'ass' is correctly used is tactless, uncalled for or infelicitous. It is rather its use *on a given occasion*, for example, in a public debate or in a formal after-dinner speech, that may be these things. And while the use of a word may become fashionable, whereas the meaning of a word may not – all that means is that the word is commonly used or used by the trend-setters in society. But that does not affect the correctness of the equation of *the way in which a word is used* with *the meaning of a word*.

In short, what Wittgenstein meant by 'the use of a word' was *the way* in which the word is *correctly used* within the speech community, or the way in which it *is to be used*. The notion of the use of a word that he was concerned with was a normative notion – that is, a notion linked to a norm or standard of correct use. It is one that is determined by accepted explanations of its meaning among competent speakers of the language. The meaning of a word is fixed by linguistic conventions, by the consensus among competent speakers in a speech community. It is what a speaker knows when he knows how to use a word, and what he explains when he explains what a word means.

Int. I see. So according to Wittgenstein, the meaning of a word is what is explained by an explanation of what it means, and an acceptable explanation of what a word means in a given context is also a rule for its use.

PMSH. Precisely!

Int. Good. I'm starting to cotton on. But now you are still leaving me in the dark. If all these objections are *not* really objections to Wittgenstein's qualified identification of meaning and use, why on earth did he say that *for most cases* of the use of the phrase 'the meaning of a word' it amounts to no more than the use of the word in the language? Why 'most uses'?

It is noteworthy that Wittgenstein emphasized that *meaning* is a 'primitive concept' (LW I §332). It is not a sophisticated technical term for linguistic theorists and semantic theory; it is an unsophisticated non-technical term for language learners and ordinary language users who want to know what a word means and whether *this* word means the same as *that* one. It is at home in paraphrastic explanations of meaning, and of course in translation from one language to another. But there are expressions in our language that – putting translation aside – do not readily lend themselves to the format 'it means a so-and-so'. If we were asked 'What does "if" mean?' or 'What does "but" mean?' or 'What is the meaning of "indeed"?', we would not answer 'It means a so-and-so' or 'It means the same as "such-and-such"', let alone 'The meaning of "if" (or "but", or "indeed") is …'. But the absence of paraphrastic explanation of meaning does not imply meaninglessness – and we should explain what 'if', 'but' or 'indeed' mean by giving examples of their correct use.

Still, one must grant that there are meaningless words in a language that do nevertheless have a use: such as 'Abracadabra' or 'Lillibulero', as well as jingles in nursery rhymes such as 'Fi-fi-fo-fum' and 'Hey diddle diddle'. So too, the venerable foxhunter's cry 'Tally-ho' has a use, namely: to signal the sighting of a fox, but no one would say that 'Tally-ho' has a meaning. In these kinds of cases, the concept of the use of a word or phrase and the concept of the meaning of a word or phrase do indeed come apart. And that is perhaps *one* reason for Wittgenstein's careful qualification.

Quite differently, one might say that the word 'walk' and its present tense form 'walks' mean the same – for they mean the same as 'perambulate'. But one must admit that 'walk' is not used in the same way as 'walks', for 'walk' is used in the first-person present tense and 'walks' in the third-person. So morphology is not an aspect of the lexicon. And that is surely as it should be. As Wittgenstein puts it (slightly clumsily), 'not every use is a meaning'.

Again, precisely because the concepts of meaning and use are not technical concepts of an exact science, their boundaries are blurred and the criteria of sameness and difference of meaning and of use are not sharply defined. Does the word 'white' in 'white coffee' mean the same, is it being used in the same way as in the phrase 'white snow'? The word 'but' is generally substitutable for 'however', but not in a parenthetical context such as 'Jill, however, went up the hill'. So do 'but' and 'however' have the same meaning or not? – It is unclear what we should say here. If someone first uses a hammer to hammer a nail into the wall, and then to shape a piece of red-hot iron, is he using the hammer in one way or two? There is no point in trying to answer such questions unless one knows why one is being asked. For one is in effect being asked to draw a sharp line where there is none. One *can* of course draw one, but to do so intelligently and non-arbitrarily, one must know what the point and purpose of doing so is.

Finally, Wittgenstein draws our attention to the fact that we often *experience* the meaning of a word, we apprehend it as having just *this* meaning as opposed to another, as when we hear the address 'Hail, Caesar', in contrast with Caesar's question to Anthony 'Is it hail or rain?' – and Anthony's answer 'Hail, Caesar'. Here we can be said to experience the meaning of the word, but no one would say that we experience the use of the word.

These are, at any rate, *some* of the reasons that Wittgenstein may have had for qualifying his equation of the meaning of a word and the use of a word.

Ostensive Definitions and the Foundations of Language

Now let me turn to the second theme of today's lecture: namely, the subject of ostensive definition. You will, I hope, recollect the second lecture on Augustine's picture of meaning and on the various more sophisticated referential and correlational conceptions of meaning that Wittgenstein associated with this picture. One common feature of such conceptions of meaning is that language somehow is *connected* to reality – that it is its *connectedness to reality* that gives content to the web of words.

The picture is this: The words of a language divide into definables and indefinables. The definable expressions in a language are defined in analytic terms, for example by a definition that specifies the necessary and sufficient conditions for the application of the word. So: 'a vixen is a female fox'; 'a bachelor is an unmarried man'; 'a circle is a locus of points equidistant from a given point'. But verbal definitions must come to an end, otherwise we could go on defining words in terms of other words *ad infinitum* and never reach an understanding. For one expression, the meaning of which we do not know, would be defined in terms of other expressions, the meaning of which we do not know. Sometime or other, it seems, we must exit from language and make contact with reality and with our experience of it. For it is the points at which language is hooked to reality that give the words of language their content. In short, there must be a semantic – meaning endowing – connection between words and world. And that semantic connection must not only be the point at which content is injected into the web of words, it must also be constituted by our experiences of the world. For only thus could we acquire a language and come to understand the words of language. Or, to put it slightly differently, the foundations of language must lie in experience.

> **Int.** Well, that seems very plausible. It is surely a first-rate empiricist principle. I mean, we surely want language and linguistic understanding to make contact with our experience! But now, what was thought to be the simple, indefinable terms in a language?
>
> **PMSH.** The most obvious examples of such terms were held to be names of simple objects, qualities and relations that we encounter in experience. In the case of qualities that we apprehend by means of our perceptual organs (our 'outer senses'), these indefinable terms included such words as 'red' and 'blue', 'sour' and 'sweet', 'loud' and 'faint', 'fragrant' and 'fetid', 'hot' and 'cold'. These surely seem to be paradigms of words which *cannot* be verbally defined, and which one can understand only if one has experienced the perceptual qualities which they signify. Somehow or other (and it was never really worked out how), *all* other expressions signifying perceptibilia must be defined in terms of these simple ones. Indefinables of introspection, or *inner sense*, were held to be such expressions as 'pain', 'pleasure', 'desire', 'aversion', 'believing' and so forth. For these seem to stand for fundamental unanalysable features or operations of the human mind, they can be named but cannot be defined. And in order to name them, it seemed evident, one must experience them by inner sense. Other names of objects of inner sense, it was thought, could then be defined in terms of these indefinable ones. So, *hope*, for example, might be defined in terms of belief in a desired future eventuality, *ambition* as desire for office and precedence, and so on.
>
> **Int.** Yes, I see. That's very good! But how was a simple indefinable expression held to be linked to what it signifies? How was *the connection* between the simple name 'blue', for example, and the simple indecomposable entity in reality – *blueness* – held to be forged?

A most common way of explaining what numerous words of different kinds mean is by pointing. If a child asks, 'What's an Alsatian', one points at one and says: 'That's an Alsatian'. If someone asks, 'What is ultramarine?', one can point at the ultramarine curtains and say: 'That's ultramarine'. And if a child asks, 'What does "circular" mean?', one may point at a coin and say, 'That's circular'. So it is natural that the idea of ostensive explanation should be invoked to elaborate the idea of the connection between words and world, names and things – and to clarify the notion of the foundations of language in experience. In the case of simple indefinable names of objects of inner sense, such as pain or pleasure, it seemed that there must be some *inner analogue* of such a public explanation of meaning – *a private* ostensive explanation. We will examine that idea carefully in a later lecture.

A public ostensive explanation, however, is not an analytic definition elaborating necessary and sufficient conditions for something to be a so-and-so. Indeed, it is not a verbal definition at all.

Int. So what exactly is it?

PMSH. Well, few philosophers dwelt on the matter. The British empiricists, such as Locke, Berkeley and Hume, argued that words in general are names of ideas. So they held that one just *resolved* to call *a given* simple idea – a simple idea given one in experience – by *such-and-such* a name. What more could be said? Early in the twentieth century, Russell, in *Principia Mathematica*, remarked that primitive, that is, indefinable, ideas are *explained* by means of descriptions intended to point out to the reader what is meant. But, he added, the explanations do not constitute definitions because they really involve the ideas they explain.

Int. What on earth did he have in mind?

PMSH. That can easily be illustrated. The colour-word 'red' is indefinable by analytic definition. So one may explain it by pointing at a red car, say, and describing the car correctly by saying 'That's red'. But, of course, to understand this true description, one must grasp what the word 'red' means – that it is the name of, or sign for, *this* colour. That is why the young Wittgenstein, in the *Tractatus*, said enigmatically:

> The meanings of primitive signs can be explained by means of elucidations. Elucidations are propositions that contain the primitive signs. So they can be understood only if the meanings of the signs are already known. (TLP 3.263)

The thought was actually perfectly simple: one can't strictly *define* primitive terms. One explains them by using them in true assertions, from which the hearer is supposed to gather what they mean. That conception is also to be found in the writings of Quine, the leading American philosopher of the twentieth century. He wrote

> Many expressions, including most of our earliest, are learned *ostensively*; they are learned in the situation that they describe, or in the presence of the things they describe.

Int. I see. So an ostensive explanation was held to explain the meaning of an indefinable by using it in a true description. And that use of the indefinable links language to reality and lays the foundation of language in experience.

Yes, that is what they all thought. And that is indeed the natural thing to think. But *it is all wrong* – as the older Wittgenstein came to realize in the early 1930s. In the first place, ostensive explanations of meaning are not confined to the so-called indefinable expressions in the language. One *can* explain what the word 'circle' means by an analytic definition such as 'the locus of points equidistant from a given point', but one is much more likely to point at a coin and say, 'That shape is a circle'. One *can* define the animal name 'cat' as *felis domesticus*, that is, by specifying the genus *felis* to which a cat belongs and the differentia *domesticus* that distinguishes the cat from lions, tigers and so forth. But one is much more likely to point at Timmy and say, 'That's a cat'. So it is wrong to suggest that ostensive explanation and analytic definition are exclusive. It is also quite mistaken to suppose that one is superior to the other – that analytic definition is superior to ostensive definition because it is sharper or less liable to misinterpretation, or that ostensive definition is superior because it lays the foundation of language. A definition is in order, Wittgenstein stressed, *if it fulfils its role* – which is to enable the hearer to go on to use the word explained correctly.

Second, sentences such as 'That's a cat', 'That's ultramarine' or 'That's circular' have two quite different uses. On the one hand, they can be used as true descriptions – to say, for example, that there is a cat over there in the garden, that the curtains are ultramarine or that the ice-rink is circular rather than oval. These are empirical propositions that *presuppose* the meanings of their constituent terms and are true or false according to whether things are as they describe them as being. On the other hand, such sentences may be used as ostensive explanations of meaning – *rules for the use of the constituent word*. Then they can be elaborated as 'That ☞ *animal* is a cat', 'That ☞ *colour* (not "those curtains") is ultramarine', and 'That ☞ *shape* (not "that coin") is circular'. These are not true or false descriptions, but rules for the use of the words. What they amount to is that the word 'cat' is correctly applied to any animal that is of the same kind as *that* ☞ one; that anything which *is* the colour of *those* ☞ curtains is correctly described as being ultramarine; that anything that has *that* ☞ shape is rightly said to be circular.

When this form of words *is* used as an explanation of word meaning, it is a rule, not a description. Indeed, it *is* a definition – only not an analytic definition. And *that* it is a definition can be seen by reflecting on the following simple truth: if one has been given such an ostensive definition of, say, 'ultramarine', then one can go on to describe something else, such as the cushions, as being ultramarine simply by saying 'The cushions are *this* ☞ colour' – pointing at the ultramarine curtains. That is, the pointing gesture, the sample pointed at – namely the curtains, and the words 'this colour' actually do service for the colour word they define, namely 'ultramarine'. So one can look on an ostensive explanation or definition as a kind of substitution rule. Just as the analytic definition 'A bachelor is an unmarried man' allows one to substitute the word 'bachelor' in any occurrence of the phrase 'unmarried man', so too the ostensive explanation 'That ☞ colour is ultramarine' allows one to substitute for the word 'ultramarine' the partly concrete symbol consisting of the pointing gesture, the sample pointed at, and the expression 'that colour'. Instead of saying 'The cushions are ultramarine', one may say 'The cushions are *that* ☞ colour', while pointing at the curtains.

So, we should conceive of an ostensive explanation as a rule, not as a true or false description. It provides a standard for the correct use of the word it explains. And what is pointed at in such an explanation of meaning is not *described* at all – it is being used as a *defining sample*. It sets the standard for what is to be *called* ultramarine, for example (or, with a different sample, Wellington blue, or Brunswick green and so on). Of course, whether something is a sample or is an object being described is up to us. We *choose* things to function as samples – sometimes just for a given occasion, as when we explain what colour indigo is by pointing, say, to a book cover, sometimes relatively permanently, as when we use a colour chart from the local paint shop, and sometimes canonically, as when we lay down samples in the International Bureau of Standards. But now notice that if we do use an object as a defining sample, then it belongs to *the means of representation* and is not something *represented*. It belongs among the instruments of language, not to the world that we go on to describe. It is a measure, not what is measured.

Int. Could you slow down a little. I don't think I follow you.

All right. Let me try to make it clearer. We can measure lengths in many different metrics – in metres and centimetres, in yards, feet and inches, in ells or in banana lengths. That is up to us. If we buy a 12-inch ruler in the nearest stationery shop, we can both explain what a foot length is, that is: what the measure 'one foot' means, and use the ruler, which is a standard sample of a one foot length, as a measure. We lay it alongside an object and read off the length of the object. The ruler functions both as a defining sample and as a measure by reference to which to apply the term 'one foot long'. So it belongs to our means of representation, not to what is represented. We do not determine *its* length, we *stipulate* it – and we use it to determine the length of *other things*. And in just the same way, if we have recourse to a colour chart to classify fine shades of colours, we use the colour samples as defining samples for the names of shades of colour, and also as measures – objects for comparison – to determine the colours and shades of colours of things around us.

This simple reminder of what we do has dramatic consequences. For if samples are to be viewed as belonging to the means of representation, if they are among the instruments of language, if they are what do the measuring and not what is measured, then the whole picture of language as being *connected* to reality, as having its *foundations* in descriptions of reality, collapses. For a sample of green or of one foot long is not *described* by the ostensive definition 'That's green' or 'That's a foot length'. It is a measure and belongs among the means of representation. Ostensive definitions do not link words (namely symbols that represent) and world (namely what is represented). Rather, ostensive definitions *remain within language*. They merely link two different kinds of *means of representation* – words and samples. In giving an ostensive explanation we are not stepping *outside* language, as it were, and *linking language to reality*, we are merely stepping outside *word* language into *gesture* language. That is why Wittgenstein wrote 'I cannot use language to get outside language' – in this sense, *there is no exit from language*.

In this sense too, language is not *semantically linked to reality*. The whole picture of the web of words *deriving its content* from links with simple entities in reality – in the domain of what is represented by means of language – is misconceived. Language is, *in this sense*, self-contained and autonomous – it owes no homage to reality. It has no foundations – but is free-floating, like the globe. Of course, that does not mean that it is not conditioned by our nature and by the nature of the world we inhabit.

Int. But does that not mean that we do not use our language to refer to reality? That would be absurd. It would be a bizarre form of linguistic idealism!

PMSH. No, no. You've got hold of the wrong end of the stick. But I'll concede that you are in good company – since a very eminent British philosopher jumped to the same conclusion. But Wittgenstein meant no such thing, and no such thing follows from his observations. Of course, we refer to reality by the words we use to describe how things are in reality. But the *meanings of words* are fixed by conventions of meaning, by rules of use and by our practices of using words – not by how things are in the world. We give meaning to the words of our language by the conventions we have and the linguistic practices we engage in. And in laying down and explaining these conventions – these rules for the use of words – we appropriate objects in the world around us to function as part of our means of representation.

Int. You mean that they are tools in the toolbox of our language?

PMSH. Very well put. Yes, that's exactly what I mean.

Family-Resemblance Concepts: Undermining the Idea of Essence

The explanation of the meanings of simple indefinable expressions, such as 'red', 'sour', 'hot', 'acrid', was one pole of the classical foundationalist conception of language. The other was the explanation of definable expressions, such as 'triangle', 'vixen', 'grandfather'. Here it was generally assumed that such expressions are properly explained only by explicit definitions that specify necessary and sufficient conditions for their application.

We have already noted that the suggested exclusiveness of these two forms of explanation is misleading. The fact that an expression *can* be sharply defined by an analytic definition does not mean that it *cannot* be explained, indeed defined, by an ostensive explanation – as in the case of such words as 'cat' or 'circle'. But Wittgenstein came to challenge the idea from a quite different angle. He noted that these two kinds of explanation are not exhaustive either – for there are other licit forms of explanation of word meaning. One of these in particular caught his attention: family-resemblance explanations of concepts that are explained by *a series of examples together with a similarity rider*. Let me try to clarify this.

He noted that some words in a language are applied to the range of things to which they do apply – that is, to what logicians call 'their extension' – despite the fact that not all the items within their extension share a set of common characteristics. So, for example, we don't call cricket or tiddly-winks 'games' because they satisfy a list of necessary and sufficient conditions for being games – after all, we have no idea what the necessary and sufficient conditions for something's being a game are. The dogma against which Wittgenstein was objecting was the idea that if something is to be deemed a so-and-so, then there must be a set of characteristic features *in virtue of which* it is a so-and-so.

The traditional idea was that if an expression 'A' is not a simple indefinable of the language, then anything that is A must be so in virtue of its having features 'F', 'G' and 'H', which *make* it an A. So, for example, anything that is correctly deemed a vixen is so because it is both a fox and female. Being female and being a fox are individually necessary and jointly sufficient for being a vixen. And if anyone is a bachelor, then it is in virtue of being both a man and unmarried. Being an unmarried man is necessary and sufficient for being a bachelor. And so on. A corollary of this conception was that the things thus defined have *an essence*, which is given by specification of the conditions necessary and sufficient for being a thing of that kind. Bachelors may be rich or poor, young or old, handsome or ugly – these are all *inessential properties*. But being a man and being unmarried are essential features of being a bachelor.

So too, triangles may be large or small, red or black, drawn on white or pink paper – all of which are inessential properties. But being a three-sided rectilinear figure in a plane the sum of the internal angles of which is 180 degrees is the essence of triangularity. In the wake of Plato, it was widely held to be the task of philosophy to *discover* the essences of things. Definitions were not mere stipulations or arbitrary conventions for the use of words – they were descriptions of the *objective essences of things*. And they were correct only in so far as they captured the objective essence of what they purported to define.

Now doubtless there are many terms like 'vixen' and 'bachelor' that *are* defined by specifying a set of necessary and sufficient conditions for their application. But there are many terms that are *not*. Wittgenstein took as an example the word 'game'. All manner of activities count as games: football, cricket, chess, snakes and ladders, tiddly-winks, hide-and-seek, bridge, 'I spy with my little eye', patience and darts. Wittgenstein held that there is no set of features necessary and sufficient for something to be a game. Some games involve teams, others only a pair of players and some, like patience, are played alone. Some are competitive and involve winners and losers, others, like hide-and-seek, are not. Some are played for fun and only for fun; others, like the games we play with children to teach them how to spell or do elementary arithmetic, are not. So, what makes something a game? In virtue of what features does a certain activity count as a game?

Wittgenstein thought that games have *no* common defining features in virtue of which they are games. Rather, all the things we call 'games' are so called because of a multitude of partially *overlapping* features. They are related to each other like the faces of members of a family: my son may have my eyes, my daughter may have her mother's mouth, their cousin may have their grandfather's forehead, their niece her aunt's chin and so on. The faces are linked by a multitude of different partly overlapping similarities, and there may well be two members of the family who have *no* Hacker features *in common*, but who recognizably belong to the Hacker family. This series of partial overlapping similarities can be compared with the fibres of a rope. There is no set of fibres or even a single fibre running through the whole rope, but a series of overlapping fibres that make it a rope and bind it together into a unity. We characteristically explain what the word 'game' means by giving a series of examples together with a similarity rider. We might explain thus: 'Cricket, bridge, chess, darts, tiddly-winks and hide-and-seek, and other things like that are games.' This series of examples with its rider is an expression of a rule for the use of the word 'game', just as a rule for an arithmetical series can be given by a sequence such as '1, 4, 9, 16, 25 and so on'. We should view the series of examples as a guide to the application of the word – and, of course, in practice we do just that. Moreover, we teach our children how to use the word 'game' by teaching them games and telling them that *these* and other similar things are games. We do not offer an analytic definition, and we do not conceive of games as having an essence given by an analytic definition.

> **Int.** But surely there *are* familiar common properties to all games – for example, they are all *activities*, indeed, they are all *played*, and at the very least, typically *rule-governed*.
>
> **PMSH.** Well, that may be true. But the fact that all games are *played* gives us no handle by which to determine whether something is a game or not. For to determine that something is a game and that it is being played is to determine one thing, not two independent things. *Being played*, one might say, is a formal characteristic of games. And formal characteristics cannot serve to identify the things of which they are a form. And although one may argue that all games are rule-governed, that does not distinguish games from endless other rule-governed activities.
>
> **Int.** But surely, with sufficient ingenuity, the concept of a game *can* be defined. It has been suggested that a game is a rule-governed activity, with an arbitrary and non-serious objective lacking significance outside the game itself, which players set themselves to attain for the sake of fun or for the satisfaction of participating in the activity.
>
> **PMSH.** That is ingenious. But it is not satisfactory. First, it is not true that the objectives of children's spelling games or of Pentagon war games are either arbitrary or non-serious. Nor is it true that all games are played for fun – modern field games are largely played for money and to entertain the crowd. But let us waive this. What is far more important is the fact that no one was ever taught the use of the word 'game' by reference to such a definition, and no one is held not to understand the word 'game' because he cannot come up with this explanation of what it means. If we do come up with a satisfactory definition that shows nothing about our *current concept* of a game or our *current practice* of using the word 'game'.

Further objections against the idea of family-resemblance concepts have been raised. We must bypass them here and bear in mind the following crucial points:

First, there *is* general consensus about the use of family-resemblance words like 'game'. We don't come to blows over whether a kind of activity is or is not to be called 'a game'.

Second, we *do not* explain such terms through analytic definition.

Third, we do not apply these terms *haphazardly* or *arbitrarily*, and do not accept any old resemblance as warranting inclusion of a new member into the family. An election, for example, is not a game despite involving a number of players, a set of rules, a clear goal, determinate winners and losers, being very exciting and needing much skill and concentration. But for all that it isn't a game.

Fourth, we *do* accept as correct explanations of such terms by means of a series of examples and a similarity rider.

Fifth, we do sometimes *extend* a family by incorporating new members in virtue of overlapping similarities to existing ones – as when we incorporate photography into the family of the arts, or hyper-complex numbers into the family of numbers.

These are our practices. We must bear in mind the fact that it is *not* the task of philosophy to explain how what is actual is logically possible. Rather, its job is to show what is wrong with the idea that it is logically impossible or conceptually disreputable.

Now, the importance of the idea of family-resemblance concepts is twofold. First, it is one step on the road to dispelling the illusion of objective, language-independent essences. Second, the importance of the notion lies in its applications. Wittgenstein was not the first to have noticed the phenomenon of family-resemblance terms – it was noted by the Scottish philosopher Dugald Stewart in the early nineteenth century. Nor was he the first to use the expression 'family resemblance' – it was used by Humboldt and Nietzsche. But he was the first to apply it to some of the central problematic concepts in philosophy. For he argued that the concept of a proposition, and the concept of number, as well as many psychological concepts, such as thinking and understanding, are family-resemblance concepts. Consequently, he also held that the quest for the essence of a proposition which he had pursued so ardently in the *Tractatus*, or for the essence of a number, or of thinking or understanding, was bound to be futile. We shall explore Wittgenstein's anti-essentialism further in the next lecture on metaphysics as the shadow of grammar.

Chapter 6

METAPHYSICS, NECESSITY AND GRAMMAR

Description and Necessary Truth

It is a part of what Wittgenstein called 'Augustine's picture of language' that sentences are ordered combinations of names. A corollary of that idea is the thought that it is by the combination of names in accordance with the rules of syntax that sentences can represent how things are. It is but one step more, in the developed forms of this conception of language, to suggest that just as it is of the essence of words *to stand for things*, so too it is of the essence of sentences *to describe how things stand*. And one may well go on to argue, as Wittgenstein did when he wrote the *Tractatus*, that the general form of a proposition – a sentence in use – is: *such-and-such is thus-and-so*. And that is clearly the general form of a description.

If we think thus, then we may be inclined to go on to say that different kinds of proposition describe different kinds of subject matter. We distinguish the subject matter of physics from that of chemistry, for example, and we distinguish the domains of physics and chemistry from that of biology. Propositions of physics describe how things are in the domain of physics. Propositions of chemistry describe how things stand in the domain of chemistry. And propositions of biology describe how things are in the realm of the biological. But if we go down this road, what are we going to say about propositions of mathematics?

> **Int.** Well, surely arithmetical propositions such as '25 x 25 = 625' are true *descriptions* of relations between numbers. They state *mathematical facts*. Just as there are physical facts in the spatio-temporal domain of physics, so too there are mathematical facts in the non-spatial and atemporal domain of numbers. Isn't that precisely what mathematicians study?
>
> **PMSH.** Good, that is indeed how most great mathematicians have thought of themselves and of the propositions they investigate. Mathematicians conceived of themselves as explorers and discoverers of the non-spatial

and atemporal domain of number – precisely analogous to physicists in the spatio-temporal domain of physical objects. Charles Hermite, a distinguished nineteenth-century French mathematician, wrote:

> I believe that numbers and functions of analysis are not the arbitrary products of our spirits; I believe that they exist outside of us with the same character of necessity as the objects of objective reality; and we find or discover them and study them as do the physicists, chemists and zoologists.

And in the twentieth century, the great Cambridge mathematician G. H. Hardy wrote:

> It seems to me that no philosophy can possibly be sympathetic to a mathematician which does not admit, in one manner or other, the immutability and unconditional validity of mathematical truth. Mathematical theorems are true or false; their truth or falsity is absolutely independent of our knowledge of them. In some sense, mathematical truth is part of objective reality. (Mind 1929)

So you are in good company with your hunches or intuitions. But now what about the propositions of logic?

Int. Well, why not argue that propositions such as 'every proposition is either true or false' – the Law of Excluded Middle – or 'No proposition is both true and false' – the Law of Non-Contradiction – are descriptions? They describe the laws of propositional relations. Just as there are laws of physics *describing* how physical objects behave in the spatio-temporal realm, so too, it seems, there are laws of logic *describing* how propositions behave in a non-spatio-temporal realm.

PMSH. I agree with you that this is a wonderful and powerful picture. Logicians have succumbed to it throughout the ages. It is very tempting to think of logic, of the laws of truth, in this way, as indeed Frege did. He wrote:

> the laws of truth are [...] boundary stones set in eternal foundation, which our thought can overflow but never displace. It is because of this that they have authority for our thought if it would attain to truth. They do not bear the relation to thought that the laws of grammar bear to language, they do not make explicit the nature of our human thinking and change as it changes. (*Basic Laws of Arithmetic*, vol. I, p. xvi)

And the great Polish logician Łukasiewicz wrote in a similar manner:

> I should like to sketch a picture connected with the deepest intuitive feelings I always get about logic. This picture perhaps throws more light than any discursive exposition would on the real foundations from which this science grows (at least as far as I am concerned). Whenever I am occupied even with the tiniest logical problem, e.g. trying to find the shortest axiom of the implicational calculus, I have the impression that I am confronted with a mighty construction,

of indescribable complexity and immeasurable rigidity. The construction has the effect on me of a concrete tangible object, fashioned from the hardest of materials, a hundred times stronger than concrete and steel. I cannot change anything in it; by intense labour I merely find in it ever new details, and attain unshakable and eternal truths. Where and what is this ideal construction? A Catholic philosopher would say: it is in God, it is God's thought.

Now, how are we to think of what goes by the name of 'propositions of metaphysics', such as 'Nothing can be red and green all over at the same time', or 'Every event is temporally related to every other event' or 'Substances are bearers of properties'?

Int. Well, as far as I know, most philosophers think of such metaphysical propositions as describing *facts that obtain in all possible worlds*. While physicists discover truths of physics, truths that *happen to hold* in our world, philosophers conceived of themselves as discovering truths that *must hold* in *all possible worlds*. Their proper domain seemed to them to be the necessary features of the world and of our experience of it. It falls to metaphysics to discover the *essential scaffolding of any possible world*, and to *describe* it in philosophical propositions.

PMSH. Yes, the picture is powerful. Moreover, it is neat and tidy too. All propositions serve to describe how things are. The propositions of the natural sciences describe how things are in the various domains of contingency – of things that happen to be so but could be otherwise. The propositions of logic, mathematics and metaphysics describe the various *domains of necessity* – of things that could not be otherwise. Propositions of logic and mathematics describe how things stand in the ideal domain of abstract objects – thoughts and numbers. Propositions of metaphysics describe what is necessarily so in the domain of our experience and the objects of our experience.

This is certainly neat and tidy – but perhaps too neat and too tidy.

One might feel suspicious – and I hope that you do. There are two evident sources of unease to which I wish to draw your attention. The first is the very idea of non-empirical facts, and the second is the very idea of a necessary truth. In both cases, we need to be much more puzzled – and to take much less for granted. We need to worry about what exactly a fact is, and in particular what a *non-empirical fact* might be. So too, we must pause at the idea of a necessary truth and wonder what exactly it *means* for a proposition to be necessarily true and not be hoodwinked by the correct but unhelpful reply that it is a proposition that could not possibly be false.

It is one thing to distinguish between different sciences, such as physics, chemistry and biology, and to say that there are distinctive propositions proper to each of them that state facts discovered by physicists, chemists and biologists. But it is quite another thing to suggest that in addition to empirical facts established by natural scientists, there are also *non-empirical facts* – such as mathematical, logical and metaphysical facts discovered by mathematicians, logicians and metaphysicists. After all, what on earth *is* a 'non-empirical fact'?

> **Int.** Surely it is a necessary truth. It is not as if the proposition that 2 + 2 = 4 is a mere contingent truth that could be different in other times or at other places. No one would hold that perhaps it is just here on earth that 2 + 2 = 4 and that on Mars 2 + 2 might make 22! And can't I say the same of the truths of logic? The law of non-contradiction is surely not something that could be otherwise. The laws of logic, as Frege said, are 'boundary stones set in an eternal foundation, which our thought can overflow, but never displace'. And metaphysical propositions such as 'red is more like orange than like yellow' or 'effects cannot precede their causes' seem to be descriptions of *necessities in the world*.
>
> **PMSH.** Beautifully put. And not only beautifully put. For what you are inclined to think is indeed the most natural way to think. And it is what very many philosophers throughout the ages have thought. But you should be starting to get used to the idea that the natural way to think in philosophy is usually the wrong way to think.

Wittgenstein spent much time and effort between 1929 and 1944 trying to deconstruct this conception of necessary truths. He thought it to be a tangled web of misunderstandings, which beautifully exemplifies the nature of conceptual confusion. It is not so much a tangle of falsehoods, but a knotted web of nonsense – that is, not of rubbish, but of claims that transgress the bounds of sense. This venerable conception of the nature of necessity needs no disproof, but disentangling – for what transgresses the bounds of sense cannot literally be disproved and thereby be shown to be false, but only dismantled and shown to make no sense.

Dismantling – First Suspicions: Facts and Propositions

Crucial to the conception we are confronting is the idea that the role of the proposition is descriptive and that it successfully fulfils its role when it describes the facts – empirical facts, mathematical, logical and metaphysical facts. Of these, some are contingent and others are necessary. Mathematical, logical and metaphysical facts are all necessary facts.

But this might give us pause. For surely a fact is precisely something *that could be otherwise*. It is a fact that Harold of England died in 1066, but he might well have died earlier or later. It is a fact that cheetahs are the fastest animals on earth, but there might have been even faster ones. It is a fact that there are no Martians, but there might have been. We take matters of fact to be matters determined by observation and investigation, including scientific observation – but we do not take logicians and mathematicians to be investigating matters of fact at all. So, are we not conjuring 'necessary facts' into existence, together with possible worlds, domains of number and realms of propositions, simply in order to satisfy a misleading picture? After all, there are no 'possible worlds', any more than there are possible people in this room and possible mountains in the landscape. Talk of possible worlds is no more than a fancy way of talking about what could have or might have been the case in this world – the one and only world. Our talk of a domain of mathematics in which numbers stand in relations to each other, and await description by mathematicians, is surely a mere fiction modelled on empirical propositions and their relation to reality. And is not Frege's talk of an atemporal realm of propositions just a misleading figure of speech? – Well, these suggestions are worth contemplating and examining. So let's do so together with our interlocutor.

PMSH. Let me start by asking you what you mean by 'a fact'?

Int. Well, we think of facts as what *correspond* to true thoughts and assertions. Facts *make* those thoughts and assertions true. Our thoughts and the assertions that express them, we think, are representations. What they represent is how things are, and they represent truly if what they describe is in fact the case – if what they state is a fact. So surely, facts are in some sense *in* the world. Thought and speech are correct insofar as they *correspond* to those facts in the world. And it seems obvious that some facts are contingent facts – which are described by the empirical sciences – and other facts are necessary facts – which is the task of logic, mathematics, ethics and metaphysics to describe.

PMSH. Yes, that is the natural and persuasive picture we are inclined to conjure up. It is immensely convincing.

Int. So I suppose that you are going to tell me that it is all wrong!

PMSH. Yes. Wittgenstein argued that this is all illusion. And it seems to me that his arguments are overwhelmingly powerful. Contrary to what he himself thought when he wrote the *Tractatus*, the world does *not* consist of facts at all. Rather, *true descriptions of the world* – that is, descriptions of how things are – consist of *statements of facts* – that is, statements of how things, *in fact*, are. Facts, unlike objects, events and states of affairs, are not to be found in the world. For one thing, they have no location. It is a fact that the battle of Hastings was fought in 1066, but that fact is not in Hastings – it is the battle that occurred there, but the fact that it occurred there is not there. And although the battle was fought in 1066, the fact that it was fought in 1066 did not take place in 1066 or at any other time – for facts do not take place and have no temporal location. To say that something is a fact is not to *classify* anything as being of a certain kind, but *to affirm an empirical proposition*. To say that it is a fact that things are thus-and-so is to say that things are *in fact* thus-and-so – that they *really are* so, or that they are *actually* so. Furthermore, facts don't *make propositions true* in the sense in which acids make litmus paper turn pink, but only in the sense in which being an unmarried man makes one a bachelor. There are not contingent facts and necessary facts – only contingent and necessary *propositions*. And the question that calls out for elucidation is what *is* a necessary proposition? For whatever it is, it is not a proposition that states or describes a necessary fact.

Now let me step back from our interlocutor. It is surely evident that when confronted by questions about necessary truths, we readily fall victim to an immensely appealing picture. So we need to probe that picture. What is it, and what are its sources? And why does it appeal to us so persuasively?

It is a picture of propositions all having (i) a uniform structure, (ii) a uniform function and (iii) all standing in a uniform relation to reality.

Their structure is a rule-governed, syntactically well-formed combination of signs or names, in which one thing is predicated *of* another.

Their function is *to describe how things stand*.

The relation in which they stand to the realities they describe is that they are made true by things being as they describe them as being – *in the relevant domain of things*.

It is precisely this essentialist conception of propositions that Wittgenstein challenged when he argued that the concept of a proposition is a family-resemblance concept. So, let us probe this thought more deeply – for it demonstrates the fruitfulness of the notion of family resemblance when it is put to work.

Let us grant that one-word utterances apart, propositions have the common form of the declarative sentence. Furthermore, in Wittgenstein's view, it is an internal property of propositions that they are either true or false – that is, we would not deem a sentence to express a proposition unless what is said by its use is either true or false. But while propositions of physics, chemistry and biology are simply different kinds of propositions, as Coxes, Pink Ladies and Braeburns are different kinds of apples, empirical, logical, mathematical and metaphysical propositions are not – in this sense – different *kinds* of propositions, but different *categories* of propositions. They differ from each other not as Coxes differ from Braeburns, but rather as Coxes differ from

Applemacs – not as one kind of railway train differs from another, but as railway trains differ from railway companies or railway tickets. They are categorially distinct – and radically unlike each other in their roles and functions.

Let me give you a few examples to show what Wittgenstein had in mind here with respect to logical and mathematical propositions – and then I shall focus upon metaphysics and elaborate his views at greater length. In his investigations into logic, Wittgenstein was criticizing, among others, the great logician of his day, Frege. Frege held that all logical propositions were perfectly general. Hence, he held that the proposition that either it is raining or it is not raining is not a logical proposition but an *application* of the logical proposition known as the Law of Excluded Middle. The Law of Excluded Middle is the logical generalization that *every proposition* is either true or false. So too, Frege did not think that the proposition that it is not both raining and not raining at the same time is a logical proposition but simply an application of the Law of Non-Contradiction – that *no proposition* is both true and false. Propositions of logic, he held, are general laws that apply to *all* propositions whatsoever – somewhat in the way that the laws of physics apply to all spatio-temporal bodies whatsoever. Laws of Logic are the laws that describe the logical relationships between propositions, irrespective of their subject matter – they are eternal truths concerning the domain of propositions.

Wittgenstein thought that was misconceived. Such propositions as the Law of Excluded Middle and the Law of Non-Contradiction are *not* generalizations over all propositions. 'Every proposition is either true or false' looks like 'All swans are either white or black' – but it is not. After all, it is not as if we have examined all hitherto encountered propositions and have discovered that they are all either true or false.

Int. Do you mean we do not *count something* as a proposition unless it is true or false?

PMSH. Yes, that's exactly right! You've hit the nail on the head. 'Every propositions is either true or false' is like 'Every natural number is either odd or even' and not like 'Every swan is either white or black'.

Int. You mean that, in principle, we might come across a red swan. But on the logicians' construal of 'proposition', it is inconceivable that we might come across a proposition that is neither true nor false, for this is constitutive of what it is to be a proposition.

PMSH. Exactly so. Now note that actual propositions of logic, as opposed to these so-called *Laws of Logic*, are indeed such propositions as 'Either it is raining or it is not raining' or 'It is not both raining and not raining'. These are indeed necessary truths – *they are true no matter how things stand*. But just because of that, they are devoid of information and tell one nothing. *To know that it is either raining or not raining is not to know anything about the weather.* Such logical propositions Wittgenstein called *tautologies*. They have *no descriptive role at all*. Moreover, all these propositions of logic have the same sense – namely *none*. For they say nothing at all. Precisely because they are uninformative, because they convey no information, he called them senseless (not nonsense, since they are perfectly well-formed) – they have, in a manner of speaking, zero sense. A corollary of this is that there can be no science of logic on the model of the science of physics. For logical propositions, unlike the propositions of physics, say nothing. They are not about any particular subject matter – as physics is. Logic is a *calculus*, not a doctrine or set of doctrines. Logical propositions – such as 'Either it is raining or it is not raining' – are not *descriptions* of anything.

Wittgenstein's remarks about the fundamental nature of arithmetical propositions are no less radical. He argued that they are not descriptions of a super-sensible domain of numbers. Indeed, he insisted, *they are not descriptions at all*. We are misled by their propositional form into thinking, for example, that the arithmetical proposition that three is greater than two is akin to the empirical proposition that Jack is taller than Jill – only about the eternal realm of numbers rather than the fleeting realm of empirical fact. But arithmetical propositions are actually *expressions of rules*. The purpose of arithmetical equations, for example, is, above all, *to provide rules for the transformation of empirical propositions about magnitudes and quantities*.

Let me give you some simple examples. That three is greater than two is not the description of a relation between numbers. It is an inference rule that allows one to infer from the fact that, for example, Jill has three apples and Jack has two, that Jill has more apples than Jack – one need not look to see. The arithmetical proposition $25 \times 25 = 625$ is an inference rule that enables one to infer from the fact that one has 25 bags of 25 biscuits each that one has 625 biscuits in all. One need not count up afresh. And should it turn out on a count that one does *not* in fact have 625 biscuits, then that is not a reason for thinking that sometimes $25 \times 25 = 624$ or 626. Rather, it is a criterion for believing that a biscuit was removed or added, or alternatively that the initial count of the bags and their respective contents was mistaken.

Similarly, geometry is not a science about super-sensible perfect figures, as Plato thought. Nor is it a theory of space, as Newton thought. It is a *grammar* for the description of spatial relations. The Pythagorean theorem that the square on the hypotenuse of a right-angled triangle is equal to the sum of the squares on the remaining two sides is a rule for transforming measurements of areas. The *whole point* of mathematics is not to achieve more and more *true descriptions* of numbers and their relations, or of shapes or of space – but to achieve ever richer *forms of transformation* of empirical propositions concerning magnitudes and spatial relations. In short, mathematics is not *a description of a super-empirical domain,* and geometry is *not a description of space.* Mathematics is the development and elaboration of a *grammar of number* and a *grammar of spatial relations* for the purposes of more refined descriptions and transformations of descriptions of things in the world. Mathematics is a *net* within which to catch quantifiable empirical truths, but mathematicians and philosophers have typically mistaken the net for a transcendent, diaphanous world of numbers and shapes, which it is their task to describe.

Necessary Truths of Metaphysics

These examples give you a very rough idea of Wittgenstein's pathway through logic and mathematics, guided by the principle that *there is no mystery here.* Rather, when things appear mysterious, then we have been taken in by appearances. This is especially striking when it comes to propositions such as 'Black is darker than white' or 'Red is more like orange than it is like yellow', or 'Nothing can be red all over and also green all over at the same time'. These propositions are surely necessary truths – for it is inconceivable that black be lighter than white, or that red be more like yellow than like orange or that something should be both red all over and also green all over simultaneously. These are not empirical observations; they are *metaphysical propositions,* which, according to metaphysicists, are true in all possible worlds.

It is striking that putatively metaphysical propositions are often cast in modal form, that is, as characterizing what is necessarily so, what is possible or impossible. So, we are prone to say that what is coloured *must be* spatially extended, that nothing *can* be both red and green all over, or that it is *impossible* to travel backwards in time. Of course, such modal forms of sentences are common in other contexts too. So, we say that what goes up *must* come down, that if an animal is deprived of food and water it *must* die. Such modal forms of sentences also have a well-established role in practical reasoning about ways and means: if you want to cool the room, we say, then you *must* open the window; if you want more light, you *must* turn on the lamp. These are surely descriptions of *physical, practical* necessities. So, by analogy, we think that the putatively metaphysical propositions are descriptions of *metaphysical* necessities. These, we are inclined to think, differ from physical necessities inasmuch as they are non-causal, much stricter than physical necessities and ineluctable. They seem adamantine. But, although they seem so, Wittgenstein argued, appearances are deceptive. For these propositions are not descriptions of anything, but *expressions of rules for descriptions.*

> **Int.** But surely that can't be right. The proposition that black is darker than white describes a relationship between black and white – a relation of *being darker than*. It is *obviously* just like the proposition that the sofa is darker than the armchair. Of course, it differs from 'the sofa is darker than the armchair' because it is *a necessary truth* about colours as opposed to *a contingent truth* about the furniture.
>
> **PMSH.** Well, yes, that is what it looks like. And that is what one is inclined to say. But what we are inclined to say when confronted by philosophical questions is not the conclusion of a philosophical argument – it is raw material for philosophical investigation.

'Black is darker than white' is actually the expression of a rule for the use of the words 'black', 'white' and 'darker than'. It is in effect an inference licence. It allows one, for example, to infer from the propositions that the sofa is black and that the chair is white, the conclusion that the sofa is darker than the chair. One does not need to look and compare. If the one is black and the other white, then the former *must* be darker than the latter – that is, *it follows* that the sofa is darker than the chair. The *must* here expresses not *a necessity in the world*, but *the legitimacy of the inference*.

Similarly, the proposition that red is more like orange than like yellow is not a *description* of the necessary features of these colours in all possible worlds, but rather a rule for the use of these colour words or colour concepts. It is a licence to describe any object that is red as more akin in colour to any orange object than it is to any yellow one. And it is not a truth that *follows* from the *nature* of red, or from the *meaning* of the word 'red' – rather it partly *determines* the nature of red, and it is partly *constitutive* of the meaning of the word 'red'. For it is the expression of a rule for the use of the word 'red' – and so part of its grammar.

> **Int.** All right, I'll grant you that. But surely the metaphysical proposition that nothing can simultaneously be both red all over and green all over is precisely parallel to the proposition that nothing can run faster than 100 miles an hour. The latter proposition describes a biological impossibility. No animal can run that fast. Surely the former proposition about colour exclusion – that nothing can be red and green all over at the same time – describes a metaphysical impossibility. Nothing can be red and green all over at the same time *because it is of the nature of colours that two different colours cannot occupy the same space at the same time*, just as two different human beings cannot occupy the same place at the same time.
>
> **PMSH.** Yes. That is what we are inclined to think. And interestingly enough, that is what Wittgenstein himself thought at one time (in 1929

in fact). But it is an illusion. And it is not easy to rid oneself of it, for it is firmly rooted in analogies that grip us. How can we escape the hold of the illusion?

Note that colours, unlike layers of paint, do not *occupy* space or *fill* space at all – they are *properties* of things, not *very thin things* like wafers. So although it is true that nothing can be red and green all over at the same time, this proposition is not at all like the proposition that Jack and Jill cannot sit in the same chair at the same time, since one will keep the other out. If the chair is red, the red of the chair does not keep green out, as Jack keeps Jill out. One might say that while Jack *excludes* Jill, red *precludes* green.

The illusion is engendered in part by the similarity in the grammatical forms of sentences such as 'Nothing can be red and green all over' and 'Nothing can run faster than 100 mph'. But we have learnt enough from Wittgenstein to know that we must always beware of attending to form and disregarding function. The proposition that no animal can run faster than 100 mph is informative – it excludes an intelligible possibility. It is *conceivable* that a living being should run faster than 100 mph, but in fact, this cannot be done. But the proposition that nothing can be both red and green all over is altogether dissimilar. It does not exclude an intelligible possibility – for it is *inconceivable* that something should be both red all over and also green all over at the same time. That is a conceptual impossibility. And a conceptual impossibility is not *a possibility that is impossible.*

Int. So if this proposition does not exclude a genuine possibility, what does it exclude?

PMSH. Wittgenstein's answer was that while it looks as if it describes a state of affairs which it then says is impossible, it is actually *the expression of a rule* – and *what it excludes* is not a possibility, but *a form of words*. It excludes the form of words 'is both red all over and green all over at the same time'. It specifies that this form of words *has no sense;* it is not a description of a possibility. But of course, it is not a description of an impossibility either. Rather, it is a nonsensical combination of words – a form of words to which no sense has been given.

Int. But that can't be right! If the proposition that nothing can be red and green all over is just a rule, and if rules of grammar owe no homage to reality, then what prevents us from making it a rule that it *does* make sense to say that something is both red and green all over.

PMSH. Nothing *prevents* us. But if we wish to make this a rule, we should be changing the rules for the use of these colour predicates, and we should then mean something quite different from *red* and *green* and *being* *the same colour*. As things are in our colour grammar, we explain that something is red all over if it is *this* ☞ colour all over (and we point at a sample of red), and something is green if it is *that* ☞ colour all over (and we point at a sample of green), and, we add, '*this* ☞ colour is not the same as *that* ☞ colour'. So we allow nothing *to count* as being both red and green all over, that is, we have given no meaning to the phrase 'is both red all over, and at the same time also green all over'. And that is what the pseudo-metaphysical proposition 'Nothing can be red and green all over' boils down to. It is not a deep insight into the essential nature of reality or the language-independent natures of redness and greenness, but a rule for the use of the words 'red' and 'green'. It is no more than an inference licence – for if we know that something is red all over, we *can infer* straight away, without looking to see, that it is not also green (or blue or yellow) all over.

So, what seem to be statements about the nature of things, what seem to be insights into necessary features of all possible worlds and what seems to be the domain of metaphysics turn out to be just more grammar.

It is important to note that statements concerning metaphysical *impossibilities* – such as 'no one can travel backwards in time', or 'no one can count through all the cardinal numbers' – are not descriptions of human frailties and limitations. Unlike 'no one can run a mile in three minutes', *they are not descriptions of things we can't do*. They are specifications of the *bounds of sense*. Reflect on the proposition 'You can't checkmate in draughts'. This does not describe a constraint under which one labours when playing draughts; rather, it is like 'There are no goals in tennis'. It does not actually describe something one *cannot* do, it says that *there is nothing to be done*. That is why it is more clearly specified by saying '*There is no such thing* as checkmate in draughts'. 'You can't count through all the cardinal numbers' does not describe something that is too difficult for us to do – it says that *there is no such thing* as counting through all the cardinal numbers, that this form of words makes no sense. So too, the statement that time-travel is impossible does not describe something we can't do, but says that *there is no such thing to do*; there is no such thing as time-travel – the phrase 'time-travel' has no meaning. Now, of course, it is not enough just to assert this – it has to be shown. For it is not immediately obvious that this phrase has no use. That can be done – although I shall not do it here. My only concern here is to make clear the *status* of such metaphysical assertions; they are not descriptions, but expressions of rules for description. And what appear to be statements of metaphysical impossibilities are merely exclusionary grammatical rules.

Grammar Pays No Homage to Reality

To be sure, this deflationary account of the adamantine truths of metaphysics may strike you as unsatisfactory. It goes against the grain. It flies in the face of all our intuitions. Nevertheless, reflect that our so-called intuitions are just hunches and guesses – they are no more than what we are inclined to say. But, to repeat, what we are inclined to say when confronted with difficult conceptual problems is usually mistaken. That is one reason why philosophy is so infernally difficult. And it is one reason why we have to dig right down to the roots of 'what we are inclined to say'. So I shall let our interlocutor have his say.

Int. Thank you. You are dead right that this flies in the face of everything I have picked up in philosophy. Surely Wittgenstein fails to do justice to the *objective truths* of metaphysics and indeed to their *adamantine necessity*! What he says just doesn't add up.

It is *true* that red is darker than pink, that causes cannot follow their effects, that every event is temporally related to every other event. But *rules are neither true nor false*! Rules are human artefacts – they are human conventions that inform our behaviour, that guide our activities, that can be adopted or rejected, that can be stipulated or that are constitutive of our practices. Moreover, *rules are not adamantine necessities,* they can surely always be changed! So how can Wittgenstein say that such propositions of metaphysics as 'Nothing can be red and green all over at the same time' or 'Red is darker than pink' are expressions of *rules*? How can he aver that such necessarily true propositions are *rules of grammar*?

PMSH. That is a very natural reaction. But if you react in this way, then you have still not grasped Wittgenstein's arguments. You are still inclined to think that metaphysical essences are described by *true* metaphysical descriptions. And – you want to say – surely *rules are not true or false*. And you infer from this that Wittgenstein's assimilation of metaphysical propositions to expressions of rules *must* be wrong! You are in the good company of many philosophers who have argued along just these lines.

Nevertheless, you (and they) are being careless. Of course, rules are neither true nor false. But *the statement of a rule* is either true or false. It is a rule of chess that the king moves one square at a time. That *rule* is not true. But it is true that the chess king moves one square at a time. That is, whereas we don't characterize rules as true or false, we do characterize the *statement of a rule* as true or false. And so the rules of our grammar and the rules for the use of the familiar words of our language are neither true nor false, but a statement of a rule of grammar, such as 'red is darker than pink', can, of course, be said to be true, no less than the statement of the rule of chess that the king moves a square at a time can be said to be true.

Int. All right. I can see that. But surely a proposition such as 'red is darker than pink' or 'nothing can be red and green all over' is a description of *the essence of colour*. And surely the essences of things are independent of language.

PMSH. That is a misconception of what the essence of something is. Of course, there is nothing *wrong* with talking about the essence of certain things. But, Wittgenstein wrote:

> I say, however: if you talk about *essence*, you are merely noting a convention. But here one would like to retort: there is no greater difference than that between a proposition about the depth of the essence and one about – a mere convention. But what if I reply: to the *depth* that we see in the essence there corresponds the *deep* need for the convention. (RFM 65)

Of course, one *can* say that being darker than pink is part of the essence of red, but all that means is that we would not *count* some object as being red if it were not also darker than any pink object – that is, any object that we *count* as pink. And that *is* a convention – a convention to which we cleave through thick and thin as long as we are talking about coloured things. The putative necessity is, as I suggested previously, merely a misleading reflection of the inference rule that we accept, namely that if A is red and B is pink, then *it follows* that A is darker than B.

Int. But surely, *grammar* (in Wittgenstein's sense) is *answerable to reality*! Surely we adopt the grammatical rule that red is darker than pink precisely *because* red actually *is* darker than pink!

PMSH. No, this is to confuse the shadow that grammar casts upon the world for the properties of what is determined by grammar. *Grammar determines what it makes sense to say* – not how things actually are. How things *actually* are is determined by reality. The world determines how things actually are; grammar determines only what it makes sense to say about reality – not what is true, but what is logically or conceptually possible.

Int. But does that not change?

PMSH. Yes, of course. It changes as our concepts and our conceptual schemes change.

Int. But then it might no longer be the case that red is darker than pink – and that means that it is not in fact a necessary truth at all. So Wittgenstein *must* be wrong!

PMSH. No, no, slow down! You are taking the fences much too fast. If we change the grammar of a word, then we are changing the concept. And if we are changing the concept, then we are speaking of something different. Let me give you a simple example. Prior to the introduction of negative numbers, it made no sense to subtract 10 from 5; you can't take a larger number away from a smaller one, it was said, for, to be sure, you can't have less than nothing! Then negative numbers were introduced, and thenceforth it made sense to subtract 10 from 5 – and to be left with -5. But, of course, that did not involve changing any adamantine necessities. For one was no longer talking of the same thing. One was talking of signed integers, not of natural numbers. So too, we might at some distant time change the grammar of the words 'red' or 'pink' or 'darker than', but then we would no longer be speaking of the same things.

This dialectic could go on for much longer. It is exceedingly difficult to shed old habits of thought, especially when our very language seems to speak for them. But, as Wittgenstein noted:

> Philosophy is a struggle against the bewitchment of our understanding by the resources of our language. (PI §109)

And you must struggle for yourselves. Wittgenstein can show the way out of the fly-bottle, but he cannot fly out for you. I should, however, like to draw your attention to two further important points, which may help you further. First, if these putatively metaphysical truths that so mesmerize us *were* descriptions of the scaffolding of the world, they should be genuine discoveries, news from the *Transcendental Times*. But now reflect:

> Whom do we tell 'White is lighter than black'? What information does it give? (RFM 76)

And second, think of Wittgenstein's remark:

> I could also have said: it is not the property of an object that is ever 'essential', but rather the [defining] mark of a concept. (RFM 64)

Now let us turn, finally, to the great metaphysical systems of the past and to Wittgenstein's response to them.

Metaphysical Systems

The great philosophers of the past were in pursuit of larger quarry than 'nothing can be red and green all over' or 'black is darker than white'. Their aim was to discover the true global nature of reality – its essential nature. Unlike scientists, they were not concerned with discovering the contingent chemical constitution of things, or the ultimate particles of which matter happens to consist or the physical nature of energy. Rather, they conceived of themselves as struggling with deeper questions – striving to discover whether reality is essentially mental or physical, whether the mind is a material substance, such as the brain, or a mental, spiritual one. They were preoccupied with the relations between appearance and reality, striving to discover whether appearances are a guide to how things really are. So they wanted to find out whether colours in general are objective or whether they are no more than subjective modifications of the observing mind. For if colours are merely the effects of material things on us, if they are merely ideas in our minds, then reality is very different from the way it appears to us. For then the world as it is in itself is a colourless array of radiation-reflecting objects in space and time. It was this striving to understand the ultimate nature of reality that gave metaphysics its aura and grandeur.

It is noteworthy that today most philosophers are inclined to be materialists, to hold that everything that exists is physical, that the mind is identical with the brain, that consciousness is a property of the brain, that the world is actually bereft of colour, sound, smell and taste – since these are merely the effects of radiation on our nerve endings. And scientists encourage them – for they share the same beliefs. Lay members of the educated public who are vaguely interested in such matters go along with this – impressed, one might say, with this scientific conception of reality. But it is not actually a *scientific* vision at all; it is a *metaphysical* one, rooted in part in the seventeenth-century metaphysics of Descartes and Locke. Reflect on the rather obvious fact that no scientific experiment can *prove* or *confirm* that *nothing* is coloured, or that there are *no* noises around when there is no one to hear them – but only sound waves. These doctrines are not the experimental results of scientific inquiry; they are *metaphysical presuppositions*. Indeed, this is *scientistic* metaphysics – a metaphysics inspired by misunderstood and misconstrued empirical science.

Wittgenstein thought that the metaphysical quest is an illusory one. Its results, conflicting and contentious as they are, are uniformly confused. Metaphysicists come up with startling news: that the world really consists only of material things, or that it really consists only of minds and ideas or – in the case of the solipsist – that it really consists only of me and my ideas. Some reported back that space and time are unreal, and others that material objects are unreal. Some, impressed by the atomic theory of matter, held that despite appearances, nothing is really solid – for matter consists of atomic particles separated by empty space. Others claimed to have discovered that the mind was a spiritual substance that can exist independently of the body, and yet others claimed that there are no minds at all – that the mind is but a fiction. And the controversies continue unresolved throughout the ages, changing, to be sure, with the fashion of the day, but never achieving any substantive knowledge of the world.

This, Wittgenstein held, is no coincidence – precisely because the quest is illusory. It is akin to Winnie the Pooh's quest for the East Pole. *There is no such thing* as *metaphysics* – only conceptual confusions dressed up in the guise of news from the *Transcendental Times*. Someone who tells us that material objects are not really solid does not hesitate to put his books down on the table – which he would do if the table were a mere hologram. He does not hesitate to pour himself a drink into a glass – which he would do if the glass were full of holes like a sieve. And he does not hesitate to walk on the floor without fear of falling through. So, there is something fishy about his claim that material things are not really solid. The scientist or philosopher who tells us that things around us are not really coloured nevertheless asks his wife to give him a red scarf for Christmas. When he avers that material objects are not really coloured, he does not mean that they are all made of transparent colourless glass. And of course, he complains that the windows of his car are so heavily tinted blue that he cannot see the beautiful colours of the landscape. So, what is going on here?

No doubt a variety of different things – different forms of conceptual confusion – contribute to controversy between philosophers who have advanced different metaphysical conceptions of the nature of the world. This is not a disagreement over facts; it is a disagreement over concepts and forms of description – masquerading as a disagreement of fact.

The materialist, who says that the world consists of material things alone, and the idealist who says that the world consists of ideas alone are actually disagreeing about *forms of description*. The materialist wants to describe the world exclusively in terms of the behaviour of material things in space. The idealist, by contrast, wants to describe the world in terms of experiences. But both wrongly express their preferences for one or another form of description as a disagreement of fact. Here Wittgenstein noted that:

> *This* is what disputes between idealists, solipsists and realists look like. The one party attacks the normal form of expression as if they were attacking an assertion; the others defend it, as if they were stating facts recognized by every reasonable human being. (PI §402)

What is clear is that the passionate metaphysical claims are not disagreements of fact at all. That is why Dr Johnson's famous refutation of Berkeley's idealism – which consisted of kicking a boulder with all his might and exclaiming loudly 'I REFUTE HIM THUS' – was not to the point at all.

The presentation of startling news from the *Transcendental Times* is the result of misunderstanding scientific discoveries. The atomic theory of matter does not show that material objects are not really solid. Wittgenstein spelt this out nicely:

> We have been told by popular scientists that the floor on which we stand is not solid, as it appears to common sense, as it has been discovered that the wood consists of particles filling space so thinly that it can almost be called empty. This is liable to perplex us, for in a way, of course, we know that the floor is solid, or if it isn't solid, this may be due to the wood being rotten, not to its being composed of [atoms and] electrons. To say, on this latter ground, that the floor is not solid is to misuse language. For even if the particles were as big as grains of sand and as close together as these are in a sand-heap, the floor would not be solid if it were composed of them in the sense in which a sand-heap is composed of grains. Our perplexity was based on a misunderstanding; the picture of thinly filled space had been wrongly applied. For this picture of the structure of matter was meant to explain the very phenomenon of solidity. (BB 45)

In short, the meaning of the phrase 'solid object' has not changed just because we have a new picture of the molecular structure of solid objects.

Similar considerations apply to the 'discovery' that things are not really coloured or that things do not actually make noises and sounds. Someone who thinks that things are not really coloured but only appear so to us is confused about the grammar of colour; but he has not discovered anything about reality. For his claim amounts to this: that colour words are to be defined purely in terms of colour appearances to normal observers in normal observation conditions. When we say that something is red, what we really mean, he argues, is that this thing looks red to any normal observer under normal observation conditions. But that is mistaken. First, the concept of *looking red* presupposes the concept of being red, and to acquire mastery of the use of the phrase 'looks red' one must already know what it is for something to be red. And indeed, we explain that what it is for something to look red is for it to look *thus* ☞, and here we point to something that *is* red. Second, we have no independent handle on the ideas of normal conditions of observation. Rather, normal observation conditions for colour are those conditions under which things look as they are. And so too, normal observers are people who can discriminate coloured things as they are under normal observation conditions. So what appeared to be a discovery about the subjective nature of colours was no more than a misconstrual of the grammar of colour words. Of course, a great deal more could and should be said on this subject. But the trajectory of the analysis is, I hope, clear.

The upshot of Wittgenstein's investigations into what are commonly taken to be metaphysical propositions and metaphysical investigations is that there

METAPHYSICS, NECESSITY AND GRAMMAR 109

is no such thing as metaphysics, only grammatical confusions. What are presented as metaphysical propositions that describe the necessary features of reality are not actually *descriptions* of anything, but at best grammatical *rules* for making descriptions. So, what seem to be objective and mysterious necessities in the world are actually no more than the shadows cast upon the world by grammar.

This demystification is altogether characteristic of Wittgenstein's later philosophy. 'All that philosophy can do', he wrote, 'is to destroy idols'. For 'A philosophical problem is an awareness of a disorder in our concepts and can be solved by ordering them.' The whole of his later philosophy is a painstaking ordering of concepts with the purpose of dispelling conceptual confusion and bewilderment and attaining an overview of a segment of our conceptual scheme.

Chapter 7

THOUGHT AND LANGUAGE

Augustine's Picture Again

You will recollect that an integral element of the conception of meaning that Wittgenstein associated with Augustine's pre-reflective picture of language is the idea that language is *connected* to reality. Augustine remarked that

> When grown-ups named some object and at the same time turned towards it, I perceived this, and I grasped that the thing was signified by the sound they uttered, since they meant to point *it* out. This, however, I gathered from their gestures, the natural language of all peoples [...]. (Augustine - Confessions I-8)

So Augustine conceived of words being connected with things by means of ostension. We have already examined Wittgenstein's criticisms of that idea. Let me briefly remind you of some of his points and take the matter forward a little.

First of all, we must distinguish ostensive training from ostensive teaching. All initial language learning is a matter of training. Parents and siblings endlessly repeat words, encourage correct reactions and reinforce correct repetition. This is not explaining what words mean, but inculcating verbal responses and reactions. Ostensive teaching can play a role in language learning only once the child has already acquired substantial linguistic skills and is in the position to start asking 'What is a so-and-so?' and 'What does such-and-such a word mean?'

· Second, we must note that the form of words 'This is so-and-so?' has two quite different uses. It may be used to make a true or false statement about the object that is pointed at – as when we are asked whether there is anything octagonal around, and in reply we point at a small side table and say 'This ☞ is octagonal'. Alternatively, we might be asked what the word 'octagonal' means, and in reply we might point at the table and say 'This ☞ is octagonal'. In the first case, our description could be paraphrased 'This ☞ table is octagonal', but in the second case our ostensive utterance is not a description but a definition.

Third, when we give an ostensive definition such as 'This ☞ – that is, this shape – is octagonal' or 'This ☞ – that is, this colour – is brown', we are using the object we point at as a sample. So used, it belongs (even if only for the moment) to the means of representation – it is on the side of what is representing, not on the side of what is represented. That sample is used both to explain what the word in question means and to provide a rule for its use. The sample is in effect an object for comparison by reference to which the application of the defined term can be judged to be correct or incorrect. This is all ground that we have covered. I now want to draw your attention to a further point on which Wittgenstein dwells.

Ostensive definitions *can be misunderstood*, for when one defines the word 'table' or 'octagonal' or 'brown' or 'mahogany' by means of an ostensive definition, one may point perfectly correctly at one and the same octagonal, brown, mahogany table. Of course, one can readily disambiguate one's utterance by saying 'This shape is octagonal', 'This colour is brown', and 'This wood is called "mahogany"', and 'This piece of furniture is called a "table"'. But that, of course, presupposes that one's addressee knows what a shape, a colour, a kind of wood and a kind of piece of furniture are. Hence Wittgenstein remarks:

> So, one could say: an ostensive definition explains the use – the meaning – of a word if the role the word is supposed to play in the language is already clear. So if I know that someone means to explain a colour-word to me, the ostensive explanation 'That is called "sepia"' will enable me to understand the word. – And one can say this, as long as one does not forget that now all sorts of questions are tied up with the words 'to know' or 'to be clear'.
>
> One has already to know (or be able to do) something before one can ask what something is called. But what does one have to know? (PI §30)

Well, one must know, broadly speaking, how words of this general kind are used – that one is a shape word, the other a colour word and the third the name of a kind of material. In short, one has to know the grammatical post at which the word being explained is stationed. This is why Wittgenstein remarks apropos Augustine's picture of language:

> Someone coming into a foreign country will sometimes learn the language of the inhabitants from ostensive explanations that they give him; and he will often have to *guess* how to interpret these explanations; and sometimes he will guess right, sometimes wrong.
>
> And now, I think, we can say: Augustine describes the learning of human language as if the child came into a foreign country and did not understand the language of the country; that is, as if he already had a language, only not this one. Or again, as if the child could already *think*, only not yet speak. And 'think' would here mean something like 'talk to himself'. (PI §32)

The idea that learning a language presupposes an antecedent capacity for thinking – or for talking to oneself in the language of thought, as it were – indeed, the more general idea that language as such presupposes thought, is a venerable one. Hobbes, for example, wrote:

> The general use of speech, is to transfer our mental discourse, into verbal; or the train of our thoughts, into a train of words. (*Leviathan* I–4)

And Locke shared the same conception:

> The Comfort and Advantage of Society, not being to be had without Communication of Thoughts, it was necessary, that Man should find out some external sensible Signs, whereby those invisible *Ideas*, which his Thoughts are made up of, might be made known to others [...] Thus we may conceive how *Words*, which were by Nature so well adapted to that purpose, come to be made out by Men, as *the Signs of* their *Ideas*. (*Essay*, II – ii - 1)

The Hobbesian and Lockean idea that we need a language not in order to think but primarily in order to translate our thoughts and ideas into a public medium of communication is popular to this day – especially among neuroscientists. So, Antonio Damasio, an eminent neuroscientist, writes:

> Language, that is, words and sentences – is a translation of something else, a conversion from non-linguistic images which stand for entities, events, relationships and inferences. Language [...] operates [...] by symbolizing in words and sentences what exists first in non-verbal form [...]. (*Feeling of What Happens*, p. 108)

And the Nobel laureate Gerald Edelman and his colleague Giulio Tononi assert that

> Concepts, in our view, precede language, which develops by epigenetic means to further enhance our conceptual [...] exchanges. (*Consciousness: How Matter Becomes Imagination*, pp. 215f)[1]

The fundamental idea is that we can think *without words* and that we need language only for communication. So thought antecedes language. This claim demands scrutiny. Can one think without having mastered a language? Do animals, who have no language, think? Do they have non-linguistic concepts?

---

[1] G.M. Edelman and G. Tononi, *Consciousness: How Matter Becomes Imagination* (Allen Lane, The Penguin Press, London 2000), pp. 215f.

Concepts and the Limits of Thought

To resolve these questions, we must travel far and wide in the grammatical landscape. Let's start with the notion of a concept. The question 'What is a concept?' is not a good one. It invites an answer of the general form 'It's a so-and-so'. That is, the question demands an answer in the form of a nominal clause. One *can* answer it by saying 'A concept is an abstraction from the use of a word or phrase' – but no one is much the wiser for that. We need to bypass the question and focus on two different but related ones instead. First, 'What is it *to possess* a concept?' Second, 'How do we *use the word* "concept"?'. The answers to these questions will resolve the puzzlement that was expressed by the unhelpful question 'What is a concept?'

When do we say of a creature that it *possesses* a given concept? Surely, only when the creature has mastered the use of a word or phrase that can be said to express the relevant concept. It is not enough for possession of a concept to have a mere recognitional ability. Birds and bees can recognize blue things; they can discriminate between things that are blue and things that are not. But that does not suffice for ascribing to them mastery of the concept of blue. To have mastered the concept of blue one must know, for example,

- that blue is a colour
- that this ☞ colour [pointing at a sample of blue] is blue
- that it is darker than white
- that if something is blue all over, then it cannot also be red (or indeed any other colour) all over
- that if any thing (as opposed to a flash of light) is blue then it is spatially extended
- that sounds, tastes, and smells cannot intelligibly be said to be blue

and so on and so forth. To the extent that these connections are not grasped, to that extent the concept of blue is not grasped either. But to grasp these logico-grammatical connections is to have grasped a set of rules – the meaning-determining rules for the use of any word equivalent to 'blue'. In other words, to have grasped the logico-grammatical connections constitutive of the concept of blue is to have grasped the use of a word, in one language or another, that means blue.

The notion of *a concept* is bound up with the ideas of application and misapplication of concepts, with the inter-substitutability of one concept for another, with the ideas of defining concepts and with inter-definability of concepts, with extending, modifying and stretching concepts. All these linked ideas are, of course, language-parasitic notions. To possess a concept is to be able to use a word or phrase that expresses the concept; it is to be able to apply the word (and to be liable to misapply it), to be able to explain it or to recognize a correct explanation of it. Someone who has mastered the use of a word that expresses a given concept is also able to extend the use of the word, for example in metaphor or metonymy, and so on. So to possess a concept is obviously not the same as to possess a recognitional ability, to apply a concept is not the same as recognizing something, and to misapply a concept is not the same as misrecognizing something. A dog can recognize a lamp post – and it responds to one appropriately in its doggy manner. It may fail to recognize a lamp post. But it does not have the concept of a lamp post and it cannot misapply a concept (remember that misapplying a concept is not thinking or saying something false, but saying something that makes no sense). Conversely, you and I have the concept of a thousand-sided polygon – a chiliagon, but we would never be able to recognize one. We have the concept of being old, but it does not mean that we can recognize old rocks of the pre-Cambrian age or Old Masters of the seventeenth century, just as we may have the concept of a fake, but that does not mean that we recognize fake Old Masters.

Words and phrases *express*, but do not *name* or *stand for*, concepts. It is important to note that to have mastered, and hence to possess, a concept is neither to have nor to have a disposition to have, a mental image before the mind. We do not determine whether someone has the concept of ultramarine, of a triangle, or of a chiliagon by finding out what images come before his mind on hearing these words, but by observing whether he uses the words correctly and responds appropriately to their use by others. If the mental image of a pram always springs to someone's mind whenever he hears the word 'perambulate', but he nevertheless uses the word correctly, and explains that it means the same as 'to walk or stroll', then he knows what it means, despite the associated mental imagery. Mental imagery is neither necessary nor sufficient for mastery of the use of a word. Consequently, it is also irrelevant to the mastery and possession of concepts.

A consequence of this, of course, is that it makes no sense to ascribe to non-language using animals possession of concepts. That is a controversial claim. So it is time to call our interlocutor to join us.

> **Int.** Thank you. You are quite right. I have the gravest qualms about what you have said. If we deny concept possession and concept mastery to non-language using animals, then does that not mean that we are committing ourselves to the view that animals *cannot think*? Surely, thinking is *operating with concepts*. Thoughts, it is often said, *consist* of or are *constituted* of concepts. So if animals do not possess concepts, then they do not think. But does that not fly in the face of the facts? Surely, when I rattle my dog's leash, and he jumps excitedly to his feet, wagging his

tail, and rushes to the door, he thinks that I am going to take him for a walk. And when my cat discovers a mouse hole in the garden and waits motionlessly for a mouse to poke its nose out of the hole, the cat thinks that there is a mouse in the hole. So surely it must possess concepts!

PMSH. No! That is much too fast. First of all, it is a confusion to suppose that thoughts – that is, *what one thinks* when one thinks something to be thus-and-so – consist of *anything*. If one says something thoughtfully aloud, one's utterance consists of words. If one talks thoughtfully to oneself in one's imagination, then one utters words in one's imagination. But *what one thinks* does not consist of words. Otherwise, John, Hans and Jean could never think the same thing – for what John thinks would consist of English words, what Hans thinks would consist of German words and what Jean thinks would consist of French words. So, they could no more think the same thought than their English, German and French utterances could be utterances of the same sentence. But that is plainly silly.

Int. But aren't *you* now going much too fast? Why should what one thinks not consist of something else – such as concepts? Don't we think with concepts?

PMSH. Well, Yes and No! One may well say that we think with concepts. Or perhaps better: that to think is to use concepts. It is obviously true that we couldn't think the kinds of thoughts we think without having mastered a rich array of concepts. But it would be at the very least mistaken and at the worst just wrong to suppose that what we think *consists* of concepts. The *verbal expression* of what one thinks consists of words, some of which – the concept words – express concepts. But *what one was thinking* is not *made of anything* and does not *consist of anything*, any more than one's beliefs, expectations and fears, when one believes, expects or fears that things are thus-and-so, consist of anything. It would be sheer nonsense to say that my expectation that you will attend the committee meeting at 7.00 o'clock *consists* of the concept of attending, of the concept of a committee meeting and of the concept of 7.00 o'clock. It is equally absurd to conceive of my thought that you will attend the meeting as consisting of these concepts.

Int. But does not denying that animals do possess concepts amount to denying that animals can think? I am very reluctant to concede that to you. It seems to me that there are endless examples of intelligent animal behaviour and intelligent animal problem-solving.

PMSH. Well, I agree with you there. But to deny that animals possess concepts does *not* commit one to the idea that animals cannot think – that it makes no sense to attribute thinking to non-language using animals.

A creature can think whatever it *can express* in its behaviour – no matter whether the behaviour is linguistic or non-linguistic.

To put the same point differently: it makes sense to say of a creature that it thinks that things are thus-and-so only in so far as there is a form of behaviour within the creature's behavioural repertoire that is a criterion for its thinking things to be thus-and-so. In the case of non-language using animals, it makes sense to say of them that they think something or other only to the extent that what they are said to think is *expressible* in their non-linguistic behavioural repertoire. So, it makes sense to say that the dog thinks it is going to be taken for a walk precisely because its behaviour – prancing around and wagging its tail upon hearing its leash being taken down – counts as a criterion for its thought process. It makes sense to say that a dog expects its master to come in at any moment, because its excited barking on hearing its master's footsteps on the path is a criterion for its expecting this. But it makes no sense to say that the dog *now* thinks that it is going to be taken for a walk *tomorrow*, or that the dog *now* expects its master to return *next Monday* – for nothing in the dog's behavioural repertoire could possibly express its thinking or expecting that. *The limits of thought are the limits of the expression of thought.* This is the crucial point. It *makes sense* to say of non-language using animals that they think this or that, *as long as their so thinking is expressible in their behaviour.* For such rudimentary thinking no mastery of concepts is necessary – but only behavioural dispositions, recognitional capacities and their exercise.

By the same token, the limits of thought of language-using creatures such as ourselves far outstrip the limits of thought of non-human animals. For the horizon of human thought is determined by the limits of human language. We can think of what will happen tomorrow or next Monday precisely because we have a language with time-indicative devices that enable us to express such thoughts and also enable us to think such thoughts without expressing them. We need not say what we think. But to think what we think, we must *be able* to say it.

Thought and Speech

So, rudimentary thinking is possible without mastery of a language. The human child prior to learning to speak can think no farther than other non-language using animals – what he can intelligibly be said to think is limited by what he can express in his non-linguistic behavioural repertoire. That is why it makes no sense to suppose, as Augustine did, that the child, prior to his mastery of a language, could grasp whether a word used by adults signified a piece of furniture, a type of wood, a colour or a shape. No, *first comes training*

– for there is no access to a first language by means of language and explanations of the meanings of words.

Now let us turn to a further item in this cluster of problems: *Is speech essentially a translation of thoughts into language for the benefit of others?*

One is surely inclined to say that it is. Certainly, many great scientists have supposed that thinking is a non-linguistic process, which is subsequently translated into words. Einstein remarked that

> The words or the language, as they are written or spoken, do not seem to play any role in my mechanism of thought. The psychical entities which seem to serve as elements of thought are certain signs and more or less clear images which can be voluntarily reproduced and combined.

And the great nineteenth-century scientist Francis Galton wrote:

> It is a serious drawback to me in writing and still more in explaining myself, that I do not think as easily in words as otherwise. It often happens that after being hard at work and having arrived at results that are perfectly clear and satisfactory to myself, when I try to express them in language, I feel I must begin by putting myself on quite another intellectual plane. I have to translate my thoughts into a language that does not run very evenly with them. I therefore have to waste a vast deal of time in seeking appropriate words and phrases.

And in our own times, Roger Penrose – an eminent mathematician and physicist – wrote:

> Almost all my mathematical thinking is done visually and in terms of non-verbal concepts, although the thoughts are quite often accompanied by inane and almost useless verbal commentary. [...] the difficulty that [...] thinkers have had with translating their thoughts into words is something I frequently experience myself.

But despite the fact that such eminent thinkers line up in this manner, the ideas that inform their remarks are altogether confused. In what might have been a reply to these confused ruminations, Wittgenstein wrote:

> In order to get clear about the meaning of the word 'think', we must watch ourselves thinking; what we observe will be what the word means! – But that's just *not* how this concept is used. (It would be as if without knowing how to play chess, I were to try to make out what the word 'checkmate' meant by close observation of the last move in a game of chess.) (PI §316)

What is he driving at?

One can observe oneself when one is in pain – that is, attend to one's pain – and report what one notes to the doctor. The description of the waxing and waning of the pain, of its phenomenal qualities and location, may help him to make a diagnosis. But the concept of thinking is not like that. To observe what goes on in one's mind while one is thinking, pondering or reflecting *is not to observe the course of one's thoughts*. To report what one observes thus is not to describe one's thinking at all – it is merely to describe what crossed one's mind *while* one was thinking. Moreover, as Wittgenstein remarked, 'it is very noteworthy that *what goes on* in thinking practically never interests us' – for these inner goings-on are not my thoughts, and only rarely would one be able to derive what I was thinking from my reports about what went on in my mind *as* I was thinking. Telling someone what I was thinking is not giving them a report on inner goings-on. *Thinking is not an experience*, and to tell another what I think is not to report the character of an experience. It may be to tell another *what conclusion* I have come to on the basis of the premises at hand, or to tell another *what chain of inferences* leads to that conclusion or it may just be to tell another *what I was ruminating on* – as when one answers another person's request: 'A penny for your thoughts'. But a conclusion arrived at, a chain of inference and a subject of reflection are not inner goings-on. *What I think* is not a mental event.

> **Int.** Why then are such great scientists inclined to insist that they don't think in words and sentences, but *in* something else, far more mysterious and nebulous – non-verbal concepts (as Penrose suggested) or psychic entities (as Einstein suggested)?
>
> **PMSH.** It is very unclear what they thought these things were – but it seems that they thought of them as being *mental images*, including images of symbols. The supposition is that thought requires a vehicle or medium – that one must think *in* something, if not in words, then in images or ideas, if not in images or ideas, then in something else, even less tangible and more mysterious.
>
> **Int.** But that seems dead right.
>
> **PMSH.** Well, it may *seem* dead right, but it doesn't follow that it *is* dead right. Why does it seem dead right?
>
> **Int.** You know, I'm not sure. It just does. I mean ... how could one think without thinking *in something*?
>
> **PMSH.** No, that is not the question to ask. What you need to ask is why is this supposition so tempting? We are tempted by this idea because we draw a false analogy between thinking and speaking – the one being a private process in the mind, the other a public process in the extra-mental world. For we note that if one speaks, one must speak in one language or another – if not in English then in German, if not in German then in French. Since we are prone to suppose, as Plato did, that thinking is the dialogue of the soul with itself, we suppose that thinking is just like speaking only private – hidden, as it were, within the mind. So it seems that just as when we speak, we must speak *in* something, so too, when we think, we must think *in* something. And if we don't think *in a*

language then we must think in something else – *in images or ideas* or something even more arcane – a special 'language of thought' as Ockham supposed in the fourteenth century and Jerry Fodor in the late twentieth century.

Int. Yes. That's exactly right.

PMSH. No, it is exactly wrong. It is a ramifying array of confusions. Let me explain.

First, note that to talk to oneself in the imagination is not in general the same as to think. It is not necessary for thinking, since one may think something to be so and conclude that something is so, without talking to oneself in one's imagination. One might simply say so to another, without first saying anything to oneself. Indeed, one might think thus without saying anything to anyone – as long as, *if one had been asked,* one *would,* other things being equal, have said it. Nor is talking to oneself in the imagination sufficient for thinking. For one may talk to oneself in the imagination precisely to *prevent* oneself from thinking – as when one mechanically recites the multiplication tables or the ABC to oneself in order to fall asleep. We may grant that when one talks to oneself in the imagination one talks in some language or other, and one may do so thoughtfully or without thinking.

Int. But surely when one thinks something one must think what one thinks in some language or other or say something to oneself in one's imagination.

PMSH. No, not at all.

Int. I really don't see this.

PMSH. It is a difficult point. So let us go at it indirectly. First, let's put pressure on the very idea of *thinking in a language*. Let's reflect on what speaking *without thought* is. One can speak mechanically, unthinkingly, thoughtlessly, without understanding. Each of these differs from the others. But in none of these cases does the absence of thought consist in one's speech lacking a covert accompaniment in one's mind. Lack of thought in speech may be manifest in the mechanical, monotonic manner in which one speaks; or in the lack of expression in one's face; or in the routine, unimaginative justification one has for what one thinks. Quite differently, lack of thought may be exhibited by one's failure to take into account the relevant factors pertinent to one's reasoning. *But that is not a matter of the absence of a mental process.* So too, thoughtlessness may be a matter of lack of tact and sensitivity – but neither tactlessness nor insensitivity are processes that might accompany speaking. So, *to speak without thought* is not to speak without a concurrent mental process of thinking. Rather, as Wittgenstein wrote: 'Speech with and without thought is to be compared to playing a piece of music with and without thought' (PI §341).

Int. All right. I can vaguely see that. But what about speaking *with* thought? If speaking *with thought* is *not* to accompany one's speech with a simultaneous covert activity of thinking, then what is the difference between speaking with thought and speaking without thinking? Isn't *speech with thought* simply speaking together with simultaneous thinking?

PMSH. No! try speaking something with thought. And now just *do what you did when you spoke with thought only without speaking* (PI §332)! – One would not know *what* to do. It would be like reading something with understanding, and then being asked to do what one did when one read the passage with understanding, only now without reading anything. To speak with thought is to speak *having taken all the relevant factors into account.* It is to have good reasons for what one says. And it is to be able to offer a justification for what one says by reference to one's reasons. It is not to speak *and to do something else at the same time.*

Int. But don't we say such things as 'I can speak in German, but I still don't think in German'? This surely makes sense, and if it makes sense, then when I speak in my native language – in English – I surely also think in it. So I *do* think in something. So thought *does* require a medium after all!

PMSH. No! You are rushing things. Take it slowly! The sentence 'I can speak German, but I can't think in German' is deceptive. It seems like 'I can speak German, but I can't write in German', but it is not. 'I can speak German, but I can't think in German' signifies that the English speaker has learnt enough German to speak the language, but that before he says anything he has first to decide what he wants to say (which to be sure he *can* say in English) and then struggle to find the right German words. It does not follow that when he speaks in English, he *also* thinks in English – for when he speaks in English, he does not struggle to find the right English words, and he does not translate anything. Of course, he may speak to himself in his imagination in English; but to speak to oneself in the imagination, as we have seen, is not necessarily to think at all.

Int. But we often say such things as 'My German is getting much better – I am even thinking in German' – and does that not show that thought needs a medium in which to think? – that we think *in* a language?

PMSH. No, it doesn't! What it shows is that as one's German gets better, one no longer needs to think what one wants to say and *then* pause to think of the right German words. Alternatively, it may just mean that he has now reached the stage at which he even speaks to himself in the imagination in German. Either way, it does not support the idea that thought without speech stands in need of a medium.

Int. Well, I see what you mean. But what about the phenomenon of hunting for the right word. That is surely common; and doesn't it show that one thinks *in* something?

PMSH. We must distinguish two apparently similar, but actually quite different, phenomena. First, we often hunt for the right word in a foreign language with which to translate an English word. Here we are indeed translating our thought, expressed in English, into another language. Second, we often look for the right word in English.

Int. Yes. Exactly. Doesn't this show that we think in something?

PMSH. No! When I want to tell my monolingual German friend that it is time to go to dinner, I may hunt around for the German word for dinner. But, of course, I can say – in English – exactly what I want to say. But when I hunt around for the right *English* word, I *cannot* say what I want to say – until I have found it. This is not because I have thought in images and have not found their correct translation. It is not as if I know exactly what I think and am hunting to find the precise words to express my subjectively perspicuous thought. Reflect on the use of the common phrase 'The word is on the tip of my tongue'. It means much the same as 'The right word escapes me, but it will occur to me in a moment'. In a similar manner, to say 'I know what I want to say, but I can't think of the words' is either nonsense or else it means no more than 'Give me another moment or two for the thought to crystallize and then I'll tell you what I think'. So too, when *someone else* finds the right words – the words that *I* was looking for to express what I think – the rightness of the words does not consist of their being a correct *translation* of my thought or of their *matching* the wordless thought I have. Rather, it consists in the words matching *the phenomenon which I was thinking about* in a way that strikes me as appropriate, and which I was trying unsuccessfully to capture myself. – 'That's exactly what I wanted to say', one may then exclaim. But that does not mean that one said it to oneself in thought, or that one thought it in some other medium and couldn't think of the right translation into words.

So, thinking is not the same as talking to oneself in the imagination. Speaking with thought is not *translating* what one thinks into words. Thinking does not *have* to be *in* anything. What *can be thought* by a creature is circumscribed by what the creature *can express* in its verbal and symbolic behaviour or *can manifest* in its non-symbolic expressive behaviour. The very question 'What do you think in?' leads us up the garden path before we have even begun. And that is altogether characteristic of trying to grapple with conceptual and philosophical problems. The mistakes occur before one has started.

Thought: Organ and Location

The concept of thinking is a constant source of intellectual confusion. We are constitutionally inclined to misconceive thought and thinking. We are impressed by the sentence 'Use your brains!' and take it for granted that we think *with* our brains – that the brain is the organ of thought. We interpret the utterance 'I wonder what is going on in his head' to mean that the locus of thinking is in the head. So we are inclined to take it for granted that not only do we think *with* the brain – as we walk with our legs – but we also think *in* the brain. But, of course, we are equally impressed by such idioms as 'A thought crossed my mind' and 'I have a thought in mind', and we are inclined to suppose that we think with and in our minds. And if that seems to clash with the idea that we think with our brains, that can easily be sorted out – for does it not patently point to the fact that the mind just is the brain?

In fact, such phrases, reinforced by popular science, lead us to have altogether the wrong picture of thinking. For the picture that informs our reflections is of an inner activity of the mind or of the brain or of what sometimes goes by the name of *the mind/brain* – an inner activity which accompanies outer activities, including speech, and that picture is confused.

First, it is confusing to suppose that the phrase 'Use your brains!' is indicative of the fact that we think *with* our brain, that the brain is *an organ of thought* just as the eyes are organs of sight. For something is an organ for engaging in a given voluntary activity if one *uses* it when one voluntarily engages in the activity. The eyes are the organ for sight in as much as we look in the direction of what we wish to see, we bring our eyes closer to see better, and shade our eyes to see more clearly in the sunshine, and so on. The legs are the organ of locomotion, precisely because it is our legs that we move when we want to walk or run. *In this sense*, the brain is not an organ of thought, although thinking is often engaged in voluntarily. We cannot move the brain, position it, direct it or use it in the same sense in which we can use our eyes and our legs. 'Use your brains!' is not like 'Use your eyes!'

> **Int.** But surely, we can't think without a brain! So the brain *is* the organ of thought after all!
>
> **PMSH.** No, for we cannot walk without the normal functioning of the brain either. But that does not mean that the brain is the organ of locomotion – that we walk with our brain. 'Use your brains!' simply *means* 'Think!'. It is mistaken to suppose that the brain is the organ of thought.

Thought has no organ in the sense in which sight and hearing, walking and talking have organs.

Int. Still, even if the brain cannot be said to be the *organ* for thinking in the sense in which the sense organs are the organs for perceiving, is it not the brain that thinks? Is the brain not the *agent* of thinking? Is that not what cognitive neuroscientists have discovered?

PMSH. No! It may be what many of them *say*, but it is not what they have *discovered*. It is not the brain that concentrates on the examination essay – but the student. It is not the brain that plays a cunning game of tennis or gives a brilliant concert performance – but the tennis player or pianist. It is the skilled debater, not his or her brain, who argues intelligently. Brains, unlike human beings, cannot be bigoted or prejudiced, but they cannot be open-minded either. It is not the brain that is the subject of thinking, but the human being whose brain it is. I shall say more on this vexatious subject in a later lecture.

Int. But don't we think *in* our brain or *in* our mind? The distinguished neuroscientists Edelman and Tononi write of 'the human head within which we have no doubt that thoughts occur'.

PMSH. That is just confusing. Neuroscientists are poor guides to conceptual structures. The answer to the question 'Where did you think of that?' is not 'In the prefrontal cortices, of course'. It is rather 'In the British Library, when I was working there last week' or 'In bed, when I was lying awake in the middle of the night'. The location of thinking is wherever one was when one thought whatever one thought.

Int. But doesn't one have thoughts in one's mind – sometimes before the mind, sometimes lurking just out of reach at the back of one's mind? – Is that not the correct location of thought? Indeed, does one not think *with* one's mind? After all, it isn't one's body that thinks – so surely it has to be one's mind!

PMSH. No, that is quite wrong. The mind is not an ethereal organ of thinking. 'Use your mind!', like 'Use your brain!' just means 'Think!' – it is not an instruction to use an immaterial organ of thinking. So too, although we use spatial metaphors when we speak of thoughts and ideas being before one's mind, at the back of one's mind or flashing across one's mind – they are just that: namely *figures of speech*. For the mind is not a space and a thought is not an occupant of space, despite the fact that it may be lurking at the back of one's mind.

Int. Surely what I think and the thoughts I have are in the mind or brain and are stored in the head. For do we not, by and large, remember what we thought? And how could we remember our thoughts unless we retained them? Memory, Locke said, is the storehouse of ideas; and the brain, the neuroscientists assure us, is the storage depot.

PMSH. That is a muddle. One may grant that if a variety of cerebral phenomena were not occurring and if a variety of cerebral structures did not obtain, then we would not be able to remember what we can remember. But neither what we think nor what we remember having thought can intelligibly be said to be in the brain. What one thinks, namely *that things are thus-and-so*, is not an object that one might store in a place. It no more has a location than *the fact that things are thus-and-so* that makes the thought true. What I think is not in my head, and it is not anywhere else either. The sentence 'Where is the thought that it rained yesterday?' is like the sentence 'Where is your visual field?' – it is quite senseless.

Of course, we may grant that the head is *conceptually* more closely connected with thinking than it is with digesting or walking. But that is not because one thinks with one's head. It is rather because one clutches one's head or beats one's head with one's fist when one racks one's brain – that is to say, when one is thinking hard, one closes one's eyes to think better. It is also important that one reads a person's thoughts *on his face* and not on his feet. It is his eyes that twinkle when he is pulling one's leg, and it is his face that lights up when he 'cottons on'. All this renders it intelligible that we should favour the *picture* of thinking as an activity or process in the head. Let me end with a marvellous remark of Wittgenstein:

> Is it not important that for me hope lives in the *breast*? Isn't this a picture of one or another important bit of human behaviour? Why does a human being believe a thought comes into his head? Or, more correctly, he does not *believe* it; he lives it. For he clutches his head; he shuts his eyes in order to be alone with himself in his head. He tilts his head back and makes a movement as a sign that nothing should disturb the process in his head. – Now, are these not important kinds of behaviour? (RPP I, §278)

But this is not a theory of any kind – and above all, it is not a theory that is now being confirmed by neuroscience. It is a picture – like the picture of love being in the heart, of loving someone with all one's heart, and of being heartbroken by the loss of someone loved. There is nothing wrong with the picture – only with misusing it ... which is what we do when we forget that it is just a picture and take it to be a theory or a hypothesis.

Chapter 8

THE PRIVATE LANGUAGE ARGUMENTS

We have surveyed Wittgenstein's reflections on the nature of language and linguistic representation, and we have looked at the destructive consequences of his conception for metaphysics. Now it is time to move on to what has rightly been said to be the most important philosophical argument of the twentieth century. It is known as 'the private language argument', and it occurs in *Investigations* §§243–315. It might better have been dubbed 'the private language *arguments*' – in the plural – since there is not one argument but a whole battery of bewilderingly interwoven ones. It links Wittgenstein's philosophy of language with his philosophy of psychology.

Wittgenstein had an uncanny ability to dig down deeper into the presuppositions of our thought than any other philosopher. It is a common philosophical failing, he said, not to put the question marks deep enough down. In the case of the *Private Language Arguments*, Wittgenstein himself put the question mark so deep down that at first glance it is exceedingly difficult to see why the question he raises matters in the slightest. Here is how he begins:

> A human being can encourage himself, give himself orders, obey, blame and punish himself; he can ask himself a question and answer it. So one could imagine human beings who spoke only in monologue; who accompanied their activities by talking to themselves. – An explorer who watched them and listened to their talk might succeed in translating their language into ours. (This would enable him to predict these people's actions correctly, for he also hears them making resolutions and decisions.)
>
> But is it also conceivable that there be a language in which a person could write down or give voice to his inner experiences – his feelings, moods, and so on – for his own use? — Well, can't we do so in our ordinary language? – But that is not what I mean. The words of this language are to refer to what only the speaker can know – to his immediate private sensations. So another person cannot understand the language. (PI §243)

So, the question Wittgenstein addresses is whether there could be a *radically* private language. A private language, as he uses the phrase, is not a language which, *as it happens*, others cannot understand (such as Esperanto, before its inventor Zamenhof, went public). It is rather a language which only its speaker can *in principle* understand.

Why on earth should anyone be interested in that question? The languages we all speak are public languages, means of interpersonal communication. Even if we are the last speakers of a language, like Chingachgook after the death of Uncas in *The Last Mohican*, or the devisers of a private language that we keep to ourselves, these are languages which could in principle be taught to, and understood by, others. So why is it worth discussing the *logical* possibility of a language that *only* its speaker could, in principle, understand? Why would anyone want such a bizarre language? *And anyway, who cares*?

This lecture will clarify why this question is not trivial but deep. If you are interested in the nature of language, if you are interested in what constitutes self-awareness and self-consciousness and if you are interested in how it is possible to know anything about other people's experiences, then you *ought* to care very much about the possibility of a logically private language.

I shall show how the tacit assumption of such a language lies inadvertently at the root of much of philosophy since Descartes and the British empiricists in the seventeenth century. It also informs a great deal of current empirical theories of language and language acquisition in linguistics, psycho-linguistics and neurolinguistics.

I shall go on to show you that if, as Wittgenstein argued, there can be no such thing as a logically private language, then the overwhelmingly dominant conception of our knowledge of our own mental states is wholly misconceived. Furthermore, the received conception of our knowledge of the mental states of others, both in philosophy of mind and in current experimental psychology, is fundamentally confused.

So, to show the assumption of the possibility of a private language to be untenable is to undermine the mainstream tradition in philosophy of language and in philosophy of psychology. It is, as we shall see in later lectures, to transform the conception of the mind, and the conception of the relation of the mind to the body and to behaviour that has dominated philosophy and science for the last four centuries. It also casts doubt on the intelligibility of much contemporary psychology, general linguistics and cognitive neuroscientific theorizing. If Wittgenstein is right, then much of contemporary philosophy and contemporary sciences of the mind is built, as it were, on a geological fault line. My purpose is to show you that he is right.

Let's start with Wittgenstein's question: Can there be a language the words of which refer to, are names of, immediate private sensations? Now, although in the immediate sequel, Wittgenstein concentrates on the example of the sensation of pain, it is evident that his concern is with subjective experience in general. He is concerned not just with the experience of pain, but also with the experiences of seeing something red, feeling something hot or hearing a sound, and so too with feeling angry or frightened, joyful or sad. So, the putative private language is a language the individual words of which refer to our own subjective experiences.

Int. But surely our *ordinary language* contains innumerable words that either *refer to* or are the *names of* our subjective experiences. After all, I often speak of *my headache* or *toothache*, of *my seeing* or *hearing* this or that, of *my feeling joyful* or *angry*, so what is problematic here?

PMSH. Take it slowly. Wittgenstein said that the words of this putatively private language are to refer to the speaker's *immediate private sensations* – that is, to something that *only he can know*. Now why might one think that only *I* can know about my pain, my visual, auditory or gustatory experiences, or my feelings?

Int. Well, because you can't have my pain. You cannot *see* how things look to me, how *I* experience red or green things, how sweet things taste *to me* and what sounds sound like to *me*? You can't have my fear or hope, my joys or sorrows. And that's why you can't really know what my pains are like. Only I can. And you can't really know what red things look like to me or how sweet things taste to me.

PMSH. Slow down. Why exactly can't I know what your pain is like?

Int. *Because you can't have my experience*! To know what my pain is like you'd have to have it, but you can't have my pain. To know what red things look like to me, you would have to have my visual experience, but you can't, as it were, 'see *my* seeing' or 'do my seeing'!

Not only can't you *have* my experience, you are not *acquainted* with it. My experience is 'immediate', but you can know of it or about it only *mediately*, by observation of my behaviour – of what I do or say. Since my experience is immediate, *I* have immediate *access* to it – and no one else does.

PMSH. This is all very interesting. I don't yet understand what you mean here by 'access'. After all, no one talks about 'access' to one's experience. How, according to your account, do I have *access* to my own experiences?

Int. Well, by *introspection*, of course. I can *peer into* my own mind and see there the experiences I am having. Only *I* can introspect my mind, no one else can have this *privileged access* to *my* mind, but only to their own. Only *I* can know what is in my mind; others can only surmise it on the basis of my behaviour. So, *only* I can have my experiences. And that's why *only* I can *really know* what it is like to have the experiences I have or what the experiences I have are really like.

PMSH. Good. That's very well put.

Few can deny that this chain of reasoning is mesmerizing. It seems overwhelmingly persuasive. Before going further, let's distinguish clearly between two senses of the phrase 'private experience' that have already been brought into play:

(A) The first signifies what we might call 'privacy of ownership'. For on the view we are going to investigate, experiences are privately and inalienably *owned* by their subject. As the great logician Frege put it wittily (but seriously): 'You can't have my pain, and I can't have your sympathy.' Experiences are *logically* private property; one cannot share them with others or give them away.

(B) The second sense of the phrase 'private experience' concerns what we might call 'privacy of knowledge' or 'epistemic privacy'. According to the conception we are going to examine, only the subject of experience can know, or *really* know, the nature of the experience he is enjoying or undergoing; others can only *surmise* what it is. For the subject of experience has privileged access to his own experience by means of introspection; others have to rely on what the subject of experience says and does. He has immediate knowledge of how things are with him; others' knowledge is indirect, mediated by their observational knowledge of the behaviour which his experience causes.

It is important to note that although many writers have embraced the idea of epistemic privacy independently of privacy of ownership, nevertheless, if one is inclined to think of experience as privately owned, it is natural to think that it is *therefore* also epistemically private – that only *I* really know how things are with me. Others have to guess or surmise it on the basis of my behaviour.

> **Int.** All right. So far, so clear. I can see why one might think that *all* names of experiences refer to items with which only the speaker is acquainted. But why should anyone think that *all* the words in a language are *names of experiences* – after all, we have a rich vocabulary with which to speak of objects, their properties and relations?
>
> **PMSH.** There is *more than one route* to the idea of *a* language – indeed of *our* language – as consisting of names of experiences and of the contents of experiences.

The first route goes via reflection on the objective nature of the world around us. Recollect a point we have already encountered: since Galileo, Descartes, Gassendi, Boyle and Locke in the seventeenth century, it has been scientific commonplace and philosophically received wisdom that perceptual qualities such as colour, sound, smell, taste, thermal and tactile qualities are essentially subjective or mental. Things around us, it is said, are not really red or green; they merely reflect light waves of certain wavelengths, which, impinging upon our retinas, cause us to have the experience of seeing colour. So too, objects do not really make sounds and noises; they merely generate sound waves, which, impacting on our eardrums, cause us to have the experience of hearing sounds. As an eminent American psychologist Irving Rock wrote not long ago:

> The perceptual world we create differs qualitatively from the physicists' descriptions because our experience is mediated by our senses and constructed internally as a representation of the world. Thus we perceive colours, tones, tastes and smells – perceptions that either have no meaning in the world of physical reality or have a different meaning. What we perceive as hues of red, blue or green, the physicist refers to as surfaces reflecting electromagnetic waves of certain frequencies. What we experience as tastes and smells, the physicist refers to as chemical compounds [...] Colours, tones, tastes, and smells are mental constructions, created out of sensory stimulations. As such they do not exist outside of living minds.[1]

The picture is by now so familiar that we are no longer astonished by it – and yet it is truly *amazing*. For if all this is true, then the world as we experience it is a *fantasy world*, far removed from the world as it really is in itself. Wittgenstein characterized it thus:

> The evolution of the higher animals and of man, and the awakening of consciousness at a particular stage. The picture is something like this: Though the ether is filled with vibrations, the world is dark. But one day, man opens his seeing eye, and there is light. (PPF §55)

Let's bypass the question of whether this received picture is correct and just examine its ramifying consequences. If the world, as it is in itself, is altogether lacking in colour, sound, smell, taste, warmth, cold and so on, then a gulf opens between experience and reality. All the colourful objects we apprehend and all the noisy events we perceive are not as we take them to be. What we know of them we know in virtue of our experiences; we experience them as multicoloured, as emitting sounds, as being hot or cold, wet or dry, as having smells or tastes. But, if this scientific picture of the world is correct, then these experiences are purely subjective and, in an important sense, *illusory;* they are not direct or correct apprehensions of the attributes of the world around us. The names of the apparent qualities of what we experience are *actually* names of purely subjective, private, mental items. 'Red' is the name of an element of the content of the experience I have when, for example, I see a tomato, 'sweet' is the name of a sensation I have when I taste honey, 'acrid' is the name of a sensation I get when I smell burning and so on.

---

1 I. Rock, *Perception* (Scientific American Books, New York, 1984), p. 4.

If all this is so, then surely I *must* have a radically 'private language' – a language the names of which refer to my private sensations, which only I can have and only I can know! These names will not be only names of sensations (such as pain) and experiences (such as seeing), but names of all the things that I can experience – for what I know of things in the world around me I know in virtue of experiencing them; experiencing them as having perceptual qualities which are in fact no more than the effect on my mind of the agitation of my nerve endings by means of radiation and impact.

So, now the picture grows larger and bolder. Is it convincing? To be sure, it has the backing of the most up-to-date science. The Nobel laureate and discoverer of the structure of DNA, Francis Crick, remarked:

> In perception, what the brain learns is usually about the outside world or about parts of the body. That is why what we see appears to be located outside us, although the neurons that do the seeing are inside the head. To many people this is a strange idea. The 'world' is outside their body yet, in another sense (what they know of it), it is entirely within the head.[2]

Another Nobel laureate and distinguished neuroscientist Eric Kandel and his colleagues James Schwartz and Thomas Jessell observed:

> We *receive* electromagnetic waves of different frequencies but we *perceive* colours: red, green, orange, blue or yellow. We receive pressure waves but we hear words and music. We come into contact with a myriad of chemical compounds dissolved in air or water but we experience smells and tastes.
>
> Colours, sounds, smells and tastes are mental constructions created in the brain by sensory processing. They do not exist, as such, outside of the brain. Therefore we can ask the traditional question raised by philosophers: Does a falling tree in the forest make a sound if no one is near enough to hear it? We can say with certainty that while the fall creates pressure waves in the air, it does not create a sound. Sound occurs only when pressure waves from the falling tree reach and are perceived by a living being.[3]

So, dare you gainsay this?

> **Int.** Well, no! Surely the scientists know what they are talking about.
>
> **PMSH.** Don't be so sure. The history of science is no less littered with conceptual confusions than other branches of intellectual activity. After all, strictly speaking, this is not experimental science, but seventeenth-century metaphysics masquerading as science. For there is and can be no *experiment* that can prove that the world is not multicoloured and

---

2 F. Crick, *The Astonishing Hypothesis* (Touchstone, London, 1995), p. 104.
3 E. Kandel, J. Schwartz, and T. Jessell, *Essentials of Neural Science and Behaviour* (Appleton and Lange, Stamford, 1995), p. 370.

noisy. How would you test whether there are noises when no one hears, or colours when there is no one around to see?

Int. Yes, I see what you mean.

PMSH. All right, let's defer that issue for the moment. What I want you to note is that *if* the story *is* true, if perceptual qualities such as colour, sound, taste, smell, warmth and cold really are no more than the result of the impact of colourless, soundless, odourless, tasteless objects on our nerve endings, then not only can we *conceive* of a logically private language, but the very language each of us speaks *is* a logically private language – for the names in our language refer to private experiences and their contents, experiences which only the subject can have and with which only the subject is acquainted.

But now reflect: *How can anyone else understand what we say?* For if you cannot have the same experiences as I have, if you are not acquainted with my experiences and cannot in principle know what they are and if the words of my language signify the experiences I have, then surely *you can't understand what the words in my language mean and can't understand a word I say!*

Int. I can see that this follows. If what I call 'red' is the content of the experience I have when I look at a tomato, if what I call 'sweet' is the taste I experience when I eat a lump of sugar, if what I call 'pain' is the experience I have when I bump my head and if you can't have my experiences – which you surely can't – then you should not be able to know what I mean by my words. That's pretty dramatic! But surely *it can't be like this*, for after all you DO understand my words.

PMSH. Yes. Nevertheless, surely *it must be like this* – for it is IMPOSSIBLE that you should understand my words!

We are torn between the two alternatives and do not know how to move. It is interesting that Wittgenstein pointed out that the form of the predicament – it must be like this, and it can't be like this – is characteristic of philosophy. We are caught like a fly in a fly-bottle and can't find our way out.

I said that there was more than one route to the conclusion that the language each of us speaks must, *in some sense*, be private. The first route went via reflection on what is widely held to be the objective scientific nature of the world, on our experience of the world and on the immediate objects of our experiences. The second goes via reflection on language and communication, and on the differences between mere sounds and meaningful symbols.

As we have seen, it was a commonplace from the seventeenth to the nineteenth century that words stand immediately for ideas in the mind. Let me remind you of Locke's famous remark:

> Words, in their primary signification, stand for nothing but the ideas in the mind of him that uses them [...] Nor can anyone apply them as marks, immediately, to anything else but the ideas that he himself hath. (*Essay Concerning Human Understanding*, III – ii – 2)

Again, at first blush, this seems very odd. Surely, words, in their primary and immediate signification, stand for things in the world around us. What led so many generations of thinkers to suppose that words stand for ideas in the mind?

As we have already seen, at least two factors were prominent:

One was the thought that there is all the difference in the world between parroting words and using words meaningfully – with understanding. Surely what distinguishes the parrot's saying 'Time for a gin and tonic!' and my saying 'Time for a gin and tonic!' is that the parrot has no idea what these words mean. The parrot just squawks these words – but then they are empty sounds without meaning. But when I speak, I associate the words I utter with ideas in my mind. In my mouth, the words are not just dead signs; they are alive with meaning; they have life breathed into them by the ideas – of gin and tonic – with which I back them up.

The second factor making it seem obvious that words stand for ideas in the speaker's mind is that *experience consists in the reception of ideas*. To have experience of the world around us is to have one's sensory organs stimulated by radiation and impact. The consequent agitation of nerve endings transmits electrical current along nerve fibres to the brain, and the upshot of the consequent neural activity is that our mind receives sensory 'ideas' or 'sense impressions'. What is, so to say, *given* in experience are *ideas*, or *sense data*, or, as contemporary cognitive scientists put it, *mental representations*. Again, Locke is an appropriate speaker for a perennially seductive conception:

> *Our Senses*, conversant about particular sensible Objects, do *convey into the Mind*, several distinct *Perceptions* of things, according to those various ways, wherein those Objects do affect them: And thus we come by those *Ideas*, we have of *Yellow*, *White*, *Heat*, *Cold*, *Soft*, *Hard*, *Bitter*, *Sweet*, and all those which we call sensible qualities, which when I say the senses convey into the mind, I mean, they from external Objects convey into the mind what produces there those *Perceptions*. This great Source, of most of the *Ideas* we have, depending wholly upon our Senses, and derived by them to the Understanding, I call *SENSATION*.
>
> The other Fountain, from which experience furnisheth the Understanding with *Ideas*, is the *Perception of the Operations of our own Minds* within us, as it is employ'd about the *Ideas* it has got; which Operations, when the Soul comes to reflect on, and consider, do furnish the Understanding with another set of *Ideas*, which could not be had from things without: and such are, *Perception*, *Thinking*, *Doubting*, *Believing*, *Reasoning*, *Knowing*, *Willing*, and all the different actings of our own Minds; which we being conscious of, and observing in our selves, do from these receive into our Understandings, as distinct *Ideas* [...] (*Essay Concerning Human Understanding* II – i – 2/3)

Ideas in the mind are furnished by experience and by reflection upon the operations of the mind. Ideas are *given*. They are also the raw materials of thought. For in thinking, we put ideas together to form thoughts. As we have seen, judging consists of affirming or denying one idea of another – as when we affirm that apples are round and deny that they are square. But for communication to be possible, words that are names of the ideas constitutive of our thoughts are necessary. A spoken sentence therefore represents a thought in the mind of the speaker, and the words of that sentence are names of the ideas constituting his thought. A hearer will understand the thought communicated if the words he hears arouse in him the same ideas, that is, the *qualitatively identical* ideas, in the *same combination* that are in the mind of the speaker. Communication by means of language is conceived to be a form of *telementation* – of generating ideas in another person's mind that are qualitatively identical with the ideas one has in one's own mind. Locke, again, articulates the picture:

> The Comfort and Advantage of Society, not being to be had without Communications of Thoughts, it was necessary, that Man should find out some external sensible Signs, whereby those invisible *Ideas*, which his thoughts are made up of, might be made known to others. [...] Thus we may conceive how *Words*, which were by Nature so well adapted to that purpose, come to be made use of by Men, as *the Signs of* their *Ideas*. (*Essay Concerning Human Understanding* III – ii – 1)

So, it is natural enough, on reflection, to suppose that words are names of ideas in the mind and that the ideas in the mind are given in experience. It does not matter whether the words in question are names of sensations, such as pain, or of perceptual qualities, such as red, or of kinds of things, such as a horse. *All* words in a language, it now seems, must be names of ideas given in experience or names of combinations of such ideas. *All* ideas are privately owned and epistemically private; but, if communication *is* to be possible, then the ideas in my mind must be qualitatively identical with the ideas in your mind.

Int. I see that this was the dominant style of thought in the seventeenth and eighteenth centuries. But isn't all this obsolete now?

PMSH. No! With but marginal changes and with updated jargon, they are as much in fashion as ever. Noam Chomsky, the leading linguistic theorist of the second half of the twentieth century, argued as follows:

> The speed and precision of vocabulary acquisition leaves no real alternative to the conclusion that the child somehow has the concepts available before experience with language and is basically learning labels for concepts that are already part of his or her conceptual apparatus.[4]

---

4 Chomsky, *Language and the Problems of Knowledge*, pp. 27f.

This has become a commonplace in the contemporary cognitive scientific investigation of language and its use. The dominant models of language acquisition and speech suppose that words are labels for (i.e. names of) concepts and that concepts are stored in the brain in a concept module. Language learning, according to this conception, is a matter of learning the words that are labels for antecedently acquired concepts. Substitute the word 'idea' for 'concept', and we are not far removed from the seventeenth century at all.

Now, if all words are names of ideas, what is the mechanism by which they are attached to the ideas of which they are names? We have seen in our previous examination of the Augustinian conception of meaning that it is most natural to suppose that words are linked with the things they name by *ostensive definition*. When it comes to names of sensations, perceptual experiences, feelings and emotions, we have nothing *external* to point at. If we think that perceptual qualities are actually subjective modifications of the mind consequent upon the agitation of nerve endings, then it seems evident that we can assign a meaning to such words as 'red', 'sweet', 'tinkle', 'warm', 'soft', 'malodorous' and so on only by, as it were, *pointing inwards* – to 'ideas in the mind' or to experiences.

Sensations, perceptions, perceptual qualities, feelings and emotions are subjective experiences. If one is to master their names, there must be some *private analogue* of public ostensive definition, and so too some *mental analogue* of a public sample. In short, there must be some procedure that we might with justice call *'private ostensive definition'*. Reflect on the simple case of pain. How do we learn the meaning of the word 'pain'? Surely, we must have a pain and learn to associate the word 'pain' with the sensation. But we need something more than random association. We need a *standard of correct use* – like a sample. So, can't we use a current pain as a sample, just like a public sample of length, such as a 12-inch ruler as a sample of 1 foot, or of weight, such as a kilogramme weight as a sample of 1 kilogramme? So when we have a pain, we can concentrate our attention on this sensation – attention being a mental analogue of pointing – and resolve that *this* is pain and that anything which is what *this* is is rightly deemed to be pain. Of course, public samples are typically physical objects. They may be stored for future use, as when we store in our files a colour chart that we have purchased from a paint shop or store in a drawer a 12-inch ruler that we have bought from the stationer's shop. But how can one store an experience that is meant to function as a *mental* sample – a sensation, such as pain, or a feeling, such as fear, or a perceptual quality as experienced, such as indigo? What can be more natural than the thought that we store such mental samples in our memory – the storehouse of ideas, as Locke called it. Again, Locke himself articulated the thought:

Such precise naked appearances in the mind, without considering how, whence, or with what others they came there, the understanding lays up (with names commonly annexed to them) as standards to rank real existences into sorts, as they agree with these patterns, and to denominate them accordingly. (*Essay Concerning Human Understanding* II – xi – 9)

So when we need to check on the meaning of such words as 'pain', 'seeing', 'indigo', 'fear' and so forth, all we need to do is to call up the *sample* or *pattern* from memory. And when we wish to assure ourselves whether what we are now experiencing is a pain or a tickle, or is indigo or purple, all we need to do is recollect the right sample, call it into our mind and use it as a *standard* for the correct application of the word that we have defined by private ostensive definition by reference to this mental sample. So, where does that leave us?

> **Int.** It seems that experiences are privately and inalienably owned. And if that's right, then they are strictly speaking known only to their subject. It seems that names of experiences must be connected with the objects of which they are names by means of a private analogue of public ostensive definition. And it seems plausible to suppose that words are names of ideas in the mind or concepts stored in the brain. And if all this is right – if we are to believe modern neuroscientists, theoretical linguists and cognitive scientists – then the language each of us speaks *is actually* a private one.
>
> **PMSH.** Yes, that's what it looks like. But what now about communication?
>
> **Int.** Surely something is awry. None of the philosophers who embraced this conception of language and its relations to experience thought that it meant that each of us speaks a private language that no one else can understand. Moreover, none of the modern linguists and cognitive scientists who embraced this cluster of ideas thought that they implied that communication is impossible. On the contrary, they thought that they were *explaining* what communication actually is – namely a form of telementation, of causing the hearer to have the same ideas in his mind as I have in mine.
>
> **PMSH.** Exactly. So they have to argue as follows:
>
> > A private language is not a means of interpersonal communication.
> > The language I speak is a means of interpersonal communication.
> > ∴   The language I speak is not a radically private one.
>
> > On the other hand, that flies in the face of all the considerations we have been advancing.
>
> **Int.** But there is another alternative. A philosopher, psychologist or theoretical linguist may argue instead:

> The language I speak is private.
> Other people do typically understand what I say.
> ∴   A private language is intelligible to others.
>
>> If the first premise (that the language I speak is private) seems irresistible in the light of all our considerations and if the second premise (that others do typically understand what I say) is a truism, then the conclusion must be that there is something awry in the incommunicability claim.
>
> **PMSH.** That's excellent. The escape route that is typically proposed is that although the experiences of others cannot logically be the same as my experiences, they can be very similar. A distinction is drawn between numerical identity and qualitative identity. Let me explain this bit of jargon: Two people can have the numerically identical car, for example, if one sells his car to another or if they are joint owners. Here there is but *one* car. Two people can have *numerically distinct* but *qualitatively identical* cars if both have cars of the same make, model, colour and so forth. Here there are *two* qualitatively identical cars. So, invoking this simple distinction, it is argued that although no two people can have the *numerically* identical experience, the experiences of different people may be *qualitatively* identical. You can't have *my* pain, but only a different pain that is *just like* mine. So there is really no barrier to communication! Since, as cognitive scientists commonly say, 'we are all wired up the same way', communication can surely take place as long as the experiences you have on a given stimulus are qualitatively the same as everyone else's, and as long as you attach the same words as others do to the qualitatively identical experiences. Is that not convincing?
>
> **Int.** Yes, immensely so. Isn't it right?
>
> **PMSH.** No, it is deeply confused; and Wittgenstein devoted much time and effort to showing it to be so.

The picture is now nearly complete. The last touches to the canvas are to highlight how extensive the ramifications of this conception of the mental, of psychological words and their meaning, of subjective knowledge and of knowledge of other minds are. Wittgenstein has dug down to the very roots of our thought. More infertile offshoots grow from these roots than one might think, and they must be pruned. Let me try to sketch these ramified confusions.

First, the ramifications of the private linguist's conception of the mental:

According to the picture we have painted, each of us enjoys access to a private realm of the mind. The mental world, it seems, consists of mental objects (such as pains), mental states (such as feeling cheerful) and mental processes (such as thinking). These are logically akin to physical objects, states and processes – only they are mental rather than physical.

To have an experience, for example, to have a headache, to feel an emotion or to make a calculation in one's head, is to stand in a certain *relationship* to such an object, state or process. 'John has a headache' is grammatically akin to 'John has a house' and so too 'I have a headache' is akin to 'I have a house'. In the case of having a house, one stands in a certain relation to a house – a relation of legal ownership. In the case of having a headache, one stands in a certain logico-metaphysical relation to a headache – a relation of *logically non-transferable ownership*. I *have* my experiences – they are *mine* – I *own* them. But unlike my house or car, I can't give them or transfer them to anyone else. They are not legally inalienable; they are *logically* inalienable. Or so it seems.

Second, the ramifications of the private linguist's conception of names of psychological attributes.

The picture we have elaborated commits us to the idea that one knows what the name of a mental entity means if and only if one knows what it stands for (and here, as you will have realized, we are firmly in the grip of the Augustinian, correlational, conception of language). One knows what the word 'pain' means if and only if one knows that it stands for the sensation of pain. And one *can* know that only if one has had the appropriate experience and linked the word 'pain' with that experience by means of a private ostensive definition. The private ostensive definition uses a representation of the experience as a defining sample. The representation is a memory image. That knowing the meaning of names of subjective experiences presupposes acquaintance with such experiences seems to be confirmed by empirical data. For surely, the fact that the blind do not know what colour words mean is to be explained by their not being acquainted with colours, that is, by their lacking the sensory experiences of seeing colours. Lacking that, they are unable to give themselves a private ostensive definition of colour words and are unable to store private mental samples of colour in their memories.

A further corollary concerns children's concept acquisition. A child learns what a name of an experience means by first *having* a certain experience. Then the child must concentrate on the experience and link it with the appropriate name, for example, 'headache', 'want', 'thirst' or 'blue'. A sample store in the child's memory ensures that the child will thenceforth associate the name with the experience of which it is a name.

Note that it is central to this picture that concepts of mental attributes are logically independent of behaviour. A person acquires psychological concepts by having, and then naming, experiences. But those experiences are completely independent of any behaviour. The mental is causally, but not *logically*, connected to behaviour.

Third, the epistemological ramifications of the private linguist's conception of the mental:

The claims made for epistemic privacy advance the view that acquaintance with one's subjective experiences is a form of direct knowledge. Indeed, it seems to be particularly *certain* knowledge. After all, when I have a pain, can I *doubt* whether I do? Does it make sense to say 'I think I have a pain, but I'm not sure. Let's see'? If I think of Jill, can I be *mistaken* about whom I was thinking? Does it make sense for me to *wonder* whether I was thinking of Jill or of $\sqrt{-1}$? Surely not. If I have the visual experience of something's seeming red to me, can I be mistaken? Might it really seem green to me even though I think it seems red? This is absurd. So it seems that when we have an experience, hold a belief or think a thought,

(i) we *know* that we do,
(ii) our knowledge is *certain*, and
(iii) it is *indubitable*.
(iv) it is *infallible*.

If that is so, then it appears that the subjective, mental realm is better known than the objective, physical realm. For our knowledge claims concerning how things are in our environment are fallible and susceptible to occasional error and illusion. So, as Descartes and the British empiricists argued, *the mind is better known than matter,* and *the mental is better known than the physical.*

Since having experiences is conceived to be a matter of *acquaintance* with mental entities, and since that relation yields knowledge, there is an inner analogue of the relation of perception to outer entities. This analogue is variously denominated *introspection, inner sense, consciousness* or *awareness*. So, when I have an experience, I am conscious or aware of it; an experience of which I was not conscious would, as Kant put it, be 'as nothing to me'. I can't have a pain, for example, and *not* be aware of it. To say 'I had a terrible pain, but luckily I wasn't aware of it' is to talk nonsense. A pain of which I am unaware, Wittgenstein jested, might even be quite pleasant!

When I have an experience, I can observe it in inner sense and report for the benefit of others what I apprehend. When I say to others that I think this or that, that I want to do this and have decided to do that, I am *describing* in words what I apprehend by introspection or consciousness. The fundamental role of first-person psychological utterances is descriptive; I describe for others how things are with me. (Again, it is evident that we are moving within the force-field of the Augustinian conception of language according to which the *essential* role of sentences is *to describe*).

Finally, the ramifications of the conception of knowledge of other minds:

According to the conception we are about to investigate, one can't know of other people's experiences as one knows one's own. One knows how things are with oneself by introspection. But to know how things are with one's friend, one observes his behaviour – his bodily movements. One then infers from these bodily movements what unobservable mental states and experiences are causally responsible for them. The actual experiences of others, not to mention their thoughts and beliefs, are hidden – inaccessible to direct observation. Even if my friend tells me in words what he is experiencing or thinking, these are just words – and anyway he may be lying. Even if my friend does behave in these and these ways – crying out, weeping, smiling and laughing – this is just behaviour, not the real experience itself – and anyway, my friend may just be dissimulating.

Human behaviour, strictly speaking, consists of bare bodily movements and the emission of sounds. The body that behaves is a physical organism subject to the very same causal laws that determine the movements of all physical bodies. Since a mental state can obtain or an experience be undergone without any corresponding behaviour being evident, and behaviour may occur without the appropriate mental state or event occurring, behaviour seems to be logically independent of the mental. Since the experiences and mental states of others are known *only* from their behaviour and since the behaviour is *not* logically connected with the mental, the inference cannot be logical. Nor can it be inductive, for in order to establish an inductive connection between two phenomena, one must be able to observe both and note their correlation. But in the case of other human beings, one cannot do so, since one can observe only their behaviour – their bodily movements – and one cannot observe their private mental states. So the nature of *that* inference from observed behaviour to underlying mental state is problematic. Whatever it is, it seems that it cannot yield genuine knowledge, but at best belief and conjecture. We can know with certainty how things are with us, but how things are with others is problematic and uncertain.

Let me summarize the state of play. We have built up a convincing case for the supposition that the very language we speak is a private one. Its constituent words apparently refer to, and are names of, experiences or of the perceptual contents of experiences. We have taken on board the thought that experiences are privately and inalienably owned and that strictly speaking they can *really* be known only by their owner. And the way in which words for these subjective mental objects, states and processes are endowed with meaning is by means of a private ostensive definition. It all seems very plausible. And we have confirmation from both seventeenth-century philosophy and from twentieth-century neuroscience, linguistics and cognitive science. So it looks as if the assumption of the conceivability of private languages is perfectly warranted. Indeed, it looks as if it is not only conceivable but actual, and not merely actual, but inevitable.

When it looks as if, Wittgenstein remarked, it is time to look out! We have, without noticing it, stepped off the highroad of good sense. But where? And why? If you have followed me thus far, then you should be puzzled and bewildered. I shall resolve the puzzlement and bewilderment in the next lectures. We'll start with careful scrutiny of the two notions of privacy, and with close examination of the idea of private ostensive definition. Our task, as Wittgenstein said, will be to transform latent nonsense into patent nonsense. Our aim will be to bring this elaborate house of cards tumbling down.

Chapter 9

PRIVATE OWNERSHIP OF EXPERIENCE

In the previous lecture, I surveyed the question that Wittgenstein posed concerning the possibility of a logically private language – that is, a language that no one but the speaker can, logically, understand. I tried to make clear that, although the question seems, at first glance, to be bizarre and of no obvious interest at all, it is in fact exceedingly important. For a large part of the philosophical thinking of the past three and a half centuries, unwittingly presupposed that the languages we all speak *are* private languages. The words of our language, it was thought, refer to our own immediate private experiences – which are something that only we can have and that only we can know. And I pointed out that mainstream ideas of contemporary cognitive neuroscience, psychology and theoretical linguistics are likewise tacitly committed to this conception of language and experience. The idea of a logically private language can be represented as a three-legged stool. The three legs are:

First, the experience is logically privately owned: Only I can have *my* experience. I cannot have your experience and you cannot have mine. Experiences are logically inalienable possessions.

Second, the experiences are privately known. Only I *really know* of my experiences. For only I have access to them by means of introspection. I have *privileged* access to my own experiences. But others can judge of my experience only on the basis of my behaviour.

Third, the mental mechanism whereby words are linked to the experiences which they name is private ostensive definition.

This is the three-legged stool of a private language. If the legs are sound, the stool will stand. If so, then it follows that the language each of us speaks is a logically private one. That will face us with the intolerable paradox that no one else can possibly understand us. For the words of the language are defined by reference to samples that no one else can apprehend.

Finally, I drew attention to the characteristic attempt to find a way out of this paradox by invoking the distinction between numerical and qualitative identity. You will remember that this distinction between two uses of the expression 'the same' or 'the identical' applies clearly to things, such as chairs or cars. If I give you my car, then the car you now have is identical with the car I previously had. It is the numerically identical car, since there is only one car, previously owned by me and now owned by you. But if we each purchase a 2023 VW of the same model and colour, then we have the very same car – and here we are speaking of two cars that are qualitatively the same. It is very tempting to ward off the paradox of the incommunicability of a private language by invoking this distinction. So one will argue that although experiences are privately owned – and one person's experience is numerically distinct from anyone else's experience – this does not mean that the private experiences of different people cannot be *qualitatively* identical. You have your pain and I have mine, but the pains may be qualitatively the same. Given that we are mercifully all 'wired up' the same way, there is indeed good reason to suppose that what I mean by 'pain' is qualitatively the same sensation as you mean by that word. So too, what I mean by 'red' is qualitatively identical with what you mean, because as long as neither of us is colour-blind, we shall have the qualitatively identical visual experience when we look at a ripe tomato.

In this lecture and the next two, I shall show you that all three legs of the stool of the private language are rotten. Today, I shall concentrate on the first leg, namely private ownership of experience.

Private Ownership of Experience: The Deceptive Picture

We think of the physical world as populated by material objects located in an objective, unified spatio-temporal framework. Material objects interact with each other, and the resultant physical processes and events can be observed by an appropriately situated spectator. A material object is an independently identifiable particular thing.

It is, however, easy to work one's way into a frame of mind in which mental things do not seem to fit readily into the physical world. Mental things, one is then inclined to argue, belong to the domain of consciousness. And consciousness, we are all told, is deeply mysterious. How can something as distinctive and strange as consciousness emerge from mere matter? – we ask. And if we have taken these few steps down this road, then it seems irresistible to think of mental phenomena as constituting an 'inner' world, distinct from the physical or 'outer' world. Gottlob Frege remarked:

> Even an unphilosophical man soon finds it necessary to recognize an inner world, distinct from the outer world, a world of sense-impressions, of creatures of his imagination, of sensations, of feelings and moods, a world of inclinations, wishes, and decisions.[1]

---

1 Frege, 'Thoughts', in *Collected Papers on Mathematics, Logic and Philosophy* (Blackwell, Oxford, 1984), p. 360.

If we think thus, we are likely to conceive of the mental world as populated by mental objects such as pain, mental events such as thoughts occurring to one and mental processes such as doing mental arithmetic. Precisely parallel to the physical world, the mental world consists of objects, events and processes. They will inevitably seem ethereal, intangible, elusive and often difficult to describe – after all, mental objects are not made of matter. What are they made of? Well, we are inclined to respond, that is difficult to say. One day we shall find out more about them. And we may even be inclined to agree with cognitive neuroscientists that it is for neuroscience to solve these mysteries. Whether that is right is questionable, and we shall investigate the matter in a later lecture. But for the moment, let us grant that mental objects are just like physical ones, only mental.

If so, it seems that the differences between mental objects and physical objects must be very general *metaphysical differences* that distinguish the mental from the physical, consciousness from matter. For, to be sure, the status of mental objects seems quite different from that of physical ones. Physical objects are independent existences. They belong to the public domain and can be perceived by all who are appropriately situated. But objects in the 'inner world' are quite different. In the first place, they seem to be *essentially* owned. To quote Frege again:

> It seems absurd to us that a pain, a mood, a wish should go around the world without an owner, independently. A sensation is impossible without a sentient being. The inner world presupposes somebody whose inner world it is. (ibid.)

One cannot find pain in the room – only people in pain. One cannot find thoughts in the drawer or under the bed. And one cannot find perceptual experiences in the street – one can only have them in the street. What appear to be 'inner objects' are essentially someone's – they are, it seems, owned by someone.

Inner objects are not only essentially owned, they are also essentially untransferable and unshareable. Each person's inner world consists, as it were, of metaphysically inalienable property. As Frege put it:

> Nobody else has my pain. Someone may have sympathy with me, but still my pain belongs to me and his sympathy to him. He has not got my pain, and I have not got his feeling of sympathy. (Ibid., p. 361)

So, each mental world is a particular person's mental world, and objects within a given mental world cannot be exported. An object within one inner world can no more migrate to another inner world than it can escape to the outer world. It is of the essence of mental objects to be owned, and they cannot exist unowned. The ownership of pain is inalienable. Not only can't you have my pain when I have it, you can't have my pain even when I have ceased to have it! If I cease to have a pain, then the pain I had ceases to exist; the pain has not only passed, it has passed away. Put thus, in the 'metaphysical mode', this seems a mysterious metaphysical fact. Mental phenomena, we might then say, are just very strange!

Peter Strawson, one of the greatest Oxford philosophers of the twentieth century, offered what seemed to be a convincing explanation. What appears to be a brute metaphysical fact, he argued, is actually a logical matter of identity. It is in the nature of experiences, such as pain, to *belong* to a subject and to be *inalienable*. This is because the very *identity* of these inner objects is bound up with the identity of the possessor of the inner world to which they belong. Pains, perceptions, feelings and intentions are *logically identified* as the pains, perceptions, feelings and intentions *of* such-and-such a person. What Strawson wrote was this:

> States or experiences, one might say, *owe* their identity as particulars to the identity of the person whose states or experiences they are. From this it follows immediately that if they can be identified as particular states or experiences at all, they must be possessed or ascribable [...] in such a way that it is logically impossible that a particular state or experience in fact possessed by someone should have been possessed by anyone else. The requirements of identity rule out logical transferability of ownership.[2]

This transforms a metaphysical mystery into a logical claim of identity-dependence. It is allegedly *because* the identity of pain turns on *whose* pain it is, that another person *cannot* have my pain. I may have a headache. If you also have a headache, it is alleged, we *call* what you have 'another headache', and we do not *say* 'You have my headache'. What you have *does not count as* my headache. In short, *another person's pain is another pain*. This, Strawson could claim, is a convention – a rule for the use of the expressions 'same pain' and 'different pain'. The demystification is admirable; but is the logic correct? Well, let us investigate!

Strawson's logical claim concerning the identity of pain can be *strengthened* by reflection on pain location. It is clearly *constitutive* of physical pain to have a bodily location. It always makes sense to ask: 'Where is the pain?' or 'Where does it hurt?', and many pains are *differentiated* by reference to their bodily location. One can't have a headache in one's back, or a backache in one's head. The location of a pain is clearly *one* criterion of identity of pain. So, if Jack has a toothache and Jill has a backache, they are both in pain, but they evidently have quite different pains. For a toothache is a different pain from a headache. And if you grant that, must you not grant that it is actually impossible for two people to have the same pain? For Jack's pains are the

---

2 P. F. Strawson, *Individuals* (Methuen, London, 1959), pp. 97f.

pains in *his* body, and Jill's pains are the pains in *her* body. And Jack's body is different from Jill's body. Their respective bodies are located in different places. If there is a pain in Jack's knee, it is Jack's pain. Jill may have a similar pain in her knee. But since her knee is not Jack's knee, the pains are in different places. So is it not *obvious* that two people can't have the identical pain? Difference in location surely implies numerical difference of the pain. The pains may be qualitatively identical, but they can't be numerically identical. Or so it seems [...] so it seems!

Private Ownership of Experience: Disentangling the Knot

A large part of philosophy consists in disentangling the knots we tie in our understanding. The smaller the knot, the harder it is to unravel. The more one pulls at it, the smaller the knot becomes. I know of few, if any, tighter and smaller knots than the one we are so readily tempted to tie in our grasp of the nature of pain and its identity. Here, the *natural* way to think is the *wrong* way to think. To unravel this tiny knot, one needs to tease it free – not to pull on a thread. The way to do so is to detect what tempted one to tie it in the first place.

Wittgenstein's response to the predicament in the *Investigations* is brief and laconic. He wrote thus:

> 'Another person can't have my pains.' – My pains – what pains are they? What counts as a criterion of identity here? Consider what makes it possible in the case of physical objects to speak of 'two exactly the same': for example, to say, 'This chair is not the one you saw here yesterday, but it is exactly the same as it.'
>
> In so far as it makes *sense* to say that my pain is the same as his, it is also possible for us both to have the same pain. (And it would also be conceivable for two people to feel pain in the same – not just the corresponding – place. This might be the case with Siamese twins, for instance.)
>
> I have seen a person in a discussion on this subject strike himself on the breast and say: 'But surely another person can't have THIS pain!' – The answer to this is that one does not define a criterion of identity by emphatic stressing of the word 'this'. Rather, the emphasis merely creates the illusion of a case in which we are conversant with such a criterion of identity, but have to be reminded of it. (PI §253)

Wittgenstein invites us to reflect on cases in which we can speak of two things being exactly the same but not identical. His example is a chair, that is, a space-occupying, movable physical object that consists of matter and persists over time. Here we may say: 'This is the very chair we saw together at the auction last week – I bought it.' Or we may say, 'This is not the identical chair that you saw last week, but it belongs to the same set, and is just the same as the other one, which is being re-upholstered.' So let us reflect, together with our interlocutor, on this simple and familiar distinction. What makes it possible to distinguish in such cases between being numerically identical and being qualitatively identical?

> **Int.** Well, I suppose it must be this: a chair is made of a certain quantity of matter, such as wood. And the wood of which this chair is made is not the same *specific* quantity of wood as the wood out of which the other chair is made – even though each chair is made of 15 pounds of mahogany. The two chairs are material space-occupants of the same kind, and the distinct quantities of matter of which they are severally made cannot be in the same place at the same time. But the two chairs may share virtually all their other properties. They are numerically distinct but may be qualitatively identical.
>
> **PMSH.** Yes, that's spot on. You have it just right.
>
> **Int.** Good! But now, *is it not just like that with pains*? If I have a pain in my knee and you have a pain in your knee, then given that being in my knee is being in a *different* place from being in your knee, my pain cannot be numerically identical to yours – since mine is in my knee and yours is in yours. Of course, the pains may be similar – that is, qualitatively identical – but not identical. So, you can't have my pain. You can't have the very same pain I have. Isn't this right?
>
> **PMSH.** Well, actually, No!
>
> **Int.** But surely, it is. You are sitting over there, and I am sitting over here. Now suppose that you have a pain in your knee, and I have a pain in my knee. Then it surely follows that you have a pain in a different place from me! Different people *obviously* can't have a pain in the same place since their bodies are in different places!
>
> **PMSH.** No, things are more subtle than that. Let's take this slowly. The location of pain is determined *by the behaviour* of the sufferer. The criterion for where a suffering person has a pain is where he *says* it hurts, where he *points* when asked where it hurts and what part of his body he *assuages*. If two people aver that their knee hurts, if they both point at their knee when asked where it hurts, and if both rub their knee to assuage the pain, then each has a pain in his knee. And now remember that this is precisely what it *is* for two people to have a pain *in the same place*. We *say* they have a pain in the same place. That is what *is called* having a pain in the same place. So it is mistaken to claim that different people cannot have a pain in the same place because their bodies are in different places. Hence too, it is mistaken to claim that two people cannot have the same pain *because* they cannot have a pain in the same place.

Int. But all your argument shows is that in *colloquial use*, the phrase 'pain in the *same* location' means the same as 'pain in the *corresponding* location'. But strictly speaking, a *corresponding* location is not the *same* location. So, after all, two different people cannot have the same pain, since even if their pain is of the same intensity and phenomenal character, the location of A's pain differs from the location of B's.

PMSH. All right. I do perhaps have more respect for the ordinary use of words than you seem to do. For it is the ordinary use of words that shows the ordinary concepts that we deploy in our thought and talk. But never mind. Let us sidestep the location issue – since that is exactly what Wittgenstein did. Rather than quibbling over the use of the phrases 'pain in the same place' and 'pain in a different place', he short-cut the issue in order to show that the heart of the matter is not the notion of pain location. Suppose a case of Siamese twins, Jack and Jill, who are joined at the knee. If both twins have a pain at the point of juncture, then they both have a pain in the knee. But now it is *the very same* knee. Each twin, when asked where it hurts, points at the knee and says 'That's where it hurts'. Here one cannot say 'Jack cannot have the same pain as Jill, because Jack's pain is in his knee whereas Jill's pain is in her knee', for they have the same knee. So, given identity of pain location, as in this case, and identity of phenomenal characteristics and intensity as avowed by the two sufferers, must we not now admit that Jack and Jill may have the identical pain? So, at least in this bizarre case, two people *can* have the very same pain, can't they?

Int. No, I don't see that at all. Jack cannot have Jill's pain, and Jill cannot have Jack's pain – and that's the end of the matter. *Another person's pain is another pain*!

PMSH. Good. I'm glad you said that. What your response shows is that the question of pain location is *a red herring*. The decisive point that moves one to support the private ownership doctrine is that you can't have my pain, *because mine is mine and yours is yours*! What determines the identity of pain is the *owner* of the pain. If someone else has a pain, it is a different pain! Now, what this amounts to is the claim that pains in particular and experiences in general are *identity-dependent upon their owner*. Having a pain, Strawson suggested, is a form of 'logically non-transferable ownership'. So two people cannot have the identical pain, only a similar one. Is that what you want to argue?

Int. Yes, that's exactly right. You can't have the same pain as I because you can't own *my* pain!

PMSH. Right. So let's pursue this idea. To do so, we must enquire into the notion of 'logical ownership'. Ordinary ownership is a *legal relation* between a person and the thing owned. The car I have belongs to me, but I might sell it to another. Then it will belong to him – *ownership is transferable*. I might share my car with my wife. Then we both own the very same car – *ownership is shareable*. Do you agree with that?

Int. Yes, of course. That's obvious.

PMSH. Indeed it is. But how do we come by the idea of *logical ownership* of experience?

Int. Well, isn't it something like this: surely *having* something here signifies a kind of *relation*. To have a car is to own a car, isn't it? Ownership of a car (or any other chattel) is a *legal* relation between a person and an object. Isn't that right?

PMSH. Yes, of course.

Int. Well, then, to *have* a pain, and more generally, to *have* an experience, is to stand *in a relation* to a pain. *Having*, in this case, is a relation of ownership too – but it is a relation of *logical*, not of *legal*, ownership. Isn't that what Strawson had in mind?

PMSH. It is certainly the *analogy* that he had at the back of his mind when he spoke of *logically non-transferable ownership*.

Int. Good. Then it is surely obvious that one and the same car may successively be owned by different owners. But pains, and experiences in general, are not like cars. They are *non-transferable*. Different owner, it seems, then different pain, no matter how similar. That is why you can't have the same pain as I, but only a pain that is just like it.

Come to think of it – I have an even better argument in support of Strawson's conception that you can't have the very same pain as mine. He argues, doesn't he, that the identity of pain is *dependent* on the identity of the person who has the pain – on the identity of the owner of the pain. Now it occurs to me that this identity-dependence of a pain on the owner of the pain is just like the identity-dependence of an event upon the object undergoing change.

PMSH. A very interesting analogy. Would you elaborate a bit?

Int. Well, take a pair of ripening apples. Say two apples slowly change from being green to being red. Now a simple event is a change to a particular thing, isn't it? So the change that takes place when an apple ripens and changes its colour is an event. *Now*, can't you see that the event that consists in *this* apple's changing from green to red is *a different event* from the event that consists in *that* apple's changing from green to red! And that is precisely because the first event is a change to *this* apple and the second event is a change to *that* apple. Events are identity-dependent upon the substance, the thing, undergoing change. Is it not like that with pains and experiences?

PMSH. I think you have put your hand on something very important. You have identified the analogy that lies at the heart of the idea that two people cannot have the same pain, that two people cannot have the same visual experience and hence that the colour you see when you see a tomato can't be the same as the colour I see. That is of the greatest importance. But now the question is: is this a good analogy? It is remarkable how difficult it is to penetrate the grammar of *having experiences*, to compare and contrast *having a pain* and *having a penny* and to see the similarities and differences between *the way in which an event is logically related to the substance the change in which is the event* and *the way in which the subject of a pain or more generally an experience stands to the pain or experience he has*. But we must try.

We need to slow things down. We need to look closely at the verb 'to have' and its complex use. We speak of *having* chattels, such as cars and houses. This is a relation of ownership. We also speak of *having* a wife and children, and we speak of 'my wife' and 'my children' – but that does not signify a relation of ownership at all, but a marital and a parental relation to another person or people. We also speak of *having* a promissory obligation, and this too is a relation, but, again, not one of ownership. Moreover, it is not a relation between us and what we have, namely: an obligation, but between us and the person to whom we made a promise. We speak of *having* a cold, a sharp tongue or a sense of humour. In these cases, no relationship between a person and an object is signified. I may have caught my cold from another (colds are eminently transferable), nevertheless, I do not *own* my cold and don't stand in a relation to the cold I have. If I give you my cold, it doesn't follow that I no longer have it. To be sure, I cannot give my sense of humour to another, but I don't therefore non-transferably *own* it either. To have a sense of humour is to be disposed to act and react in certain ways to what is comic, not to own anything.

So, *having* need not be *owning* and need not be a relation at all. Now, does the phrase 'to have a pain' signify a relation to a pain? Why is one tempted to think it does? One obvious reason, on which we have been dwelling thus far, is the grammatical similarity between the phrase 'to have a pain' and 'to have a pin' and between 'his pain' and 'his pin'. But a deeper reason is that 'I have a pain' is synonymous with 'I feel a pain', and *feeling* is commonly a relation to what is felt. I may feel a pin in the cushion, or feel the warmth of the fire. That is a perceptual relation between the perceiver and what is perceived.

Int. Is *feeling a pain* not a matter of perceiving a pain?
PMSH. No! Here too superficial similarity of grammatical form conceals important logical differences:

'I feel a pain'

and

'I feel a pin'

look alike. The two sentences have the same grammatical structure. Nevertheless, feeling a pain, unlike feeling a pin, is *not* a form of tactile perception. One can feel a pin in the cushion only if there is a pin in it to be felt. If there is no pin there, then it may *seem* to one that one feels a pin. Furthermore, one may *feel for* the pin with one's fingertips and fail to find it, even though there is a pin there. But to feel a pain *is* to have a pain – one cannot feel it and *not* have it. Nor can one *have* a pain and *not feel* it. And it cannot *seem to one* that one has a pain although one has none. Although one can always replace the 'has' in the phrase 'has a pain' with the verb 'feels', neither the word 'has' nor the word 'feels' here signify a perceptual relation between a person and a pain.

So, it is now evident that the sentence 'A has a pain' is not a relational sentence like 'A has a pin' despite the grammatical similarity. So the word 'pain' in the sentence 'A has a pain' does not signify a *relatum*. To have a pain is to be in pain – to suffer. Despite Strawson's claim to the contrary, to have a pain is not to *own* anything. The pain I have is not something that *belongs* to me.

Int. I see. That is fascinating. I would not have realized it had you not shown me the different kinds of logical and grammatical relations that you spelt out. It is amazing how difficult it is to bring to mind the wholly familiar conceptual links – I mean, after all – I know all this perfectly well.

PMSH. Indeed. If you didn't, then what I say would be wrong. For all I am trying to do is to clarify *your*, and of course *our*, concept of pain and more generally concept of experience. And that concept is exhibited in the ways in which you (and we) use the word 'pain' and more generally names of experiences – ways which are altogether familiar to you. If they weren't familiar, then I would not be accurately characterizing your (and our) concept.

Int. Still, you have not yet answered the question of whether my pain is not identity-dependent upon me. Isn't experience in general identity-dependent upon the subject of the experience, as Strawson argued? I mean ... do you *really* want to say that you can have *my* pain?

PMSH. Take it slowly; and don't get too excited. We know from the Siamese twins example that the location question is *irrelevant*. We have cast doubt on the idea that having a pain is a *relation* between a sufferer and a pain. And we have repudiated the idea that the subject of pain is the owner of his pain. What now remains of the claim that my pain *must* differ from yours? If my pain tallies with yours in phenomenal qualities such as burning, throbbing, stinging, nagging, if it has the same intensity and has a corresponding location, what differentiates my pain from yours?

Int. Well, *mine is mine* and *yours is yours*.

PMSH. Yes, that is the heart of the matter, and the rest is really irrelevant. What this amounts to is that the property that differentiates my pain from your pain is *the property of belonging to me*. But that, in effect, is treating *the subject of pain* as *the differentiating property of the pain* – and that is absurd. *I* am not a property of my pain, and nor is it *being mine*.

Belonging to me is a property of my car, precisely because legal ownership is a genuine relation. It is a relational property of my car which it has now and will lose when I sell it. But *belonging to me* is *not* a property of my pain, precisely because *having* in the phrase 'having a pain' does not signify a relation at all. To say that *being mine* is an identifying relational property of my pains is like saying that it is an identifying property of the blue colour of this chair that it *belongs* to the chair. For here too, we are absurdly taking the bearer of a property (or, to be pedantic, *being* the bearer of a property) to be a property of the property. And that is absurd.

Int. Why exactly is that absurd?

PMSH. Well, think it through! One may not argue that two different objects cannot be of the same colour because the colour of A belongs to A and the colour of B belongs to B. That *would be* absurd, making the coloured substance (or belonging to the coloured substance) an identifying property of its colour. If two objects have a colour of the same hue, intensity and saturation, then they have the same colour – neither numerically the same, nor qualitatively the same, but just the same. For the distinction between numerical identity and qualitative identity is a distinction that applies to material substances such as a chair but has no application to colours. *And this is precisely parallel to pains.*

Int. Yes, I see ... but surely that can't be right. I have a very powerful objection. Indeed, it seems to me to be a clinching objection that will force *you* back to the drawing board.

PMSH. All right – I'm all ears.

Int. I mean Jack and Jill can't possibly have the same headache, because if Jack takes an aspirin and ceases to have a headache, Jill's headache won't cease. So *they don't have the same headache*. If they had the same headache, then when Jack takes an aspirin and his headache disappears, then Jill's would disappear too. Since it doesn't, they obviously have different headaches.

Actually, come to think of it, your arguments *must be wrong*. For I still think that pains are identity-dependent upon the person who has them. They aren't like colours, I grant you – they are like axes of rotation! I mean nothing other than the Moon can have the axis of rotation of the Moon! The identity of the axis of the Moon is identifiability-dependent on the Moon. There!

PMSH I see you have been reading some *very* sophisticated philosophers. But you need to read very slowly and think very hard. After all, the greater the sophistication, the greater the sophistry!

This piece of legerdemain seems persuasive until the logical sleight of hand is revealed. For to argue thus is to beg the very question at stake. What Wittgenstein is *denying* is that the distinction between numerical and qualitative identity applies to pain. But your counter-argument about the disappearing headache *explicitly invokes that very distinction*. If, *per impossibile*, Jack's pain *were* numerically identical to Jill's, then, of course, if it disappeared, then by the same token Jill's pain would disappear. But as we have shown, pains are not like pins or pens. The distinction between numerical and qualitative identity *has no application to pains*. Rather, Jack and Jill may have the same headache – just as they may have the same-coloured hair. If Jack takes an aspirin and his headache disappears, then they no longer have the same headache – just as, if Jill dyes her hair, Jack and Jill will no longer have the same-coloured hair. – But that does not mean that they did not have the same-coloured hair before. That would be as absurd as arguing that this blue chair cannot be the same colour as that blue chair, because if one paints this one red, the other one will remain blue!

Int. Oh! [*pause*] ... But I said that pains aren't like colours – they're like axes of rotation! You haven't shown me what is wrong with that!

PMSH. What is wrong with it is very similar to what is wrong with the idea that the colour of an object is identity-dependent upon the identity of the coloured object. Just as you do not identify the colour of an object by telling me which object is coloured, so too you don't tell me what the axis of rotation of the Moon is by telling me that the Moon has an axis of rotation. If you say: 'no other satellite can have the axis of rotation of the Moon, since the axis of rotation of the Moon uniquely belongs to the Moon', I reply: 'So what *is* the axis of rotation of the Moon?' And if you now tell me that it is 15 degrees, I can reply 'That's interesting – that is the very same axis of rotation as that of the third Moon of Jupiter'. So these two satellites have exactly the same axis of rotation – neither numerically the same, nor qualitatively the same, just the same!

This delivers the *coup de grace* to the private ownership doctrine, including the initially persuasive Strawsonian variant of the doctrine.

This has further consequences. If the distinction between numerical and qualitative identity does not apply to experiences, then the idea of resolving the paradox of the incommunicability of a private language by invoking *that* distinction is foreclosed. One *cannot* argue that although human beings all speak a private language the words of which refer to their own private experiences, nevertheless the experiences of different people in the same circumstances are qualitatively identical and *that* is why communication is, after all, possible. The paradox of incommunicability remains – and something further has to give.

It is noteworthy that Wittgenstein remarks: 'In so far as it makes *sense* to say that my pain is the same as his, it is also possible for us both to have the same pain.' We should pause to reflect on this careful qualification. Why the 'in so far as'? What is Wittgenstein alluding to?

First, *being mine* does not, contrary to the private ownership conception, play any role in the criteria of identity for pain. The phrases 'being mine', 'being yours' and 'being his' do *not* specify a property that identifies a pain – 'A has a pain' identifies a sufferer from pain, but it does not identify his pain. That is why Wittgenstein exclaims 'My pains – what pains are they?' The criteria of identity of pain turn on questions of phenomenal character, intensity and location.

Second, one can speak of 'my pain' and also of 'the pain I have'. But, it makes no sense to say 'I have my pain'. For the phrase 'My pain' is synonymous with the phrase 'the pain I have'. So to say 'I have my pain' is equivalent to saying 'I have the pain I have', which is to say nothing at all, except perhaps that I have a pain. So if someone says 'You can't have my pain', we could reply 'And you can't have your pain either'. What we should *not* reply is 'I *can* have your pain'? Rather, we should reply exactly as Wittgenstein replies: 'Your pain? What pain is that?' – and if we get a response such as 'A dull, throbbing headache in the left temple' *then* we may respond 'I have the same pain'.

Third, while it makes sense to say that you have the same headache as if one has reason to suppose that your headache, like mine, is dull, throbbing and in the left temple, it makes no sense to suppose that we *share* the same pain, as we might share the same house. And for us to have the same pain does not mean that you have my pain as you might have my keys. Above all, we must be careful not to project upon experiences the logical characteristics of objects, such as material things. With that proviso, of course, two people can have the same experience.

Fourth, it makes sense to say 'I have the same pain as you' as long as we do not think that by this we mean that we have either the numerically identical pain or the qualitatively identical pain.

So, the subject of a pain does not determine the identity of the pain. The criteria of identity of a pain incorporate three dimensions: intensity, location and phenomenal qualities such as sharp, dull, burning and throbbing. But it is noteworthy how elastic these criteria are in our practices. For sometimes we drop one – as when we say that we have the same rheumatic pain in our hand as in our ankle, disregarding the difference in location. And sometimes change of intensity is irrelevant – as when we say that the dreadful burning pain we had before is now less intense. It is the same pain, but not so bad. And sometimes we may say that the burning pain we had has become dull. So a phenomenal quality may change, yet the pain remain the same pain. Well, if we measure with an elastic ruler, so be it – that too is an important datum. (Don't be surprised at elastic rulers – we use them all the time. Having a fluctuating exchange rate is having an elastic ruler to measure the values of exports and imports.) Our task is to describe the concepts we have, not concepts that we do not have – and if a certain concept is thus elastic, so be it.

A final comment on Wittgenstein's compact remark. The last paragraph, you will recollect, runs as follows:

> I have seen a person in a discussion on this subject strike himself on the breast and say: 'But surely another person can't have THIS pain!' – The answer to this is that one does not define a criterion of identity by emphatic stressing of the word 'this'. Rather, the emphasis merely creates the illusion of a case in which we are conversant with such a criterion of identity, but have to be reminded of it. (PI §253)

One must surely admit the temptation to respond thus (the person in question was G. E. Moore). And that, in itself, is of great interest. For it inclines one to think that merely having a pain and attending to it provides one with a criterion of identity for pain. That is as misconceived as thinking that one can acquire the concept of a negative number by having debts. The emphasis upon 'This' inclines one to think that by giving oneself a pain, one has also provided oneself with a private criterion of identity. That is a deep illusion. There is no such thing as a logically private criterion. Moreover, when one says that one is in pain, one employs no criterion at all – one just says so. And other things being equal, one's word goes! How can that be? We shall examine the matter in a later lecture.

We have spent a great deal of time in this discussion unravelling a tiny knot in our understanding. We have been concerned with just one facet of the grammar of nouns signifying experiences. We have focussed upon a couple of assertions. The first was the common-or-garden one: 'I have the same pain as you.' The second was the more bizarre assertion: 'You can't have my pain.' And the irresistible character of the latter assertion trapped us into misinterpreting the former one. To unravel this tiny knot, we have had to travel a long way in the grammatical landscape. We had to survey aspects of the grammar of location of sensation, of numerical and qualitative identity and of simple sameness. We had to compare the grammar of experiences with the grammar of material objects, events, colours and axes of rotation. In fact, we have had to circle round the problem, examining it from different directions. As Wittgenstein remarked, if we shine light on a problem from one side, that casts long dark shadows on the other. And that is why we *have* to circle round until it becomes clear to us how all the pieces fit together.

Chapter 10

EPISTEMIC PRIVACY OF EXPERIENCE

Epistemic Privacy

You will often have heard someone on the radio say 'Of course, it is impossible *really* to know what other people feel'. Neuroscientists, such as Colin Blakemore, observe that 'Although I assume that other human beings think in much the same way as I do, I have no direct evidence about their conscious minds.' Francis Crick, Nobel Laureate, wrote 'Strictly speaking, each individual is certain only that he himself is conscious' and cannot be completely certain about the consciousness of others. Benjamin Libet, another renowned neuroscientist, wrote: 'Conscious experience, as an awareness of some thing or some event, is directly accessible only to the individual having that experience, not to an external observer.' If you examine legal casebooks, you will find judges making remarks such as: 'Neither you nor I can ever look into the mind of the accused person and say, with positive certainty, what his intention was at any particular time' (*R. v. Charlson* [1955] I All E. R. 859, at 861*)*. This very common conception, which I have called 'epistemic privacy of experience', is the doctrine that only *I* really know that I am having a given experience. Others can at best surmise but cannot *really* know that I am or cannot know it with the certainty with which I know it.

The doctrine of the epistemic privacy of experience is one of the legs of the three-legged stool of the idea of a private language – the others being *private ownership of experience*, which we discussed in the last lecture, and *private ostensive definition*, which I shall discuss in the next lecture. Today I will examine the widespread idea of epistemic privacy.

Wittgenstein introduces the theme in this passage:

> In what sense are my sensations *private*? – Well, only I can know whether I am really in pain; another person can only surmise it. – In one way this is false, and in another nonsense. If we are using the word 'know' as it is normally used (and how else are we to use it?), then other people very often know if I'm in pain. – Yes, but all the same, not with the certainty with which I know it myself! – It can't be said of me at all (except perhaps as a joke) that I *know* I'm in pain. What is it supposed to mean – except perhaps that I *am* in pain?

> Other people cannot be said to learn of my sensations *only* from my behaviour – for I cannot be said to learn of them. I *have* them.
>
> This much is true: it makes sense to say about other people that they doubt whether I am in pain; but not to say it about myself. (PI §246)

As is so common with Wittgenstein, a great deal is packed into a few sentences. So I shall first unpack it and then slowly examine the different points.

We are faced with an epistemological claim that has two complementary parts:

First, *only I can know whether I am really in pain*.

Why so? Because *I* feel it – no one else can feel *my* pain. I am *directly aware* of it. I am *conscious of* my own pain. When I am in pain, I *cannot doubt* whether I am in pain – I am *absolutely certain* that I am.

And second, its corollary is that:

Others can only surmise whether I am in pain – so they may believe I am, but cannot really know whether I am. Or they may know that I am, but not with the certainty that I have.

Why so? Because they *can't feel* my pain. They merely see my grimaces, see me clutching my injured limb, hear me groaning or screaming – and that's just pain-behaviour, not the pain itself. They can't be certain that I am in pain as I can. Doubt may gain a foothold in their considerations in a way in which it can't in mine.

Wittgenstein's response to this bipartite claim is that in one sense it's false and in another it's nonsense. What does he mean?

Well, it's false that others can't know whether I am in pain. Given the ordinary use of the verb 'to know', one person often knows whether someone else is in pain. This is surely indisputable. If someone falls off a high ladder and lies on the ground with an *obviously* broken leg, screaming in pain, does one not *know* that he has hurt himself? Can one seriously say 'He might be pretending'? Surely not. First, pretence itself is something that has to be *learnt*. It would make no sense to say of a baby, crying after having hurt himself, that he is pretending, for he has not yet *learnt* to pretend. Second, there are limits to the idea of *pretence* – in circumstances of incurring a patently severe injury, such as falling off a ladder and breaking one's leg, *nothing would count as pretending*. Could anyone in such a case seriously say: 'He's *probably* in pain'? No, that would be a misuse of the adverb 'probably'. 'What do you mean *probably*', we might reply, '– can't you *see* that the poor fellow is in agony?' This is straightforward, and I'll say no more about it today.

In what sense is the bipartite claim nonsense? Wittgenstein asserts that it can't be said of one at all that one *knows that one is in pain* – that this is nonsense. This remark is startling. It runs contrary to what we are all inclined to say – 'Surely I must know whether I am in pain or not!' is how we're all likely to respond. And it runs contrary to the whole empiricist tradition of the modern era, which argued that human knowledge rests on the bedrock of our knowledge of our own perceptual experiences. Surely, one's sensations, perceptions, emotions, felt attitudes and desires are just the sort of thing that one *does* know about oneself with *absolute certainty*! But Wittgenstein is even more startling. For he not only implies that it is *wrong* to say that I know with certainty whether I am in pain, he then goes on to deny that I cannot doubt whether I am in pain. This seems doubly baffling, since surely it is just *because* I can't doubt whether I am in pain that my knowledge that I am in pain is certain! – What on earth is going on here? We need to take a step backwards and think.

Although the idea of private ownership of experience – the idea that no one else can have my pain – gives powerful support to the notion of epistemic privacy, the idea that only I really know how things are subjectively with me has numerous other roots. The criticism of the idea of private ownership of experience has not damaged these. The idea of *privileged access* remains in place, the idea of *introspection* as a form of inner sense is still intact, and the thought that *I* know how things are with me *directly*, whereas others have only *indirect knowledge* via my behaviour is firmly entrenched. It is these that need careful scrutiny.

It is tempting to think that I am *directly acquainted* with my pain, or, more generally, with my experiences, whereas others can perceive only my behaviour. This picture was nicely articulated by Bertrand Russell:

> When I see the sun, I am often aware of my seeing the sun; thus 'my seeing the sun' is an object with which I have acquaintance. When I desire food, I may be aware of my desire for food; thus 'my desiring food' is an object with which I am acquainted. Similarly, we may be aware of our feeling of pleasure or pain, and generally of the events which happen in our minds. This kind of acquaintance, which may be called self-consciousness, is the source of all our knowledge of mental things. It is obvious that it is only what goes on in our minds that can be thus known immediately.[1]

Mental objects and events are or occur in the mind. According to Russell, one is *acquainted* with them. One is, it seems, immediately *aware* or *conscious* of them. *Introspection* seems to be a form of private perception, a faculty of inner sense by means of which we observe what is in our minds. Indeed, this idea has the imprimatur of contemporary science. Nicholas Humphrey, an eminent psychologist and evolutionary theorist, suggested that

---

1 Russell, *The Problems of Philosophy* [1912] (Oxford University Press, Oxford, 1967), pp. 26f.

a revolutionary advance in the evolution of the mind occurred when, for certain social animals, a new set of heuristic principles was devised to cope with the pressing need to model a specific section of reality – the reality comprised by the behaviour of kindred animals. The trick which nature came up with was *introspection* […] [the] examination of the contents of consciousness.[2]

According to this conception, introspection informs one about the contents of one's own mind. One can then observe how one's own experiences are related to one's behaviour: for example, that when one is in severe pain, one groans or screams. On this basis, one can, it is widely held, construct *a theory of other minds;* for example, when others injure themselves and groan or scream, it is very probable that they are in pain, just as one would be oneself. Or so it seems.

Many philosophers have held that such introspective knowledge is also peculiarly *certain*. Thomas Reid is a good representative of this natural view:

> When a man is conscious of pain, he is certain of its existence; when he is conscious that he doubts or believes, he is certain of the existence of those operations.
>
> But the irresistible conviction he has of the reality of those operations is not the effect of reasoning; it is immediate and intuitive. The existence therefore of those passions and operations of the minds, of which we are conscious, is a first principle, which nature requires us to believe upon her authority.
>
> If I am asked to prove that I cannot be deceived by consciousness – to prove that it is not a fallacious sense – I can find no proof. I cannot find any antecedent truth from which it is deduced, or upon which its evidence depends. It seems to disdain any such derived authority, and to claim my assent in its own right.[3]

Whence the authoritative knowledge? Well, can one be in serious pain and not know it? If, like Macbeth, one takes oneself to see a dagger before one, then one is mistaken, since there is no dagger there. But can one be mistaken in thinking that *it visually seems to one just as if there were a dagger before one*? Does it make sense to say 'It seems to me that there is a dagger before me, but I might be mistaken – perhaps it actually seems to me that there is a dragon before me'? Surely that is nonsense. That things perceptually seem to me to be thus-and-so appears to be something I know with absolute certainty. My knowledge of my subjective experience is direct, immediate and indubitable.

This conception of the epistemology of the subjective has dramatic ramifications. Consciousness seems to deliver both *knowledge* and *certainty*. Awareness seems a form of indubitable inner perception. Introspection seems to be a cognitive faculty – a source of knowledge about one's own subjective experiences. Frege is a good spokesman for this picture:

---

2 N. Humphrey, *Consciousness Regained* (Oxford University Press, Oxford, 1984), p. 30.
3 Thomas Reid, *On the Intellectual Powers of Man*, Essay VI, chapter V.

> I cannot doubt that I have a visual impression of green, but it is not so certain that I see a lime leaf. So [...] we find certainty in the inner world, while doubt never leaves us in our excursions into the external world.[4]

Consequently, *the mental*, as Descartes too averred, *seems better known than the physical*. It seems that our subjective experience gives us a bedrock of certainty. And it is upon this bedrock that our objective knowledge concerning the world is constructed. Surely, I know that there is a red chair in the corner of the room because *it visually seems to me that there is. That it so seems to me* is something I know with *absolute certainty*. And so seeming to me is the firm evidential ground upon which my objective belief that there is a chair there rests.

This conception of the source of empirical knowledge lies at the heart of empiricist epistemology. All knowledge is derived from experience, and the bedrock of certainty upon which our knowledge of, and beliefs about, the world rests is our knowledge of how things perceptually seem to us to be.

This idea is given powerful support by reflection on the scientific nature of perception. We readily conceive of our visual, auditory and other forms of perceptual experience as being caused by the impact of things and of light and sound waves upon our perceptual organs. I see the chair in the corner because light reflected off it hits my retina, agitating the sensitive cells so that minute electrical current is transmitted along the optic nerve to the 'visual' striate cortex. The upshot of this is *that I have a visual experience* – an experience that seems best described as 'the experience as of seeing a chair' or as 'its visually seeming to me just as if there were a chair there'. Similar considerations apply to the other sense organs and sense experiences; sound waves impact upon our eardrums, molecules in the air agitate the olfactory nerve endings in our nostrils and so on. The impact of the physical world upon our nerve endings yields *subjective perceptual experiences*, which are known directly and with certainty. It is these subjective experiences that provide us with the evidence for things in the world around us being, for the most part, as they sensibly seem to us to be. This *causal theory of perception*, ingeniously advocated in the last century by such clear-thinking philosophers as Peter Strawson and Paul Grice, has powerful scientific support. A distinguished neuroscientist, Antonio Damasio, wrote recently:

> When you and I look at an object outside ourselves, we form comparable images in our respective brains [...] The image we see is based on changes which occur in our organisms [...] When the physical structure of the object [we are looking at] interacts with [our] body [...] The object is real, the interactions are real, and the

---

4 Frege, 'Thoughts', p. 367.

images are as real as anything can be. And yet, the structure and properties in the image we end up seeing are brain constructions prompted by the object.[5]

So, a very specific conception of the causation of subjective experience, of consciousness of subjective experience, and of the evidential relationship of subjective perceptual experience to how things are in the world around us lies at the heart of a whole world view. So, in tracking down the idea that only I can know whether I am in pain, we're not hunting an insignificant little mouse, we're hunting big game: the nature of our knowledge of the mental attributes of other people (the 'theory-theory' as contemporary psychologists call this doctrine), and the foundationalist – causal theory – of our knowledge of the world around us. Both these grand and scientifically popular accounts rest on the pivot of a very specific conception of subjective experience and our allegedly privileged knowledge of our experience.

This conception of subjective experience and its epistemology is Wittgenstein's target. He argued that it is confused in every particular. It involves

- Misconceptions about introspection, about inner sense or inner perception, and about the mind's eye.
- A misunderstanding of *consciousness* and *awareness* as involved in subjective experience, for example, 'I am conscious of a pain'.
- A misconstrual of the use of the verb 'to know' in scientific and philosophical theorizing in such sentential contexts as 'I know I am in pain'.
- A conflation of the *privileged status* of a person's avowal of experience, for example, 'I have a pain' or 'I seem to see a chair' with the confused idea that the person has *privileged access* to a private peepshow and reports back to us what they have seen in it.
- A misapprehension of the *role* of utterances of the form 'It visually seems to me just as if …' or 'It sensibly appears to me that …'.

The consequences of these misconceptions are deep and ramified. Indeed, they nicely exemplify the principle that in philosophy, a small knot in one's understanding here may lead to complete entanglement in the web of grammar elsewhere. Or, to put it differently, in logic – in the logic of our concepts – there are no *small* mistakes. *All mistakes are big mistakes!* We shall follow through some of these big mistakes in later lectures. But first, together with our interlocutor friend, we must get to grips with Wittgenstein's arguments.

---

5 Antonio Damasio, *A Feeling of What Happens* (Heineman, London, 1999), p. 320.

Introspection: Wittgenstein's Elucidations

Int. Surely Wittgenstein can't deny that there is such a thing as introspection! After all, wasn't it William James who wrote 'The word introspection need hardly be defined – it means, of course, the looking into our own minds and reporting what we discover there. *Everyone agrees that we discover states of consciousness.*'[6]—Now that seems to me to be dead right.

PMSH. No! That's dead wrong. You and James are being misled by a metaphor. The metaphor embedded in the etymology of the verb 'to introspect' is misleading. For there is no such thing as *looking* into one's mind, or as *seeing* what is in one's mind. The mind is not a space in which anything is visible, audible or tangible. We can wonder about our currently seeing whatever it is that we are seeing and we may note that our eyesight is blurred, but we cannot *see our eyesight*. I may tell my oculist that when he puts that lens before my eyes, I see things in a blurred manner, but I do not aver this on the grounds of *my seeing the blurred manner in which I see*.

Int. Oh, all right. That would be pushing things too far. But surely James is right that we *perceive* what is in our minds.

PMSH. No. He is dead wrong – although I admit that he is wrong in very august company. It was Locke who, in the modern era, introduced talk of *perceiving our perceptions*, and it was Leibniz who coined the term *apperception* as a translation of Locke's 'perception of perception'. But that does not make it any less erroneous. *Introspection is not a form of perception at all.* To perceive something involves the use of *perceptual organs*, such as eyes or ears. It requires appropriate *observation conditions*. And it involves *observational skills*.

But introspection, even when misconceived as a faculty of knowledge of the 'inner', nevertheless patently involves no *perceptual organ* – one does not use one's eyes or ears to be able to say whether one has a pain, what one's mental images are like or what one thinks or expects, wants or intends. Nor are there *observation conditions* for introspection – no 'More light, please' or 'Let me look closer'. And there are no *observational skills* that make one better at spotting a pain or identifying a thought.

Of course, we speak of *the mind's eye* – but that too is a metaphor. Moreover, we should remember that we see things *in* our mind's eye, not *with* our mind's eye. And we don't hear things in our mind's ear. We

---

6 W. James, *Principles of Psychology* [1890] (Dover, New York, 1950), vol. I, p. 185.

must not confuse the ability to *say* how things are with us with the ability to *see* how things are with us.

Int. But now it looks as though you are denying that we have any experiences. I mean, surely it is by looking into, or if you don't like the word 'looking', then it is by *apprehending* what is *in the mind* that we can say with confidence, indeed with certainty, that we are having such-and-such an experience?

PMSH. Oh, come now, you are getting irritable! I never even intimated that we don't see and hear, feel tired or in pain, get excited and feel passions. The moot question, however, is why we are prone, when thinking about these problems, to suppose that our experiences are *in the mind*. After all, when I see something, what I see is not in the mind but in the room, the street or the field. And my seeing what I see does not take place *in my mind* either – although it may take place in the room or outside in the open. So why are we inclined to conceive of the mind as 'populated' with perceptible experiences?

One reason is doubtless because of the phenomenon of mental imagery. For we can conjure up visual images in our imagination or in our memory. And we can talk to ourselves in the imagination, just as we can vividly recollect how Brendel played the 'Moonlight Sonata'. But to visualize something is not to see anything, and to rehearse a tune in the imagination is not to hear anything. If I imagine Brendel playing louder than he actually did, that does not mean that it sounded louder in my reproductive imagination than it did in the concert hall. It means that if I hear a recording of his performance, I should say: 'I thought he played that passage louder.'

Int. All right. I see what you mean, and it seems reasonable. But what about Nicholas Humphrey's claim that introspection is a crucial step in the evolution of higher species – that it is what explains how animals can socialize and cooperate. *Now that is science, not philosophy.* I don't see how your grammatical nit-picking can gainsay evolutionary theory.

PMSH. Now calm down. I don't know why you are getting so upset. First of all, my grammatical descriptions are not nit-picking; they are reminding you of the way *you* use the expressions that are pivotal to the arguments we are examining. Second, Humphrey's claims are not science at all; they are just conceptual confusions that are introduced into scientific writing in the guise of a plausible hypothesis. Now my contention is not that the hypothesis is not actually plausible but implausible. That is not my point at all. What I am suggesting is that it is not a hypothesis at all, because a hypothesis, plausible or implausible, must *make sense*. And Humphrey's hypothesis that nature came up with a faculty of introspection to facilitate animal communication and cooperation is a conceptual confusion, not an implausible empirical hypothesis.

Int. I don't see why you say that. It seems to me to be a very plausible hypothesis, and I can't understand why you say it doesn't make sense!

PMSH. Oh, then I have been going too quickly. I'm sorry. Look, contrary to what Nicholas Humphrey suggested, the ability *to say* or indeed just *to think* how things are with us, to say or think 'It hurts', 'I'm frightened', 'I want a drink' is not something nature came up with in evolutionary development of animals, but something *we* came up with in the social development of language.

To be sure, social animals, such as elephants, meerkats or chimpanzees, are sensitive to the feelings of other animals in their social group – *but not on the basis of their ability to introspect*, since genuine introspection, as we shall see in a moment, *presupposes mastery of a language*. Nor can such social animals apprehend the feelings of other animals of their kind on the basis of their own ability to say how things are with them, since, with the exception of human beings, *they cannot say how things are with them*. The evolution of empathy, on the one hand, and awareness of emotions and purposes, on the other, is not to be explained in terms of the construction of theories of any kind. Animals are not in the theory-constructing business. And small children do not respond to their mother's love because of infantile theories based on their own introspective knowledge. They have no introspective knowledge, and they have a very long way to go before they can begin to theorize about anything.

Incidentally, the empirical psychologists' 'theory-theory' account of children's slowly growing appreciation of what others think and feel is a non-starter too, and the invocation of deficiency in the child's ability to construct such a theory is not an explanation of autism, but merely a misleading redescription of it. This will be discussed in Lecture 13.

Let me break off the discussion in order to pull the threads together. Of course, there is such a thing as introspection, and there are introspective people. In one sense, the introspective person is someone who reflects on himself, his character, his moods and feelings, his springs of action and his attitudes. He thinks about his reasons for doing what he has done, wonders about his motivation and probes the rationale of his attitudes. And, of course, one cannot think about, wonder about or probe such things without having the *concepts* of reasons, motivations and attitudes. In this sense, *introspection is a form of reflexive thought*, not of perception. Some people, such as Marcel Proust, are better at introspective reflection and its articulation than others. In this sense, introspection is a route to self-knowledge and self-understanding, even if it is one beset with the perils of self-deception.

To be sure, there is such a thing as *self-knowledge*. But it is not exhibited in saying what sensations one has, what one seems to see or hear, that one is feeling cheerful or irritable. Doubtless, the ability to say how things are with one is integral to one's capacity for self-knowledge, but in itself it is not a manifestation of self-knowledge at all. That a child has learnt to say that he has hurt his finger, that he is hungry or tired, that he thought he heard Daddy upstairs does not mean that he has begun to achieve *any* self-knowledge. To do that, the child would, precociously, have to discern his own character traits and reflect on them, come to understand his motives, reflect on the reasons for his likings and dislikings and the rationales for his passions.

There is a second sense of 'introspection'. In this sense, introspection is not a form of reflection but of attention – to one's current emotional state, one's sensations and feelings. One may attend to the waxing and waning of a pain in the course of the afternoon, perhaps in order to be able to report back to the doctor. Jack may attend to the changes in his feelings for Jill, noting perhaps that he is no longer excited at her coming, no longer so eager to listen to her views and no longer so taken with her smile. But that is not a matter of *perceiving* or *observing* one's emotions and attitudes; it is a matter of taking note of them and paying attention to them. *Self-observation*, one might say, is not really a kind of observing.

Consciousness and Awareness: Wittgenstein's Elucidations

So, we have dealt with introspection. Now we must, together with our interlocutor friend, probe our natural inclination to invoke consciousness in place of perception to explain our knowledge of how things are currently with us within our minds.

> **Int.** Yes. I can see that it was a mistake to invoke introspection as a form of inner perception. But surely, we are all *conscious* of how things are with us – that is how we *know* that we are seeing or hearing, feeling pain or pleasure and so on. And since only *I* can be conscious of my pain, or my seeing or my feelings, *only I can really know* how things are inwardly with me. I mean ... *you* can't be conscious of my pains, only I can, and you can't be conscious of my seeing, only I can. So even if Humphrey is misusing the term 'introspection', still, he is absolutely right. What nature came up with was *consciousness*. We, and all the higher animals, are *conscious* of our experiences.

PMSH. I think not. Now you are misconstruing the concept of consciousness no less than you were previously misconstruing the concept of introspection.

Int. But surely you aren't denying that when I have a pain, I am conscious of it. I mean, *I can't have a pain and not be aware of it!*

PMSH. No, you can't. I quite agree with that.

Int. So you agree that if someone were to say 'I had a dreadful pain, but I was not aware of it' or 'I had a frightful toothache, but I was not conscious of it', we should remonstrate that this is impossible.

PMSH. Yes, I agree.

Int. And do you agree that if you have a dreadful pain, then you *must* be aware of it; you can't have a frightful toothache and not be conscious of it?

PMSH. Yes, I agree to that too. But this statement is not an empirical generalization based on the observation of innumerable cases of dreadful pain, *all* of which were accompanied by awareness and consciousness of the pain. It is simply a grammatical statement that excludes a form of words from use, namely the words: 'to have a pain and to be unaware of it'. 'I had a pain, but I was unaware of it' is nonsense. We have no use for this form of words.

By the same token, 'I had a pain and I *was* aware of it' is nonsense too – for the negation of a nonsense is a nonsense. For *to have a pain, to be aware of a pain* and *to be conscious of a pain* are the very same thing – just as *having a pain* and *feeling a pain* are the very same thing. One cannot have a pain and not feel it. But this is not because one's sense of feeling is so good, but because *to feel a pain* is not to exercise one's sense of feeling (one's tactile perception) at all. To feel a pain is unlike 'to feel a pin'. One can seem to feel a pin in the cushion, even though there is not one there, and there may be a pin there, although when one felt for it, one felt nothing. But pains are not like pins, and feeling a pain is not a form of tactile perception. One cannot have a pain and not feel it and one cannot feel a pain and not have one. That is not an empirical truth. Nor is it a metaphysical one – since there are no metaphysical truths – only metaphysical confusions. It is simply a proposition about what it makes sense to say.

Int. All right. But how does that bear on being conscious of having a pain?

PMSH. Well, it follows that one cannot argue that *I* am conscious or aware of my pain as no one else can be, and therefore *I know* that I have a pain in a way in which no one else can know this. For, on the one hand, to be aware or conscious of pain just *is* to have a pain. And, on the other hand, other people – such as the nurses in the hospital who are caring for me – are aware of my suffering and are certainly conscious of the fact that I am in pain. They show their awareness in their solicitude, in the care with which they move me and in their concern for me.

Int. But surely, they can't be conscious of my pain!

PMSH. But surely they can! If you want to deny that another person can be conscious of your pain, you must ask yourself what exactly you are *excluding*. That is, what would it be for someone else to be conscious of your pain? What is the impossibility that you are excluding?

Int. Well, to be conscious of my pain, he'd have to have my pain.

PMSH. Now we're going round in circles. We have already agreed that he *can* have exactly the same pain as you.

Int. Yes, but *that* would not make him conscious of my pain. He might not even know that we both have the same pain.

PMSH. Of course not. So what *would* count as his being conscious of your pain? Isn't it obvious that it is simply that he should be aware of your being in pain – that is what it *means* for one person to be conscious of another person's suffering. And there is nothing problematic about that.

Knowing That One Is in Pain: Wittgenstein's Elucidations

Now let's turn to the curious sentence 'I know I'm in pain'. Or, more generally, 'I know I think, believe, fear that such-and-such', or 'I know that I want, hope, intend to do so-and-so'. According to Wittgenstein, the utterance 'I know I have a pain' is either just an emphatic or concessive assertion that I am indeed in pain or – in the philosophical context in which one is likely to encounter the utterance – philosophers' nonsense.

There is nothing wrong, in appropriate circumstances, with saying 'I know I am in pain', but it is not what the philosophical tradition takes it to be. It is not the expression of an item of indubitable first-person subjective knowledge. So too, there is nothing wrong with the utterance 'I know what I think'; it could be the expression of *having come to a conclusion* on whether things are thus-and-so. For unlike 'I don't know what he thinks', 'I don't know what I think' is not a confession of ignorance. It is a confession of lack of any well-formed opinion. And to remedy things what I need to do is not to 'introspect' in order to observe my own thought on the subject at hand, but rather *to examine the evidence* for and against the matter in question and *come to a conclusion*. Similarly, 'I don't know what I want' is altogether unlike 'I don't know what she wants'. But that is not because I have to find out what I want by examining *what is going on in my mind*. Rather it is because I need *to reflect on the merits of options available to me*, and *to make a decision*.

Because we do use the verb 'to know' in these ways, we are inclined to think that we are in the same ball-game as when using such sentences as 'I know that he is in pain' or 'I know what she thinks'. And then we extend the courtesy to such sentences as 'I know that I am in pain' and 'I know how things seem to me to be' and think that they are expressions of indubitable knowledge. It is *this* illusion, which lies at the root of foundational theories of knowledge, that Wittgenstein is trying to undermine. It is important to realize that *he is not legislating on linguistic usage*. He is pointing out that the use of such sentences does not belong to the language-game to which it seems to belong. There is nothing at all wrong with saying 'I know what I think, but I'm not going to tell you' or 'I know what I want, but it is a secret' – all they amount to is 'I do think something, but I am not going to tell you what I think' and 'I do actually want something, but I won't tell you what'. What is wrong is to suppose that such utterances belong to a class of utterances about subjective experiences that form the basis of all *empirical knowledge* and the *analogical basis for theorizing about other people's experiences.* Wittgenstein nicely remarked:

> If I say 'This statement has no sense', I could just point out statements with which we are inclined to mix it up, and point out the difference. This is all that is meant. – If I say 'It seems to convey something and doesn't', this comes to 'it seems to be of this kind, and isn't'. This statement becomes senseless only if you try to compare it with what you can't compare it with. What is wrong is to overlook the difference.[7]

If we take 'I know I am in pain', 'I know what I think' or 'I know that it seems to me just as if I were seeing a dagger' as being akin to 'I know he is in pain', 'I know what he thinks' and 'I know that it seems to him just as if he were seeing a dagger', *then* we are crossing two different language games. And the result is nonsense. Remember that it doesn't follow from the fact that one is playing a game on a chessboard and has a king on the board that one is playing chess – it may be draughts.

To clinch the argument, we should note the logical conditions for an epistemic use of the verb 'to know' as affixed to a humdrum, common-or-garden, empirical sentence to make sense. I will mention five conditions:

(i) 'A knows that things are thus-and-so' makes sense only if it *excludes the genuine possibility* of A's being *ignorant* of whether things are thus-and-so. So, for example, 'A knows that the sun is shining' makes sense, and so too does 'A doesn't know that the sun is shining'. For A might well be ignorant of what it's like outside. That possibility is excluded by A's *knowing*

---

7 Wittgenstein, 'The Language of Sense-Data and Private Experience' [1936], edited by Rush Rhees, repr. in J. C. Klagge and A. Nordman, eds. *Ludwig Wittgenstein: Philosophical Occasions 1912-1951* (Hackett, Indianapolis, 1993), p. 359.

that the sun is shining. Part of the information that is conveyed by telling someone that A knows such-and-such is that A is *not* ignorant of the relevant fact. But if it is *logically impossible* for A to be ignorant, if it *makes no sense* to say that A is ignorant of such-and-such, then what information *could* be conveyed by saying that he knows? There is, so to speak, nothing to exclude!

(ii) If 'A knows that things are thus-and-so' makes sense, then 'A believes (suspects, guesses, surmises) that things are thus-and-so' also *make sense*. So, for example, it makes sense to say that Jill knows that Jack is in pain. And, as we have just observed, it also makes sense for Jill *not to know this*. But if it is possible for Jill to know this, and also possible for her not to know it, then it must also be possible for Jill to believe, suspect, guess or surmise that Jack is in pain. In general, what one can know to be so is also what one might believe, suspect, guess or surmise to be so.

(iii) If 'A knows that things are thus-and-so' makes sense, then the sentences 'A doubts whether things are thus-and-so' and 'A is certain that things are thus-and-so' must also make sense. It makes sense to say that Jack knows that Jill is in pain, and obviously it *makes sense* to say that Jack doubts whether Jill is in pain, and that Jack is certain that Jill is in pain. In general, what we know to be so is also what we can be certain to be so, and what we might, in appropriate circumstances, doubt to be so.

(iv) If 'A knows that things are thus-and-so' makes sense, then 'A thinks he knows that things are thus-and-so, but he is mistaken' must make sense too. So, for example, it makes sense to say that A knows that it is going to rain tomorrow. And so too, it makes sense to say that A *thinks* that he knows that it will rain tomorrow (and, of course, he may be right or wrong). Similarly, 'It *seems* to A that things are thus-and-so, but he is mistaken' must make sense too.

(v) If 'A knows that things are so' makes sense, then 'A satisfies himself that things are so' and 'A verifies, confirms, that things are so' must, other things being equal, make sense too. So, for example, it makes sense to say that Jack knows that it rained yesterday, and it also makes sense to say that he verified, confirmed or satisfied himself that it rained yesterday.

All these conditions hold for knowing that *another person* is in pain, thinks, hopes, fears, wants or intends. For I may *not* know whether Jack is in pain. I may guess, suspect, surmise, or believe that he is, and I can often satisfy myself, verify or confirm that he is (or is not) in pain. Thinking Jack a malingerer, I may doubt whether he is in pain; or, seeing Jack screaming in evident agony, I may be certain that he is in pain. I may think that I know he is in pain, but be wrong – for, unbeknownst to me, he may be pretending. It may seem to me that he is in pain, and yet I may be mistaken.

So far, so good. Now let us look at the problematic sentence 'I know that *I* am in pain'. Does it belong to the same language-game as assertions of knowledge? Does it satisfy the five conditions that we have just elaborated for the intelligible use of 'I know' when applied to ordinary empirical sentences? Clearly, we have no use for a first-person confession of ignorance. If we were to ask Jack whether he is in pain and he were to reply, 'I don't know', we should not understand what he was trying to tell us. It makes no sense to assert that Jack is in pain, but luckily for him, he doesn't know he is. Could we imagine circumstances in which we could *informatively* impart to him the knowledge that he is in pain? 'Do you realize that you are in dreadful pain' is an utterance without a use – that is, a senseless form of words. But that is *not* because when one is in pain one *always knows* that one is. On the contrary, it is because it *makes no sense* to be in pain and *to be ignorant that one is* that it also makes no sense to know that one is in pain. For there can be no knowledge where *ignorance* is *logically* ruled out anyway. If *there is no such thing* as ignorance of whether one is in pain, there is nothing for *knowledge* to exclude.

So, 'I know I am in pain' is, as Wittgenstein said, either just an emphatic assertion that one is in pain, or else it is philosophers' nonsense. Similarly, we have no use for such sentences as 'I believe, think, guess, surmise, that I am in pain'. One cannot intelligibly say 'I think I am in pain, but I am not sure. Let's try to find out'. So too, there is no such thing as being in pain and doubting whether one is. If someone were to say 'I am a notorious malingerer, so I doubt whether I am in pain' we should take him to be joking. The sentence 'I doubt whether I am in pain' is not false but nonsense. For doubt is *logically* excluded here. And precisely because doubt is *logically* excluded, so too is certainty. For, again, if there is no such thing as doubting that one is in pain, then there is nothing for certainty to exclude. 'I'm sure that I am in pain' and 'I'm certain I'm in pain, but of course, I may be wrong' are surely nonsense. We labour under an understandable illusion here, for we mistake *the categorical absence of doubt* for *the presence of complete certainty*. Whereas in fact *both* doubt *and* certainty are *grammatically excluded*. Further, it cannot *seem* to me that I am in pain, even though I am not. There is no such thing as being mistaken over whether one is feeling a pain. The role of the phrase 'it seems to me' is to qualify an utterance, typically when one thinks that things may not be as they appear to be. But such a qualification has no place in such utterances as 'I am in pain'. For there is no such thing as *its seeming to me as if* I were in pain, even though I am not.

So, Wittgenstein has made a very powerful case for his claim that 'I know that I am in pain' is philosopher's nonsense. Still, there are objections to his account. I want to mention three just to show that they rest on the very mistake that Wittgenstein was keen to eradicate:

- First, one might worry about the following point: I can and often do know that another person, my wife say, knows that I have a headache (after all, I truthfully told her that I do). But can I know that another person knows something without myself knowing what they know? If I know that you know that the battle of Hastings was fought in 1066, then surely I too must know that it was fought in 1066! So if I know that my wife knows that I am in pain, then surely I too must know that I am in pain!

  That seems, at first glance, a good objection to Wittgenstein. But note that the condition 'without myself knowing what she knows, namely that I am in pain' *presupposes* that it makes sense for me to know that I am in pain – which is precisely what is at issue. In fact, when I know that another knows such-and-such, what is logically excluded is that I be *ignorant* of what they know. And of course, in this case I am not *ignorant of my being in pain* – for ignorance is no less excluded by grammar than knowledge. It is *senseless* to say that I am ignorant of my being in pain, and by the same token, it is *senseless* to say that I know that I am in pain.

- A second, initially persuasive objection is this: it surely makes sense for me to remember that I was in pain yesterday. But memory is knowledge retained. To remember something is to know it now *because one knew it previously*. So, if I remember that I was in pain, then I know now that I was in pain, and I know that now because I knew it previously. So when I was in pain, I knew I was. Q.E.D.? Well, actually – no! Although this analysis of the proposition 'I remember that *something is thus-and-so*' is attractive, it must not be dogmatically applied. In the case of remembering one's own subjective experiences, the analysis has to be – and can easily be – modified. 'I remember that I was in pain' is to be construed as 'I know now that I was in pain, and I know this now *because I was in pain previously.*' (Not: 'because I previously *knew* that I was in pain' – for that is nonsense).

- A third objection seems similarly convincing. It is easy to imagine circumstances in which I might rightly say that I know that no one in the room is in pain – for example, at a party when everyone is laughing merrily. But if I know that no one in the room is in pain, and I am in the room, does it not follow that I know that I too am not in pain? No! That again presupposes that it makes sense to say that I know I am, or am not, in pain, and hence too that it makes sense to say that I am, or am not, in pain but am ignorant of the fact. But these sentences make no sense. Rather, if I am at the party and am not in pain, and, looking around, I can see that no one else is in pain, then I can rightfully say that I know that no one in the room is in pain, since I am not, and I know that no one else is either.

Other objections can be dealt with similarly.

We may therefore conclude that Wittgenstein has successfully shown that such sentences as 'I know that I am in pain' do not belong to the same language-game as 'I know that he is in pain' and 'He knows that I am in pain'. They do not belong to epistemic language-games. And if one takes them epistemically, one will produce nothing but well-concealed philosophical nonsense. That conclusion applies to a considerable range of the experiential vocabulary. And that is altogether non-trivial. For, among other things, it means that the idea that empirical knowledge rests on the solid and certain grounds of our knowledge of how things perceptually appear to us to be is a non-starter. Although the sentence 'It visually *seems to me* that there is a vase of flowers on the table' makes sense, the sentence 'I *know* (or I am certain) that it visually *seems to me* that there is a vase of flowers on the table' is philosophers' nonsense. For could things seem thus-and-so to me *and I be ignorant of the fact?* But if *there is no such thing* here as ignorance, then there is no such thing as knowledge either. The verb 'to know' has no work to do and no information to convey in this sentential context. Furthermore, sentences of the form 'It perceptually *seems to me* that things are thus-and-so' do not serve to elaborate rock-solid certainties, but to indicate uncertainties. Far from 'It seems to me just as if ...' introducing something certain, it normally functions to indicate that I am *uncertain* whether things are thus-and-so – even though they seem to be.

Privileged Status rather than Privileged Access

I want to conclude by noting an important conceptual truth that is misconstrued by the traditional introspectionist conception of the 'inner'. It is this: the *privileged status* of certain kinds of first-person utterances concerning the speaker's subjective experiences is systematically misrepresented. It is misrepresented by a mistaken *explanation* in terms of *privileged access* to a hidden domain that only its 'owner' can apprehend. But the correct explanation is not epistemological, but logico-grammatical. It is perfectly true that the subject's *word* carries special weight. If the patient sincerely says he is in pain, no doctor can gainsay him. If an observer sincerely says that such-and-such looks thus-and-so to him, no one can rightly say 'No it doesn't'. If someone says that he is feeling in the dumps, no one can licitly reply 'No you're not, your feeling cheerful'. The explanation of the privileged status of a person's avowal of experience is not by reference to a private peepshow that only he can peer into. It is rather that his utterance is an *expression* of the experience he is undergoing.

An avowal of experience is not a description of a private observation of the 'inner'. It is typically *an expression* or *manifestation* of experience – although it may in appropriate circumstances, be *a report*. Such verbal expressions of experience, even if they are reports, enjoy the same grammatical status as natural expressive behaviour – in the following sense. They constitute not *inductive evidence* for the 'inner', but *logically good evidence* – which Wittgenstein called 'criteria'. Pain-behaviour, for example, is not inductive evidence for someone's being in pain – for if it were, we should have had to observe people's pains and their painbehaviour and noted that there is a good inductive correlation between the two. But there is no such thing as observing the pain of another and correlating it with his behaviour.

Of course, in one's own case, one can note that one expresses one's pain in characteristic pain-behaviour. And it has seemed to many philosophers and psychologists that one can extrapolate from this single sample to the rest of humanity. But the objection is not to the smallness of the sample, it is rather that even to note a correlation in one's own case presupposes that *one possesses the concept of pain*. Otherwise, one would not be able to correlate one's own pains with one's behaviour. So the crucial question must be: what, at the end of the day, is requisite for possession of the concept of pain? Here we are naturally inclined to reply – well, surely, one has to *have a pain* and *to associating the word 'pain' with the sensation one has*! Alas, our natural inclination here is to take the wrong turnings in the jungle of grammar and to lose our way. In the next lecture, I shall show how this natural inclination leads us astray.

Chapter 11
PRIVATE OSTENSIVE DEFINITION

The Third Leg of the Three-Legged Stool

The idea that our language is private inasmuch as its words refer to what only the speaker can have and to what only he can know is, as we have already noted, akin to a three-legged stool. Two of these legs – namely the idea of private and inalienable ownership of subjective experience and the idea of private and privileged knowledge of subjective experience – have been shown to be rotten. Today we shall deal with the third leg – private ostensive definition.

We shall focus on the manner in which words signifying subjective experiences, such as 'pain', are supposedly given a meaning by the private linguist. Our critical task is to examine the cogency of the accounts of language and linguistic meaning given by philosophers who assume that words have a meaning by virtue of standing for ideas in the mind or 'internal representations'. Our constructive task is to remind ourselves how words signifying subjective experiences are *actually* used and explained and to give a surveyable representation of this domain of the grammar of our language. We shall touch on this today and discuss it at greater length in the next lecture.

    Int. Before you begin, I would like to ask something.
    PMSH. Yes, by all means. What is worrying you?
    Int. Well, why does Wittgenstein bother to continue? I mean, since he has shown that the first two legs of the three-legged stool of the private language are rotten through and through, as you explained in the last two lectures, why bother with the third leg? I mean, it is already obvious that with the assumptions of private ownership of experience and of epistemic privacy, the putative private language would not be intelligible to anyone other than the speaker. If the words of my language were to refer to things that only I can have, and only I can know of, then *obviously* no one else could understand it! Now that is surely absurd, since the languages we speak are obviously understood by others. The languages of mankind are shared, common languages. So, once it has been shown

that such a language would be radically private, the whole idea should disintegrate and that would be the end of the matter.

PMSH. You are perfectly right. But you must bear in mind the fact that, as we have seen, the typical response to the incommunicability argument is simply *to challenge it* – to insist that after all, there must be something wrong with the thought that if the words of our languages are names of our ideas, then we wouldn't be able to communicate with each other.

Int. Ah, yes. I see. You mean that, at any rate, if the scientists and philosophers are right about the subjectivity of colours, sounds, smells and tastes, as well as tactile qualities, then words *must* be names of ideas. If colours, sounds, smells, tastes, hot and cold and so forth are no more than ideas in our minds, then words for colours, sounds, tastes and all the rest *must* be names of these internal representations.

PMSH. Just so! If the neuroscientists and philosophers in the empiricist tradition are right, then what we are given in experience *are* ideas, sense impressions and internal representations. Such sense data are accordingly the only things that the words of our languages *can* name *directly*. So people persuaded by this *picture* – for that is all it is: *a picture* – will go on to argue as follows: Communication consists in associating words with ideas in my mind, and then using those words to generate the same – the qualitatively identical – ideas in the mind of my hearer. John Locke, in Book III of the *Essay Concerning Human Understanding*, articulated the idea perfectly:

> The chief end of language in communication being to be understood, words serve not well for that end, neither in civil nor in philosophical discourse, when any word does not excite in the hearer the same idea it stands for in the mind of the speaker. (III – ix–4)

Communication is accordingly a form of *telementation* – a matter of producing certain ideas in the mind of another.

Int. Yes, I see. So they accept the doctrine of epistemic privacy and privacy of ownership of experience, and nevertheless maintain that we can understand each other's language *despite* not having the same experiences as others and not having access to their experiences.

PMSH. Yes, that's right. They argue that since we can communicate with each other – and that's obviously right – then the twofold privacy cannot be a barrier to communication.

Int. But how can they argue that?

PMSH. Let me remind you. They will insist on trying to apply the distinction between numerical and qualitative identity to experiences – where, as we have seen, it can no more apply than it can to colours

– and they will go on to argue that since we are all members of the same biological species, we are, as they repulsively put it, 'all wired up the same way'. So, they argue, it is a fair bet that what you have when you hit your finger with a hammer will be the qualitatively identical sensation I have when I do so. Communication is arousing in your mind the qualitatively identical ideas that I have in my mind in association with the words of my language.

Int. Yes. I see. So there is just a stand-off!

PMSH. That's right. One side insists on what the other side has shown to be incoherent. That is, defenders of the thought that experience is privately owned and epistemically private back their case by reference to the thought that this is how things *must be* since we *do* succeed in communicating.

Int. You mean that if Wittgenstein were right about privacy, then we wouldn't be able to communicate, but we can communicate, so he must be wrong!

PMSH. Exactly!

Int. So what is to be done? Wittgenstein insists that the dual assumptions about privacy imply a language no one else could understand, and his opponents insist that, despite these assumptions, which still seem wholly compelling to them, we *can* all communicate – which is obvious, since we *do* communicate. So, where do we go from here? How does Wittgenstein prove that a language that refers to what only I can have and only I can know is not a possible means of communication?

PMSH. It is a mark of Wittgenstein's genius that he bypassed this controversy altogether. The really deep issue is not whether such a language could or could not be understood by others – it is whether it could be understood by *the speaker himself*. The central question is whether *I* could understand a language the words of which are names of my own 'private' experiences – my sensations, perceptions, felt desires and emotions, with which no one else is acquainted. If it can be shown that *even the speaker* could not understand such a putative language, then the question of whether others could understand it falls by the wayside – for then it is evident that *there can be no such language*. That is, the imagined language fails to satisfy the logico-grammatical conditions for counting as a language at all. And it is precisely this that Wittgenstein sets out to show.

Naming Private Experiences

This is how Wittgenstein introduces the problem:

> Now, what about the language which describes my inner experience and which only I myself can understand? *How* do I use words to signify my sensations? – As we ordinarily do? Then are my words for sensations tied up with my natural expressions of sensation? In that case my language is not a 'private' one. Someone else might understand it as well as I. – But suppose I didn't have any natural expression of sensation, but only had sensations? And now I simply *associate* names with sensations and use these names in descriptions. (PI §256)

Here two moves are made: First, Wittgenstein reminds us of what he had already noted earlier, namely that in our public language, names of sensations –

> are connected with the primitive, natural, expressions of sensation and used in their place. A child has hurt himself and he cries; then adults talk to him and teach him exclamations and, later, sentences. They teach the child new pain behaviour. (PI §244)

That is how *the connection between name and thing named* is, so to speak, set up here. And that nexus is an integral part of the language game with 'pain'. When human beings injure themselves, fall, bump against things, cut themselves, when they are hit or wounded, they naturally cry out, clutch the injured limb, writhe and groan, and their face is contorted in a characteristic way. It is this kind of natural expressive behaviour, in circumstances of injury or illness, that we *call* 'pain-behaviour', or – less artificially – 'moaning (screaming, writhing) in pain' or 'grimacing with pain'. It is this kind of behaviour, in such circumstances, that *warrants* saying of the person 'He is in pain'. *Acculturated* expressive pain-behaviour includes *verbal* pain-behaviour – exclamations such as 'Ouch!' or 'Ow!', utterances such as 'That hurts' or groaning 'Oh, I have a headache'. The verbal behaviour is integrated into the non-verbal behaviour. If someone avowed that he is in pain, and then stood around laughing and joking, we would take him to be pulling our leg. If someone said, 'I have a dreadful pain in my foot, but I don't mind it' and did not limp but walked as a normal person does, we would not know what he meant and would ask for explanation. A natural manifestation of pain and a pain utterance in appropriate circumstances are reasons for helping the suffering person, and reasons for commiseration. In this, and numerous other related ways, the use of the word 'pain' is bound up with the natural behavioural expression of pain.

Second, Wittgenstein emphasizes that according to philosophers who in effect (and often unwittingly) advance the conception of a private language, the concept of pain and concepts of experience in general are *logically detached* from all behavioural manifestation. For names of experiences are conceived to stand for the experiences themselves, to which the subject has privileged access, of which he has private knowledge and of which he is the sole and inalienable owner. So how, in *this* case, are we to envisage the words being connected to the experiences that they supposedly signify? 'Well', Wittgenstein replies for the private linguist, 'I simply *associate* names with sensations, and use these names in descriptions'.

Notice how Wittgenstein links the idea of a private language with the Augustinian conception of meaning. According to this conception, the fundamental role of words is to name objects, and the fundamental role of sentences is to describe how things are. So, it should be unsurprising that the first point Wittgenstein addresses here is the very idea of *naming* a sensation.

> But what does it mean to say that he has 'named his pain'? – How has he managed this naming of pain? And whatever he did, what was its purpose? – When one says 'He gave a name to his sensation', one forgets that much must be prepared in the language for mere naming to make sense. And if we speak of someone's giving a name to a pain, the grammar of the word 'pain' is what has been prepared here; it indicates the post where the new word is stationed. (PI §257)

This remark harkens back to Wittgenstein's discussion of naming and of ostensive definition, which we examined earlier. Let me remind you of the salient points.

Naming is a preparation for the use of language. Recall for a moment Wittgenstein's favourite analogy between speaking a language and playing a game. Giving a piece in a game a name or explaining the name of a piece achieves next to nothing, unless it is clear what game we are speaking of, and how this piece is to be moved in the context of this game. So too in the case of giving names to things in general and explaining their names. We can point at a person and say, 'That's Jack', point at an object and say, 'That's a table', point at a colour and say, 'That's red'. If our ostensive explanation is to be understood, then the first case, 'That's Jack', must be understood *as giving a person's name*, that is, it is to be used in introducing him, calling him, addressing him, talking to him, attributing responsibility to him, accusing him, congratulating him and so forth. The second case, 'That's a table' must be understood as *giving the name of an artefact* – it has no use in introducing the thing, calling it, addressing it, talking to it, since we don't introduce inanimate things to people, we don't call or address them. The name of an artefact is used in quite different but equally distinctive language games. The word 'table' is employed in telling people to set the table, or in telling them that something is on the table or that this table is a Sheraton, or in asking someone to polish the table or move it, or in buying or selling tables. In the case of the word 'red', we are introducing *a colour word*, not the name of a person or of an artefact. And it is integrated into an altogether different, although often overlapping array of language games – of asking for something to be painted red, of expressing a desire for a red so-and-so, of describing things as being red, of identifying a thing as the red so-and-so, of inferring that this thing is darker than the pink one we saw yesterday and so forth.

So, the place in grammar for the word 'pain' has to be prepared before it can even make sense to give the sensation of pain a name. For names of such sensations are names of what sentient creatures suffer from; such sensations have a somatic location, wax and wane, have phenomenal qualities such as stabbing, burning, throbbing, nagging and so forth. They are ascribed to people on the grounds of pain-behaviour. They are self-ascribed without any grounds at all – my saying that I am in pain does not rest on any evidence. And a pain utterance is itself a *manifestation* of pain (whereas a colour ascription is not a manifestation of colour, and the identification of a table is not a form of complaint). So, *one* difficulty for the private language theorist is that the mere idea of *giving a name to a sensation or experience* is far more problematic than it seems *in the context of naming something that only the speaker has and only he knows about*. We think that to name a sensation requires no more than

> pronouncing the name while one has the sensation and possibly concentrating on the sensation, – but what of it? Does this name thereby get magic powers? And why on earth do I call these sounds the name of a sensation? I know what I do with the name of a man or a number, but have I by this act of 'definition' given the name a use?
>
> 'To give a sensation a name' means nothing unless I know already in what sort of game this name is to be used. (LPE 240)

So much for the first criticism, which concerns the very idea of naming.

The second major critical point concerns the idea of association and definition. Wittgenstein introduces this by means of the following passage:

> Let's imagine the following case. I want to keep a diary about the recurrence of a certain sensation. To this end I associate it with the sign 'S' and write this sign in a calendar for every day on which I have the sensation. – I first want to observe that a definition of the sign cannot be formulated. – But all the same, I can give one to myself as a kind of ostensive definition! – How? Can I point to the sensation? – Not in the ordinary sense. But I speak, or write the sign down, and at the same time I concentrate my attention on the sensation – and so, as it were, point to it inwardly. – But what is this ceremony for? For that is all it seems to be! A definition serves to lay down the meaning of a sign, doesn't it? – Well, that is done precisely by concentrating my attention; for in this way I commit to memory the connection between the sign and the sensation. – But 'I commit it to memory' can only mean: this process brings it about that I remember the connection *correctly* in the future. But in the present case, I have no criterion of correctness. One would like to say: whatever is going to seem correct to me is correct. And that only means that here we can't talk about 'correct'. (PI §258)

The natural thought of the defender of the idea of a private language, and of anyone who is moving in the force-field of the Augustinian conception of meaning, is to suppose that words are connected to the world by means of ostensive definitions. Ostensive definitions seem to *pin* language to reality. It is the gesture of pointing at the item one intends to name and meaning *that very thing* while one utters the sentence 'That is S', which seemingly makes 'S' the name of that thing. Isn't it the same in the case of words signifying a subjective experience – be it a sensation, a colour impression, a mood or emotion? There surely seems to be a perfectly intelligible mental analogue of a public ostensive definition in which one points at a sample and says, 'That's indigo' or 'That's a table'. The only differences, it *seems*, are

that in this case the sample is a mental one, a sensation or an impression in the mind,

and

that there is here no pointing with one's finger.

But there *seems* to be a surrogate for pointing, namely focussing one's attention on the sensation one is naming and *meaning* it.

Well, the road to philosophical perdition is paved with *seeming* stones. So we must walk very carefully! We must examine two things. First, whether there is a private analogue of pointing. That is straightforward. Second, whether a sensation can fulfil the function of a sample in an ostensive definition. That is much more complicated and subtle.

Private Ostensive Definition and Mental Samples

So, first, is there a private analogue of pointing at a thing when giving a public ostensive definition? Let's include our friendly interlocutor in the discussion.

> **Int.** Good. Well, why can't the private linguist point at his pain when he is explaining to himself what he means by the word 'pain', or even when he is giving the word 'pain' a meaning?
>
> **PMSH.** But look, he can't literally point to his pain with his finger. The most he could do would be to point to the *place* that hurts – but that is not the pain.
>
> **Int.** No, no – of course not. I don't mean that he should point at his pain with his finger. What I mean is that it is easy to think of an internal surrogate for pointing, namely: *concentrating one's attention on one's pain*. Or *meaning one's pain* by the word 'this' when saying 'That is pain' or 'This is what is to be called "pain"'. Isn't that just like pointing? When one gives a public ostensive definition, say of a colour word like 'magenta', one points at an object, says 'That's magenta', and *means* the colour. Isn't

it like that in the case of the word 'pain'? Can't the private linguist just concentrate on his pain and *mean* that sensation?

PMSH. No! In a public ostensive definition, one *can* point at an object, say a piece of fruit, and say, 'That is S' and mean its shape, or its colour, or its taste and so forth – but *only* if one already *has the concepts* of a shape, or a colour or a taste. For it is they that determine the grammatical place of the word one is introducing. But the private linguist may not presuppose the concept of sensation, for that too is a concept in a public language that is essentially bound up with behaviour. So, he could mean the sensation only if he already possessed the concept of sensation. But in so far as he conceives of sensations as epistemically private and privately owned, the very same question arises for the explanation of the meaning of the word 'sensation'. Anyway, meaning something by a word is not a kind of pointing, but a kind of intending.

Int. But that's just what I said. Why can't he *intend*, that is, *mean*, his sensation?

PMSH. Because you can mean one thing as opposed to another *only if you possess the concept of the things in question*. But here we are trying to explain how the very concept is acquired and mastered, and we cannot presuppose its possession.

So far, so good. But this does not go *very* deep.

Int. All right. I see that there isn't much of an analogy between outer pointing and inner attending. I suppose that one is readily misled by the fact that outer attending, that is directing one's attention, in particular one's gaze, can function as a kind of pointing. For if one's outer attending is rather like pointing, then why should one's inner attending not be so too.

PMSH. Excellent. I'm sure you have put your finger on one of the features that lead us down the garden path here.

Int. Right. But let's look at something else here. Public ostensive definition, Wittgenstein taught, commonly involves the use of a sample. A coloured slip of paper on a colour chart functions as a public sample of a given colour. And a metre rule functions as a public sample of a metre length. Now why shouldn't a sensation function as a *mental sample* in a manner analogous to that in which a colour patch on a colour chart or a metre rule function as public samples? Why can't we explain the meaning of a sensation word like 'pain' or any other name of an experience by reference to a private sample?

PMSH. Well, we must examine the logical or logico-grammatical conditions that something has to satisfy in order to count as a sample. You remember that a sample in a public ostensive definition fulfils a function in *explaining the meaning of the word being defined*. It also commonly fulfils the function of *an object of comparison* that can, and often does, play a role in the technique of applying the defined word. Furthermore, something *can* fulfil the role of a sample only if it *can be used again* (think of colour samples, or samples of fabric or carpet or samples of length such as rulers and tape measures) or alternatively *if it is readily reproducible* (think of sample sounds produced by a tuning fork, or smells and tastes produced by determinate substances). In short, something *can be* a sample only if it *satisfies the conditions* for being a sample, and something *is* a sample only if it is *used* as a sample.

Int. Wait a moment. Have I got that right? Something that fulfils the role of a sample if (a) it's used to explain the meaning of the expression it defines, (b) it can fulfil the role of an object of comparison, and (c) it can be used again on a later occasion, or at least can be reproduced in a regular and reliable manner. Is that right?

PMSH. That's perfect. Now, bearing these three points in mind, let's see whether something like a pain, a tickle, the experience of seeing something red, a feeling of joy or of sorrow could fulfil the role of a sample. The first objection to the idea of private mental samples that might play a role in private ostensive definitions is that they would not *persist*.

Int. Oh, that seems pretty trivial. Why can't one simply remember mental samples.

PMSH. Indeed. They would have to be 'stored', so to speak, in one's memory and conjured up in one's reproductive imagination when needed. It is striking that Locke nicely sketched this idea in a passage that I've already mentioned to you:

> Such precise naked appearances in the mind, without considering how, whence, or with what others they came there, the understanding lays up (with names commonly annexed to them) as standards to rank existences into sorts, as they agree with these patterns, and to denominate them accordingly. (II-xi-9)

Int. Well, doesn't that make sense?

PMSH. It is very interesting that Wittgenstein, despite never having read Locke, wrote:

> One cannot take the image [idea] as a sample, for it would be like a sample that will be destroyed and so is of no use. But a memory can help me only in so far as it is ratified as 'memory'. (MS 119, 134r)

Int. I don't understand. What does he have in mind?

PMSH. The point is a difficult one. So concentrate hard. Suppose that I have an experience, any experience – a Something, and denominate it

'S' and then, as it were, file away this Something in my memory – my storehouse of ideas. In short – I commit the sample to memory. What now has to fulfil the function of the defining sample is *a mnemonic representation* of the Something I had, by reference to which I gave a meaning to the sign 'S'. 'I commit it to memory' has to mean: I remember *correctly* the connection between the sign 'S' and the S-experience (the Something). But, Wittgenstein objected, *I have no criterion of correctness* for remembering the meaning of 'S'. That is, if I try, so to say, to recollect what I associated with the sign 'S', then *whatever mental image comes to mind* is right. If I press the key 'S' on my mnemonic cash register, as it were, then a label pops up. But there is no determinant of what is to count as the right label. For *whatever seems to me right* is right – and that means there is no such thing as right.

Int. I don't see that. I mean, why shouldn't I just remember what sample I previously named 'S'? Is Wittgenstein worried about memory scepticism?

PMSH. No, no, that is *not* the point. He is not the slightest bit worried about defects of memory, let alone about the absurdities of scepticism about memory. But one can *recognize, re-cognize*, only what one previously *cognized*. One can remember only if there is something *to* remember. What am I being called on to remember here?

Int. Well, I have to remember what I named 'S', that is, what *sample* I introduced in a private explanation of what 'S' means.

PMSH. Exactly, and the moot question is whether in going through this ceremony I did indeed succeed in naming *anything* S. After all, there is more to naming than concentrating one's attention and making a noise. If I go out into the garden on a summer's night, gaze at the Moon and make the sound 'Oo-oo-woo', I have not named the Moon!

Int. Well, I grant you that. But surely all I have to do is *undertake to use the sign 'S' in the same way again*!

PMSH. Yes. That is what one is tempted to say. But now ask yourself: what is to count as the *same way*. After all, you haven't yet introduced *a way of using* 'S'! You have merely made the sound 'S' and had a mental image or representation at the same time, on which you focussed your attention. But that does not introduce a way of using the sign 'S', nor does it provide a criterion for using 'S' correctly.

Int. I vaguely see what you are driving at; but only vaguely. Can you elaborate?

PMSH. All right. Note two important points. First, Wittgenstein's exclusive concern is with *the meaning of the sign 'S'* – not with the putative empirical judgement that he has S again. Let me explain.

The judgement that one has S again *presupposes* the meaning of the sign 'S'. But our question comes in earlier than making judgements *with* the sign 'S'. For our concern is whether 'S' has been given a meaning at all. Wittgenstein hammers home this point in a justly famous passage about a dictionary in the imagination:

> Let us imagine a table – something like a dictionary – that exists only in our imagination. A dictionary can be used to justify the translation of a word X by a word Y. But are we also to call it a justification if such a table is to be looked up only in the imagination? – 'Well, yes; then it is a subjective justification.' – But justification consists in appealing to an independent authority – 'But surely I can appeal from one memory to another. For example, I don't know if I have remembered the time of departure of a train correctly and to check it I call to mind how a page of the time-table looked. Isn't this the same sort of case?' No; for this procedure must now actually call forth the *correct* memory. If the mental image of the time-table could not itself be *tested* for correctness, how could it confirm the correctness of the first memory? (As if someone were to buy several copies of today's morning paper to assure himself that what it said was true.)
>
> Looking up a table in the imagination is no more looking up a table than the image of the result of an imagined experiment is the result of an experiment. (PI §265)

Clearly the mental dictionary is supposedly akin to a private chart of samples correlated with names.

Int. Absolutely. That is exactly what I meant. If there can be public physical charts (such as colour charts), surely there can be private mental charts too! Concentrating one's attention on a private sensation, meaning by the name 'S' that very sensation, and then storing this private sample in memory is *surely* the mental analogue of making a table of samples!

PMSH. No! That makes *no* sense. Justification, Wittgenstein explains, consists in appealing to something independent – otherwise 'whatever is going to seem right to me is right. And that means that here we can't talk about right'. The intelligibility of appealing to memory presupposes that something *counts* as remembering *correctly*.

Int. But we *can* appeal from one memory to another. As in Wittgenstein's example of checking my memory that the first train to London after lunch is the 13.42 by calling up my memory of what the timetable looked like. So why does he say that we can't do so in the case of the remembered sample of 'S'?

PMSH. Think carefully now! In the case of the railway timetable, the mnemonic image of the timetable can have a confirmatory role precisely because it is an image of something objective and can itself be tested for correctness. Here there is a manifest difference between remembering correctly and remembering incorrectly.

Int. Yes, exactly. But isn't there a manifest difference in the case of remembering the meaning of 'S'? After all, all the private linguist has to do is call to mind the same sensation S! I don't see the problem!

PMSH. That is because you are tacitly presupposing precisely what you have to prove. You are assuming that the private linguist already has the concept of S, that he already knows what the word 'S' means. But that is precisely what is being questioned. After all, this procedure of private mental definition is supposed to explain how the concept of S is introduced – *so it cannot presuppose the concept of S as given.*

Int. I don't see why you say that the concept of S is being presupposed.

PMSH. It is being presupposed because you have to appeal, as indeed you did, to the notion of *the same sensation.* That requires *criteria of identity* for sensation S – and criteria of identity are precisely what are supplied by the grammar of the word 'S', which has not yet been determined.

Int. Oh yes! Now I see. That's why Wittgenstein says that there is no difference between being right and seeming to be right – between remembering what 'S' means and mis-remembering what 'S' means.

PMSH. Exactly. In the case of the dictionary that exists *only* in the imagination, as in the private diarist's case, there is no such distinction. The private diarist endeavours to remember what a word means *only* by reference to his memory of what it means. There is here no *possibility* of an appeal to something independent. So nothing *counts* as correct *or* incorrect. That is why it is like buying a second copy of the *Times* to check what is written in the first copy of the same newspaper. As Wittgenstein concludes: the balance on which impressions are weighed cannot be the impression of a balance.

Int. So the issue is really not one of fallibility of human memory at all.

PMSH. No. To the extent that our memories are fallible – which they are, that is something we live with in the case of a public language too. His point does *not concern memory scepticism* about the meanings of words. It is rather a demand for the intelligibility of a distinction between remembering correctly and remembering incorrectly what a word means. Wittgenstein elucidated the matter thus:

> I cannot remind myself in my private language that this was the sensation I called 'red'. There is no question of my memory's playing me a trick – because (in such a case) there can be no criterion for its playing me a trick. If we lay down rules for the use of colour-words in ordinary language, then we can admit that memory plays tricks regarding these rules.[1]

---

1 Wittgenstein, 'The Language of Sense Data and Private Experience', p. 8 (Klagge and Nordmann, p. 296).

So, let me sum up thus far. The private linguist must be able to give a meaning to the words of his putative language, and must be able to explain, at any rate to himself, what he means by his words. The way in which he envisages doing this is by linking words to the subjective experiences he has. That connection, it seems to him, must be by way of a private ostensive definition by reference to a private sample – namely an experience that only he has and only he can know of. Wittgenstein's response is that the conditions for an ostensive definition are not met. First, there is no genuine analogue of pointing. Second, an experience does not satisfy the conditions for functioning as an explanatory sample, and the memory of such a putative sample *thus conceived* cannot be either correct or incorrect.

Private Samples Could Not Function as Objects for Comparison

Wittgenstein hints at a third argument against the private linguist's conception. The third argument turns on the idea of the technique of using a word. This is what Wittgenstein wrote:

> In order to establish a name-relation we have to establish a technique of use. And we are misled if we think that it is a peculiar process of christening an object which makes a word a word for an object. This is a kind of superstition. So it's no use saying that we have a private object before the mind and give it a name. There is a name only where there is a technique of using it. – The technique can be private, but this only means that nobody but I knows about it. (MS 166, 165)

So, how does the private linguist think to lay down a technique for using 'S'? Well, Wittgenstein suggests, he 'must inwardly resolve to use the word in such-and-such a way'. But how does he resolve this? Does he *invent* the technique of applying the word (PI §262)? Obviously, he supposes that one can read the grammar of a word off the object the word stands for – as is supposed by the Augustinian conception of language. But we have already seen that this is an egregious misunderstanding.

Thus far Wittgenstein. But I wish to go further. Reflect that something that functions as a sample in the explanation of the meaning of a word is also something that can function as a measure in the application of the word.

Int. Slow down. What do you mean by 'a measure' here?
PMSH. Well, in the case of a colour chart, the sample that defines 'peach-blossom pink', say, also functions as a standard or measure in applying the name 'peach-blossom pink'. We place the sample next to the object we want to describe and look at both for match or mismatch. If the object we want to describe *is* the colour of the sample, then we

describe it as being peach-blossom pink. The possibility of doing this is an integral part of the technique of using this colour word.

Int. Yes, I see. That is rather like using a ruler. If we want to measure the length of an object, we place the ruler next to the object and read the length off the graduating marks on the ruler.

PMSH Absolutely right! This is part of the technique of using expressions for lengths such as 'a metre long'. What is important to note is that a sample must be *capable* of functioning as a standard of comparison for the correct application of the expression it helps to define. And to master the use of that expression, one must grasp the technique of using it – know how it is to be laid alongside reality, so to speak.

Now, let's waive all the previous arguments. Let's suppose that I *do* define the word 'pain' by reference to the sensation in my hand. Let's shelve all our worries about whether there is any difference between remembering the sample correctly and mis-remembering it. The only question I want you to concentrate on is this: *Can we use what I have in my hand to determine whether what I have in my head is correctly to be called 'a pain' or 'a headache'?*

Int. You mean: Is there an analogue here of using the sample as a measure in the way in which we use a colour sample of peach-blossom pink as a measure? In the case of the colour name, we lay the sample alongside the curtains, say, and see whether the curtains match the sample – that is: whether the curtains *are* the colour of the sample. If they are, we say that the curtains are peach-blossom pink.

PMSH. Exactly. And now the question is: Is there an analogue of this in the case of pain?

All right. Let's consider this carefully. I am using my injured hand as a sample of pain, in a manner analogous to that in which I use a piece of card on a colour chart as a sample of peach-blossom pink or use a metre rule as a sample of a metre length. So, the sensation I have in my hand is what I call 'pain'. Can I use this as a measure – as a standard for the correct application of the expression 'pain'?

Int. I don't see why not?

PMSH. Well, what am I supposed to do to determine whether what I have in my head is a pain? Am I to hold my hand up against my forehead to determine whether what I have in my head is what I have in my hand? But how should I do that? After all, unlike the case of a colour determination, I cannot *see* the pain sample in my hand, and I cannot *see* the sensation in my head.

Int. Can't I *feel* them and compare what I feel?

PMSH. No. You have forgotten something we have already clarified. To feel a pain is not to perceive a pain – it is just to have a pain. Pains are not perceptibilia.

Int. But surely, I very often find that I have the same pain in my wrist as in my ankle – I have rheumatism in both.

PMSH. Of course, but that *presupposes* possession of the concept of pain. One says truthfully that one has a rheumatic pain in one's wrist and also that one has a rheumatic pain in one's ankle. Here one applies the concept of pain, and the concept is given. The application of the concept to wrist and to ankle respectively involves no sample. One then says that the pain in one's ankle is the same as the pain in one's wrist. But that judgement of sameness *does not use any sample whatsoever*. Obviously, if one has a rheumatic pain in one's ankle and an indistinguishable rheumatic pain in one's wrist, then one has the same pain in both wrist and ankle. *But this judgement of sameness does not rest on comparison with a sample.*

Int. So what does it rest on?

PMSH It does not *rest* on anything – one just sincerely *says* that the pains are the same. Moreover, one's sincere word is a criterion *for others* to say that one has the same pain in one's wrist and ankle.

Int. But *that* presupposes that one already has the concept of pain.

PMSH. Of course. And it also shows that we were barking up the wrong tree in supposing that the word 'pain', and indeed any word that signifies a subjective experience is given a meaning by private ostensive definition.

But I am rushing things. Let's go back to the idea of using a putative mental sample as an object of comparison and nail it once and for all. Let's look at the supposed case of storing a sample in one's memory for future use. Suppose I have a Something in my foot, and I call up the mnemonic image that is supposed to function as a sample of 'S'. *How am I supposed to lay my memory image alongside my foot* to determine whether what I have in my foot is what is defined by my memory image? I hope you will agree that we have now descended to charades.

Int. Yes, I see. That really is the *coup de grace*.

PMSH. Well, it is a deadly blow, but there is one final move. Not only is there no criterion of identity for the putative mental sample, nor a method of comparison between sample and what instantiates the concept it is meant to define ostensively, but one *cannot* juxtapose a mental image and what it is an image of.

Int. I don't understand you.

PMSH. Look, when you compare a colour sample with an object in order to determine whether the object has or is what the sample is a sample of, then you must be able to perceive both. You hold the colour sample next to the curtains, or next to the material you are thinking of buying in order to see whether the curtains or the material *is* the colour of the sample. And you lay the ruler alongside the object that is to be measured, to see whether the object is thus-and-so long. Now forget about the technique of comparison for a moment – we have already dealt with that. The point I now wish to draw your attention to is that you cannot have a mental image of what you are currently perceiving.

Int. Why on earth not? All you have to do is call to mind the right mental image.

PMSH. Well, that is the suggestion. And we have seen that there is no criterion of correctness for being the right mental image. But that too is not my concern at the moment. The point I am making, which as far as I know Wittgenstein did not make, is that you cannot simultaneously have the mental image of, say, red and also see something red. You cannot have mental image of a house and at the same time be looking at the house.

Int. How extraordinary! I confess that now, as I am looking at you, I cannot conjure up an image of your face in my imagination. I can do so when I shut my eyes, but not if I am looking at you. How bizarre! Is this so for others too?

PMSH. Oh, indeed. This is *not* a weakness of your reproductive imagination. The impossibility is not an empirical impossibility. It is not too difficult for us. Rather, it is logically impossible.

Int. But why? I know I can't do it. But why is that just not a limitation of our powers of reproductive imagination?

PMSH. Because it is like trying to win a race that you have just won. There *is no such thing*! You cannot, logically cannot, try to win what you have already won, or try to kick a goal you have just kicked. It is not *too difficult* for you to do, *there is no such thing to do*.

Int. Ah! I see. It is like trying to visualize something that you can see or trying to call to mind in your imagination a musical phrase that you are at that very moment listening to.

PMSH. Exactly. So, you see, sensations cannot, *logically cannot*, fulfil the function of samples as standards for correct application of the words defined by reference to them.

Beetles and Private Objects

All right. So far the refutation of the idea of a radically private language. But Wittgenstein does not stop here, for two reasons.

First, he has not yet clarified the articulations of our public language with respect to words signifying experiences such as pain or emotions or felt desires and so forth. We shall discuss this in the next lecture.

Second, the idea is immensely tenacious. One, very natural, response is this: Is Wittgenstein not in effect saying that *pain*, the sensation itself, has no role in the grammar of the word 'pain'? And if so, does that not mean that he is a logical behaviourist – that he thinks that there aren't really any pains – only pain-behaviour? And is that not absurd?

Well, Wittgenstein certainly seems to deny that the word 'pain' signifies anything 'inner' at all. Look at the following passage in which he repudiates the idea that everyone knows what the word 'pain' means only from their own case:

> Suppose everyone had a box with something in it which we call a 'beetle'. No one can ever look into anyone else's box, and everyone says he knows what a beetle is only by looking at *his* beetle. – Here it would be quite possible for everyone to have something different in his box. One might even imagine such a thing constantly changing. – But what if these people's word 'beetle' had a use nonetheless? – If so, it would not be as the name of a thing. The thing in the box doesn't belong to the language-game at all; not even as a *Something*: for the box might even be empty. – No, one can 'divide through' by the thing in the box; it cancels out, whatever it is.
>
> That is to say: if we construe the grammar of the expression of sensation on the model of 'object and name', the object drops out of consideration as irrelevant. (PI §293)

Wittgenstein's point is that, on the one hand, if the word 'pain' were the name of a radically private object, then it could play no role in communication, and, on the other hand, if the word 'pain' has a communicative use, then it cannot be as a name of the private something.

Now, it is crucially important to pay attention to the final sentence of this remark: 'if we construe the grammar of the expression of sensation on the model of "object and name", the object drops out of consideration as irrelevant.' For this identifies the target – the misconstrual of the grammar of sensation words, and indeed of subjective experiences in general, on the model of name and object. And the model of name and object is the model according to which the name of the object can be given by an ostensive definition in which the object is pointed at, and functions as a sample or paradigm. If one does not grasp this, then it will sound as if Wittgenstein is denying that there are any pains. Or as if he is denying that utterances of pain concern pains. Hence his interlocutor objects indignantly:

> Right; but there is a Something there all the same, which accompanies my cry of pain! And it is on account of this that I utter it. And this Something is what is important – and frightful. (PI 296)

And again:

> 'But you will surely admit that there is a difference between pain-behaviour with pain and pain-behaviour without pain.' – Admit it? What greater difference could there be? – 'And yet you again and again reach the conclusion that the sensation itself is a Nothing.'

To which Wittgenstein replies:

> Not at all. It's not a Something, but not a Nothing either! The conclusion was only that a Nothing would render the same service as a Something about which nothing could be said. We've only rejected the grammar which tends to force itself on us here. (PI §304)

We have to reject the grammar that forces itself upon us here, the grammar that belongs in another, quite different language-game, the language-game with ordinary physical objects and perceptual properties. And we have to attain an overview of the grammar of experience and its expression. For to try to construe the language-game with the expression of experience on the model of the grammar of name and object is to try to play football with a tennis racket on a tennis court – shouting 'Goal' whenever the ball hits the net.

Let us now put the private language aside. What is crucial for a clear overview of our public language of subjective experience is the realization that no sample or paradigm of pain plays any role in the language-game. In very difficult passage, Wittgenstein draws our attention to this:

> It is – one would like to say – not merely the picture of the behaviour that belongs to the language-game with the words 'he is in pain', but also the picture of the pain. Or, not merely the paradigm of the behaviour, but also that of the pain. – It is a misunderstanding to say, 'The picture of pain enters into the language-game with the word "pain".' Pain in the imagination is not a picture and *it* is not replaceable in the language-game by anything that we'd call a picture. – Imagined pain certainly enters into the language game in a sense; only not as a picture. (PI §300)

In our language-game with sensation words such as 'pain', the behaviour that exhibits pain can be pointed out and can itself function as a sample of pain-behaviour. That is, one can point at someone manifesting pain or at a picture of someone in pain and explain 'That's what is called "pain-behaviour"!' But there is no comparable paradigm or picture of pain. A mental image of pain in the imagination cannot, logically, fulfil the function of a defining sample or picture. How then does imagined pain enter our language-game? Well, we tell each other how awful this or that pain must be, we empathize with each other, saying 'I can well imagine it, it must have been dreadful' and so on.

So, in our public language, the sensation of pain itself and its mnemonic reproduction in the imagination play no role in the grammar of pain. And it is unintelligible to suppose that they might play a role as a defining sample in a 'private' language. For sensations and experiences cannot play the role of samples, since they do not satisfy the conceptual conditions for something's counting as a sample. So the third leg of the three-legged stool of the private language is as rotten as the other two. So the very idea of a private language is incoherent. Why is that important? Because the possibility of such a language – indeed its actuality – is tacitly presupposed by numerous accounts and theories in philosophy, psychology, cognitive science and cognitive neuroscience. Moreover, even where such a putative language is not tacitly presupposed, the ideas of private ownership of experience and of epistemic privacy lie at the roots of numerous theories in psychology and cognitive neuroscience. So, if Wittgenstein is right, then those accounts and theories must be rejected or refashioned. I shall show you this in due course.

I have taken you on a long and difficult trek in this lecture. But we have emerged from the forest and started to climb higher. In the next lecture, I shall try to show you that the trek was worth the effort. The view that you will see from the mountain top is very different from what you expected before you plunged into the jungle of the *Private Language Arguments*. For we are now in a position to see clearly the conceptual relations between the mental and the behavioural, the inner and the outer, first-person utterances of subjective experience and the ascription of experiential attributes to others.

Chapter 12

MY MIND AND OTHER MINDS

In the previous four lectures, we introduced the idea of a private language, the words of which purport to refer to subjective experiences, which only the speaker can have and only the speaker can really know about. We showed that the two notions of privacy: *private ownership of experience* and *private knowledge of experience* are both incoherent. We also showed that the idea that names of experiences are given their meaning by association with the experiences which they name and that the form of association is a private analogue of a public ostensive definition is likewise incoherent. So much for demolishing houses of cards.

Our present task is to complement the destructive analysis with a constructive account of the logical character of words signifying subjective experiences. This is an important task. For clarifying their logical character is simultaneously to clarify the nature of subjective experiences. Our account must highlight the logical differences between first-person avowals and reports of experience, such as 'I have a pain', on the one hand, and third-person ascriptions of experience, such as 'He has a pain', on the other. Moreover, it has to weld these two aspects of use together into a single unified concept of experience and experiential attributes. For we must, at all costs, avoid finding ourselves in the position of arguing that the word 'pain' or 'joy' means something different when it is applied to oneself from what it means when it is applied to others.

Other Minds

We feel sensations and emotions, perceive things and have desires and appetites. Being mature language users, we can give expression to our subjective experiences in linguistic form. We can also express our purposes and intentions, our thoughts and beliefs, which, of course, are not *experiences*. Being self-conscious creatures sometimes given to introspection, we can reflect on our experiences, as well as on our intentions, dispositions and tendencies, and express our reflections in words.

On traditional philosophical views, each of us has special privileged knowledge about his or her subjective experiences. We have seen that Wittgenstein disputed the claim that when one is in pain one knows that one is, and the further claims that such knowledge is unique, certain and indubitable. But for present purposes, we can sidestep this dispute by limiting our remarks to the fact that each of us is in a position to *say* whether we are having this, that or the other subjective experience. For that much is agreed by all parties. On the traditional view, we can say this because we are conceived to have privileged access to the contents of our own minds. The form that privileged access takes is *introspection* – incorrectly conceived to be a kind of 'inner sense', analogous to perception of the outer. So our knowledge of how things are subjectively with us, or our ability to say how things are subjectively with us, is privileged. For no one else can introspect my mind to see what experiences I am enjoying, or what thoughts are crossing my mind, or what intentions I have formed. That is something only I can do. My mind is, as it were, a private peepshow into which only I can peer. Again, we have seen that Wittgenstein rejected this conception of introspection – there is no inner sense, and our ability to say how things are with us does not rest on the exercise of any special faculty. It presupposes only the mastery of a sufficiently rich language that contains psychological and mental predicates.

So much by way of reminders. Now let's consider the question of our knowledge of other people and their subjective experiences, thoughts, and intentions. To be sure, we can't say how things are with others by 'looking into their minds'. Rather, we observe what they do and say. And we may then be in a position to say that they are in pain, are feeling cheerful, are thinking of this or that, have formed an intention to do something or other. But now – how can that be? Does it follow from the observed behaviour that there is an inner experience behind it, as it were?

Consider: If I want to find out how many among us in the room feel pain, I can stick a pin in everyone. But now, only when I stick a pin into *myself* do *I* feel pain – when I stick a pin into the others, all I can observe is that they flinch! – I don't feel any pain at all. So how can I possibly conclude that they have what I have when I have a pain?

Again, suppose that I feel a severe pain in my left knee, and my left knee trembles uncontrollably; then my right knee starts to tremble uncontrollably too – but without my feeling any pain. And now everyone else's knees start to tremble. But isn't that just like what is the case with my right knee? So how on earth can I be in a position to ascribe pains to others – or indeed to ascribe any other experience to them?

To put the question in traditional idiom: how is knowledge of other minds possible?

The Argument from Analogy and the 'Theory-Theory'

The traditional answer was: *by analogy with my own case*. When I stick a pin in my hand, I feel a pain, and I flinch and cry out. When I stick a pin in another person's hand, he flinches and cries out – and I feel nothing. But *by analogy with my own case*, I infer that he too feels pain, just as I do. After all, we are biologically similar – as cognitive scientists say today: we are all wired up the same way! This simple argument is known, rather grandly, as the argument from analogy for the existence of other minds. An eminent spokesman for it was John Stuart Mill:

> I observe that there is a great multitude of other bodies, closely resembling in their sensible properties ... this particular one, but whose modifications do not call up, as those of my own body do, a world of sensations in my consciousness. Since they do not do so in my consciousness, I infer that they do it out of my consciousness, and that to each of them belongs a world of consciousness of its own, to which it stands in the same relation in which what I call my body stands to mine, ... Each of these bodies exhibits to my sense a set of phenomena (composed of acts and other manifestations), such as I know, in my own case, to be effects of consciousness, and such as might be looked for if each of the bodies has really in connection with it a world of consciousness.[1]

That is beautifully put, very powerful – and completely wrong.

The same conception is alive and flourishing in current psychology, where it goes by the name of the 'Theory of Mind' theory. The most common explanation of the deficiencies of sympathy with, and understanding of, others exhibited by autistic children is that, for neurological reasons, they fail to develop a proper theory of mind. But, it is argued, normal children do develop such a theory by the age of four, and hence can sympathize with others and predict the behaviour of others on the basis of their theory of mind. An excerpt from the Wikipedia Encyclopaedia illustrates a contemporary version of the argument from analogy updated to the needs of twenty-first century empirical psychology:

> Theory of Mind is a 'theory' insofar as the 'mind' is not 'directly observable'. The presumption that others have a mind is termed a 'theory of mind' because each human being can only prove the existence of his or her mind through introspection, and no one has access to others' minds. It is typically assumed that others have minds by analogy with one's own, and based on the reciprocal nature of social interaction, as observed in joint attention, the functional use of language, and the understanding of others' emotions and actions. Having a theory of mind allows one to attribute thoughts, desires, and intentions to others, to predict or explain

---

1 J. S. Mill, *An Examination of Sir William Hamilton's Philosophy*, in *Complete Works of John Stuart Mill* (University of Toronto Press, Toronto, 1963–91), vol. IX, p. 192.

their actions, and to posit their intentions. As originally defined, it enables one to understand that mental states can be the cause of – and thus be used to explain and predict – others' behaviour ... If a person does not have a complete theory of mind it may be a sign of cognitive or developmental impairment. (*Wikipedia*, 'Theory of Mind', 2009)

This is an extraordinarily interesting passage. It presents the claims that the mind of another person is not directly observable, that one can prove the existence of one's own mind by introspection, and that no one has access to other minds but only to their own, as *obvious truisms*. But, as I hope is slowly becoming evident, these observations are either false or plain nonsense.

> **Int.** Well, you are certainly making me wary of such claims. In fact, you are making me feel as if thinking about all these subjects one is walking through a conceptual minefield. Still, is it *so* mistaken to claim that I can observe my own mind?
>
> **PMSH.** Yes – in the sense that is being proposed, it is! That really should be clear to you by now. But it merits further clarification and elucidation, since old habits of thought are so very difficult to shed – and that is precisely what Wittgenstein is trying to get us to do.
>
> Insofar as 'observe' signifies intentional perception, looking, listening, feeling, and so forth – then this claim is nonsense. For I cannot *perceive* my mind or what is going on in my mind. I cannot *look into* my mind, and although I can talk to myself in my imagination, I do not *hear* what I say to myself. But, of course, I do not fail to hear what I say to myself either. The 'cannot' here is logical – it does not signify inability or circumstantial prevention or obstruction. Rather, it is like 'I can't checkmate in draughts' – that is: *there is no such thing* as checkmate in draughts. There is nothing here that one cannot do. Rather there is no such thing *to do*. So too the assertion that one can't hear what one says to oneself in one's imagination does not signify a deficiency in one's hearing. Rather, *there is no such thing* as not hearing, or not catching, what one says to oneself in one's imagination. (The figure of speech 'I can't hear myself think' means no more than 'I cannot think in all this noise'.) If there is no such thing as not hearing, then by the same token, there is no such thing as hearing either.
>
> **Int.** But surely there is some sense in which I can observe what passes in my mind, isn't there? After all, Jill can keep a record of her feelings for Jack, and when I am ill, I can keep a record for my doctor of how I am feeling in the course of the day.
>
> **PMSH.** Of course. But note that in so far as the sentences 'I can observe my own mind' or 'I can observe what experiences I am undergoing

and what thoughts cross my mind' *do make sense*, they don't signify a form of *perception* of the inner at all. Rather, they are figurative expressions of *a form of attention and reflection*. So, in one sense, I can't observe my own mind – but that is no limitation, since in *that* sense, there is no such thing as *observing* one's own mind. But in another sense, I *can* observe my mind and what goes on in it. I can attend to what I am feeling or thinking and reflect on it. I can *say* what I am feeling, tell you what I think or imagine, let others know my plans and expectations. But equally, *I can very often attend to what others are feeling or thinking* and reflect on it. And I can often say what they are feeling, tell you what they think or imagine, inform you of their plans and expectations. So, *in so far as it makes sense* to observe the minds of others, it is just false that one cannot do so. Conversely, in the sense in which I *cannot* observe the minds of others, *they cannot observe their minds either*. In short, it makes no sense to construe 'observing the mind' on the model of 'observing the body'.

Int. Yes, I see. That really does take the wind out of the sails of a great many theories of the mind. What about the second claim proponents of the 'theory-theory' conception of the mind advance as a truism?

PMSH. Which one was that?

Int. It is the claim that I cannot prove the existence of the minds of other people but only of my own, and that I can prove the existence of my own mind by introspection.

PMSH. That is doubly misconceived. First, the very idea of proof here is out of place since nothing could possibly *count* as a proof.

Int. I don't see why it is *out of place*. I mean, isn't it right and proper to demand that we vindicate the proposition that human beings in general have minds and are subjects of experience?

PMSH. No. You are conflating and confusing an empirical proposition with a grammatical one. That human beings are proper subjects of psychological attributes is not an empirical proposition at all. It is an a priori proposition about *what it makes sense to say*. One can say of a human being that he is in pain, but it makes no sense to say this of a stone or a cloud. That is a matter of grammar, in Wittgenstein's extended sense of the term. That Jack is in pain or that Jill is worried is a straightforward empirical proposition. But that human beings can be said to suffer pain and undergo anxiety is a statement about what makes sense.

Int. But can't one suppose that these people in the street are not really human beings, but just automata or zombies?

PMSH. No, that makes no sense. First of all, they are, as you just said, *people* – and people – human beings are precisely beings to whom mental predicates can intelligibly be ascribed. Second, what would really *count* as supposing this? Just try having a conversation with them while telling yourself that they are really automata who can neither see nor hear, neither know anything nor understand what you are saying!

Int. Yes, I see. It is just pretending to suppose – one can't really *suppose* it. Still, can't I *prove* that *I* have a mind?

PMSH. Well, just stop to think about it. Is it really intelligible?

Int. But for sure, Descartes tried to prove it – first proving that he existed and then proving that he is essentially a thinking thing. Even I know that. And isn't his proof a good one?

PMSH. No. Descartes' famous *cogito ergo sum* – I think therefore I am – is misconceived. For *it makes no sense to doubt whether one exists.* Doubt is here excluded by grammar, not by an irrefutable proof that I do exist. 'I wonder whether I exist' or 'I doubt whether I exist' are nonsensical forms of words – not doubts that can be laid to rest by an existence proof. We are so used to the Cartesian formula that we fail to note just how bizarre it is. For one might respond: 'I think WHAT, therefore I am'. If a philosophy student were to say: 'I think that there are tigers in India, therefore I exist' one wouldn't understand what he was talking about. If he were to explain: 'Well, I wondered whether I existed, and so I thought that there are tigers in India, and from this I drew the conclusion that I exist', one would pat the poor fellow on the shoulder and tell him that he has been doing too much philosophy and needs a holiday.

Int. All right. I see that the *cogito* is too quick and all wrong. But surely, I can *prove* that I have a mind *by introspection*! And I can't prove that other people have minds by introspection – I just presume that they are like me. That seems absolutely straightforward.

PMSH. No, that is doubly confused. As we have seen, introspection is not a form of inner sense, but a form of reflection. I can't *perceive* my own mind.

On the other hand, I *can* perceive that another person has seen something, is looking at something, is in pain, is overjoyed or racked with grief and so on. That's the bit that is straightforward.

However, the thought that it is merely a *presumption* that other human beings are subjects of experience is incoherent. It is akin to the idea that it is merely a *presumption* that the external world exists. If it *were* merely a presumption, we should have to be able to render intelligible the thought that other human beings *are* mere automata or that the external world does *not* actually exist, but *that* one cannot do.

Int. Yes … But what about the idea that one has access to one's own mind, but not to the minds of others?

PMSH. We have actually been over similar ground before. But I agree that it is not easy to make the moves Wittgenstein makes when one's mind is so accustomed to the traditional modes of thinking.

The idea that one has *access* to one's own mind but not to the minds of others is nonsense. It is nonsense that results from failure to reflect on what counts as *access* to something. The thought is that one has privileged access to one's own mind in as much as one can say how things are with one *without behavioural evidence*. One does not have to hear what one says in order to find out what one thinks, and one does not have to see what one does in order to find out whether one is in pain. So one is tempted to say that one *knows directly* how things are with one. One has *direct access* to one's mind. But others can know only *indirectly*, on the basis of what one says and does.

But this is a muddle: in order to have a pain and be able to say that one does, one need not have access to anything. One has access to a library if one is permitted to use it; one has access to the closed garden if one has a key to the gate; one has access to the President if one is allowed to see him on request. But there is nothing comparable to this in the case of one's ability to avow a pain when one has one. Moreover, the inability of a baby to avow a pain is not a result of lack of access to anything, but a result of lack of mastery of a language. To have a pain and to be able to say that one is in pain is not *to have access* to anything. It is equally misconceived to suppose that one has only *indirect access* to the experiences of others. There are no *more direct* grounds for saying that another is in pain than the fact that he is screaming in pain in circumstances of injury. There is no more direct way of knowing what another human being thinks than from his sincere confession. What might legitimately be called 'knowing indirectly what another thinks' is knowing what he thinks on the basis of hearsay. But there is nothing indirect about hearing it from the horse's mouth.

I shall have more to say on these matters when we come to consider the idea that the mental is hidden behind the overt behaviour. But for the moment, note how easy it is to start on the wrong foot; and once one has done that, one may never regain one's balance.

The Need for Criteria for the Ascription of Experience

Now let's focus on the analogical argument and its contemporary cousin, the theory that one needs a theory of mind in order to be able to ascribe mental attributes to others. In the course of his *Private Language Arguments*,

Wittgenstein confronts such misconceptions, and we must look at his remarks. I shall dwell on two of his critical observations before examining his own account of the matter.

The first is this:

> If one has to imagine someone else's pain on the model of one's own, this is none too easy a thing to do: for I have to imagine pain which I *don't feel* on the model of pain which I *do feel*. That is, what I have to do is not simply make the transition in the imagination from pain in one place to pain in another. As from pain in the hand to pain in the arm. For it is not as if I had to imagine that I feel pain in some part of *his* body [...]
>
> Pain-behaviour can indicate a painful place – but the person who is suffering is the person who manifests pain. (PI §302)

We ascribe pain and other psychological attributes to others. We are warranted in so doing by their behavioural manifestations of pain. But *not* on the basis of extrapolation from our own case. That is, if pain ascriptions to others were analogical, then I would indeed have to suppose that when others injure themselves – cut or burn themselves – they have what I have when I injure myself. Well, what do I have? Surely, I have *this*! – I have *this pain*. But how am I to imagine another having *this pain*? If I imagine another's having *it*, must I not imagine feeling this pain in the other person's body? For if that is not what is meant (and it clearly is not) then how am I to imagine pain that I don't feel on the model of pain that I do feel? Are we not back to the trembling knee case? Pain in another person's knee is pain *that I do not feel* – so how am I to imagine it?

> **Int.** I'm a bit bewildered by this. Of course, I can imagine another person having pain in his knee. And I can *assert* that another person has pain in his knee. So what is Wittgenstein fussing about?
>
> **PMSH.** He is, in his subtle way, repeating the point that we have already encountered – that the pain I have *provides no criterion of identity for pain*. The concept of pain is *not* like the concept of red or green either. It is not defined by reference to a sample. Whereas one can say that something is red if and only if it is *this* colour [and here we point at a red sample], one cannot say that someone has a pain if and only if he has *this* [and here we concentrate our attention on our pain]. One can say that two things are red, that is, have the same colour, if they are both *this* colour [and here we point at a colour sample of red]. But as the argument against private ostensive definition shows, a pain or a mnemonic copy in the imagination of a pain cannot function as a sample. That is why Wittgenstein wrote:
>
>> It is a misunderstanding to say 'The picture of pain enters into the language-game with the word "pain"'. Pain in the imagination is not a picture, and

it is not replaceable in the language-game by anything that we'd call a picture. – Imagined pain certainly enters into the language-game in a sense; only not as a picture. (PI §300)

Int. You know, there is something you have left out of the story altogether. You have shown me convincingly that one cannot explain the meaning of mental or psychological predicates by reference to private mental samples and by private ostensive definitions because there can't be any such thing as a private mental sample and there is no such thing as a private ostensive definition. I accept all that. But you have not explained at all how we do apply such predicates, and how their meaning is taught and explained. Nor have you explained how it can be that we can say of another that he has the same pain as I do. For you laboured hard to explain to me that despite one's initial inclinations, there is nothing awry in saying that someone else has the same pain as I do. But how can I be in a position to say this?

PMSH. Yes, you're quite right. Since there is no such thing as a defining sample of pain, we have yet to make clear the grounds upon which we *can* say that another person has a pain, and the criteria that *would* warrant us in saying that he has the same pain as I do. Wittgenstein puts the point wonderfully in another passage:

> 'But if I suppose that someone has a pain, then I am simply supposing that he has just the same as I have so often had.' – That gets us no further. It is as if I were to say, 'You surely know what "It's 5 o'clock here" means; so you also know what 'It's 5 o'clock on the sun' means. It means simply that it is just the same time there as it is here when it is 5 o'clock.' – The explanation by means of *sameness* does not work here. For I know well enough that one can call 5 o'clock here and 5 o'clock there 'the same time', but do not know in what cases one is to speak of its being the same time here and there.
>
> In exactly the same way, it is no explanation to say: the supposition that he has a pain is simply the supposition that he has the same as I. For what's surely clear to me is *this* part of grammar: that one will say that the stove has the same experience as I *if* one says: it's in pain and I'm in pain. (PI §350)

So, the experience of pain does not give one the concept of pain, any more than being in debt gives one the concept of a negative number. Nor does the experience of pain give one a sample of pain by comparison with which one can say that someone else is in pain.

What we need is a criterion for the ascription of pain to a person, and criteria of identity to determine when different people have the same pain and when they have different pains. That seems evident from these reflections. But we are inclined to feel cheated. After all, when I say that I have a pain, I *do not do so on the basis of any evidential criteria at all*. As Wittgenstein remarks:

> It is not, of course, that I identify my sensation by means of criteria; it is, rather, that I use the same expression. But it is not as if the language-game *ends* with this; it begins with it. (PI §290).

Let's dwell on this remark for a moment. What Wittgenstein is driving at is that the utterances 'I have a pain', or 'I'm in pain' or even the simple 'It hurts', are *the first move in a language-game*. They are *unlike* the assertion 'The table is brown and the curtains are blue' which is the upshot of looking and seeing, and then, as it were, reading the description of the coloured objects off what one sees. But 'It hurts' is an *expression* of pain, and is no more the end of a language-game than a groan of pain. Rather, it provides a ground *for others* to say of one that one is in pain, a reason for others to express sympathy and to help one. *I* don't identify my sensation by reference to any criterion – *I don't identify my sensation at all. That* is why there is no such thing as my *misidentifying* my sensation – or being *mistaken* as to whether it is a pain. There is here *neither recognition nor misrecognition*, any more than a groan of pain is preceded by a recognition or misrecognition of pain. I just express my pain in a groan or in an avowal or utterance of pain. So too, I don't recognize my thoughts and beliefs and identify them before I express them, and there is no such thing as *misrecognizing* my thoughts or beliefs or as misidentifying them. The expression of what I think or believe is the beginning of numerous language games – of arguing, disputing, justifying, explaining, drawing conclusions, and making decisions. My utterance of pain, my expression of belief, my avowal of want or expression of intention are *criteria for others to say of me* that I am in pain, that I believe this or that, that I want and intend to do so-and-so.

Of course, a condition for one's utterance of pain or expression of one's thought or one's avowal of wanting something to count as a criterion depends upon circumstances and the surrounding behaviour. Someone who avows a severe pain but carries on joking and laughing will not be understood. Someone who expresses a desire for a drink but refuses one when given it has some explaining to do. That is: the evidential force of a verbal manifestation or expression of the inner may be annulled by circumstances and surrounding behaviour. If the circumstances are inappropriate or the accompanying behaviour incongruent, that may warrant one in withholding the psychological ascription. Now, there is a great deal more to be said about the notion of behavioural criteria for psychological attributes, and I shall elaborate further in a moment.

What Are the Conditions of the Possibility of Groundless Self-ascription of Experience?

> **Int.** Wait. I still have some very serious qualms. You have explained that Wittgenstein emphasized that such utterances as 'I'm in pain',

expressions of belief such as 'I think he is in London' and avowals of intention like 'I'm going to visit him' are *groundless*. If I understand you correctly, what that means is that they are uttered without using any evidence or criteria at all. What that seems to amount to is that barring slips of the tongue, there is in such cases no such thing as identifying or misidentifying and recognizing or misrecognizing. But if that is so, why cannot the private linguist respond, 'If *you* can do this, if *you* need neither evidence nor sample for self-ascription of experience, *why can't I do the same?*' If we speakers of a *public* language can ascribe experiences to ourselves without samples or behavioural evidence, why was the private linguist damned for lack of criteria or sample in his case?

PMSH. Yes, you are quite right. This is a capital point – it is indeed one critical source of the impression that Wittgenstein is engaged here in some form of legerdemain. So we must probe it carefully and in detail.

Note that the question amounts to the following: *What are the conditions that license groundless self-ascription of experience* (and of thoughts, purposes and intentions)? *How can it be* that in the case of first-person present-tense articulations of experience we may rightly utter the words we utter *without any justification?*

Int. Yes, that's exactly what I meant to say.

PMSH. Wittgenstein's brief answer is that to say something without justification *does not mean that one says it wrongfully*. Groundless self-ascription of experience is possible precisely because such utterances are bound up, *logically* bound up, with behaviour. In the context of an examination of the logical exclusion of expressions of doubt or ignorance with respect to self-ascriptions of pain, Wittgenstein wrote:

> That expression of doubt has no place in the language-game; but if expressions of sensation – human behaviour – are excluded, it looks as if I might then *legitimately* begin to doubt afresh. My temptation to say that one might take a sensation for something other than it is arises from this: if I assume the abrogation of the normal language-game with the expression of sensation, I need a criterion of identity for the sensation; and then the possibility of error also exists. (PI §288)

Int. Well, yes. But I don't see the connection between groundless self-ascription and behaviour.

PMSH. The connection is this. The *expression* of the inner in non-linguistic behaviour and linguistic behaviour alike is *essentially* a ground for ascribing an appropriate psychological attribute to the living being. This connection is partly *constitutive* of the meaning of the psychological predicate – behaving in *this* way is what is called *manifesting pain*, behaving *thus* is what is called 'listening to the music', 'tasting the food', 'smelling the scent'.

This essential linkage is precisely what was conspicuously *missing* from the private linguist's tale. For according to the private linguist, there is *no* conceptual connection between inner and outer, between the mental and the behavioural. In his view, psychological concepts are wholly explained by reference to defining mental samples. Once that is fixed, then the connection to behaviour is something that can be discovered. And *that* is precisely what Wittgenstein denied and, as we have seen, *refuted* by argument. He argued that, on the contrary, inner, the mental, is *logically*, or *conceptually*, connected with behaviour.

Int. But I still don't grasp your point. How does Wittgenstein bring into view this essential connection between the psychological and the behavioural in the first-person case, where behavioural criteria are not used at all? I mean, when I exclaim 'I'm in pain', I *don't* look to see how I am behaving. As you have emphasized, my utterance is *groundless*. So where is the connection between the groundless avowal and the pain-behaviour that is indeed a logical criterion for others to ascribe pain to a person?

PMSH. In the case of pain, Wittgenstein makes clear the conceptual connection between pain and pain-behaviour here by emphasizing the roots of the language-game in natural expressive pain-behaviour. Pain utterances, such as 'Ow', 'Hurts', 'It hurts', 'My head hurts', 'I have a pain' should be seen as grafted onto natural pain-behaviour. They are extensions of, and partial substitutes for, such behaviour. And it is not a *discovery* that pain utterances in circumstances of injury are a ground – a criterion – for ascribing pain to the speaker. It is something we learn as we learn the use of the word 'pain' and acquire the concept of pain.

Int. Yes, I see. That's really ingenious. Pain-language is really an extension of natural pain-behaviour. Yes, of course. ... But you can't make that kind of move for all psychological predicates. I mean 'I see this, that, or the other' or 'I hear a noise' is surely not grafted onto natural perceptual behaviour. And surely 'I think this or that' is not an extension of natural thoughtful behaviour?

PMSH. You're absolutely right. Each kind of psychological predicate has to be examined in its own right in order to obtain a clear picture of the conceptual structure in this domain. For the patterns are not uniform or even homologous. Nevertheless, it is not difficult to see how Wittgenstein's account can be extended. Let me give you three examples:

First, in the case of perceptual verbs, utterances such as 'I see the mountains', 'I can hear a noise' or 'I smell roses' are *integrated into*, rather than *grafted onto*, perceptual behaviour associated with the use of the appropriate sense organs in appropriate circumstances. One may view them not as extensions of natural perceiving and observing behaviour, but rather as *operations on observation statements* such as 'There are mountains in the distance', 'There was a noise', or 'The roses have a lovely scent'. Only when one has mastered the use of elementary observation statements does one proceed to the use of such prefixes as 'I see ...', 'I can hear ...' or 'I smell ...', one function of which is to specify the source of one's knowledge.

Int. You mean that once the child has learnt to say, 'There is a bird on the lawn' or 'Mummy is cooking bacon for breakfast', it can go on to learn how to answer the question 'How do you know?' by saying 'I can see it' or 'I can smell the frying bacon'.

PMSH. Exactly. *One* use of the perceptual verb prefixed to such an observational sentence is precisely to indicate the source of one's knowledge. For, of course, the perceptual faculties *are* sources of knowledge – they are *cognitive faculties*. And prefixing them to an observation statement indicates how one knows or came to know what one is asserting.

Int. Yes, that must be right.

PMSH. I think so. But you must be aware of differences. 'I want' is quite unlike 'I see'. Just as 'I have a pain', 'It hurts' and 'I am in pain' are extensions of natural pain-behaviour, so too 'I want' is an extension of natural *conative* behaviour – that is, of *trying to get* something. The small child learns the use of 'want' by learning to replace its frustrated cries and efforts to reach something by 'Want!' and later, for example, 'I want a banana'. So 'I want ...' is more like 'I have a pain' than like 'I can see a horse in the field' – for, like 'I have a pain', it can be said to be grafted onto natural expressive behaviour rather than onto pre-existing linguistic behaviour.

Int. Yes, that's very plausible. I remember that when my little nephew was learning to speak and learnt how to use 'Want', he didn't bother with any further words for the next three weeks, because 'Want' did everything he needed!

PMSH Very good! Let me give you one more example that is quite unlike the ones we have looked at so far. In a striking example, Wittgenstein suggested that *expressions of intention* are unlike expressions of wants and desires. They are not substitutes for natural conative behaviour, but rather are learnt as *heralding behaviour*. The most primitive form of expression of intention is 'I'm going to'. The child learns that when one says, 'I'm going to do so-and-so', then one must go on and *do* so-and-so. Imagine a parent and child playing with a ball: the father, holding the ball, says to the child, 'I'm going to throw you the ball – here: Catch!' and he proceeds to throw the ball. An expression of intention is, in its primitive form, *an announcement*. In the primitive language-game in which expressions of intention are rooted, it is an essential part of the language-game that *one goes on to do* what one has declared that one is going to do. Of course, in the developed language-game things are far more complex, since one may have intentions for the distant future, one may change one's mind, and so forth. But the roots of the language-game lie in elementary announcements of action.

Let me sum up. In general, psychological predicates are linked more or less directly, in different, more or less complex ways, *with behaviour*. Severed from their essential connection with behaviour, as they are in Cartesian doctrines, in idealism and in much current psychology and cognitive neuroscience, they lose all sense.

So, we apply a wide range of present-tense psychological verbs to ourselves without any grounds whatsoever. But *a condition for this to be intelligible* is that this groundless use in the first-person be *bound up with behaviour* in a twofold manner:
- First, it must be appropriately integrated with the speaker's behaviour in the circumstances. For the first-person utterance is itself a form of behaviour and this must cohere with the rest of the speaker's behaviour.
- Second, the first-person utterance is itself a criterion for others to ascribe the relevant psychological attribute to the speaker.

What Is a Criterion?

I have used the term 'criterion' in this discussion, and it is time to say a few words about it. The word 'criterion' is a perfectly ordinary expression signifying 'a mark of'. So, something is said to be a criterion for another thing if it is evidence for it. In Wittgenstein's usage, however, it becomes a quasi-technical term. For in these contexts, he distinguished sharply between what he called 'symptoms' and 'criteria'. It is important to be clear about the difference between the two – for in using the term 'criterion' as he did, he drew a novel distinction.

We say that a blotchy rash and a high temperature in a child are symptoms of measles. We may also say that rising damp in a wall is evidence of a damaged damp course, and dark lowering clouds are signs of impending rain. In such cases, we are speaking of inductive evidence. Note four important points about inductive evidence:

First, inductive evidence is *discovered through experience*. So, something's being inductive evidence for another thing is not a *logical* relation. It is something known a posteriori, not a priori. It is discovered by noting the systematic correlation of two phenomena – clouds and rain, rising damp and broken damp courses, rash and fever, and the presence of the rubeola virus. Hence,

Second, it presupposes the *independent identification* of the relata and the discovery of their correlation in experience. That is, we can identify rising damp independently of cracked damp courses and can identify cracked damp courses independently of rising damp – and then we can find out that the former are very well-correlated with the latter. And having correlated them, we can use our observation of rising dampness as evidence for cracked damp courses.

Third, inductive evidence *falls short of entailment*. Being a bachelor, for example, *entails* being unmarried. The proposition that Jack is a bachelor *logically implies* the proposition that Jack is unmarried. If he is a bachelor, *no additional evidence* can annul the conclusion that Jack is unmarried. By contrast, the presence of a symptom does not *logically* imply that what it is a symptom of is present. It is possible to have a rash and fever *without* having measles; rain clouds *need not* precipitate rainfall; and rising damp *may* have other causes than a broken damp course.

Fourth, inductive evidence can be defeated. For it can be overridden by countervailing evidence. For example, if 97 per cent of the dentists in Oxford are male, then the fact that T. A. Jones is an Oxford dentist is a good ground for thinking that Jones is a man. But if we then discover that Jones is a member of the YWCA, then that evidence is overridden.

So, to summarize:

A symptom, according to Wittgenstein's usage, is
  i. inductive and, hence, non-logical evidence,
  ii. it is discovered through experience,
 iii. it presupposes independent identification of the relata,
 iv. it falls short of entailment inasmuch as it can be overridden.

By contrast, a criterion is *logical evidence*. Given that it is an evidential relationship, it is not surprising that it shares some features with inductive evidence. Given that it is logical, it is equally unsurprising that it shares some features with logical relations. But unlike inductive evidence, a criterion is not discovered through experience – it is a priori, not a posteriori. It is *necessarily*, not contingently, *good evidence* for that of which it is a criterion. It is not discovered through experience by independent identification of the relata and observation of their regular association that, for example, pain-behaviour is good evidence for being in pain. We learn the criteria for the ascription of pain in learning the use of the word 'pain' – in acquiring the *concept* of pain.

We do not learn to identify pain in our own case and then correlate our pains with our cries and groans in circumstances of injury. We don't *identify* pain in our own case at all – we express it. And we learn to ascribe pain *to others* on the grounds of their behavioural manifestations and utterances of pain. These are the criteria for ascribing pain to another. It is not a coincidence that pain is manifest in crying out, groaning, screaming, in assuaging the injured limb, and so forth. It is not as if pain might well have been exhibited by laughing and smiling. It is not as if we have pain here, and pain-behaviour there, and the two happen to go together. No – they are conceptually linked. What we call 'pain-behaviour' is *logically necessarily good evidence* for pain.

Let me give you another example. The criteria for someone wanting an apple, for example, are that he goes to the fruit bowl to get one or buys some apples at a greengrocer's and then eats one, or that he says 'I want an apple' or that he asks someone for an apple. But we do not learn the meaning of the word 'want' by correlating an experience of wanting with trying to get something, let alone with saying 'I want'. We learn to express or report our wants by saying 'I want …' or 'I would like …' or 'Could you …?' and we learn to ascribe wants to others when they say such things too. There is a conceptual link between wanting something and endeavouring to get it. If people expressed their wants, but *never* seized opportunities to get what they want and were never *pleased* to get what they said they want, or never *did anything* with the thing they said they want once they got it, the word 'want' would lose its meaning.

Let me summarize the differences and similarities between criterial evidence and inductive evidence:

Criterial evidence *differs* from inductive evidence:
i. In being a priori rather than a posteriori.
ii. In being a logical relation rather than an empirically discovered one.

Unlike an inductive relation, a criterion is not established by correlation of independently identified relata – like clouds and rain, or smoke and fire. Rather, that certain behaviour is a criterion for a psychological attribute is partly constitutive of the meaning of the corresponding psychological expression – it is, as Wittgenstein puts it, part of its grammar.
iii. In being *logically necessarily good evidence*, not empirically good evidence.

But criterial evidence *resembles* inductive evidence in the following important respects:
i. It falls short of the logical relation of entailment. Pain-behaviour, for example, does not *entail* being in pain. Someone may be play-acting or trying to deceive. An avowal of pain may be a lie. Consequently,
ii. The criterial relation, like inductive evidence and unlike entailment, is *defeasible*. It can, in certain circumstances, be undermined by additional evidence.

I have emphasized that for something to be a criterion for something else is for it to stand in an evidential relationship to it. Nevertheless, it is important to note that in one sense criterial ascription of a psychological attribute to another person is *not* typically evidential. This seems surprising and startling after all that I have just said. But let me explain. There *are* grounds for the ascription of a psychological attribute to another person. There *are* answers to the question 'How do you know?' that cite behavioural criteria. But it would be profoundly misleading to think that typical ascriptions of psychological attributes are *inferences* from behavioural evidence. When we see someone writhing in pain after having broken his leg, we do not say 'He was groaning and screaming, and he had broken his leg, so I *inferred* that he was in pain'. No – we can see the pain in the poor man's face, hear the pain in his voice. We make no *inference*. But we may later answer the question 'How did you know?' by citing his behaviour and what he said. The criterion is *a justification*. Similarly, if someone tells us that he is afraid, we do not later say 'He told me that he was afraid, so I *inferred* that he was frightened'. And if someone tells me that he is going to London tomorrow, I do not then *infer* that he intends to go to London tomorrow. But if I were later *asked* why I thought he would be in London the next day, I should reply by giving the justification for my belief, namely that he told me that this is what he was going to do. So, there is nothing at all odd about the statement that psychological attributes are ascribed to others *on the grounds* of behavioural criteria, but that the ascription is not inferred. On the contrary, it is the suggestion that it *is* inferred that would be very odd. To have *a warrant* for an assertion does not imply *drawing a conclusion* and *making* an inference. Rather, one typically asserts what is obvious, and one can justify what one asserts by citing the criteria.

So, to sum up. It is a cardinal point of Wittgenstein's philosophy of psychology that psychological predicates require behavioural criteria. Such expressions as 'pain' or 'tickle', 'see' or 'hear', 'feel cheerful' or 'feel sorry', 'want' or 'intend', 'believe' or 'think' are all Janus-faced. They are typically applied to oneself without any evidential grounds at all, but they are applied to others on the grounds of behavioural criteria that exhibit the inner. 'Inner states stand in need of outer criteria' Wittgenstein noted. And it was this requirement that was not met by the putative private language, and that was not understood by mainstream writers on psychology and philosophy of psychology prior to Wittgenstein. Its consequences, both within philosophy and for the psychological sciences, are dramatic. We shall explore some of these in the next lecture, starting with its implications for the 'theory-theory' account of children's awareness of the mental states of others. For if Wittgenstein is right, this psychological theory must be awry.

Chapter 13

THE INNER AND THE OUTER – BEHAVIOUR AND BEHAVIOURISM

Recapitulation

In the last lecture, we examined the Janus-faced character of certain psychological predicates. In the first-person present, they are used groundlessly – without reference to any outer criteria (that is, behaviour) and without reference to an inner criterion either. By contrast, ascribing such psychological predicates as *being in pain, feeling frightened, wanting a drink* to others involves reference to what they do and what they say in the circumstances – in other words, to behavioural criteria. These two aspects of psychological predicates are indissolubly welded together by the essential connection between a given mental attribute and its constitutive forms of behavioural manifestation. The criterionless first-person use is possible only because of a threefold connection with behaviour:

- First, the first-person utterance has to be congruent with the rest of the speaker's behaviour. Pain utterances, for example, mesh with groaning, crying out and assuaging the injury.
- Second, the roots of first-person utterances lie in *expressions* and *manifestations* of experiences, beliefs, intentions and so forth. So, pain utterances are rooted in natural behavioural manifestations of pain. Explicit expressions of believing and thinking are learnt as qualifying operations on empirical assertions. Expressions of intention are rooted in announcement of plans and projects. And so on.
- Third, a first-person utterance of an experience, belief or intention is itself a behavioural criterion for others to ascribe the predicate to the speaker.

In the previous lecture, I remarked that this account of the logico-grammatical character of such psychological predicates has multiple consequences. Here I shall start by indicating some of them. Then I shall move on to examine the correlative notions of behaviour and of the mental that are involved.

For a widespread misconception about what counts as behaviour in such contexts feeds on and is fed by a further misconception of the mental as *inner*, that is, as *hidden* or *concealed* behind the observable. I shall then make some remarks about behaviourism.

Unfinished Business: The Argument from Analogy and 'Theory-Theory'

First of all, let's pick up the threads of the two accounts of knowledge of other minds which I introduced in the last lecture: the traditional philosophical explanation known as 'the argument from analogy for the existence of other minds' and the contemporary psychological explanation known as 'theory-theory' – namely, the claim that our ability to ascribe psychological predicates to others rests on a theory that we developed when we were children about the behaviour of other people.

The traditional argument from analogy for the existence of other minds asserted that we ascribe mental predicates to others by analogy with our own case. We are, it is claimed, introspectively aware of pain when we injure ourselves. We make an inductive correlation between our being in pain and our own pain-behaviour. We observe that when others injure themselves, they cry out. And we infer that they feel pain just as we do – even though we cannot introspectively observe their pain and cannot feel their pain.

Now, after having been exposed to Wittgenstein's style of thinking for quite a while, doesn't this account strike you as fishy? Surely there are some very bizarre things going on under the surface here!

> **Int.** [*hesitantly*] Well, I'm not sure what kinds of thing you have in mind. But one thing that does strike me is that the argument seems to be an analogical argument from *one single case*! I mean, we're generalizing here not from a wide range of observed cases to the rest of humanity, but we're generalizing just from *my* case to the whole of humanity. I can't think of any other argument that engages in such a wild generalization from such a slender basis.
>
> **PMSH.** Yes, that is exactly right. Indeed, in so far as we want to ascribe a range of psychological predicates such as being in pain, being hungry or thirsty, being angry or frightened, to non-human animals too, the scope of the generalization is even greater than you suggest. And one certainly can't find any such generalizations in the sciences. So it certainly smells bad.
>
> Now, are there any further grounds for suspicion?
>
> **Int.** ... I'm not sure.

PMSH. Well, how would one go about validating this sweeping generalization? I mean, what would count as confirming it, and what as disconfirming it?

Int. Ah, yes. I see. On the assumptions that inform this 'theory of our knowledge of other minds', only *our own* judgements about *our own* minds are really verifiable. One can never *really* verify the claim that others have experiences just as I do.

PMSH. That's right. The analogical inference must, by its own lights, remain unverifiable in principle. For the analogy is needed only because we are held *not* to be able to observe the experiences of others, but only the experiences that we ourselves have. Only *our own* judgements concerning *our own* experiences are, on this account, directly verifiable.

Any other points? ... What about the use of 'observe' and 'observation'? Do you recollect our previous discussion of this concept?

Int. Oh yes. Of course. It is misconceived to say that when I am in pain I *observe* that I am in pain, and that's how I know I am. For on the one hand, I can't be said to *know* I am in pain in the sense in which I can indeed know that someone else is in pain – when for example, he is screaming in agony. And on the other hand, I often do observe another person's pain – as in that case, or as in the case of a nurse, who observes her patient.

PMSH. Yes, that's right. The argument from analogy misuses the expressions 'to observe my pain' and the expression 'to observe someone's pain'. Remember that there is such a thing as observing my pain – as when I make notes of its waxing and waning in the course of the afternoon. But here one might paradoxically say that observing my pain is not a case of observation – it is a case of taking note.

Any further points? What about introspection?

Int. Yes. The argument from analogy invokes the incoherent conception of introspection that you have already discussed with me. I mean, the defender of the argument conceives of introspection as a kind of *inner sense* by means of which one *knows* whether one is in pain, is frightened or wants a drink, say. But that, as you explained, is quite wrong, since introspection is not a kind of seeing, but a kind of reflecting. And anyway, we don't need to invoke any such faculty of inner sense to explain how we know we are in pain, since it is confused to suggest that we either know or are ignorant of being in pain when we are in pain. Being able to say truthfully that one is in pain does not require internal quasi-perceptual knowledge. All it requires is mastery of the concept of pain.

PMSH. Very good. So we have four major objections to the argument from analogy. First, it is a wild generalization from one's own case.

Second, it can neither be confirmed nor be disconfirmed. Third, it involves misuse of the concept of observation. And finally, it involves a similar misuse of the concept of introspection.

Over and above *these* flaws, the analogical argument presupposes the intelligibility of learning the first-person use of psychological expressions independently of mastering their third-person use. *That is absolutely fundamental.* Consequently, it is a tacit assumption of the argument from analogy that psychological predicates such as 'to be in pain' have a meaning *independently of any logical nexus with behaviour.* But, as we have seen, the connection between a psychological attribute such as *pain* and its behavioural manifestations in groans and screams is *partly constitutive* of the meaning of the phrase 'is in pain'. To learn the meaning, the use, of the word 'pain', one must learn that screaming and groaning in circumstances of injury warrant ascribing pain to another.

Let me try to make this clearer. The argument from analogy takes it for granted that one can *identify* the sensation of pain in oneself and then correlate it *inductively* with one's own behaviour. That is, it is assumed that our knowledge of the regular connection between our own pain (in circumstances of injury) and our pain-behaviour is the upshot of independent identification of the two relata: we identify the pain we have, we observe our own pain-behaviour and we note their regular concomitance. But if we have to *identify* our own pain, that presupposes:

- First, the intelligibility of misidentification and mistake – since there is no such thing as *identifying* without also the possibility of *misidentifying*, and there is no such thing as getting something right without the possibility of getting it wrong, that is, making a mistake.
- Second, the availability of a private criterion of identity for pain – there must be *some* mark of identifying pain correctly as opposed to making a mistake.

Wittgenstein spells this out in a powerful passage in which he tries to imagine a subject's having a pain without even the *logical possibility* of pain-behaviour. One might try to imagine this in one of two ways: one might imagine that one has become a disembodied spirit, and then wonder what it would be to have a pain without a body and hence too without *anything* that could even *count* as manifesting pain. Or one might imagine turning to stone while having frightful pains, bearing in mind the fact that stone statues *cannot behave*. The two cases are exactly akin – since both involve trying to imagine pain severed from the logical possibility of any behavioural expression of pain. Wittgenstein chose the second scenario. This is what he wrote:

> I turn to stone and my pain goes on. – What if I were mistaken, and it was no longer *pain*? – But surely I can't be mistaken here; it means nothing to doubt whether I am in pain! – That is, if someone said 'I don't know if what I have is a pain or something else', we would think, perhaps, that he doesn't know what the English word 'pain' means […]
>
> If he now said, for example, 'Oh, I know what "pain" means; what I don't know is whether *this* that I have now, is pain' – we'd merely shake our heads and have to regard his words as a strange reaction which we can't make anything of. (It would be rather as if we heard someone say seriously, 'I distinctly remember that sometime before I was born I believed […]')
>
> That expression of doubt has no place in the language-game; but if expressions of sensation – human behaviour – are excluded, it looks as if I might then *legitimately* begin to doubt. My temptation to say that one might take a sensation for something other than what it is arises from this: if I assume the abrogation of the normal language-game with the expression of sensation, I need a criterion of identity for the sensation; and then the possibility of error also exists. (PI §288)

So, if one tries to imagine turning to stone and one's pain continuing, then the question of mistake and doubt *could* arise – for now a criterion of identity for pain would be needed in the first-person case. And, of course, *there can be none*. So one is imagining a nonsense. Thus, pain is essentially connected with the logical possibility of its behavioural manifestation.

What this means is that the argument from analogy assumes that groundless self-ascription of experience is possible but *fails to confront the question of the conditions of its possibility*. In fact, it takes it for granted that having a pain and associating the word 'pain' with the pains one has is sufficient for mastery of the concept of pain. But, as Wittgenstein's argument against private ostensive definition shows, that is unintelligible. Rather, he explains, mastery of the groundless first-person present-tense use of 'pain' is one side of a single coin, the other side of which is mastery of the third-person use. There is no such thing as mastery of the concept of pain independently of mastering the conditions of its application to others.

Int. [*Admiringly*] That's a real *tour de force*!

PMSH. Yes, I think it is. It is the most remarkable piece of philosophical analysis in the twentieth century. It digs deeper down into the presuppositions of thought about the nature of the mind than anything I have ever come across.

Now let's turn to the psychologists' 'theory-theory'. This is the doctrine that children learn to ascribe psychological attributes to other people by constructing a *theory* of human behaviour, a theory according to which psychological attributes may be ascribed to others on the grounds of what they do and say in given circumstances. According to some psychologists the theory is innate, according to others the theory is tacitly formed, and according to yet others it is actively learnt. On the latter view (advanced, for example, by Gopnik and Meltzoff (*Words, Thoughts and Theories* (MIT, 1997)), the young child develops a theory of human behaviour in much the same way as a scientist develops a scientific theory. Let me very briefly raise some qualms:

- Notice, first, that the idea of an *innately* known theory is more than a little questionable. What would it be like to know the theory of gravity innately? Or to have innate knowledge of ionic theory? One would like some examples of innately known theories just in order to understand what is meant by 'knowing a theory innately'. And if someone tells us that we have innate, though implicit knowledge of the theory of gravity inasmuch as we can walk, we should reply that this is confused. One needs no *theory* in order to be able to walk.
- Second, the thought that a theory of other minds is *tacitly* formed is bizarre. One would like an example of a known theory, like the theory of evolution, that could be conceived to be tacitly known. What would be the difference between tacit knowledge and ignorance? What could confirm the presence of tacit knowledge, independently of the reactive behaviour? A cat perceives when another cat is angry and responds accordingly. Does it too have a theory of mind? A dog commonly senses whether its master is angry or sad – is this because it invokes a theory of mind and tacitly reasons that given its master's tone of voice, his demeanour and facial expression, it is probable that he is angry?
- Third, the very idea of a three-year-old child being in the business of forming theories is prima facie unintelligible. One must know far more and have mastered much more language than a three-year-old has, before one can start forming testable theories about anything. The idea that a child could *need* a theory to explain that when mother hits her thumb with a hammer and cries out, then she has hurt herself is absurd. As Wittgenstein observed

  > Being sure that someone is in pain, doubting whether he is, and so on, are so many natural, instinctive, kinds of relationship towards other human beings, and our language is merely auxiliary to, and further extension of, this behaviour. Our language-game is an extension of primitive behaviour. (For our language-game is behaviour.) (Instinct.) (Z §545)

- Finally, note the gross misuse of the term 'theory'. We have all learnt at school that it is part of the theory of gravity that bodies attract each other according to the inverse square law. We have all learnt that the theory of evolution explains the origin of species by reference to natural selection. But is there any acceptable sense of the word 'theory' according to which it is part of a theory that when one injures oneself, one commonly cries out in pain? Or that when one wants something, one normally acts in order to obtain it?

Of course, these qualms need to be elaborated and refined. That is not my concern at the moment. What I wish to draw your attention to is that the theory-theory account of the mastery of third-person use of psychological predicates takes it for granted that mastery of the first-person use is *independent of grasping the conceptual nexus with behaviour.* And that, as we have seen, is incoherent. It makes no sense to suppose that a language user should use and understand psychological predicates in the first-person present tense without also having mastered their third-person use. For these are just two sides of one coin – not two coins linked by an inductive or hypothetico-deductive chain. The thought that the child might have grasped the concept of being in pain, of thinking or of being frightened and so forth *prior* to constructing a theory of when and on what grounds to ascribe pain, thinking or being frightened to others is akin to supposing that a child might have mastered the moves of a chess knight by grasping that it moves two squares forward or sideways. *There are no 'half moves' in chess,* and there is no mastering the concept of pain, thinking or being frightened, without grasping the criteria for its application to others.

I noted in the previous lecture that the theory-theory in psychology is invoked to explain the difficulties that autistic children of the age of four have in ascribing a false belief to another person. This is allegedly to be explained by a failure in the child's theory of the mind. I have no idea why autistic children have such difficulties. But I think that whatever the explanation may be, it cannot possibly be due to a failure in theory formation, any more than poor balance is to be explained by reference to failure in theory formation in physics. For neither normal children nor indeed adults have anything that could be called *a theory of mind.* They have mastered, or have to master, an array of psychological *concepts.* But these are not theoretical concepts and mastering them involves no theory.

Behaviour

One misconception that fuels such doctrines as the argument from analogy or the theory-theory is that in observing the behaviour of others, all we observe are physical movements or 'bare bodily behaviour', and from this we have to infer an inner mental cause. *If* that is what one thinks, *then* it may well seem that one needs an inferential ground for concluding that another person is in pain, sees a mountain in the distance, is hungry or believes that it is time to go home.

In the heyday of behaviourist psychology, it was common to think that *really* all we observe of other people is their 'bare bodily behaviour', or their 'colourless movements' as the distinguished neo-behaviourist psychologist Clark Hull put it. Hull's goal was to show how the psychological concepts of purpose, intention, desire and so forth can be 'constructed' out of colourless movements and 'mere receptor impulses'. But this is a misrepresentation of our daily experience *and* a misconstrual of psychological concepts. Do we not *see* expressions of curiosity, puzzlement, amusement, anger, sadness and joy on people's faces? Do we *strictly speaking* see only movements of facial muscles, of mouth and eyes, and *infer* from these that the person in question is curious, puzzled, amused or angry? That is incoherent. The supposition that we do not really see anger, joy, sorrow or amusement in a person's face is as absurd as the idea that we do not really see the furniture in the room but only colours and shapes from which we infer the presence of pieces of furniture.

What counts as behaviour is *not* mere bodily movement. It is smiles of friendliness, cries of joy or grief, snarls of anger or contempt – just as what we hear when we hear people speak is not mere sounds. Rather, we hear them say things, assert things to be so, express their opinions, ask for things, answer questions, give orders and so on and so forth through a list of myriad different speech acts that human beings perform. Behavioural criteria of the mental include not merely moving one's hand or hands in a huge and virtually indescribable range of bare physical motions, but rather waving goodbye, shaking hands, caressing and gesturing. We inhabit a human world; we are surrounded by our fellow human beings – language-using beings living in distinctive cultures, not automata. It is quite extraordinary how easy it is to forget this when theorizing and philosophizing. The following passage, written by two mainstream philosophers, is instructive:

> human beings move in a bewildering variety of ways. Nevertheless, we often succeed in predicting what they will do. How do we do this? By observing what they do and say, we arrive at views about what they are thinking, what they desire, and closely associated views about their characters, mental capacities and in general about their psychological profiles [...] We have, then, great facility in moving backwards and forwards from behaviour in situations to mental states. Think of what is involved in playing a game of tennis, crossing a road at traffic lights, or organizing a conference. The antecedent probability that Jones will move her body in such a way that the ball will land where you have most trouble retrieving it, or that drivers will move in such a way that their cars will stop when the light turns red, or that a number of human bodies will move from various corners of the globe to end up at the same time in one conference centre, is fantastically small. Yet we make such predictions successfully all the time [...] The fact that we can make the predictions

shows that we have cottoned on to the crucial regularities – otherwise our predictive capacities would be a miracle. They show that we have an implicit mastery of a detailed, complex scheme that interconnects inputs, outputs and mental states.[1]

It is, of course, true that we make numerous predictions about each other. But our predictions rest on *understanding each other* and knowing *what counts as a good reason for acting*. We understand that if Miss Jones is playing in a tennis tournament, she will try to win. And, of course, we know the rules of tennis. So we know that she will try to respond to her opponent's shots by placing her shot in such a way that her opponent is unable to return it. But we do not, and commonly cannot, predict 'how she will move her body'. We may predict that Mr Jones will brake as he approaches the red traffic light, because we know, and we know that he knows, the traffic code. We know that the light's being red is a compelling *reason* for braking the car. But we do not, and by and large cannot, predict how exactly Mr Jones will 'move his body'. And if Mr Jones is playing chess, we may predict his next *move*, but not his next *movement*. What we typically predict are not movements, but actions. And our predictions of action do not rest on *observed regularities* of the form: if human bodies receive bits of paper with such marks on them then they regularly move their bodies in such-and-such ways. We don't predict that a number of human bodies will move from various corners of the globe to end up at a conference centre in New York, but rather that various scholars who have accepted an invitation to a conference will take steps to arrive on time. Our predictions rest on our knowledge of human customs, institutions, practices and on our understanding of practical reasoning.

The fact that we can make predictions does not show that we have 'cottoned on to crucial regularities' of movement. It is not as if we can predict that when someone in our culture goes into a shop and takes a product to the counter, he or she will pass a small circular piece of metal to the shopkeeper *because that is what human beings regularly do*. It is true that this is what people regularly do, but they regularly do it because the price of the good is £1, because they want to buy the good from the shopkeeper and to do so they give him or her a £1 coin since buying something involves paying for the good, and so on. That is, our predictive abilities turn on our understanding of myriad customs, conventions and rules of human conduct.

If we were capable only of registering the physical movements of others and of hearing only sounds that they emit, then it is more than just doubtful whether we could master the language of human beings, and indeed whether

---

1 D. Braddon-Mitchell and F. Jackson, *Philosophy of Mind and Cognition* (Blackwell, Oxford, 1996), pp. 56f.

we ourselves would be human at all. If we try to imagine this, then one might indeed argue that such beings would need a theory of some kind to link the slight movement of the lips and crinkling around the eyes with a feeling of friendliness, or with amusement. The idea that the psychological is *hidden* or *concealed* behind observable behaviour conceived as bare bodily movement is a misconception. The mind, human emotions and moods, desires and purposes, thought and belief are no more hidden behind their behavioural manifestations than the meaning of a word is hidden behind the utterance of the word. So, we need to say more about the notions of the inner and the outer, the concealed and the revealed.

The Inner and the Outer

The thought that what we see when we observe our fellow human beings is bare bodily movement feeds a correlative array of misconceptions about experience and the mental. Let me remind you of the passage from John Stuart Mill that you heard in the previous lecture. Mill wrote as follows:

> I observe that there is a great multitude of other bodies, closely resembling in their sensible properties [...] this particular one, but whose modifications do not call up, as those of my own body do, a world of sensations in my consciousness. Since they do not do so in my consciousness, I infer that they do it out of my consciousness, and that to each of them belongs a world of consciousness of its own, to which it stands in the same relation in which what I call my body stands to mine, [...] Each of these bodies exhibits to my sense a set of phenomena (composed of acts and other manifestations), such as I know, in my own case, to be effects of consciousness, and such as might be looked for if each of the bodies has really in connection with it a world of consciousness.[2]

Here the thought is that what Mill calls *a world of consciousness* is connected with my body, and, by analogy with my own case, I infer that other *worlds of consciousness* are connected with the human bodies that I see around me.

Now, we must not lose sight of the fact that it is misguided to hold that what we see around us when we are engaged with our fellow human beings are *human bodies*. We may see human bodies in a morgue. But what we see around us in society are human beings, living creatures, going about their business. But if we think as Mill did,[3] then it is almost irresistible to conceive of the mental or 'inner' as something hidden 'within' the bodies we observe. We

---

2 Mill, *An Examination of Sir William Hamilton's Philosophy*, vol. IX, p. 192.
3 In fact, Mill was in a much worse position, since he advanced a phenomenalist view, according to which bodies, including the bodies of other human beings, are no more than permanent possibilities of perception. This piles incoherence upon incoherence.

cannot *perceive* the minds or experiences of others, but only their bodies and bodily behaviour. And we then think of bodily behaviour as no more than the movements of a physical object in space. *Then* the inner seems to be 'hidden' behind the outer. It has to be inferred from perceptible physical movements.

Wittgenstein was highly critical of the philosophical misconstrual of the metaphor of 'inner' and 'outer'. And it is surely suspect. I mean, would you think of toothache as something 'inner'? As something mental?

> **Int.** [*hesitantly*] Well ... it's surely not something 'outer'!
>
> **PMSH.** Perhaps not. But does it follow that it is something 'inner'? Maybe it's neither 'inner' nor 'outer'. Maybe these metaphors are just totally misleading. After all, no one, except when doing philosophy, would ever say that toothache is something 'inner'. After all, what is toothache supposed to be in? In the mind? Of course not. Toothache is, by definition, a pain in a tooth.
>
> Now what about 'mental'? Is pain something mental?
>
> **Int.** I'm not really sure what to say.
>
> **PMSH.** But surely you don't want to claim that when you have a toothache, you have something mental in your tooth.
>
> **Int.** Well, no. That really would be bizarre.
>
> **PMSH.** Of course. We speak of *physical* pain and *contrast it* with mental suffering, such as anguish and grief. The important question here is why we are so tempted to say that pain is something inner, something mental. Wittgenstein noted that we *compare* toothache and its behavioural manifestation with 'internal' and 'external'. And it is easy to see why the comparison comes so readily to mind. For I don't say that I have a toothache *on the basis of observing my own behaviour*, whereas I judge that another has a toothache when I see him clutching his swollen jaw and groaning with pain. But, Wittgenstein remarked,
>
>> We must get clear about how the metaphor of revealing (outside and inside) is actually applied by us; otherwise we shall be tempted to look for an inside behind that which in our metaphor is actually the inside. (LPE 223)
>
> That is a wonderful diagnostic observation: we shall be tempted to look for an inside *behind* that which in our metaphor *is actually the inside*.
>
> **Int.** I'm afraid I don't understand. What does he mean?
>
> **PMSH.** Well, just think. Someone may have a toothache and not show that he is in pain. One may see something but not tell anyone what one has seen. And one may think something but not voice one's thoughts. But when one groans with pain, points out what one sees and says what one thinks, then one *has* 'revealed' what, *in our metaphor*, is the inner.

If a person cries out with pain when the dentist prods his tooth, one cannot then say 'Well, that is only behaviour – his pain is still concealed'. If someone sincerely asserts his opinion, one cannot go on to say – 'But these are only words – he has kept his thoughts to himself'. And if someone shows us what he sees, then we too can see what he sees, even though we don't 'look inside his mind', as it were. In each case, what was, metaphorically speaking, 'inside' is exhibited, so to say, 'outside'. This is what is *called* 'exhibiting pain', 'revealing one's opinions' and 'showing what one sees'. For it is not as if, in such cases, one always leaves something unsaid which one keeps to oneself.

Let me try to sum up. Having a mild toothache and not telling anyone is not concealing anything. Being slightly annoyed but not expressing one's irritation or thinking something but not telling anyone are not cases of concealment or hiding either – any more than wearing a shirt is hiding one's vest or sitting in an armchair is concealing one's back. We need to call to mind here what is *called* 'hiding'. I hide my pain when I stifle my groans. But by the same token, I reveal my pain when a scream bursts from my lips. I conceal my anger when I exercise self-control and speak calmly. But I reveal my feelings when I give vent to my anger. That's what is *called* 'showing one's feelings'. I don't conceal my thoughts when I am in a brown study, that is, when I am thinking and not saying what I think, although it is true that others will not know what I am then thinking unless I tell them. Even refusing to tell another what I think is not so much *concealing* my thoughts as not revealing them. But one *can* be said to conceal one's thoughts if one writes them down in code, or keeps one's diary under lock and key, or when one communicates one's thoughts to one's spouse in a language the children cannot understand or when one lies. And, of course, if the code is broken, the diary read, the foreign language understood and the lie disclosed, then one's previously hidden thoughts are revealed.

The Inner as a Cause of Behaviour

Now let's turn to a different epicycle on these orbital movements of erroneous thought. It seems evident that what lies within is the cause of corresponding behaviour. Don't people cry out *because* they are in pain? And is not pain something 'inner'? People reach for a glass of water *because* they are thirsty. They make assertions that things are thus-and-so *because* that is what they believe. It seems overwhelmingly plausible to suppose that *the inner is the cause of the outer*. But if that is so, then an inference from behaviour to a thought or experience that lies behind it is in effect an inference from an observable effect to a hidden cause. So we are prone to think of human behaviour as akin to the movements of a puppet manipulated by hidden strings. Dualists will think of the strings as being in the hands of the mind. The mind *causes* the body to move in desired ways to achieve the goals one has. Materialists think of the strings of the somatic puppet as being in the hands of the brain.

The causal conception of the mind and the mental is far too large a subject to tackle comprehensively here. All I wish to do is draw your attention to it, and – as usual – to warn you not to take it for granted that this common way of thinking is correct.

We may certainly concede that we say such things as 'I said that precisely because it was what I thought', or 'I cried out because it hurt', or 'I insisted on the point because I remember seeing it happening', or 'I did it because I wanted to'. It is common to assume that these *becauses* are causal *becauses*. But that *is far from obvious*. The expression 'because' is the most general connective employed to link an explanation to something that needs explaining. And not all explanations are causal – as is obvious in such examples as 'This angle of the triangle must be a right angle *because* the sum of those other two angles is 90 degrees', 'This blade won't break as the last one did, *because* this one is made of hardened steel', or 'He will speak first, *because* he is the prime minister'.

'I said it, because that was what I thought' does not imply that the inner event of my thinking what I thought caused me to say what I said. Rather, such an explanation is given in order to distinguish my sincerely expressing opinion from, say, being insincere, pulling someone's leg, being deliberately provocative or acting as devil's advocate. So too, 'I insisted that things were thus-and-so because I remember seeing it happening' is not a causal explanation of my insistence, as if my remembering the event caused me to insist that things were thus. Rather, my explanation specifies the source of my knowledge in prior perception, and so distinguishes my assertion from mere hearsay. Of course, we often shrink from something because we are afraid, or reach for something because we want to have it. But it does not follow that these explanations are causal. We contrast shrinking from something out of fear with shrinking from it out of disgust. Such explanations *characterize the action* – they do not explain it by reference to a causal hypothesis. Dancing with joy is not a matter of one's inner feeling of joy causing one's outer behaviour of dancing. Chortling with amusement is not a case of an inner experience of amusement causing an outer emission of chortling noises. And weeping with grief is not an outer event of tear emission caused by an inner feeling of grief. These kinds of behaviour are *expressions* or *manifestations* of joy, amusement and grief. They should be compared not with the flipping of a switch causing the light to go on, or the heating of the water causing it to evaporate, but with plaintive, joyous or triumphant music. For these are not music *caused by* the plaint, joy and triumph of the composer – nor are they music that *causes* inner feelings of plaint, joy or triumph.

> **Int.** But surely, when one hurts oneself, the pain *causes* one to cry out?
>
> **PMSH.** Take it slowly! The relationship between pain and the expressive behaviour that manifests pain is not akin to the relation between heating a kettle and the kettle's boiling. Of course, when one hurts oneself, one cries out *in* pain. Of course, when one bites on a badly infected tooth, one *can't help* crying out – for one can't stifle the cry. But it does not follow that the pain *caused* one to cry out. If anything causes one to cry out in the sense in which heating water causes it to evaporate, then it is biting on the infected tooth. The pain is not, as it were, a third object that mediates between biting on the tooth and crying out in pain. It is altogether misleading to conceive of crying out in pain as crying out plus an inner experience that is its cause.
>
> To be sure, this thought needs extensive elaboration and objections from causalist conceptions of action need to be rehearsed and refuted. But this is not the place for such an undertaking. All I can do here is warn against the temptations of the obvious. As Wittgenstein remarked: 'If it looks as if, then you need to look out.'

Behaviourism

As we have seen, the concept of behaviour looms large, in Wittgenstein's accounts of language and of psychology.

- He held that initial language learning is founded on brute training and association, and rests upon natural reactions and behavioural propensities.
- He insisted that 'words are deeds' and that 'our language-game is behaviour' (*Zettel* §545).
- He argued that psychological concepts are *essentially* bound up with behaviour.
- He granted that the 'inner' is *essentially verified* by reference to the 'outer', and that doubts about the 'inner' (e.g. about dissimulation) are settled by reference to more evidence from the 'outer'. For we determine whether someone is pretending to be in pain or frightened, for example, by reference to his *further* behaviour.
- He denied that the empirical study of human psychology is to be pursued by means of introspection – and then reporting what one observes for the benefit of the psychologist. According to Wittgenstein, the psychologist

does *not* study the 'inner' at one remove – examining unobservable mental states and processes by registering their effects on behaviour, as one might indirectly observe particles in a Wilson cloud chamber when studying particle physics.

All this is congenial to the school of thought known as behaviourism. Let me remind you of what behaviourism is. As a school of empirical psychology, behaviourism originated with the work of John Watson in the United States in the 1910s. Watson repudiated the prevailing conception of psychology as the study of consciousness. Indeed, he asserted that *there is no such thing as consciousness*. He wrote:

> The belief in the existence of consciousness goes back to the ancient days of superstition and magic [...] [The scientific psychologist] can do without the terms 'mind' and 'consciousness' – he can find no objective evidence for their existence [...] [So] the behaviourist recognizes no such things as mental traits, dispositions, or tendencies.[4]

Psychological science must focus on what is observable, namely human behaviour. Its explanations, like those in the physical sciences, must rest on functional dependencies between observable data. It seeks law-like correlations between external stimuli and behavioural responses. Explanations of behaviour are to be sought in terms of stimulus conditioning and drives. Thoughts, intentions, purposes and desires are mere fictions. Watson nicely summarizes this bleak and dehumanized conception of human nature and of understanding of human behaviour:

> It is part of the behaviourist's scientific job to be able to state what the human machine is good for and to render serviceable predictions about its future capacities whenever society needs such information. (Ibid., p. 271)

Psychology, Watson held, is the study of human behaviour. Its ultimate goal is the control and prediction of behaviour.

Watson's behaviourism may be called *ontological behaviourism* in as much as it claims that minds, consciousness and mental states and processes *do not really exist*. They are no more than *fictions* – like unicorns, dragons and witches. A milder version of behaviourism emerged with Clark Hull, who espoused *methodological behaviourism*. This did not deny the existence of consciousness and mental states but held them to be irrelevant to a respectable science. For they are 'subjective' and so not open to *inter*-subjective confirmation as proper scientific data must be. The data for scientific psychology must be limited to what is objectively observable, namely stimuli and behavioural responses.

---

4 J. Watson, *Behaviourism* (Norton, New York, 1924), pp. 2, 18, 98.

Psychological behaviourism was prominent in experimental psychology between the First World War and the 1950s. Unsurprisingly, it caught the attention of philosophers. Hence a third kind of behaviourism arose: *logical behaviourism*. This was a philosophical doctrine advanced by some members of the Vienna Circle in the inter-war years on the continent and after the Second World War in the United States. Logical behaviourists argued that propositions concerning the mental are *reducible* to propositions concerning behaviour and dispositions to behave. So, for example, 'Jack is in pain' means roughly speaking: 'Jack is groaning or is disposed to groan after having injured himself'. This is a translatability thesis: any sentence containing a psychological predicate can be translated, without any loss of meaning, into a sentence or combination of sentences which contain *no* psychological predicate but only predicates signifying behaviour and dispositions to behave. So all talk of the mental is really no more than a feigned fiction. Logical behaviourism was briefly espoused in the United States by Rudolf Carnap, Herbert Feigel and Carl Hempel – three distinguished logical positivists who had fled to the United States in the 1930s. Whatever remote plausibility it has for the analysis of third-person sentences about mental states, it altogether lacks when it comes to the analysis of first-person ones. You will perhaps remember the old joke about the behaviourist making passionate love to his mistress, and then saying 'That was great for you. What was it like for me?'

Was Wittgenstein a logical behaviourist, or an ontological behaviourist? Would he have sympathized with Hull and agreed that the data for scientific psychology must exclude personal avowals? Let's see what he said about the matter himself:

> 'But you will surely admit that there is a difference between pain-behaviour with pain and pain-behaviour without pain.' – Admit it? What greater difference could there be? – 'And yet you again and again reach the conclusion that the sensation itself is a Nothing.' – Not at all. It's not a Something, but not a Nothing either! The conclusion was only that a Nothing would render the same service as a Something about which nothing could be said. We've only rejected the grammar which tends to force itself on us here.
>
> ... (PI §304)
>
> 'But you surely can't deny that, for example, in remembering, an inner process takes place.' – What gives the impression that we want to deny anything? When one says, 'Still, an inner process does take place here' – one wants to go on: 'After all, you *see* it.' And it is this inner process that one means by the word 'remembering'. – The impression that we wanted to deny something arises from our setting our face against the picture of an 'inner process'. What we deny is that the picture of an inner process gives us the correct idea of the use of the word 'remember'. Indeed, we're saying that this picture, with its ramifications, stands in the way of our seeing the use of the word as it is. (PI §305)

> Why ever should I deny that there is a mental process? It is only that 'There has just taken place in me the mental process of remembering [...]' means nothing more than 'I have just remembered [...]' To deny the mental process would mean to deny the remembering; to deny that anyone ever remembers anything. (PI §306)
>
> 'Aren't you nevertheless a behaviourist in disguise? Aren't you nevertheless basically saying that everything except human behaviour is a fiction?' – If I speak of a fiction, then it is of a *grammatical* fiction. (PI §307)

This should be clear enough. But, of course, one has to understand it – as Wittgenstein's critics evidently have not.

First, he emphasizes that he is not denying the difference between pain-behaviour without pain and pain-behaviour with pain. What he is denying is that the difference between the two cases consists in the presence or absence of a 'private object' that is privately owned and epistemically private. And obviously he also denies that such a 'private object' could be used as a sample in a private ostensive definition of 'pain'. *That* would be something about which nothing could be said. And that is the *grammatical fiction* that he is denying.

Second, Wittgenstein does not deny that people, for example, remember things. Nor does he claim that remembering is mere behaviour. What he denies is that by the word 'remembering' one means an introspectively observable inner process. What he insists is that the form of words 'There has just taken place in me the inner process of remembering' means no more than 'I have just remembered'.

Wittgenstein did not deny that one may have a pain and not show it, think a thought and not tell anyone. Nor did he deny that one may pretend to be in pain, or that one may insincerely say that one thinks such-and-such. Pain-behaviour is a criterion for being in pain, but it is *defeasible* – it does not *entail* that the person is in pain. And so too, the expression of one's thoughts is a criterion for what one thinks – but it does not guarantee sincerity. So Wittgenstein was clearly opposed to the logical behaviourist claim that sentences about the inner can be *translated* into sentences about the outer without any loss of meaning. He patently denied anything like Watson's view that the inner is sheer ontological fiction.

What of Hull's methodological behaviourism? This too, Wittgenstein thought, rested on confusion:

> So does psychology deal with behaviour, not with human states of mind? If someone does a psychological experiment, what will he report? – What the subject says, what he does, what has happened to him in the past and how he has reacted to it. – And not: what the subject thinks, what he sees, feels, believes, experiences? – If you describe a painting, do you describe the arrangement of paint strokes on the canvas and *not* what someone looking at it *sees*? (RPP I, §287)

In short, behaviourism has a misconceived idea of *behaviour*. If behaviour is mere bodily movements, then obviously we observe much more than behaviour, we observe human actions in the circumstances of human life. And correspondingly, we do not merely hear others emitting sounds, we hear them saying things, and we understand what they say.

It is a salutary lesson to be learnt from Wittgenstein that the Cartesian and empiricist traditions passed on to us do not merely advance a misguided conception of the mental as the domain of consciousness, of private ownership and privileged access, but also an equally misguided conception of behaviour and of what is observable in observing human behaviour. Behaviourism reacted rightly against the traditional conception of the mental. But it embraced the no less pernicious counterpart conception of the behavioural. And *both* mentalism *and* behaviourism need to be rejected.

Chapter 14

'ONLY OF A HUMAN BEING AND WHAT BEHAVES LIKE A HUMAN BEING …': THE MEREOLOGICAL FALLACY AND COGNITIVE NEUROSCIENCE

The Subject of Psychological Predicates

Wittgenstein argued that there is a conceptual connection between psychological attributes, such as being in pain, being afraid, wanting an apple, and their behavioural manifestation. But he denied that this connection amounts to entailment. *Investigations* §281 opens with the accusation that Wittgenstein is in effect espousing a form of behaviourism: 'Doesn't what you say amount to this', his interlocutor queries, 'that there is no pain, for example, without *pain-behaviour*?' To this Wittgenstein replies:

> It amounts to this: that only of a living human being and what resembles (behaves like) a living human being can one say: it has sensations; it sees; is blind; hears; is deaf; is conscious or unconscious.

This brief and quite general remark is profound and consequential. It is noteworthy that Wittgenstein was anticipated by Aristotle in his great book *De Anima*, which we shall discuss in a moment, and also by George Henry Lewes (the partner of George Eliot) in his 1877 book *The Physical Basis of Mind* (p. 441) in which he wrote: 'It is the man and not the brain that thinks; it is the organism as a whole, and not one organ, that feels and acts.' It is easy to misinterpret Wittgenstein's remark. So, as is our wont, let's take it slowly.

Wittgenstein is denying that the connection between pain and pain-behaviour is as close as the behaviourist suggests. What he in effect is doing is *modalizing* the connection – that is, linking pain not directly to pain behaviour in each and every instance, but to the *possibility* of pain behaviour. So, don't say:
- There is no pain without pain-behaviour.

What we want is a looser connection that invokes modality – in particular, *possibility*. What about:
- There is no pain without the possibility of pain-behaviour.

That is not yet right, since clearly, someone completely paralysed (e.g. by an injection of curare alkaloids prior to surgery) may nevertheless feel pain. But our concern is surely not with circumstantial possibility. 'Possibility' here must be taken as 'logical possibility'. As we have seen, *logical possibility* amounts to *intelligibility* – to what makes sense. To say that something is logically possible is to say that the sentence in question makes sense – that it expresses a proposition and may be either true or false. So we may rephrase the modal move thus:

- It makes sense to ascribe pain to a being only to the extent that pain-behaviour is within its normal behavioural repertoire.

One can indeed *intelligibly* ascribe pain to a being that is not displaying any pain-behaviour. That ascription will be false, if the creature is in fact not in pain. Equally, if the creature is in fact in pain but not manifesting it, the ascription will be true. But it can be true or false only if the pain-ascription *makes sense* – and it makes sense only if the animal *can* exhibit pain, only if pain-behaviour lies within *its natural behavioural repertoire*, only if some form or other of its logically possible behaviour would *count* as manifesting pain.

So, only of a living human being (not a corpse), and what behaves like a human being, does it make sense to attribute psychological attributes *or their negations*. A human being may be in pain or may not be in pain. But it makes no sense to say of a lump of stone that it is in pain – *or that it is not in pain*. Only of a being that *can be* in pain can one intelligibly say that *it is not in pain*. Of a human being, or of a dog or a cat, we may say that he or she sees and also that he or she is blind. But a tree or a table *neither sees nor is blind*. One cannot intelligibly say of a table that it *does not* see the books that are lying on it. One may perhaps say that tables *cannot* see. That is a grammatical remark signifying that it makes no sense to ascribe sight to a table, and equally, that it makes no sense to ascribe blindness to it. A robot that responds to verbal instructions does not hear, and if it is malfunctioning, it is not deaf. A computer, no matter how complex and sophisticated, is neither conscious nor unconscious.

> **Int.** You are going too quickly. Surely, in a fairy tale a pot too can see and hear – so this surely makes sense! Of course, it's obviously not *true* that pots can see or hear – but it is not nonsense. Because if it were nonsense, we would not understand the fairy tale!
>
> **PMSH.** Well, things are not as simple as that. In a fairy tale, a pot can also talk – but then, in the fairy tale (and in drawings that illustrate it) the pot *has a face*. Is it *obvious* that it is false, rather than nonsense, to say that the pot talks? Do we really have a clear idea of the circumstances in which we'd say of a pot that it talked? Of course, we enjoy

fairy tales – but why should we not enjoy listening to certain kinds of nonsense? Not all nonsense is like the babble of a child.

We enjoy looking at Morits Escher's etchings of buildings with perpetually ascending staircases that return to their starting point, or with walls that are both behind and in front of a portico. That's just the same. These are nonsense pictures.

Int. Oh come now. The fairy tale and Escher's etchings are not at all alike. Escher's pictures aren't nonsense. They are pictures of impossible objects.

PMSH. Now you've put your foot in it! Recall our old principle: a logical impossibility is not a possibility that is impossible. And now apply it to the case of Escher's etchings. These are not pictures of impossible objects. An impossible object is not a possible object that is impossible. Escher's etchings are not pictures of logically impossible objects. They are pictures that make no sense. They systematically and amusingly transgress the rules of perspectival representation. So they are pictorial nonsense – although not in the same way in which mere scribbles are pictorial nonsense. So too, fairy tales in which the pots talk, hear and see are nonsense stories that deliberately transgress the rules of intelligible sentence formation for the sake of entertainment.

Int. All right. But what about ascribing psychological attributes to inanimate things? Do we not say of a doll that it is tired and wants to lie down, that it has hurt itself and needs a bandage? This is what children playing with dolls say, and the adults who are playing with the children go along with it. Are they talking nonsense?

PMSH. Again, things are not that simple. We, and our children, do speak thus when we're playing with dolls – but playing with dolls is a very special kind of language-game. It involves what Wittgenstein called 'a secondary use' of psychological expressions – a use which is parasitic on their primary use in application to human beings and creatures that behave like human beings. The parasitism is evident if one reflects on the intelligibility of ascribing pains *only* to dolls. Would anyone then understand what the word 'pain' means? And note that although an adult playing dolls with a child will commiserate with a doll who has, so to say, hurt itself, and help the child bandage the doll, the adult does not telephone the doctor. Imagine the child's bafflement were mother to rush to the car, bundle child and doll in the car and drive helter-skelter to the hospital!

Int. R i g h t ... But there is another matter that you must clarify. You said that Wittgenstein wrote that psychological attributes can be truly or falsely ascribed only to human beings and *what behaves like human beings*.

But how like is like? How far must the resemblance reach? I mean, do fish behave like human beings? Do computers and robots behave like human beings?

Let us try to tackle this. Do computers behave like human beings? Or, at any rate, sufficiently like them to be the logically appropriate subjects of cogitative predicates? Wittgenstein confronted the question in the mid-1930s.

> 'Is it possible for a machine to think?' [...] the trouble which is expressed in this question is not really that we don't yet know a machine which could do the job. The question is not analogous to that which someone might have asked a hundred years ago: 'Can a machine liquify gas?' The trouble is rather that the sentence, 'A machine thinks (perceives, wishes)' seems somehow nonsensical. It is as though we asked, 'Has the number 3 a colour?' (BB 47)

Wittgenstein's point is not that thinking, being in some sense ethereal, cannot be the property of a machine, because it must of its nature be the property of something with a 'spiritual nature', such as the mind. On the contrary – thinking is ascribable to living human beings and to what behaves like a living human being in the relevant respects. His point was that the question of whether machines can think is a *conceptual*, not an empirical, one. Does *it make sense* to ascribe thinking to a machine?

It might seem that the Turing Test resolves the question. Alan Turing, the great mathematician and inventor of the computer, proposed a test for whether a machine can think. It is a test that, at first glance, seems very persuasive. Turing envisaged constructing a computer into which one can type questions. The computer is so programmed that it presents answers to these questions on its screen. If these answers in general are indistinguishable from the answers that a human being might give, then, Turing suggested, there are adequate grounds for ascribing thought to the computer. And surely here we must say that the computer is behaving like a human being!

Is this persuasive? Yes – very. Is it right? No – it is altogether wrong. It takes more to perform a speech act than making a noise or generating an inscription on a screen. Human beings are no more uncomprehending display-generating machines than computing machines have a form of life. The appearance of a typed message on a screen may be the product of a human being typing it; or it may be the product of a computer programmed to type it. But either way, it is not itself a *form of human behaviour* at all.

Calculating devices were invented long before computers, ranging from the humble abacus to the slide rule and to the cylindrical mechanical calculators of the nineteenth century. No one was tempted to say that these gadgets could literally calculate or think. Are electronic calculators any different? It is tempting to think that they are, not only because the tasks which they can be used to carry out are so much more complex, but also because they surely follow rules – just as we do. For don't we programme them with ever more sophisticated algorithms, and do they not follow these instructions meticulously? — No! They do no such thing. There is no such thing as a calculator or even a computer *following a rule*! One can no more literally *instruct* a computer to do anything than one can instruct a tree to grow. One cannot make a computer that will *follow* a rule, but only make one that will produce results that *accord* with a rule. A machine can execute operations that *accord* with a rule, provided all the causal links built into it function as designed and assuming that the design ensures regularities that accord with the relevant rules. But for something to follow a rule more is needed than a mere regularity – otherwise we could say that the planets follow Kepler's three laws and obey Newton's laws of gravity. But planets do not obey anyone and they do not follow rules – rather their movements are describable by reference to Kepler's laws and Newton's theory of gravitational force.

Remember that neither a calculator nor a computer can understand the results it generates on its screen. They do not know what the symbols they display mean – for they neither understand nor know anything. Wittgenstein wrote:

Does a calculating machine *calculate*?

> Imagine that a calculating machine had come into existence by accident; now someone accidentally presses its knobs (or an animal walks over it) and it calculates the product of 25 × 20. (RFM 257)

Would anyone or anything have literally made a calculation?

We use our machines and our computers to save us the labour of calculating and to produce the answers to a calculation with great rapidity. But it does not follow that our machines calculate in the sense in which human beings calculate – for to say that a calculating machine calculates is a secondary use of the verb 'to calculate'. No one thought that slide rules could literally calculate. No one thought that when one turned the crank on a cylindrical calculating machine the machine began thinking and calculating. Indeed, it is nonsense to claim that a machine infers, draws conclusions, or indeed that it literally calculates. We are fooled into believing that our calculators and computers calculate and think primarily because we can't see anything happening, and because the results appear so incredibly swiftly.

With regard to the animal kingdom, there is no difficulty with the higher animals. They clearly perceive, feel hunger and thirst, feel fear and anger, like and dislike things – all of which is visible in their behaviour. But when it comes to the boundaries, for example insects or molluscs, there is no clear answer. That is not due to our *ignorance*. Our *concepts* of perceptual faculties, of sensation, consciousness, wanting, and so on, are essentially indeterminate at this boundary. It makes no sense to attribute sight or blindness to a telescope. It makes no sense to ascribe pain or lack of pain to a plant. But is there a clear answer to the question of whether a wriggling fly that has scorched itself feels pain? Here, Wittgenstein says, the concept gets a *foothold* – but no more. Do we have any conception of what it would be for a fly to have aching joints, or a headache? In short, living beings are said to feel; stones and other inanimate things are not. Wittgenstein immediately raises another objection:

> Couldn't I imagine having frightful pains and, while they were going on, turning to stone? Indeed, how do I know, if I shut my eyes, whether I have not turned into a stone? – And if that has happened, in what sense will *the stone* have pains? In what sense will they be ascribable to a stone? Why indeed should the pain here have a bearer at all?!
>
> And can one say of the stone that it has a mind, and *that* is what has the pain? What has a mind, what have pains, to do with a stone?
>
> Only of what behaves like a human being can one say that it *has* pains. (PI §283)

That is a powerful and convincing passage. But do not think that assent to it is trivial. For if it makes no sense to ascribe psychological attributes to a stone or any other inanimate being, what of the body – or the mind?

Wittgenstein confronted the question of the ascribability of psychological attributes to the body. This is what he wrote:

> But isn't it absurd to say of a *body* that it has pain? – And why does one feel an absurdity in that? In what sense does my hand not feel pain, but I in my hand?
>
> What sort of issue is this: Is it the *body* that feels pain? – How is it to be decided? How does it become clear that it is *not* the body? – Well, something like this: if someone has a pain in his hand, then the *hand* does not say so [...] and one does not comfort the hand, but the sufferer: one looks into his eyes. (PI §286)

> How am I filled with pity *for this human being*? How does it come out what the object of my pity is? (Pity, one might say, is one form of being convinced that someone else is in pain.) (PI §287)

One may be revolted by another's injury or diseased limb, but one feels pity for the injured human being. One may try to assuage the pain in another's limb, but one commiserates with the human being.

Now, if one's body is not the subject of psychological predicates, is it the mind? To be sure, as Wittgenstein remarked, a stone, even a stone into which I have turned, does not have a mind – for, as he put it: 'What has a mind ... to do with a stone?' But doesn't my mind feel pain, have perceptual experiences, think thoughts and make decisions, as Descartes insisted? Wittgenstein does not pursue this question directly. But it is noteworthy that Aristotle had already done so – and in a manner that would surely be wholly congenial to Wittgenstein.

In *De Anima*, Aristotle's great work on the philosophy of psychology, he discussed the *psuchē* at length. Now the term '*psuchē*' is commonly translated as 'the soul'. But that is misleading, since the notion of *psuchē* as Aristotle used it is *a biological concept*, not a theological or ethical one. All living things, including plants, have *psuchē*. The *psuchē* is, in effect, the set of fundamental capacities of a living being. In the case of plants, their vegetative *psuchē* includes the powers of nutrition, growth and reproduction. Non-human animals have the basic vegetative powers too, but also the powers of self-movement, perception and desire, which Aristotle termed 'the sensitive *psuchē*'. Humans possess, in addition to the vegetative and sensitive *psuchē*, the powers of rationality – the rational *psuchē*, that is: the ability to engage in practical and theoretical reasoning and the power to act, think and feel for reasons.[1] In a passage that is cousin to Wittgenstein's remark in *Investigations* §281, Aristotle wrote:

> to say that the *psuchē* is angry is as if one were to say that the *psuchē* weaves or builds. For it is surely better not to say that the *psuchē* pities, learns, or thinks, but that the man does these things with his *psuchē*. (*De Anima* 408b12–15)

Doing something with one's *psuchē* here is to be understood not on the model of doing something with one's hand, but rather on the model of doing something with one's talents. The *psuchē* is best conceived as the active and passive powers of a living being, not as the entity that has those powers. What possesses the powers that Aristotle calls the *psuchē* is the living animal. It makes no sense to ascribe the powers of a living being to the set of powers itself – that would be to reify the powers. And it makes no sense to ascribe the *exercise* of the powers of a living thing to the powers themselves. One's ability to think is not what thinks – it is what one exercises *when* one thinks.

Aristotle's observations on the *psuchē* apply equally to our notion of the mind. It is not my mind that sees and hears, that feels joyous or sad, that wants and intends; it is I – the living human being. Despite all that Descartes said, it is not my mind that thinks – I think, *by using my mind*. My mind is not a thinking thing – it is the distinctive capacities *of* a thinking thing – namely of a human being. It is no more my mind that has a pain than it is my body; I may have a pain in my hand, but my mind does not have a pain in *its* hand – since my mind *does not have a hand*. It is not the mind that manifests thought and desire, memory and will, emotion and volition *in behaviour* – it is the living human being.

---

1 The powers of the intellect' Aristotle refers to as '*nous*'.

Associated Fallacies

Wittgenstein has argued that psychological predicates are predicable only of humans and other beings that behave like humans. They are *not* predicable of inanimate objects, or of the body a human being has or indeed of the mind of a human being. We can distinguish here a number of further, related, confusions.

The first is the incoherence of ascribing to a faculty the acts which the faculty is the power to perform. As we have seen, this was pointed out by Aristotle. It is not a trivial matter. The incoherence is one into which the most eminent theoretical linguist of our times, Noam Chomsky, regularly falls. This is what he wrote:

> The language faculty is a component of the mind/brain, part of the human biological endowment. Presented with data, the child, or, more specifically, *the child's language faculty, forms a language*, a computational system of some kind that provides structured representations of linguistic expressions that determine their sound and meaning. [...] Universal grammar attempts to formulate the principles that enter into the operation of the language faculty. The grammar of a particular language is an account of *the state of the language faculty after it has been presented with data of experience*; universal grammar is an account of the initial state of the language faculty before any experience.[2]

But it is as absurd to say that a faculty 'forms a language' as it is to say that the *psuchē* pities, learns or thinks, or to say that my mind reasons or thinks.

> **Int.** [*excitedly*] Yes, that's very good. I see that. *Faculties are not agents*. So, what you're saying is that psychological attributes are not ascribable to the faculties the exercise of which manifests attributes *of the chap* who has the faculty.
>
> **PMSH.** Exactly. So when you read the works of Chomsky and his followers, read slowly and carefully, and with a large pinch of critical salt.
>
> When Wittgenstein asserted that psychological attributes are ascribable only to humans and to beings that behave like humans, his main concern was to make it clear that it is neither a human being's body nor his mind that is the proper subject of psychological attributes. With the exception of verbs of sensation, such as 'hurts', 'tickles', 'itches', we do not ascribe psychological predicates to our body or parts of our body. My body may be strong or weak, healthy or diseased, thin or fat, sunburnt

---

2 Chomsky, *Language and Problems of Knowledge*, pp. 60f; emphasis added.

all over or covered with dirt, but it makes no sense to say that my body is in pain, is conscious or unconscious, sees or hears, thinks or intends.

Int. I'm sorry, that was a bit too quick for me. I didn't get your point about verbs of sensation.

PMSH. I'm just reminding you of something you know perfectly well. Look, you would happily say that your hand aches, that your foot hurts, or that your back itches, wouldn't you?

Int. Yes, of course.

PMSH. Right. But you wouldn't say that your hand has an ache, that your foot has a pain, or that your back has an itch, would you?

Int. No, that sounds very odd.

PMSH. Indeed it does. For we happily ascribe *verbs* of sensation to parts of the body, but we don't ascribe their nominal equivalents to parts of the body. It is the agent, not parts of his body, that has pains, aches, tickles and itches *in* parts of his body. I have a pain in my leg, but my leg cannot be said to have a pain *in it*.

Int. Hmmm. I see your point, and I agree that we don't talk that way. But isn't that just arbitrary? Indeed, isn't the more general point you are making, namely that we ascribe psychological predicates to the human being as a whole and neither to the mind he has nor to the body he has, arbitrary, haphazard or mere coincidence?

PMSH. If it were, it would be astonishing that this linguistic practice is so widespread in different cultures and languages.

Int. Well, I agree that other languages also follow this convention. But I don't see why? I mean, it might still be arbitrary, even though it is common to many languages.

PMSH. What makes it non-arbitrary is the manner in which our psychological language itself is an outgrowth of our natural, pre-linguistic reactive behaviour. These primitive sorts of behaviour are, Wittgenstein remarked, 'the prototype of a way of thinking and not the result of thought' (Z §541). Just look at a mother tending her child, and equally at a child's natural reaction to his mother having hurt herself. It is the child who expresses or manifests pain in his behaviour – he cries out, contorts his face, groans, nurses the injured part. And our reactions are to the child, not to his parts – we look into his face with sympathy, we commiserate with him, put our arm around his shoulder to comfort him. And what goes for pain goes for other psychological attributes too. In general, it is human beings, not their sense organs that see, look around, watch and observe what is in view. A person sees *with* his eyes, and we can say whether he sees and what he sees by noting how he keeps a moving object in sight, avoids impediments in his path or looks for things. It is his behaviour that provides a criterion for saying of *him* 'He sees, looks, has noticed …'.

A corollary of Wittgenstein's observation is that it makes no sense to ascribe psychological predicates to *parts* of a human being, *as opposed to the human being as a whole* (and, of course, the same applies to other animals). To do so exemplifies what I have elsewhere called 'a mereological fallacy'.[3] *Mereology* is the logic of parts and wholes – incorporating such principles as 'Parts are smaller than the wholes of which they are parts' or 'If something is part of a part of a thing then it is a part of that thing' and so forth. What I am here calling a *mereological fallacy* is the fallacy of ascribing to parts of a being predicates that can intelligibly be ascribed only to the being as a whole.

Int. What do you mean?

PMSH. Well, let me give you a couple of straightforward examples. Although an aeroplane would not fly but for its engines, it is not the engines that fly, but the aeroplane. Similarly, an antique bracket clock would not keep time but for its fusée or great wheel, but nevertheless, it is the clock that keeps time, not its fusée or great wheel. Or again, but for the souped-up carburettor, the car would not be able to do 120 mph. But still, it is the car that does 120 mph, not the carburettor.

Int. Yes, I see. But what has this got to do with psychological predicates?

PMSH. Well, a special case of the mereological fallacy is the ascription of psychological predicates to *parts of a human being* in cases where it makes sense to ascribe them *only to the human being as a whole*. It is not our eyes that see – rather, we see with our eyes. To be sure, we speak of sightless eyes, but sightless eyes are not eyes that cannot see; they are eyes with which a person cannot see, or they are eyes of the dead. So too, we speak metonymically of warnings falling on deaf ears, but it is not the ears that do not hear, but the person who refuses to listen. We speak of a heart being heavy with grief, but it is the person who grieves, not his heart. Metaphors, metonyms and figures of speech apart, it makes no sense to ascribe psychological attributes to parts of the body. In particular, it makes no sense to ascribe perceptual, cogitative or cognitive predicates to the brain. This is a point of great importance, since this confusion is rife in contemporary cognitive neuroscience.

---

3 See M. R. Bennett and P. M. S. Hacker, *Philosophical Foundations of Neuroscience* (2nd extended edition, Wiley-Blackwell, Oxford, 2022), chapter 3.

The Mereological Fallacy in Neuroscience

Francis Crick, one of the discoverers of the structure of DNA and a prominent neuroscientist, wrote as follows:

> What you see is not what is *really* there; it is what your brain *believes* is there. [...] Your brain makes the best interpretation it can according to its previous experience and the limited and ambiguous information provided by your eyes. [...] the brain combines the information provided by the many distinct features of the visual scene (aspects of shape, colour, movement, etc.) and settles on the most plausible interpretation of all these various clues taken together. [...] what the brain has to build up is a many-levelled interpretation of the visual scene [...] the brain [...] guess[es] a complete picture from only partial information – a very useful ability.[4]

Accordingly, the brain *has experiences, believes things, interprets clues* on the basis of information made available to it and *makes guesses*. Colin Blakemore, an eminent British neuroscientist, wrote comparably:

> We seem driven to say that such neurons [as respond in a highly specific manner to, e.g., line orientation in the visual field] have knowledge. They have intelligence, for they are able to estimate the probability of outside events – events that are important to the animal in question. And the brain gains its knowledge by a process analogous to the inductive reasoning of the classical scientific method. Neurons present arguments to the brain based on the specific features that they detect, arguments on which the brain constructs its hypothesis of perception.[5]

So the brain *knows* things, *reasons* inductively, *constructs hypotheses* on the basis of arguments and its constituent neurones are *intelligent,* can *estimate probabilities* and *present arguments.* J. Z. Young, a distinguished biologist, shared much the same view. He argued that

> we can regard all seeing as a continual search for the answers to questions posed by the brain. The signals from the retina constitute 'messages' conveying these answers. The brain then uses this information to construct a suitable hypothesis about what is there.[6]

Accordingly, the brain *poses questions, searches for answers* and *constructs hypotheses*. Antonio Damasio claimed that

---

4 Crick, *The Astonishing Hypothesis,* pp. 30, 32f., 57.
5 C. Blakemore, *Mechanics of the Mind* (Cambridge University Press, Cambridge, 1977), p. 91.
6 J. Z. Young, *Programmes of the Brain* (Oxford University Press, Oxford, 1978), p. 119.

our brains can often decide well in seconds or in minutes, depending on the time frame we set as appropriate for the goal we want to achieve, and if they can do so, they must do the marvellous job with more than just pure reason.[7]

And Benjamin Libet suggested that

> the brain 'decides' to initiate, or at least, to prepare to initiate the act before there is any reportable subjective awareness that such a decision has taken place. ('Unconscious cerebral initiative and the role of conscious will in voluntary action.')[8]

It is noteworthy that psychologists are not far behind. J. P. Frisby contended that

> there must be a symbolic description in the brain of the outside world, a description cast in symbols that stand for the various aspects of the world of which sight makes us aware.[9]

So there are symbols in the brain, and the brain presumably makes use of and understands symbols. And Richard Gregory conceived of seeing as

> Probably the most sophisticated of all the brain's activities: calling upon its stores of memory data; requiring subtle classifications, comparisons and logical decisions for sensory data to become perception.[10]

So, there is a widespread tendency among scientists to ascribe psychological predicates to the brain, that is, to a part of a human being. Such ascriptions are not mere *façon de parler* (manners of speaking) nor just a *form of presentation* (like speaking of the life cycle of a star (that has no life)) that can readily be paraphrased away. For they are invoked in order to explain aspects of human behaviour: human capacities and deficiencies in their exercise. A characteristic form of explanation in cognitive neuroscience is to invoke the brain's alleged powers of perception, knowledge, belief, memory, intention and decision *in order to explain* the human being's psychological powers and their exercise. In particular, lesions to the brain are held to affect the brain's ability to know, believe, guess or decide, and that in turn is held to explain the deficiencies in the human being's exercise of his or her natural powers.

It is important to note that this form of explanation in neuroscience is not the upshot of an unexpected empirical discovery that brains have a wide

---

7 A. Damasio, *Descartes's Error – Emotion, Reason, and the Human Brain* (Papermac, London, 1996), p. 173.
8 B. Libet, *Behavioural and Brain Science*, 8 (1985), p. 536.
9 J. P. Frisby, *Seeing: Illusion, Brain and Mind* (Oxford University Press, Oxford, 1980), pp. 8f.
10 R. L. Gregory, 'The Confounded Eye', in R. L. Gregory and E. H. Gombrich (eds), *Illusions in Nature and Art* (Duckworth, London, 1973), p. 50.

range of psychological and cognitive powers. It is not at all like the genuinely unexpected discovery that bonobo chimpanzees can apparently master the use of up to four hundred words and can combine words into rudimentary sentences. What happened was this: mainstream cognitive neuroscientific research prior to the Second World War adopted a broadly Cartesian view of the relationship between the mind and the brain. The Newton of neuroscience in the twentieth century, Sir Charles Sherrington, followed Descartes in ascribing all psychological attributes to the mind, holding the mind to stand in an as yet poorly understood causal relationship to the brain. And his distinguished pupil, Sir John Eccles, like his teacher a Nobel laureate, held that there were liaison areas in the dominant cerebral hemisphere where the mind interacts with the brain. After the war, enthusiasm for Cartesianism waned. Without much further reflection, neuroscientists began to attribute psychological attributes to the brain rather than to the mind – leaving the rest of the Cartesian conception of the mental intact. It is not the mind, conceived as an immaterial substance, that thinks, reasons, knows, believes, perceives and decides to act – it is the brain. Indeed, some neuroscientists went so far as to identify the mind and the brain, while others simply dispensed with the mind in favour of the brain. Francis Crick went so far as to advance what he termed 'the astonishing hypothesis' – that

> You, your joys and sorrows, your memories and ambitions, your sense of personal identity and free will, are in fact no more than the behaviour of a vast assembly of nerve cells and their associated molecules.[11]

And Colin Blakemore wrote:

> We are machines, but machines so wonderfully sophisticated that no one should count it an insult to be called such a machine [...] The sense of will is an invention of the brain. Like so much of what the brain does, the feeling of choice is a mental model – a plausible account of how we act, which tells us no more about how decisions are really taken by the brain than our perception of the world tells us about the computations involved in deriving it.[12]

So, instead of Cartesian mind/body dualism, neuroscientists advanced a form of brain/body dualism according to which the brain exercised a wide range of psychological functions previously ascribed to the mind. They purported to explain aspects of behaviour and features of the so-called conscious mind by reference to *the exercise of cognitive powers by the brain*. But, as should be evident from Wittgenstein's arguments, this is a deep and disturbing conceptual confusion.

---

11 Crick, *The Astonishing Hypothesis*, p. 3.
12 C. Blakemore, *The Mind Machine* (BBC Publications, London, 1988), pp. 270–272.

It makes no sense to ascribe psychological predicates or their negations to the brain. The brain neither sees nor is it blind – just as sticks and stones are not awake, but they are not asleep either. The brain does not hear, but it is not deaf either – any more than trees are deaf. The brain does not remember things or register things in its memory, but nor does it forget things or fail to register some fact in its memory, since it makes no sense to say that the brain has a memory. The brain makes no decisions, but nor is it indecisive – for only what *can* decide can be indecisive. The brain is neither conscious nor unconscious – it is only human beings, and what behaves like human beings, that can be said to be conscious or unconscious. In short, *the brain is not a proper subject of psychological predicates.*

It makes no sense to ascribe psychological predicates to the brain, save figuratively. If one mistakenly does, then the resultant form of words does not say something false; rather, it says nothing at all, for it lacks any sense. Psychological predicates are predicates that apply essentially to the animal as a whole, not to its parts. It is neither the eye nor the brain that sees; it is the human being that sees with his eyes. Of course, we would not see but for the proper functioning of our brain. But equally, we would not walk but for the proper functioning of our brain. And no one would say that it is really our brain that walks, or even that we walk with our brain – we walk with our legs. The brain is not the organ of locomotion.

Int. Well, that's a pretty damning and deep criticism. I mean, if you're right, then they're very confused indeed. But I still don't quite see why it is such a conceptual confusion to try to extend the psychological vocabulary to the brain and its parts.

PMSH. For the very simple reason that the brain and the parts of the brain do not behave in ways that warrant the ascription to it of psychological expressions. It is not the brain that peers through a keyhole in order to find out what is in the locked-up room, it is not the brain that ducks when it sees a cricket ball hurtling towards it, and it is not the brain that skirts carefully around a puddle in the road. For the brain has no eyes with which to see, no head to duck and no legs with which to avoid treading in puddles. It is not the brain that exhibits its mnemonic powers by rattling off the dates of the kings and queens of England. It is the pupil who has memorized the dates. It is not the brain that is in two minds whether to go to the cinema tonight, who makes up its mind to go, and who changes its mind when its best friend turns up. The brain does not have a mind – and it is not the mind either.

Int. Oh, I see what you mean. The brain doesn't satisfy the *criteria* for the ascription of psychological attributes.

PMSH Very good. That is exactly the point. And it is not just that the brain does not satisfy the criteria for the ascription of psychological predicates – rather, the brain *can't* satisfy the criteria. And this is a *logical* 'can't'. There is nothing the brain can do that could warrant the application to it of psychological predicates. For the behavioural repertoire of the brain includes *nothing* that could count as a criterion for the application of psychological predicates to it. Though neural phenomena are well-correlated with a person's being in pain, the brain does not exhibit pain-behaviour – it does not moan or groan, assuage its injuries, shed tears or grimace. The *neural phenomena* that are concomitants of an animal's suffering pain are not forms of *pain-behaviour* at all. They are forms of neural activity *inductively well-correlated* with the animal's being in pain. The correlation is *a discovery* that *presupposes the concept of pain* and its connection with pain-behaviour exhibited by the animal.

Similarly, it makes no sense to ascribe thinking, believing or remembering to the brain. These are cognitive attributes of human beings and the higher animals, who exhibit their cogitative and mnemonic powers in what they do and say. We do not observe the brain in a brown study, but rather the thinker sunk in thought. We do not see the brain's credulity, but a person's belief or disbelief may be written all over his face as he listens to another's tale. We can, to a very limited extent, correlate a person's thinking this or that with localized brain activity which we detect by means of positron emission tomography and by functional magnetic resonance imaging. But these devices do not show that the brain is thinking, reflecting or ruminating. It shows that such-and-such parts of a person's frontal cortices, say, are active *when the person is thinking*, reflecting or ruminating. What one sees on the scan is not the brain thinking – for there is no such thing as a brain's thinking. Nor do we see a person thinking on the scan – to see a person thinking one must look at someone who is sunk in thought, problem-solving or concentrating on a complex task. What we see when we look at an fMRI scan is the computer-generated image of the blood oxygen level dependency signals emitted in the vicinity of cells in the frontal cortices that occur *when the person is thinking*.

It follows that common forms of explanation among neuroscientists of human behaviour and deficiencies in human behaviour are either vacuous or simply misconceived. J. Z. Young was confused when he wrote:

> we can regard all seeing as a continual search for the answers to questions posed by the brain. The signals from the retina constitute 'messages' conveying these answers. The brain then uses this information to construct a suitable hypothesis about what is there.

Brains cannot pose questions, they cannot receive or understand information, and there is no such thing as a brain constructing hypotheses. Only a language user can pose a question, understand information, or construct an explanatory hypothesis. And – incidentally – to perceive something is not to *construct a hypothesis* about what lies within one's visual field.

The standard explanation of the strange dissociative behaviour that is consequent upon hemispherectomy is that, as Francis Crick wrote:

> When the callosum is cut, the left hemisphere sees only the right half of the visual field [...] both hemispheres can hear what is being said [...] one half of the brain appears to be totally ignorant of what the other half sees.

But this makes no sense. For a hemisphere of the brain neither sees nor hears. The severing of the corpus callosum prevents electrical impulses from crossing over from one hemisphere to the other. But that cannot be described as preventing one hemisphere from telling the other what it can see – that is truly unintelligible. And it does not explain the dissociative phenomena; it merely redescribes it in misleading terms.

Colin Blakemore wrote:

> The brain [has] maps, which are thought to play an essential part in the representation and interpretation of the world by the brain, just as maps of an atlas do for the readers of them.[13]

But this is incoherent. One can, in certain cases, map features in the visual field onto the firing of cells in the 'visual' striate cortex. But the mapping is an inductive correlation, not a conventional one. There are no maps in the brain, nor could there be unless a human being inscribed them there. For a map is a symbolic representation constructed according to conventional rules of representation. In order to make use of a map, one must be familiar with the conventions of mapping, for example, whether the mapping is Mercator or Azimuthal; one must be able to read it and know how to navigate by it. And it certainly makes no sense to suppose that the brain is acquainted with a set of projective conventions for map making, or that it can make use of a map without knowing or understanding the cartographical methods of projection.

Examples could be multiplied, but these three suffice to illustrate the manner in which a conceptual confusion can lead distinguished scientists to

- misdescribe the phenomena they are studying,
- raise pseudo-questions that need to be dissolved rather than solved by way of experimentation,

---

13 C. Blakemore, 'Understanding Images in the Brain', in H. Barlow, C. Blakemore, and M. Weston-Smith (eds.), *Images and Understanding* (Cambridge University Press, Cambridge, 1990), p. 265.

- advance illusory explanations of human capacities and their exercise — explanations that are at best no more than a redescription of the phenomenon to be explained, masquerading as an explanation.

If that is right, then you can see that conceptual confusion can have substantive consequences in the empirical sciences. It is one of the tasks of good analytic philosophy to arraign scientists before the Tribunal of Reason when they transgress the bounds of sense.

Objections Fielded

It has been suggested that these criticisms are misplaced, since neuroscientists are, in effect, employing homonyms. Of course, brains do not really think, believe, infer, interpret or hypothesize. Rather they think*, believe*, infer*, interpret* or hypothesize*. They do not have or construct symbolic representations, but only symbolic representations*. But this cannot be right, since neuroscientists and others draw inferences from their ascription of psychological attributes to the brain which cannot be drawn from innocuous homonyms. When Crick asserts that 'what you see is not what is *really* there; it is what your brain believes is there', it is important that he takes the verb 'believes' to have its normal meaning and not be understood as a homonym. For it is part of Crick's story that the brain's alleged belief is the outcome of an *interpretation* based on previous *experience* and *information*, not the outcome of an interpretation* based on previous experience* and information*. When a neuroscientist such as Semir Zeki remarks that acquisition of knowledge is a 'primordial function of the brain', he means knowledge, not knowledge* — otherwise he would not think that it is the task of future neuroscience to solve the problems of epistemology (but only, one can but suppose, of epistemology*, whatever this might be). When John Young writes of the brain's containing *knowledge* and *information*, which is encoded in the brain 'just as knowledge can be recorded in books or computers', he means knowledge, not knowledge*, since it is knowledge and information, not knowledge* and information*, that can be recorded in books or computers.

A different objection is that neuroscientists are merely *extending* the existing psychological vocabulary in fruitful ways as is commonly done in the sciences — as, for example, in the extension of the hydrodynamical vocabulary of rate of flow, pressure, density and temperature from hydrodynamics to electricity. This extension proved fruitful in the development of the theory of electricity, even though electrical current does not flow in the sense in which water flows, and electrical wires are not kinds of pipes. So the moot question is whether the application of the psychological vocabulary to the brain is an analogical extension akin to that of electrical theory. But there is nothing comparable in neuroscientific doctrines. The application of the psychological vocabulary to the brain does not come with a new theory replete with functional, mathematical relations expressible by means of quantifiable laws comparable to what we find in the theory of electricity. When neuroscientists such as Sperry and Gazzaniga speak of one hemisphere of the brain making choices, generating interpretations, of its knowing and observing things, it is clear from the sequel that these psychological expressions have not been given a new meaning. Otherwise, it would not be said that a hemisphere of the brain is 'a conscious system in its own right, perceiving, thinking, remembering, reasoning, willing and emoting, all at a characteristically human level'.

A third objection might be ventured. It has been suggested (by Colin Blakemore) that neuroscientists don't really believe that brains think and reason, feel emotions and interpret clues, make guesses and contain maps. All this is mere figurative and metaphorical speech. But one cannot claim that talk of the maps is purely metaphorical and then go on to speak of such maps as playing 'an essential part in the representation and interpretation of the world by the brain, just as the maps of an atlas do for the readers of them'.

A Further Objection Fielded: The Limiting Case of a Mutilated Human Being

> **Int.** That's all very impressive if you're right. These neuroscientists are evidently very confused and have a dire need for philosophical treatment. But for all that, I still have qualms. We can imagine our old friend Jack losing his legs. Dreadfully, we might imagine him also losing his arms. If we allow science fiction to run amok, we might even imagine that all that remains of this poor chap is his head, duly connected to appropriate machinery that keeps this head alive. We might even imagine that the machinery that keeps his head alive also enables him to see and hear, and to engage in discourse with us. That is disgusting, but it is surely intelligible, is it not? But if it is intelligible, then surely we can imagine that all that is left of poor Jack is just his *brain*, duly immersed in an appropriate vat and wired up to an appropriate array of life-support machinery and electronic gadgetry that will still enable him to see and hear, and to speak by means of an electronic voice box. And if this brain engaged with us in intelligent conversation, would this not show that the brain, which is all that is left of our old friend Jack, is seeing and hearing, thinking and believing, asking and answering questions? And does this thought experiment not *prove* that all these Wittgenstein-inspired ruminations that we have engaged in are, will be or might conceivably be disproved by the onwards march of science?

PMSH. I don't think so. A human brain is not a human being. Nor is the human brain *a limiting case of a mutilated human being*. When a brain is removed from a cadaver and put into a jar of formalin, what the jar contains is not a human corpse or the mutilated remains of a human being. Human beings have brains, but human brains do not have brains – they are brains. Human beings have bodies, but a human brain does not have a body (any more than the mind has a body) – it is *a part* of the human body. Human beings have a mind, but a human brain does not have a mind. The fact that human beings have the distinctive capacities constitutive of having a mind is indeed dependent upon the normal functioning of their brain. But that no more shows the brain to be a human being or a limiting case of a mutilated human being than the fact that an aeroplane's capacity for flight depends upon the normal functioning of its engines shows that an engine is a limiting case of a damaged aeroplane.

Int. But what about all the science fiction scenarios that have been discussed by philosophers over the last few decades? They write endlessly about brains in vats. What they imagine is that a brain might be removed from the skull and inserted into a vat with complex gadgetry connected to it that will support its continued existence, hooked up to prosthetic eyes and ears, maybe even limbs, and a computerized voice box. Then surely the brain will be able to see and hear, to move its prosthetic limbs and to talk! Does this not show that the brain thinks, remembers, wants and intends?

PMSH. No! it shows that this imaginary being, which we might call a *cerebroid* (on the model of 'android'), composed partly of neural tissue and partly of plastic and silicon chips, thinks, remembers, wants and intends. For it is *this cerebroid* that manifests thought, perception, and will.

Int. Ah, yes, I see. It is not the brain in the vat, but *the whole being* that thinks and speaks.

PMSH. Exactly. Brains are neither thoughtful nor thoughtless. Only beings whose behavioural repertoire includes thoughtful behaviour can be said, *truly or falsely*, to think. A logical condition for the literal, intelligible, application of cogitative predicates to a being is that the being could, logically, satisfy the behavioural criteria for the ascription of such predicates.

Magritte might have painted a brain on a pedestal, with a 'bubble' coming out of it and 'cogito ergo sum' inscribed in the bubble. But this would be a joke – not the illustration of a deep truth. Brains are not even candidates for thinking.

Chapter 15

WITTGENSTEIN'S CONCEPTION OF PHILOSOPHY - I

Prolegomenon

'I destroy! I destroy! I destroy!', Wittgenstein wrote in one of his pocket notebooks in the early 1930s.

His destructive side is manifest in his criticisms of a wide range of philosophical conceptions of language and linguistic meaning. It is seen in his critique of metaphysics, and it is evident in his demolition of dualism, behaviourism and mentalism in the philosophy of mind. The upshot of these critical investigations is the destruction of what he called 'houses of cards'. His aim was to expose philosophical illusions, to undermine grand theories modelled on theories in the natural sciences and to reveal the chimerical character of metaphysical systems. He did not show these theories and systems to be *false* but to be *nonsense*. By 'nonsense' I don't mean stupid rubbish. It is *very* important to be clear about this. I mean that such philosophical theories and systems subtly *transgress the limits of language and bounds of sense*. The task of philosophy, Wittgenstein held, is to transform *latent* nonsense into *patent* nonsense – to make it clear exactly where and why the bounds of sense are transgressed.

Nevertheless, there is also a constructive side to Wittgenstein's later philosophy. Side by side with the exposure of nonsense, Wittgenstein gives us, from one domain to another, an overview of the network of concepts that make up the ways in which we think. We have seen this first, in the domain of language, meaning and linguistic understanding. There he displayed for us the warp and the weft of the concepts of word and name, sentence and description, the meaning of words and the meaning of sentences, use and practice, explanation of meaning and definition, meaning of something by words and understanding the meanings of words and so on and so forth. We have also examined aspects of his philosophy of psychology in which he gives us an overview of psychological concepts, their first-person present-tense use and their third-person ascription, their asymmetries regarding knowledge, doubt and belief, their link with behavioural criteria, the concepts of mind and of body, the misleading pictures of outer and inner and so on through a broad and ramifying weave of interlocking concepts. Wittgenstein's constructive achievement was to give us luminous descriptions of the forms of our conceptual scheme in different domains of thought and language.

What we have not yet done is to confront head-on Wittgenstein's conception of philosophy, of its nature and of its limits. This has been deliberately postponed. His views on this subject are *so* radical that it is best to see how he goes about applying his philosophical methods before examining his principles. Now that we have become acquainted with some of his methods and seen the results of applying them, we are in a position to examine what is, in many ways, the *most* revolutionary aspect of his later philosophy.

Wittgenstein's remarks on the nature of philosophy are most likely to be referred to by contemporary philosophers with indignation. This anger is commonly rooted in lack of understanding, and sometimes in gross *misunderstanding*. In this and the next two lectures, I shall present Wittgenstein's remarks on philosophy. I shall illustrate what he meant with examples drawn from his work with which you are already familiar, and I shall show how some of the standard criticisms of his delineation of the scope and limits of philosophy are to be rebutted.

The Prevalent Tradition: Philosophy as a Cognitive Discipline

The great tradition of Western philosophy conceived of philosophy as a cognitive discipline with a subject matter of its own. It was thought to be a part, perhaps indeed the most fundamental part, of the quest for knowledge of the world. But what precisely the subject matter of philosophy is and how philosophy is to be distinguished from other forms of pursuit of knowledge were disputed at the dawn of the subject and continue to be hotly disputed to this day. Within this whole tradition from Plato onwards, there was *one unshakeable conviction* – namely that philosophy is a discipline dedicated to the pursuit of knowledge – a *cognitive discipline*. This conviction is exhibited in two related theses:

- First, that there are *philosophical propositions*.
- Second, that such propositions, if true and well-grounded, express *philosophical knowledge*.

> **Int.** But isn't that right? I mean, if philosophy does not result in new knowledge, then what is the point of doing it? If it isn't a cognitive discipline, then what can be learnt from doing philosophy?

PMSH. Well, let's take it slowly. If philosophy is a cognitive discipline, if there are *philosophical propositions* just as there are propositions of physics and chemistry, then philosophy must have a distinctive *subject matter* of its own, just as physics and chemistry do.

Int. [*Indignantly*] But surely philosophy *does* have a subject matter of its own. I mean Descartes certainly thought it did – philosophy was supposed to construct the whole of human knowledge on the absolutely firm foundations of metaphysically certain and indubitable propositions. So it had both a subject matter and a task. And Locke thought that the subject of philosophy was the nature of human knowledge, and its task the determination of its scope and limits. And Hume thought that philosophy was the science of the mind. Now, what was wrong with that?

PMSH. Slow down! Of course, I am not denying that past philosophers *thought* that philosophy had a unique subject matter and a unique task, and indeed thought that there was such a thing as philosophical knowledge. But what became of these conceptions? They all came a cropper.

Int. Oh – isn't that a bit much!

PMSH. No, not at all. Just reflect: if there are no *absolutely* certain truths that are both (i) resistant to hyperbolic doubt and (ii) provide the foundations of science, then the Cartesian project of founding science on such absolute certainties collapses. And indeed there aren't, and it does!

If empirical psychology becomes the accredited science of the mind and its experimental methods of testing and measuring become the accepted methods for achieving such knowledge, then Hume's philosophical project of discovering the nature of the mind by introspective scrutiny and reflection becomes redundant. And indeed, quite irrespective of the birth of empirical psychology with its experimental methods, the Humean project rested on a profound misconception of the mind, of introspection, of meaning and understanding.

Int. All right. I grant you that the Cartesian and classical empiricist endeavours came to nothing. But Kant already showed that in the eighteenth century, didn't he? But he still thought that philosophy had a subject matter of its own, and he certainly thought that there were philosophical propositions concerning the a priori conditions of the possibility of conceptualized experience. He thought that there could be philosophical knowledge all right. After all, it was his avowed goal to set metaphysics 'upon the true path of a science' – and if that is not a commitment to the idea that philosophy is a cognitive discipline, then I don't know what would be!

PMSH. Yes, of course, that is what Kant thought. But his enterprise was challenged too. His idea that there are *synthetic a priori propositions* that are preconditions of the possibility of empirical knowledge has surely been undermined. His Copernican Revolution of holding that the world we experience must conform to the a priori conditions of the possibility of experience has been virtually universally rejected. And his conception of noumena – of things as they are in themselves, independently of space, time and causality – is generally held to be incoherent. Now, if all that is right, then the whole Kantian project of discovering and vindicating synthetic a priori truths that are the general conditions of the possibility of experience disintegrates.

And the same applies to later philosophers. If logic is neither a science of the most general truths about the universe (as Russell had supposed) nor a science concerning the most general truths concerning propositions (as Frege thought), then the Fregean and Russellian projects disintegrate. Husserl tried yet again to find a new subject matter for philosophy – in phenomenology, that is, in the description of the subjective character, the inner feel, of human experience. This promised a subject matter upon which the natural sciences seemed unlikely to encroach. And investigation of this subject matter, Husserl thought, would yield insights into the essences of things. Phenomenology aspired, as philosophy has always done, to achieve grand and important truths about essential natures. But it too proved a broken reed.

Each great philosophical system, advanced by a visionary thinker, began by promising a new beginning that would achieve philosophical knowledge and ended in the dust. The endeavours were glorious, but all seemed doomed to fail. And philosophy was left in the outer darkness, lacking a genuine subject matter of its own. That is indeed what happened.

Int. Yes, I can see that the historical story is a bit depressing. But then, as you have shown me, philosophy is just *very difficult*. I can see that the Cartesians and empiricists were barking up the wrong tree. And I can see that Kant, for all his greatness as a critic of the Cartesian and empiricist traditions, did *not* put philosophy onto the true path of a science. But surely we have done so today! I mean, just look at the amazing researches going on in philosophy of logic and language, and the enterprise of discovering a theory of meaning for a natural language that will clarify once and for all the nature of meaning and of understanding, and solve all the problems about meaning that have plagued philosophers throughout the ages. And look at the emergence of cognitive science. Isn't this a grand new science of the mind that makes old-style philosophy of mind obsolete? Not to mention work on modality and possible worlds that proves that everything that is the case is necessarily the case. Does that not show that philosophy can discover new truths and is part of the grand project of discovering the ultimate nature of the mind?

PMSH. I fear that you may be over-impressed by the noise in the current marketplace of ideas. The vendors do indeed display their wares with great enthusiasm and panache. But remember – so did Descartes and then Locke. So did Hume. And following him, Kant. Russell thought to put an end to the age-old scandal of not producing any results in philosophy by introducing what he called 'the scientific method in philosophy'. So there is nothing new about the noise – only about the projects. But are these projects any better than the old ones?

A theory of meaning for a natural language was supposed to yield a theory that would enable one, from a stock of definitions or 'axioms' concerning word meanings in a language and a set of formation rules for sentences of that language, to derive the meaning of any arbitrary sentence. This enterprise appeared to be continuous with theoretical linguistics, only much more general. And its advocates promised widespread insights into all other branches of philosophy, once the principles of the semantics of natural languages were clarified. But let me point out to you that despite 40 years of endeavour, we are no nearer having such a theory of meaning for any language or indeed of agreeing on the principles that should guide it. Moreover, it is far from clear whether any such theory *could achieve* what it aims at – namely a deductive axiomatic theory that can *informatively* deliver the meaning of any well-formed sentence of a natural language. And it is even less clear why such a theory would shed light on any *philosophical* problem. And it is quite clear that so far no serious philosophical question has been solved or resolved as a result of researches on a theory of meaning for a natural language.

Int. Oh! ... Are you sure about that? I mean, you're just saying so!

PMSH. I agree, I am just asserting it to be so. But I would challenge anyone to show us a single deep traditional philosophical problem, for example, about substance, causation, space or time, personal identity, knowledge, belief, memory, imagination, that has been solved as a result of elaborating principles of a theory of meaning for a natural language. To show you in detail why I think the enterprise is futile is a task for another occasion. What I would like to encourage you to do is to look upon such projects with a modicum of scepticism. After all, you have studied enough of Wittgenstein's ideas about linguistic meaning to realize that questions about meaning, about what it is for a word to have a meaning, what it is for a sentence or utterance to have a meaning, what it is for a speaker to mean something by his words, how linguistic meaning is related to a speaker's meaning and so forth are to be resolved by

>   *connective analysis*, not by making propaganda for an imaginary theory of meaning.
> **Int.** Yes, I see. If Wittgenstein's reflections on language and linguistic meaning are right, then the whole enterprise of modern philosophical semantics loses its lustre ... But what about cognitive science? You haven't said anything about that yet.
> **PMSH.** *Cognitive science* was conceived as a new discipline in which philosophers would work together with psychologists, theoretical linguists, artificial intelligence theorists, computer engineers, and neuroscientists. This subject would, it was hoped, replace the philosophy of mind with a genuine science of the mind that would reveal the nature and scope of human knowledge and experience. The implicit assumption seemed to be: if one can't find a unique subject matter for philosophy, perhaps it can cooperate with *other sciences* in a joint endeavour. But if you examine what philosophers who have jumped onto this bandwagon actually do, it turns out, I think, to be just a highly questionable philosophy of mind – which is eminently challengeable, although I fear that I can't challenge it now.

But let's disregard whatever qualms one may have (and I certainly have) about currently popular projects. Surely, you must admit that there is something very odd about the tale. Every other cognitive discipline has, in the fullness of time, achieved a substantial amount of knowledge of fact and of well-confirmed explanatory theory about its subject matter. There are whole libraries full of established theories and confirmed truths in physics, chemistry, and biology. But if one were to ask a philosopher for a handbook of well-established truths of philosophy – there is none. As Wittgenstein remarked:

> I read '... philosophers are no nearer the meaning of 'Reality' than Plato got ...'. What a strange business. How extraordinary that Plato could get even that far! Or, that we couldn't get farther? Was it because Plato was so gifted? (BT 424)

Those who think that the absence of consensus on the subject matter of philosophy and the patent absence of established results and theories are due to the sheer difficulty of philosophy ought to find the subject profoundly depressing. Two and a half thousand years, and virtually nothing to show for it other than false theories! Of course, hope rises eternal in the human breast! And each generation produces false prophets who announce in triumphal tones that *with them* philosophy has finally, at long last, arrived at the point at which it may attain genuine knowledge. But this song has been heard so often in the past, by Descartes, Locke, Hume, Kant, Russell, Husserl and others, that it no longer carries conviction. Is it not plausible, Wittgenstein suggested, to suppose that we need to look at the whole enterprise afresh, and from a radically different perspective?

In opposition to the whole philosophical tradition, Wittgenstein argued that philosophy, by contrast with the sciences, is not a cognitive discipline at all. It is neither *below* nor *above* the sciences. Its task is not to provide the *sure foundations* upon which the sciences rest, or which legitimate the scientific quest. But it is not a *super-science*, as metaphysicists were prone to think, either. And it is not continuous with the sciences, as Russell and Quine thought, and as many current philosophers suppose. It does not aim to add to the sum of human knowledge about the universe or about the workings of the human mind. Philosophy is a quest for a particular kind of *understanding*, not for knowledge. It is a tribunal of sense before which scientists may be arraigned – not for producing falsehoods, but rather for presenting claims that transgress the bounds of sense.

The Revolution

You will recollect that when Wittgenstein returned to philosophy in 1929, he found that his first philosophy in the *Tractatus* was deeply and irremediably flawed, and he proceeded to unravel it.

With the progressive disintegration of the *Tractatus* philosophy, a new vision and a new method emerged. I shall consider the new vision now and postpone until the next lecture the description of the new method or methods.

Wittgenstein characterized the change in his conception as a transition from questions about truth to questions about sense. It was a shift from the pursuit of apparent metaphysical *truths* about the nature of the world, of language and of representation by means of language to investigations of the *sense* of putative metaphysical, metalogical and metapsychological questions and statements. Wittgenstein moved from a preoccupation with the illusory *scaffolding of the world* to a preoccupation with the scaffolding *from which we describe the world*. It was a move from *Wesensschau* (insight into essences) to grammar. Wittgenstein came to think that it was an illusion to suppose that the metaphysical essence of the world is reflected in the depth grammar of any possible language. It was an illusion to suppose that the world *has* a metaphysical essence. It was an illusion to suppose that all languages have a common depth grammar, or indeed that any language has a depth grammar – grammar, like topography, is all surface. It was an illusion to suppose that the grammar of natural language reflects the essence of the world at all. In so far as the world can be said to have an essence, its essence is no more than *the shadow cast upon the world by grammar*. Where traditional metaphysicists entered the magical caves of philosophy and found there sparkling diamonds and rubies, glittering emeralds and sapphires, the task of philosophy is to take this jewel-encrusted golden treasure out into the sober light of day and show that it is no more than rusty old metal and worthless pebbles. And what replaces these illusions is what Wittgenstein called 'a surveyable representation of grammar'.

Wittgenstein self-consciously engendered a revolution in philosophy. On the one hand, he considered himself to be the destroyer of the great tradition of Western philosophy. In an apocalyptic moment he remarked that he would perhaps be remembered only like the man who destroyed the great library at Alexandria (MS 183, 63). The systematic destruction of the deepest ideas that informed the *Tractatus* evidently seemed to him also to be the destruction of the deepest presuppositions of Western philosophy. For he was not only destroying metaphysics, he was destroying the very idea of philosophy as a discipline that can deliver *any* truths about reality at all. He came to deny that there can be any such thing as philosophical knowledge analogous to knowledge in the sciences.

On the other hand, he thought of himself as transforming philosophy into something new. In his 1930 lectures, he said that 'the nimbus of philosophy has been lost'. It can no longer be thought to be the Queen of the Sciences. It has lost its sublimity. It cannot aspire to investigate the objective (language-independent) essence of all things, since there is no such thing. What he was now doing, he asserted, is a new subject, and not merely a stage in a continuous development. It is one of the *heirs* of what used to be called 'philosophy'. There was now, he said, a *kink* in the development of human thought, comparable to that which had occurred when Galileo invented dynamics. For a new method had been discovered. There could no longer be great philosophers, he said, but now, for the first time, it was possible to have *skilled* philosophers. These are dramatic remarks. Four questions need answering:

- First, what exactly was the transformation that Wittgenstein effected or tried to effect?
- Second, what was the new method?
- Third, why did the discovery of a new method mean that there could no longer be great philosophers, but that there could – for the first time – be skilful ones?
- Fourth and finally, was this new form of philosophy the *sole* heir to traditional philosophy or was it merely one among a variety of different ways of doing philosophy?

I shall try to answer these questions in the course of this and the next two lectures. Let's turn first to the transformation that Wittgenstein thought he was effecting.

The transformation of philosophy that Wittgenstein had in mind was the abandonment of all that had seemed sublime about the aspirations of the subject from Plato until Frege, Russell and the author of the *Tractatus*. Those aspirations rested on a multitude of illusions. These were, to invert Plato's famous metaphor of the cave, not the shadows of a transcendent reality of Platonic ideas, but the shadows *of grammar*, dancing upon the walls of the cave. And at the heart of these illusions was the assumption that philosophy is a cognitive discipline with a genuine subject matter. Our whole way of thinking, Wittgenstein now argued, must be turned around (PI §108). We must reject the old idea of the great Western philosophers that there are two kinds of problems in the field of knowledge: the *essential* metaphysical ones – which it is the task of philosophy to investigate – and the *inessential*, quasi-accidental ones – with which the empirical sciences deal. There *are* no *great essential* problems, only great and compelling *illusions* of such problems (BT 407). But if so, Wittgenstein himself queried:

> Where does this investigation get its importance from, given that it seems only to destroy everything interesting: that is all that is great and important? (As it were, all the buildings, leaving behind only bits of stone and rubble.) But what we are destroying are only houses of cards, and we are clearing up the ground of language on which they stood. (PI §118)

Int. But surely he didn't mean that there aren't any real *problems* in philosophy, did he?

PMSH. No, of course not. Philosophy, he said, is just philosophical problems. But they are altogether distinctive – and altogether unlike empirical problems in the sciences. Philosophical problems stem from a disorder in our concepts. They are to be solved by ordering those concepts (BT 421). The questions of philosophy cannot be answered by the empirical sciences since they are not empirical questions. Nor can they be answered by the mathematical sciences since they are not questions demanding proofs of new theorems. They are not practical questions. Augustine was puzzled about the very possibility of measuring time, given that the past no longer exists, the future does not yet exist and the present is no more than an extensionless point. So how *can* one measure time? – after all, one cannot measure an extensionless point! But Augustine's puzzlement would not be solved by showing him how a clock works (BB 30f.). Zeno was baffled that Achilles can overtake a tortoise who is given a head start, since the space separating him from the tortoise is infinitely divisible. How, Zeno wondered, can one traverse an infinite number of spaces in a finite time? But the bafflement is not diminished by pointing out that all Achilles has to do is to put one foot down after the other as he moves forward. Such questions manifest a *conceptual unclarity*, and it is that unclarity that needs to be pinpointed and dispelled.

Philosophical questions are commonly questions in search of a sense, rather than of an answer. Sometimes they are to be resolved not by answers, but by further questions that will dissolve them. Sometimes, when 'a confusion is expressed in the form of a question that does not acknowledge the confusion', then 'what *releases* the questioner from his problem is a particular alteration of his method of expression' (PG 193). More generally, they are resolved by attaining an overview of a segment of the grammar of our language that will enable one to recognize where one went astray.

Int. Why did he say that what he was doing should be conceived as an 'heir' to what used to be called 'philosophy'?

PMSH. He gave various reasons. It resembles traditional philosophy
- in its generality,
- in its being fundamental to ordinary life and to the sciences,

and
- in its being independent of any special results of science. (M 113)

One may further add:
- in its being an a priori investigation that is independent of *experimental* confirmation and disconfirmation.

There is an *analogy*, Wittgenstein said, between what he does and what Plato was doing. It *takes the place* of what Plato was doing. The new activity *dissolves* the problems that the old one tried to *answer* (cf. AWL 27f.). For the same problems that occupied the Greeks in an important sense unavoidably still occupy us:

> One keeps hearing the remark that philosophy really makes no progress, that the same philosophical problems that had occupied the Greeks are still occupying us. But those who say that don't understand the reason why it is so. The reason is that our language has remained the same and seduces us into asking the same questions again and again. As long as there is a verb 'to be' which seems to function like 'to eat' and 'to drink', as long as there are adjectives like 'identical', 'true', 'false', 'possible', as long as one talks about a flow of time and an expanse of space, etc., etc., people will continue to bump up against the same mysterious difficulties, and stare at something that no explanation seems able to remove. (BT 424)

How then can these problems be characterized?

Philosophical Problems and Their Sources

Philosophy, as I just remarked, is, according to Wittgenstein, nothing but philosophical problems (PG 193). Philosophical problems are best characterized by examples, for they form a family that is not fruitfully circumscribed by an analytic definition.

Int. Can't one say that they are *conceptual, a priori, problems*?

PMSH. Of course. That serves to distinguish them from scientific problems and to differentiate philosophy from natural science. But it does not demarcate them from things that have nothing to do with philosophy, such as mathematics.

Int. Oh! ... I see. Mathematics is also concerned with conceptual, a priori problems. So what is the difference?

PMSH. Mathematics, unlike philosophy, is *concept formation*. Very roughly speaking, it forms new mathematical concepts by means of theorems that make conceptual connections between two hitherto conceptually unconnected mathematical expressions. But philosophy contains no theorems and produces no deductive proofs within an established proof system as mathematics does. If one can say that mathematics is essentially concept formation, then one might also say that philosophy is essentially *concept clarification*. This is correct as far as it goes, but it does not go very far. Lexicography, after all, clarifies concepts by offering explanations of what words mean – but philosophy is not a branch of lexicography nor a form of super lexicography.

Int. So what differentiates philosophical clarification from common-or-garden lexicographical explanations?

PMSH. I'll try to make the matter clear. Now, superficially, it is obvious that philosophical discussion doesn't even look like a lexicographical clarification. Despite Platonic quests for definitions, in fact, philosophical problems and puzzles are not resolved by coming up with novel definitions. Remember, we have discussed at some length what the nature of the mind is. But our discussion was not at all like the entry for the word 'mind' in the *Oxford English Dictionary*. In order to see the reasons *why* philosophical clarification is unlike lexicography, one must first attain a firm grasp of *why* certain concepts stand in need of philosophical clarification in the first place – that is, *why philosophical problems arise?*

Philosophical problems and difficulties rest on conceptual misunderstandings (MS. 109, 298). They do not require new scientific discoveries. Philosophical doors *do* open – not by constructing a theory of philosophical locks but by finding the right key and turning it the right way. It is not the task of philosophy to set up a 'system of the world' as the great metaphysicists of the past tried to do, but only to intervene where conceptual difficulties emerge (VoW 125).

Int. So why *do* these difficulties emerge? What is the source of these philosophical problems?

PMSH. The primary, but *not the only*, source of philosophical problems is our language itself. For the grammar of our languages is *not readily* *surveyable*. As we have seen, what strikes us, and what deceives us, is what comes immediately to the eye or ear – the surface grammar of words. Note here that surface grammar does not stand in contrast to depth grammar, but to what we might call 'topographical' or 'connective' grammar. Here I wish to draw your attention to three recurrent features that give rise to confusion and misconception:

- First, expressions with different uses look alike, and expressions with similar uses may look very different.
- Second, often a fragment of one language-game is *analogous* to a fragment of another; nevertheless, the two are not *homologous* – that is, they do not share the same pattern of logical relations.
- Third, verbal pictures embedded in our language the quasi-pictorial forms by which we so commonly represent things, like *having*, that is, *possessing*, a pain, *being under* an obligation – which then weighs on one, having something *at the back of* one's mind – which may then *cross* one's mind – readily mislead us.

Int. Oh, I say! That seems awfully tame. You don't really mean that such trivialities are the real source of philosophical problems, do you?

PMSH. If that seems tame, reflect that bacteria, which are too small for the naked eye to see and were only discovered when the microscope was invented, also look tame. How could anything *that* small cause such trouble and suffering!? But they do. And these three features of the superficial, surface grammar of our languages are the source of great philosophical problems and deep conceptual puzzlement. I am not suggesting, and Wittgenstein does not hold, that these are the *only* source of philosophical problems. But they are the main source.

Actually, I'm surprised that you should find this surprising after all our discussions. I'll remind you of some of them as we go along!

I said that the first recurrent feature in the surface grammar of our languages that is a great source of philosophical problems and confusions is that expressions with different uses look alike, and expressions with similar uses may look very different. This is anything but trivial or tame. Let me remind you of such a case that kept us hard at work for a whole lecture. 'To have a pin' looks and sounds like 'to have a pain'. This is one (but only one) reason why we are prone to project upon the concept of pain the grammar of things or objects. That is why we so readily conceive of *having a pain* as a form of ownership – 'logically non-transferable ownership' as you will remember Strawson called it. And so, we are deluded into thinking that two people cannot have the same pain. One might say that the *form* in which we represent pain in our language is that of ownership – that is the *representational form* of the grammar of pain. But this representational form is *altogether misleading*. For to have a pain is not to own anything – not even non-transferably.

Int. Yes, of course. I should have remembered that. It is very important and very difficult to grasp without Wittgenstein's help.

PMSH. That's right. Let me remind you of another kind of case which we have discussed, and which you should have remembered. 'Bachelors are unmarried' looks grammatically like 'Bachelors are unhappy' – but *the role* of the two propositions is wholly different. 'Bachelors are unmarried' is *a constitutive rule* – not a true or false proposition. *It is a rule for the use of the word* 'bachelor' which entitles us to infer from 'Jack is a bachelor' to 'Jack is unmarried'. But 'bachelors are unhappy' is *an empirical generalization*, which may be true or false, and may intelligibly be denied. But if someone were to deny that bachelors are unmarried and insist that, on the contrary, he knows many married bachelors, we should wonder what on earth he meant. So, *similarity of form* leads us to overlook fundamental differences in the use of propositions, and we fail to notice the *normative* character of what Wittgenstein called *grammatical propositions*. And that lies at the root of a whole host of philosophical problems and confusions about necessity and putatively metaphysical propositions.

Int. Yes, of course. That is one of the sources of the mistaken idea that such a proposition as 'red is darker than pink' is a metaphysical proposition describing a necessity in the world – when in fact it is just a rule presented in the guise of a description of what *seems to be* a necessary fact. Similarly, 'Nothing can be red and green all over' looks like a description of an objective necessity in the world, and so we confuse a rule of representation with what appears to be a representation of a necessary fact.

PMSH. Good. Now you're beginning to think. You must bear in mind that trouble is caused not only by expressions with utterly different uses looking alike but also conversely by expressions with very similar uses looking different.

Int. What do you have in mind?

PMSH. For example, 'I have a pain in my foot' and 'My foot hurts'. Or, again, 'Red is a colour' and 'Whatever is said to be red can also be said to be coloured'. And so too, to recall an example we have examined before at some length: 'It is impossible for a thing to be red all over and also green all over at the same time' looks unlike 'There is no such thing as being red and green all over at the same time' and also unlike 'The words "is simultaneously red all over and green all over" are excluded from use.' But actually, all three propositions typically have the same function.

Let me try to pull this stage of the discussion together. Because – or partly because – such superficial similarities in grammatical form conceal differences in use, and superficial differences in grammatical form mask similarities in use, *we draw wrong inferences and jump to wrong conclusions*. Because the expression 'the mind' is a substantive like the expression 'the brain', we are inclined to think that the mind is a substance, and even to wonder whether it might in actual fact not simply *be* the brain. But, as we have seen, the mind is not a substance at all, neither an immaterial one nor a material one. Partly because arithmetical sentences have a propositional form, we are inclined to think that '3 is greater than 2' is a description of a relation between numbers just as 'Jack is taller than Jill' is a description of a relation between people. But, as we have seen, it is not a description at all, but *a rule for giving descriptions*. For the mathematical proposition '3 is greater than 2' is a rule that allows one to infer, for example, that if Jack has 3 apples and Jill has 2 apples then Jack has a greater number of apples than Jill. Or, slightly less trivially, '25 × 25 = 625' is not a description, but a rule that allows one to infer that if we have 25 bags of 25 marbles per bag, then we have 625 marbles in all – and we need not count up afresh.

Int. Yes, I should have remembered. Just imagine that instead of presenting arithmetical equations in the form of declarative sentences, that is, in the form of *statements*, we actually presented them in the form of quasi-imperatives such as 'Let 3 be greater than 2' or 'Let 25 × 25 be 625'. Then things would look very different!

PMSH. Indeed they would. We might not be misled in the ways in which we all are to think of arithmetical equations as descriptions. That's very good.

Now, not only do we jump to unwarranted conclusions, we also ask *misconceived* questions. Because 'to understand' looks like a verb of action such as 'to undersign', we ask such seemingly deep questions as 'How does one understand sentences one has never heard before?' – a question which lies at the heart of Chomsky's theories of language. But, as we've seen, that question begs the question – for understanding *is not an act or activity one performs*. It *seems as if* we can ask 'How do you do it?' Then it *seems as if* understanding were a hidden mechanism in the mind or the brain or, as Chomsky would misguidedly have it, the mind/brain. And then it appears as if we were asking *how the mechanism works*. But, as we have seen, to understand an utterance is not to *do* anything, but to *be able to do* a variety of things – such as to respond appropriately to what was said, to act on an utterance or its content, to explain what was said and so forth. But whereas one can ask how one came to be able to do something, one cannot ask how one *does* being able to do something. Because the term 'mental image' appears akin to the term 'painted image', we are inclined to think that just as painted images are visible objects, so too mental images are visible objects – the only difference being that painted images are public and visible *to all*, whereas mental images are private and so visible only to the eye of the mind. But the mind has no eyes, and one 'sees' things *in* the mind's eye, not *with* the mind's eye. Mental images are not visibilia at all – they are 'had' but not seen.

Int. Yes, I see. These similarities in the superficial grammar of expressions are anything but trivial.

PMSH. I'm glad you can now see that. Now I want to draw your attention to the second recurrent feature of surface grammar that is a constant source of conceptual confusion. Often, a fragment of one language-game is *analogous* to a fragment of another. Nevertheless, the two are not *homologous* – that is, they do not share the same pattern of logical relations. But we are commonly taken in by the analogy and overlook the lack of homology. And then we project features of one language-game onto another and draw inferences and raise questions about one domain which make sense only with respect to the different domains.

Int. I don't see what you mean.

PMSH. Let me give you an example. We say:
- It is certain that the curtains are red.
- It is certain that the Ruritanian social democratic party will win the next election.
- It is certain that $25 \times 25 = 625$.
- It is certain that $e = mc^2$.

And in our philosophical moments, we agree with Descartes that
- It is certain that I am thinking, I cannot be mistaken about whether I am thinking.

We take it for granted that these certainties are, if distinct at all, distinct only in degree. Mathematical truths – we are inclined to think – have the highest degree of certainty. Observation statements, such as 'The curtains are red' are less certain. And empirical predictions are even less so. But this is confused.

Int. I don't see why that's confused. It seems to me right. I mean, surely $25 \times 25 = 625$ is absolutely certain – a lot more certain than that those curtains over there are red. I mean, it might be some sort of illusion or some special hidden light that makes them look red even though they're not. But $2 + 2 = 4$, or $25^2 = 625$ they're dead certain.

PMSH. No, you're quite wrong! The propositions I listed are not, or at any rate need not be, propositions with different *degrees* of certainty. Rather, they are different *kinds* of proposition with different *kinds* of certainty. It is not *less* certain that I am now giving you a lecture than that 2 + 2 = 4 – but it is a *different kind of certainty*. Different kinds of certainty have different kinds of *grounds*. And *what it is* that is certain is, in each such case, a *categorially different kind of proposition*. The grounds for mathematical certainty are deductive proofs, and mathematical propositions are rules, not descriptions. The certainty of a perceptual statement such as 'The curtains are red' lies in its being evident to the senses – look and see! The certainty of an empirical prediction is determined by its conclusive empirical evidence. And the certainty of a highly theoretical proposition of science, such as $e = mc^2$, is determined by the holistic confirmation of the theory of which it is a part. And finally, in Wittgenstein's view, the apparent certainty of propositions such as 'I am in pain' or 'I am thinking of Descartes' is illusory – for we mistake the grammatical exclusion of doubt for the empirical presence of certainty.

Int. Wow! Well, that puts the cat among the pigeons. I'm amazed. I'd never have thought of that move. I must think about it.

PMSH. Good. Do! And let me give you another startling idea from Wittgenstein. What applies to certainty applies also to truth. We speak of it being true that it will rain this afternoon, that it is true that 12 × 12 = 144, that it is true that red is darker than pink and that it is true that one must keep one's promises. And we are prone to think that what *its being true* amounts to is exactly the same from case to case. Does it not simply mean that the proposition that is said to be true is a proposition that corresponds to the facts? Or that things are as the proposition describes them as being?

Int. Well, yes. Isn't that what it is to be true?

PMSH. What is correct is that the adjective 'true' in all these sentential contexts is unequivocal. But while what it is for an empirical proposition to be true may indeed be said to be that the proposition corresponds to the facts (without any commitment to the so-called correspondence theory of truth) – one cannot say that of a moral proposition. To what *fact*s does the proposition that *killing is wrong* or that *love is better than hate* 'correspond'? And whereas one can say of a true empirical proposition that things are in fact as the proposition describes them as being, one cannot say this of a mathematical proposition since the mathematical proposition is *a norm of representation* – a *rule*, not a description or statement of fact. The truth of a mathematical proposition is no more akin to the truth of an empirical proposition than a chess king is akin to a king.

Int. So the word 'true' has the same meaning, but what it is for categorially different kinds of propositions to be true is deeply different?

PMSH. Exactly. And that also serves to show some of the ramifications of Wittgenstein's insistence that the concept of a proposition is a family-resemblance concept. Empirical propositions, mathematical propositions, logical propositions and ethical propositions are categorially different. And that's why what it is for propositions of categorially different kinds to be true is also so different, even though the term 'true' is unequivocal.

Int. I see. That didn't cross my mind when you explained that the concept of a proposition is a family-resemblance concept.

PMSH. Well, think about it now.

I said that there are three kinds of sources of conceptual confusion that are rooted in the surface grammar of our languages. Let me end today with the third of the three sources. This is the linguistic phenomenon of verbal pictures embedded in our language – the quasi-pictorial forms by which we so commonly represent things. For our language is run through with figurative forms of representation. We have had many occasions to observe the manifold confusions generated by the possessive form. We speak of *having* a penny and also of *having* a pain. We speak of *having* a mind and of *having* a body. So we are prone to think that we stand in a *relation* of non-transferable ownership to our sensations. So too we think that we stand in a *relation* of ownership to our bodies, as if our body were a possession we have, and we are *in it* like a sailor in his ship or a driver in his car. Here we fail to see that we are being taken in by pictures – by emblematic representations. It is as if we were to represent death pictorially by a skeleton, and then think of our fear of death as a form of fear of skeletons. So we fail to note grammatical *differences*. We overlook the fact that I can give you the penny I have, but cannot give you the pain I have, only bring it about that you will have the same pain as I. I can sell you the pin I have, but I can't sell you the pain I have – and that is not because my ownership is inalienable, nor because you wouldn't want to buy it. On the other hand, I can sell my body – but it doesn't cease to be my body when I do so. For 'to sell my body' means to sell sexual services – and what I then lack is a choice, not a body. I have a mind. And I can indeed lose it. But if I lose it, it is no use going to the Lost Property Office to see if anyone has found it.

There are *hundreds* of misleading pictures embedded in our language. We speak of memory as a store of knowledge – and then we wonder how our memories can be stored in the brain, and neuroscientists encourage our confusion by trying to tell us in which part of the brain our memories are stored. But a memory is knowledge retained, not knowledge stored. Knowledge is akin to an ability, but abilities cannot be stored *anywhere*. We speak of the stream of time, conceive of time as a flowing river and wonder how fast it flows and how the speed at which it flows can be measured. But to measure time is not to measure the speed of anything. We speak of obligations as binding us, of duties as weighing upon us – and correspondingly of being released from our obligations and relieved of the burden of our duties. And these too are merely pictures or emblematic representations.

There are other grammatical sources of confusion, but these suffice to drive home Wittgenstein's point. We pursue chimeras and erect castles in the air. Although we are masters of our native tongue, there is a profound sense in which we do not know our way around the grammar of our language. Wittgenstein put the point nicely:

> Language contains the same traps for everyone; the immense network of well-kept false paths. And so we see one person after another walking the same paths and we know already where he will make a turn, where he will keep straight ahead without noticing the turn, etc., etc. Therefore, wherever false paths branch off, I should put up signs which help one get by the dangerous places. (BT 423)

And that was indeed what he tried to do.

In the next lecture, I shall turn to examine other sources of conceptual and philosophical confusion besides the misleading features of the grammar of our language.

Chapter 16

WITTGENSTEIN'S CONCEPTION OF PHILOSOPHY - II

Non-Linguistic Sources of Philosophical Problems

In the last lecture, I discussed three ways in which we are prone to be misled by the surface grammars of our languages:
1. Similarities of grammatical form mask differences in usage.
2. Analogies between fragments of different language games conceal logical differences.
3. Misleading pictures embedded in our language lead us astray.

Before turning to non-linguistic sources of conceptual confusion, I would like to draw your attention to a further important point.

Contrary to the idea that all languages have the same underlying depth grammar, Wittgenstein now denied the *very idea* of a hidden depth grammar and acknowledged differences in the logico-grammatical features of expressions in different languages. Grammatical forms need not be linguistic universals. Philosophical problems that are prominent in one language may not even arise in other languages. We deal with the philosophical problems that arise in our culture, in our language and in our times. These *may be* very similar to the problems that confronted Plato and Aristotle, but they may not be. Philosophers of Greek antiquity, as Wittgenstein pointed out, were just as puzzled about the nature of existence, or of truth, or of the good as we are – after all, they had verbs corresponding to 'to exist' and 'to be' and adjectives corresponding to 'true' and 'good'. But unlike the medievals, they were not concerned with proofs of the existence of the God of monotheism, nor worried about how the God of Christianity can be three persons but one substance. And unlike us, they were not concerned with whether machines can think or how we can understand sentences we have never heard before. Philosophy, one might say, is concerned with *treating diseases of the intellect*, and the viruses that affect people at one place and time *may* differ from those that affect other people at other places and times. This change in perspective is obviously a corollary of abandoning the philosophical quest for knowledge of the putative language-independent essence of all things or the ultimate perfectly general nature of the universe and the transformation of philosophy into the clarification of our forms of representation or conceptual schemes and the dissolution of conceptual puzzlement.

I shall begin by examining *non-linguistic* sources of philosophical problems. One great source of conceptual entanglement is to be found in something characteristic of the modern era rather than of antiquity. It is above all the advance of science that has marked Western civilization for the last four centuries. If theology was, throughout the Middle Ages, one of the main sources of metaphysics, today one of the main sources are the natural sciences. Their success has transformed both the world we live in and our knowledge of it. Small wonder that philosophers should be mesmerized by its methods. It was in the early 1930s that Wittgenstein wrote:

> Philosophers constantly see the method of science before their eyes, and are irresistibly tempted to ask and answer questions in the way science does. This tendency is the real source of metaphysics, and leads philosophy into complete darkness. (BB 18)

Int. That's a very curious claim. I can think of lots of people who would find that very offensive indeed. What on earth was Wittgenstein thinking of?

PMSH. Wittgenstein was probably thinking of Russell's advocacy of what he called scientific method in philosophy, exhibited in his 1914 book *Our Knowledge of the External World as a Field for Scientific Method in Philosophy*; perhaps also of Whitehead and the Vienna Circle. But if it was true in the early 1930s, how much more apt it is today, when scientism has swept the field of philosophy.

I agree that very many people, philosophers and scientists alike, would find his remark offensive. But then these are the very people who do indeed think that if a problem is serious, then it has a scientific answer, and if it has no scientific answer, then it cannot be a serious problem!

Int. Well, I agree; that *is* pretty crude. But disregarding such crudities, why is science a *source* of metaphysics and metaphysical confusions?

PMSH. Isn't that patent? Even in Wittgenstein's day, scientists were telling laymen that they had discovered that nothing was really solid, since it is made of atoms, which consist largely of empty space between the electrons. So although the floor seems solid it isn't really. And ever since Galileo, Locke and Boyle, scientists have happily been telling us that the world around us, despite appearances, is not multicoloured at all, indeed, there are no colours in the material world, and there are no sounds or smells either. And psychologists such as John Watson, the founding father of behaviourism, were telling everyone that the mind is a primitive fiction, that no one has a mind, since minds are on the same level as witches. Now that's bad enough. But things have got very much worse since Wittgenstein died.

Int. [*indignantly*] How so? Contemporary science seems to me to be making the most amazing discoveries in the history of human culture.

PMSH. Well, I agree that various sciences are making amazing discoveries. But they are also making the most nonsensical claims, and I don't mean that they are making silly or stupid claims. I am not suggesting that they are talking rubbish. As always, my point is that they are making claims that *make no sense* – that the sciences, in particular sciences of the mind and brain, are transgressing the bounds of sense, and that their most publicized and headline-catching announcements commonly transgress the bounds of sense.

Int. What do you have in mind?

PMSH. Just look at the daily press. Listen to the radio. And watch documentary television programmes. We are exposed to constant bombardment of news from cognitive neuroscience. We are told that science shows that the brain thinks and calculates, that the brain knows and believes things, that one hemisphere of the brain tells the other hemisphere of the brain what it sees, and this – which is no mere *façon de parler* – is held to explain a variety of puzzling kinds of dissociative behaviour consequent upon commissurotomy. Is this not a scientific metaphysics of mind? After all, we have discussed the mereological fallacy of ascribing cognitive powers to the brain. Similarly, look at theoretical linguistics that purports to be an empirical science. If you listen to Chomsky or his follower Stephen Pinker, you will be told that there is a language gene, that there are rules of grammar deeply buried in the mind/brain, that we are all guided in our speech by rules that we have never even heard of, and could not even understand if we had and so on. Is that not metaphysical nonsense?

Int. Yes, I see what you mean.

PMSH. All right. That is, I think, the kind of thing that Wittgenstein meant when he said that today science is the greatest source of metaphysics, that is of metaphysical nonsense.

I said that we live in an age of *scientism* in philosophy. Let me explain. There are distinctive features characteristic of successful science that infect philosophers with misguided conceptions of the methods of their subject and lead them to advance scientific forms of metaphysics. I would like to draw your attention to four such features:

- The first, of course, is the success of the natural sciences in attaining new knowledge of the natural world. It is difficult for philosophers to accept the fact that they are not participants in this grand enterprise. We discussed this point in the last lecture and need to say no more about it.
- Second, the success of the sciences is manifest above all in the powerful general theories that they have produced. Small wonder that philosophers should conceive of past philosophical endeavours as having produced false theories and to think of their own current work as finally, at long last, attaining true theories – true theories of meaning for natural languages, or true theories of cognitive science, or even true theories of morality. The great advances in science began only in the seventeenth century. Perhaps philosophy in the twenty-first century will at last start producing true theories about something or other!
- Third, the natural sciences not only produce powerful predictive theories, but they also produce powerful *explanations* of natural phenomena. Surely, if philosophy is to deserve the name of a cognitive discipline, it too must produce general explanations. Just as natural scientists commonly explain phenomena by inference to the best explanation – as when invisible bodies are postulated to explain the motion and behaviour of visible ones, or new kinds of micro-particles are postulated to explain the behaviour of other particles – so too, it is thought, philosophy may have recourse to such forms of explanation. As we have seen, it is tempting for both philosophers and psychologists to explain our knowledge of other minds by reference to an inference from bare bodily behaviour to hypothesized mental states that supposedly cause it. And it is equally tempting, for both philosophers and natural scientists, to explain our knowledge of the external world as inferred from our subjective sensory experiences – thus postulating the existence of objects in the external world as causes of our experiences.
- Fourth, it is characteristic of the natural scientists to make discoveries. Philosophers have craved the same dignity – although their putative discoveries have been some very bizarre entities indeed, such as Platonic Forms, Leibnizian monads and Kantian noumena, not to mention *Tractatus* simple objects, and, among current philosophers and cognitive scientists, qualia. But, of course, these are not really discoveries, and their existence is not a confirmable or refutable hypothesis either.

Int. So was Wittgenstein opposed to science?

PMSH. No. He didn't oppose science – although he did not think much of the world and the society that has resulted from the triumph of scientific technology. But that is another matter altogether. Wittgenstein was no enemy of the natural sciences or of scientific explanations. But he was a passionate opponent of *scientism* – that is, the attempt to apply science and scientific methods in domains to which they are inapplicable. In particular, he was opposed to scientism in philosophy. The natural sciences can no more solve or resolve a philosophical problem than experiments or observations in physics can prove a mathematical theorem. Philosophy is concerned with clarifying logical space – science is concerned with discovering which parts of it are occupied. Or, to put matters less metaphorically, philosophy is concerned with what does and does not make sense; the sciences are concerned with what is or is not the case – with truth, not sense. Hence, the natural sciences *presuppose* the conceptual framework which is the task of philosophy to illuminate when conceptual difficulties arise.

Int. Well, that seems reasonable enough. Why would philosophers object to that claim?

PMSH. For a number of different, although related, reasons. In the first place, we live in the age of the triumph of science and technology. It is perhaps depressing, but not unnatural, that philosophers should wish to participate in the great scientific endeavour of discovering the nature of the world around us – and hence that they should think of their subject as a cognitive discipline that can add to the sum of our knowledge of the world. This we have discussed. It is also only natural that they should wish to share in the glory of the sciences – to think of themselves as involved in the same adventure.

Int. You mean that they want to receive the same kudos?

PMSH. To put it rather bluntly, Yes. But to put matters less offensively, philosophers are prone to try to emulate, within the confines of their subject, the methods of the empirical sciences. So, for example, philosophers are tempted to think that their task is to construct theories on the model of the sciences. A few observations on linguistic use and on the use of the word 'meaning', they may exclaim in indignation, won't get one anywhere without some sort of general theory of meaning and use. What we need in philosophy is a general theory of the mind, a general theory of causality, a general theory of space and time and so forth.

Int. But what exactly do they mean by a 'theory'?

PMSH. Yes, that's exactly the question to ask. It is unclear what is *meant* here by the expressions 'theory' and 'general theory'. The paradigm of a theory is provided by scientific theories – of gravity, for example, or electricity, or thermodynamics. Such theories involve the construction of hypotheses which may be more or less correct, that are modifiable in the light of new facts, and that may achieve greater or lesser accuracy in predictions. If successful, these hypotheses may, in certain cases, be deemed general laws of nature that are valid at all times and places. But in this sense of 'theory', there are surely no theories in philosophy. Of course, we may concede that a few observations on use and meaning will get us nowhere – what is needed is a description, a surveyable representation, of the network of concepts linked to the concepts of meaning and use, or to the concept of mind or to the concept of a cause. And, to be sure, this is what Wittgenstein provided – sketches of the conceptual terrain in problematic areas.

Int. You said that it is characteristic of the empirical sciences to advance hypotheses. But aren't there hypotheses in philosophy? I mean, isn't it supposed to be an explanatory hypothesis that we all tacitly know a theory of meaning for our language and employ it in the process of understanding new sentences?

PMSH. Yes. Some theorists of meaning and many theoretical linguists hold that to be so. And that is just the sort of hypothesis that Wittgenstein excludes from philosophy. I'll explain this shortly, but it would involve a detour here, and for the moment I should like to continue to explain Wittgenstein's position on the differences between philosophy and the empirical sciences, for these are very important methodological issues.

Let me elaborate. In Wittgenstein's view, there are, and indeed can be, *no hypotheses in philosophy. For philosophy moves around in the domain of the meaning-determining rules of grammar.* It *cannot* be a hypothesis that a form of words that one understands and uses correctly makes sense – just as it cannot be a *hypothesis* that the chess king moves a square at a time. Remember that the meaning of an expression is given by explanations of meaning acknowledged by competent speakers. Such mundane explanations of meaning are standards of correct use. There is nothing hypothetical about these, for a hypothetical rule is not a rule, but merely a possible rule. And it is not a hypothesis of a competent speaker that one uses a word thus-and-so any more than it is a hypothesis of a chess master that the chess king moves a square at a time. Of course, the rules for the use of words are manifold, and it is not always easy to bring the right ones to mind. Care is needed, and one must trawl far and wide for relevant examples of usage. This is why Wittgenstein insisted that there is indeed a sense in which philosophy is a matter of recollection – for one has to *call to mind* how we use a word or phrase in different contexts.

Just as there is no room for hypotheses in philosophy, so too *there is no room for theory-based predictions*. What could philosophy possibly predict? Scientific theories allow for both approximation and idealization. But an approximation to sense is one form or another of *nonsense*. And an idealization is a *falsification* – a misrepresentation of the use of a word and a distortion of its meaning. If we idealize the concepts we have, we produce different concepts, and then we mask the source of our difficulties and do not resolve them at all.

Just as there is no room for hypothetico-deductive predictions in philosophy, so too *there is no room for theoretical explanations on the model of science*. In particular, *the idea of inference to the best explanation is excluded*. Metaphysicians have indeed tried to explain conceptual phenomena on the model of scientific inference to the best explanation. In so doing, they have conjured into existence a wide variety of strange things – such as Platonic Forms, Leibnizian monads and Kantian noumena – in order to explain how something can be as it is or how we *can* do something that we *do* do. Even the young Wittgenstein had succumbed to this tendency when he wrote the *Tractatus*. For he introduced the idea of *simple sempiternal objects* that constitute the substance of the world in order to explain how a proposition can be false but nevertheless meaningful, and to explain how we can think what is not the case. That there should be such simple objects seemed to him to be a condition of the possibility of representation by means of language, and to be presupposed by logic. But, as he later realized, this parody of scientific procedure is absurd. Scientific inferences to the best explanation can be

- *confirmed by experiments*

and

- *have experiential consequences.*

They commonly lead to new discoveries, enable predictions and new explanations, and they often have technological applications. But metaphysical postulates are no more than painted stage props supporting castles in the air. There are no experiments in contemporary philosophy and cognitive science to confirm the existence of monads or noumena, no tests to show that grass is not really green or poppies red and none to confirm the existence of *qualia*.

Not only is inference to the best explanation on the model of science excluded, but all explanations on the model of scientific explanation are excluded. *There are no such explanations in philosophy*. 'We must know what *explanation* means', he wrote (BT 418), 'There is a constant danger of wanting to use this word in logic [i.e. in philosophy] in a sense that is derived from science.' An explanation is *whatever renders intelligible something that was otherwise puzzling*. In this very general sense of explanation, Wittgenstein does of course offer explanations. For he explains in rich and elaborate detail the nature and sources of numerous philosophical problems and confusions. But his explanations are *grammatical explanations* – not *scientific* or *pseudo-scientific* ones. They explain *by description*, not by hypothesis. And what they describe (or, more accurately, state) are *grammatical rules for the uses of words*. If the appropriate grammatical rules are selected and properly arranged, they dissolve our puzzlement. Wittgenstein was perfectly aware that, in this sense, philosophy does explain. He wrote:

> The man who says that one can't step twice into the same river [i.e. Heraclitus] says something false; one *can* step into the same river twice. – And an object sometimes ceases to exist when I cease to look at it, and sometimes not. – And we do *know*, sometimes, what colour another person sees when he observes a given object, and sometimes we do not. And this is what the solutions to all philosophical difficulties look like. Our answers, if they are correct, must be ordinary and trivial. – For the answers, as it were, make fun of the questions. (TS 220, §111)

And he added, 'But not the explanations, which make the problem intelligible'. For it is the *grammatical* explanations that shed light on the problem and solve or dissolve it.

The natural sciences are characterized by the fruitful discoveries they make. But, Wittgenstein held, there are no *discoveries* in philosophy. If it is the task of philosophy to remind us of, and to marshal, rules of grammar that give the meanings of expressions that we use, then nothing can be hidden, awaiting discovery. For if anything is hidden, it cannot guide us in our linguistic behaviour and cannot function as a standard of correct use and determinant of meaning. There can be no such thing as hidden rules which await discovery – only unknown regularities that have no normative, standard-setting, guiding, function. As Wittgenstein noted in the *Investigations*, 'Everything lies open to view' (PI §126).

It is a sobering thought that while scientists may often plead lack of information to excuse their inability to explain a phenomenon and wait upon future discoveries of fact, *that* excuse is never available to philosophers. Everything a philosopher needs to know for the purpose of the resolution of a general philosophical problem – namely the correct ways of using the words of his language – he already knows. And if he fails to solve or dissolve the problem, that is his fault. It is never due to lack of information, only to inability to survey the web of grammar and see how to bring it to bear upon the problem at hand. That is why there is a sense in which one can rightly say that in philosophy, if it's news – if it is a new discovery – then it is wrong. The right response to a new scientific explanation is often 'Good heavens, who would have thought of that!'. But the correct response to a new philosophical resolution of a conceptual problem is always 'Yes, *of course*, I should have thought of that!'. The problems, confusions and misunderstandings that characterize philosophy never arise through *lack of information*. We already have all the information we need. What we lack is an overview of the grammatical terrain, and the skills needed in order to select the right grammatical data and marshal them in the right way that will dispel or resolve the problem with which we are struggling.

> **Int.** Well, that is striking. And powerful ... And it really is revolutionary. I'm not surprised that it upsets so many philosophers. It robs them of their white coats and halo!
>
> **PMSH.** [*chuckling*] Yes, it does indeed. Well put ... You know, there is nevertheless something paradoxical about the animus towards Wittgenstein. You're obviously right that the current generation of philosophers, particularly the *avant garde* philosophers engaged in cognitive science and consciousness studies or those engaged in philosophical semantics and theories of meaning, get very upset when told that they're not metaphysicists or super-scientists, and not even in the same business as the scientists. On the other hand, it does seem ridiculous to continue to believe that despite twenty-five centuries of failure to produce a solid body of philosophical knowledge, we are just now, at long last (as Michael Dummett, erstwhile professor of logic at New College, Oxford, claimed) on the brink of doing so. Are we so much cleverer than Plato and Aristotle, Aquinas and Descartes, Leibniz and Kant? Are the problems of philosophy so much more difficult than the problem of the structure of matter, the origin of life or the nature of the brain? Wittgenstein's vision of philosophy as a non-cognitive discipline that is concerned with conceptual problems and confusions should have been immensely liberating. But it ran contrary to the spirit of the times.
>
> **Int.** You mean to scientism?
>
> **PMSH.** Yes. But much more than just that ...

Subjective Sources of Philosophical Errors

> **PMSH.** ... Well, this is not the place for general cultural ruminations. Let's get back to our theme. The model of the natural sciences leads us astray in philosophical reflection. But Wittgenstein laid just as much emphasis on sources of philosophical confusion that *lie in us*.
>
> **Int.** What do you mean 'in us'?
>
> **PMSH.** I am referring to our natural intellectual tendencies of thought – what Kant called 'natural dispositions of reason'. Let me explain.
>
> First, we are rightly impressed by the *generality of explanation*. The more general an explanation or explanatory theory, the more powerful it is in putting order into a mass of otherwise bewildering and often apparently unconnected data. So, we have a perfectly intelligible *craving for generality*.

When we engage in science, this is an admirable spur to ingenuity in devising ever more general theories. It is hardly surprising that in philosophical investigation we should likewise wish to indulge our craving for generality. But here we need to be much more wary. We are not engaged in explanation in the sense in which the sciences are.

Int. Yes, of course. Looking back over all our discussions and all Wittgenstein's clarifications of problems that you have explained, it's obvious that the main task is careful description of grammatical connections between particular concepts – not the subsumption of phenomena under ever more general laws.

PMSH. Quite so. And very often only particularity can be achieved, and generalization is falsification. For concepts are not made to a pattern.

Second, corresponding to our craving for generality, we also have *a craving for unity*. As we saw in our discussion of family resemblance, we are prone to assume that everything that falls under a given concept does so by virtue of possession of common characteristics. For, as Plato thought, if two things are just, for example, then there must be something in virtue of which they are. If there are no such common features in virtue of which different things both fall under the term 'just', say, then the word 'just' must be ambiguous, like the word 'port'. This is a very tempting line of thought. But, as we have seen, Wittgenstein held it to be quite mistaken. The unity of a concept rarely consists of a set of necessary and sufficient conditions for something to fall under it. Often (as Aristotle had already pointed out) there is a centre of variation and surrounding it a multitude of variations connected in many different ways to the centre – as healthy food, healthy exercise and healthy appearance are differently connected to the idea of a healthy living being. And sometimes there is not even a centre of variation, but rather a set of only partially overlapping similarities – as in the case of family-resemblance concepts. So the philosophical quest for definitions in terms of necessary and sufficient conditions may often be inappropriate. Our natural appetite for unity must often be suppressed if we are to make any progress in philosophical clarification.

Int. Yes; sometimes there is not just one centre of variations, but a number of different centres of variation – as we saw in the case of our examinations of the concept of meaning.

PMSH. That's right. Now this brings me to a third point concerning our natural dispositions of thought. Our craving for unity is manifest in the philosophical quest for definition. But quite apart from the fact that many concepts are not and cannot be defined in terms of necessary and sufficient conditions for their application, the quest for *any definition at all* may be out of place.

Our typical inclination to think that our philosophical problems would be resolved *if only we could find a definition* must be curbed. From Socrates onwards, philosophers have typically seen a major part of their task to be the quest for definitions. This was no coincidence. One of the greatest intellectual achievements of the Greeks was geometry. This seemed to them to provide a paradigm for all genuine knowledge. So it seemed to them that true knowledge consisted in disclosing the real essence of things. And that, they held, is done by *real definition*, which is not a matter of registering rules for the use of this, that or the other *word* (in Greek, say), but rather a matter of determining *the true nature of things*. But, Wittgenstein argued, definitions are not expressions of insights into objective essences; rather, they *are* rules for the use of words. They do not *disclose* the essence of things; they *determine* them. They lay down rules that fix the conditions under which something is to be *called* a so-and-so – and such rules may or may not specify a set of necessary and sufficient conditions. As we have seen, in the case of focal concepts (like *health*), family-resemblance concepts (like *a game*), as well as numerous psychological concepts, such as *belief* or *thought*, they do not. Furthermore, it is an illusion that philosophical problems are typically resolved by a definition. Augustine's puzzle about time and the measurement of time would not be resolved by giving him a *definition* of time. If we are bewildered by the idea of the good, a *definition of goodness* is not going to make us any less bewildered. And nor is the declaration that it is a simple and *indefinable* idea – as Wittgenstein's colleague at Cambridge, G. E. Moore, suggested. What is needed is a careful examination of the precise nature of our confusion, and its resolution by the disclosure of the misleading analogies and grammatical misuses that lie at the heart of our misunderstandings.

Int. So the centuries' long pursuit of definitions was chasing a red herring? It was all based on a misguided analogy with geometry!

PMSH. Up to a point, Yes. I don't mean that it was all a futile waste of time, since in many cases much light was shed upon philosophical and conceptual matters. But in essence, it involved a misconception of what can and needs to be achieved by conceptual clarification.

Now, let me move on to a fourth source of conceptual confusion and entanglement that lies in us and in our natural tendencies of thought.

We are bewitched by WH-questions, in particular by '*why*?' and '*what*?'. The first exemplifies our tendency to search for causal explanations. We have already examined the scientism to which this leads in philosophy. In so far as anything is explained in philosophy, it is explained by grammatical description, analogies and disanalogies in usage. The problems of philosophy, the conceptual unclarities that bewilder us, and the knots we tie in our understanding of conceptual relationships will not be clarified or disentangled by theoretical explanation, but only by patient arrangement of grammatical data, which will make clear their formal relations and the confusion we have generated by transgressing the bounds of sense.

The second WH-question, the question 'What?', exemplifies our tendency to think that we are in pursuit of essential natures. For we are prone to phrase our puzzlement in the form of questions such as 'What is belief?', 'What is the mind?' or 'What is a number?'. But it is important to note that in philosophy this may often be either an unanswerable question or one which leads to a philosophically futile answer. There is no doubt that the question invites the search for an answer of the form 'Belief is a ...' or 'A mind is a ...', or 'A number is a ...'. When the expression that bewilders us is a substantive, as in these three cases, we are naturally inclined to think that there must be a corresponding substance or thing. *Belief* we think, must be *something* – after all, it is not nothing! The mind, we conjecture, must be a substance of some kind – if not a material one, then an immaterial one. And a number must surely be the abstract correlate of a substance – an abstract object! In these, and other, ways, we confuse ourselves by the very form of our question. What we need to do is examine how words are used. We need to ask not 'What is belief?', but rather: 'Under what circumstances do we say that someone believes something?', 'What is the role or function of the word "believe"?' – 'Why do we need this expression, and what would we miss without it?' and 'What is the grammar of this problematic term?' We need to cast our net wide over the seas of grammar – to investigate how belief is related to thinking on the one hand and to conviction on the other, why 'to believe' has no continuous tense, why one can be in a state of ignorance but not in a state of believing? Why one can know something well but not believe it well, whereas one can believe something firmly or even passionately, but cannot know something either firmly or passionately. In short, what is needed is not a definition, but a survey of grammar. For it is this that will resolve or dissolve our questions.

A fifth natural intellectual tendency that needs to be curbed and controlled when doing philosophy is *the myth-building tendency to which we are prone*.

> **Int.** What on earth do you mean? I would have thought that myths about Gods and avatars are neither here nor there in philosophy. If anything, myths are often a primitive alternative to answering conceptual questions by means of conceptual analysis.
> **PMSH.** Now ... don't rush! Let me explain. 'In philosophy', Wittgenstein wrote, 'we are always in danger of giving a mythology of symbolism, or

of psychology: instead of simply saying what everyone knows and must admit' (PR 95). We invent a new calculus – as Frege and Russell did – and then create a *mythology of symbolism* to represent the depth grammar of natural languages. We are puzzled about features of language acquisition and create a *mythology of an innate Language of Thought* to resolve our puzzlement about how infants can learn to speak. We make highly interesting discoveries about functional localization in the brain and then conceive of the brain as a thinking thing – for we claim that it is the brain that knows and believes things, the brain that stores information and calls information to mind, the brain that perceives or misperceives – in short, we construct *neural mythologies* of the thinking brain. Good philosophy, Wittgenstein remarked, works against this myth-building tendency of our understanding.

Int. Ah yes. I see now. Wittgenstein was comparing these misguided and misconceived philosophical explanations to myths, precisely because they are not just false theories, they actually make no sense.

PMSH. Good! That is right. If what goes by the name of the Language of Thought hypothesis were really a hypothesis, then even if it is false, it might have been true. That is, we would have a clear grasp of what would have to be the case for it to be true. But, of course, if Wittgenstein's criticisms, both direct and indirect, are correct, this supposed hypothesis *makes no sense*. It is not true, but it is not false either – rather like the myth of God creating Eve out of Adam's rib, or the myth of the birth of Venus.

The Idea of an Overview or Surveyable Representation

So much for some of the sources of philosophical problems. Wittgenstein, as we have seen, boldly announced in 1930 that 'a new method has been found'. Later he wrote more circumspectly that just as there are many methods of treating diseases, so too there are many methods of philosophy (PI §133). There is no conflict between the two remarks. What I should like to do is to give you an overview of the new method, and then briefly sketch a variety of specific methods that it subsumes.

In the *Investigations*, Wittgenstein wrote:

> A main source of our failure to understand is that we don't have an *overview* of the use of our words. – Our grammar is deficient in surveyability. A surveyable representation produces precisely that kind of understanding which consists in 'seeing connections'. Hence the importance of finding and inventing intermediate links.
>
> The concept of a surveyable representation is of fundamental significance for us. It characterizes the way we represent things, how we look at matters. (Is this a 'Weltanschauung'?) (PI §122)

'We' and 'us', in this quotation, are, of course, the 'royal' 'we' and 'us'. The concept of a surveyable representation is of fundamental significance to HIM – that is, to Wittgenstein – for it characterizes the way HE looks at philosophico-grammatical matters, and the way in which HE represents them.

We have, of course, come across what Wittgenstein called *deficiency in surveyability*. What he meant was that the surface similarities of logically different kinds of expression mislead us. The personal pronoun 'I' seems, in its surface grammar, to be just like 'he' or 'she'; whereas the latter pair are genuine referring expressions, the former is primarily an *index* for others – not a referring expression at all. 'I know what I want' looks like 'I know what he wants' – but it isn't: the latter is a knowledge claim whereas the former typically expresses a decision. 'Red is a colour' and 'Red is my favourite colour' look alike, but the latter is a description, whereas the former is the expression of a rule for the use of the constituent words. And so forth.

What then counts as a surveyable representation? In particular, what counts as a *surveyable* manner of representing *the grammar of an expression*? Wittgenstein explained that by a *surveyable representation* he meant perspicuously tabulating the *relevant* rules of grammar that would shed light on the problem and be capable of being taken in easily. A long list of rules for the use of an expression would *not* be surveyable: it would not be capable of being readily taken in. Moreover, many of the rules might well be irrelevant to the problem at hand. So Wittgenstein's conception of a surveyable representation must involve a *selection* from a range of rules, the selection being guided by *relevance to the problem at hand*. So, for example, Wittgenstein reminds us that the expression 'the meaning of a word' signifies much the same as the phrase 'the use of a word'. This by no means exhausts the logically significant connections of the concept of meaning with related concepts, for example with the concepts of *explanation of meaning*, of *understanding the meaning of an expression*, of *meaning something by an expression* and so forth. But the logical connection between the notion of *the meaning of a word* and that of the *use of a word* is most pertinent for dispelling the illusion that the meaning of a word is the object it stands for.

The skilful philosopher must not only *select* the salient relevant rules for the use of a conceptually problematic expression, he must also *marshal* them in a way appropriate to the problem. He must arrange them and present them in a manner that will shed light on the difficulties at hand. Moreover, the elaboration of a surveyable representation will typically involve comparisons that will *exclude* certain connections. So, for example, we need to point out that the meaning of a word is *not* the object it stands for, since if the object is destroyed, the word does not cease to have meaning. Similarly, in attempting to give a surveyable presentation of *belief* one will need to point out that belief is *not* a mental state (since one does not cease to believe whatever one believes when one falls asleep, whereas one *does* cease to be in a cheerful state of mind or in a state of intense concentration when one falls asleep). If we are faced with difficulties concerning the concept of *meaning something by a word*, we shall have to point out that meaning something by a word is *not* an act or activity (since one cannot begin or finish meaning something by one's words, and one cannot be interrupted in the middle of meaning) and so on.

Further light can, I think, be shed on the matter by invoking a characterization advanced in a different context by Peter Strawson. He introduced the term 'connective analysis' or 'connective elucidation'; although he did not characterize Wittgenstein's methods thus, it seems to me to be a helpful characterization of what Wittgenstein had in mind. The connective analysis of a concept consists in displaying its logical connections and its logical differences, its relations of implication and exclusion, compatibility and incompatibility with other concepts and conceptual forms that lie, as it were, in adjacent fields. Or, to shift the metaphor, connective analysis describes the network within which the problematic concept is embedded in the web of words. So, for example, we need to locate the concept of the meaning of a word in the appropriate place in the net, since it is adjacent neither to the node of *standing for*, nor to that of *a thing* or *idea in the mind*. Once we have correctly located the concept in the net – in close proximity to the node of 'use', we need to describe the connections it has with adjacent nodes. In the case of the concept of word meaning, as we have seen, it is adjacent to that of *explanation of meaning*, which is in turn linked with that of *a rule for the use of a word*, and it is adjacent to two further nodes in the web, namely of *knowing the meaning of* and also of *understanding* a word. It is also proximate to the nodes for 'signifies' and '… is the word for …' which are adjacent to the node for 'stands for', and this is a source of further confusion which requires careful eradication.

It is important to note that a perspicuous representation thus conceived is *not*, or at the very least *need not*, be context-free. It must be tailored to the problem that we are dealing with. For not *all* the logical connections of a given concept need be relevant to every single difficulty it presents. As we shall see in the final lecture, Wittgenstein liked the analogy between conceptual clarification and cartography. The philosopher is like the cartographer in as much as what he does is designed to help people find their way around – not in the geographical landscape but in the conceptual landscape. The comparison is apt and is also helpful in the present context. For the cartographer can make a topographical map of a land, replete with mountains and valleys, contour lines and mountain peaks. He may also make a road map, with different classes of roads and distances along the roads. And he can make a geological map, indicating the deposits in the landscape; or an agricultural map depicting the kinds of crops grown; or a map of annual rainfall; and so forth. But he cannot intelligibly synthesize all these into *one single map*. Each is designed relative to a particular interest. So too in giving a surveyable representation of a fragment of grammar – the overview is at least typically drawn with a specific array of difficulties in mind. What sheds light on one problem may be inappropriate for another.

This, I think, is what Wittgenstein meant in 1930/31 when he said that 'a method had been found' – a method of solving, resolving and dissolving philosophical problems by connective analysis.

Logical analysis on the model of Frege, Russell and the *Tractatus*, in *different* ways, treated natural language as the surface of a pool – beneath which the reality of thought and language lay. But the pool is actually a mirror, which has *only a* surface – and what appears to be in the depths is actually no more than reflections on the surface and distortions caused by misunderstanding.

Metaphysics craved to penetrate appearances in order to describe the ultimate realities behind the surface of things. But what seem to be ultimate realities are no more than shadows cast by grammar on the world. The new method is to describe grammar in order to see that the metaphysical structure of the world *is* just shadows, and to show how the shadows take us in.

Methods

This conception of philosophy is perfectly consistent with Wittgenstein's later claim that 'There is not a single philosophical method, though there are indeed methods, different therapies, as it were' (PI, boxed remark following §133). I shall mention some with which you are now familiar, since they have been illustrated again and again in previous lectures.

- Most obvious is the method of simple reminders of usage and of grammatical combinatorial possibilities. We say, 'He ceased feeling anxious when he fell asleep' not 'He ceased believing you when he fell asleep'. We say, 'I was interrupted while I was talking to you' but not 'I was interrupted while I was meaning you'. We say not only 'I just remembered that we went there last year' but also 'I just remembered that we have to go there next year'. And from such trivial reminders of combinatorial possibilities and impossibilities, we can draw conclusions that dispel illusions. For example, that believing something is not a mental state like feeling anxious; or that meaning something is not an act or activity like saying something; or that memory need not be of the past but may be of the future (as when we remember that the party is next Wednesday).

- Less obvious is the method of reminders of comparative and contrastive use. This is worth emphasizing, for although every competent speaker has, by definition, mastered the use of the language he speaks, mastery of the use of a word is not the same as having an overview of its *comparative use*. In order to know how to use the words 'nearly' and 'almost', one need not have *realized* how they differ. But when I remind you that when you want some more gin in your gin and tonic, you would never say 'There isn't almost enough gin in this drink' but only 'There isn't nearly enough gin in this drink' – you will say 'Of course'. So, in philosophy, we all know how to use the word 'believe' and also how to use the word 'think' – but are hard-pressed to state the differences between believing something and thinking something. But that is very often exactly the kind of thing that is needed. For we commonly assimilate an expression of one logico-grammatical type to an expression of another completely different one – as when we assimilate sensation to perception and blindly speak of perceiving our pains (after all, we *feel* them!); or think that because we *have* both pennies and pains, therefore we own or possess both pennies and pains. Describing comparative and contrastive use is crucially important; it may bring us to realize why an analogy we invoked is wrong or misleading.
- Just because mastery of use does not imply command of comparative use, it is often helpful to draw our attention to analogies. For sometimes we see difficulties with one grammatical structure and need to have our attention drawn to another domain of grammar that displays a similar feature without bothering us at all. And this often suffices to dispel our bafflement. So, for example, we plague ourselves with the thought that another person cannot possibly have the same pain as we do. So we should have our attention drawn to the fact that we do *not* think that another object cannot possibly have the same colour or weight as this one! We think that mathematical propositions cannot possibly be rules of representation because rules are neither true nor false, but mathematical propositions are surely either true or false. So we need to have our attention drawn to the fact that we feel no unease with the fact that it is a rule of chess that the king moves one square at a time, and yet it is perfectly licit to say that it is true that the chess king moves a square at a time. So there is no inconsistency in claiming that the mathematical equation '$25 \times 25 = 625$' is the expression of a rule, and also saying that it is true that $25 \times 25 = 625$. Rules are indeed neither true nor false, but the content of a rule, for example, that the chess king moves a square at a time can perfectly licitly be said to be true. That is not to say that this is a true rule, but rather to say that this is truly a rule.

- Because use is so intimately bound up with context, we often need to be reminded of the contexts in which the use of a word or sentence is appropriate, quite irrespective of whether what is said is true or false. We must note that in certain cases, it requires a special context for an expression to apply *either truly or falsely*. It is neither true nor false that when I look up from the dinner table in ordinary circumstances, I recognize my wife. A special context is needed for the question of recognition, misrecognition or failure of recognition *even to arise*. And the same applies to such phrases as 'It visually seems to me just as if …' – which is a crucial matter in the philosophical analysis of perception. For philosophers typically wrench this expression, and its cousins 'It looks as if …' and 'It appears …', out of the very special contexts in which they have a role and assume that *whenever* one perceives something, it also seems to one just as if … And that is radically mistaken.
- Wittgenstein placed considerable emphasis on describing simplified imaginary language games to function as illuminating objects of comparison to shed light on our much more complex language games. So it is useful to imagine a number system that reaches no farther than 100 or a language that consists only of simple orders. Similarly, it is sometimes useful to envisage language games that are importantly different from ours and try to follow through the consequences of conceiving things thus. So we might imagine a colour vocabulary that consists of verbs rather than colour adjectives (in which we would speak of something's greening or blueing), or a system of measurement with elastic rulers and so forth.
- In our philosophical reflections, our imagination is commonly driven by implicit misleading analogies that we often fail even to notice. So, we have noted the question that plagued philosophers in the last 30 years of the twentieth century and that provides the drive shaft of much of theoretical linguistics – namely: 'How can we understand sentences we have never heard before?' But it was rarely, if ever noticed by philosophers or linguists, that at least part of the puzzlement derives from the implicit supposition that understanding is something we *do*. For the question 'How can we understand sentences we have never heard before?' sounds like 'How can we start a motor car without a key?', that is, How can we *do* something? But to understand something is not anything *done* – it is to be able to do something. So, it makes no sense to ask *how* we do it. Furthermore, if we think of understanding as a hidden process of calculating the meaning of a sentence from the meanings of its constituent words and their mode of combination, then the upshot of understanding a novel sentence will seem analogous to knowing the result of a calculation – like knowing that

the answer to the question 'What is 25 x 25?' is 625. But that is precisely *disanalogous* to understanding an utterance. Understanding a sentence is like understanding the *question* 'What is 25 x 25?', not like knowing its *answer*. To understand something is not *to calculate* anything.

To be sure, that is not the end of the puzzles about understanding utterances, but it is the beginning of the end.

There are many more methods that Wittgenstein devised for clarifying features and comparative features of our conceptual scheme, and for solving and dissolving philosophical confusions and perplexities. But this selection suffices to show that all these diverse methods can reasonably be accommodated to his startling remark in 1930/31 that 'a new method has been found'.

Chapter 17

WITTGENSTEIN'S CONCEPTION OF PHILOSOPHY - III

The Goals of Philosophy: Conceptual Geography and Intellectual Therapy

In the last two lectures, we saw that according to Wittgenstein, philosophy has both positive and negative aims.
- *Positively*, philosophy aims to give an overview – a surveyable representation of a conceptual field. Wittgenstein compares this task of philosophy to conceptual cartography.
- *Negatively*, philosophy aims to disentangle conceptual confusions, to destroy metaphysical illusions, to undermine mythologies of symbolism and of psychology (both within philosophy and within the sciences).

So, let's start with the positive objective. To give a synopsis of the use of an expression, describing its salient logico-grammatical features and rendering a surveyable account of its conceptual affinities and disaffinities, is a positive achievement. One who has an overview knows his way around in the grammar of the problematic expression and is in a position to clear up associated philosophical confusions. The point of striving for an overview is to clear up philosophical difficulties – to make the troubles disappear. Where there are no conceptual difficulties, as in, say, culinary discourse, there is no point in striving for an overview of concepts. For where there are no such troubles, there is nothing to make disappear. The field of philosophy is limited by the range of our philosophical troubles.

> **Int.** Yes, I think I understood that in our last meeting. But now I am a bit confused. I thought that it was Gilbert Ryle who talked about *logical geography* in his famous book *The Concept of Mind*.
> **PMSH.** You're quite right. Ryle did use this phrase in *Concept of Mind*. That book was published in 1949. But Wittgenstein invoked the metaphor of *logical*, or *conceptual*, *geography* much earlier. The philosopher, he wrote, wanted to master the geography of concepts: to see every locality

in its proximate and its distant surroundings. In the early 1930s, he said to his pupils

> One difficulty with philosophy is that we lack a synoptic view. We encounter the kind of difficulty we should have with the geography of a country for which we had no map, or else a map of isolated bits. The country we are talking about is language and the geography its grammar. We can walk about the country quite well, but when forced to make a map, we go wrong. (AWL 43)

In his 1939 lectures, he used a similar metaphor:

> I am trying to conduct you on tours in a certain country. I will try to show you that the philosophical difficulties which arise in mathematics as elsewhere arise because we find ourselves in a strange town and do not know our way. So we must learn the topography by going from one place in the town to another, and from there to another, and so on. (LFM 44)

Int. So do you think that Ryle took this figure of speech from Wittgenstein?
PMSH. Oh, I've no idea. It may be so. But you should always remember that it is possible for two people to have the same idea independently of each other. What is interesting is not who used it first, but that they both used it. For it is, after all, a very illuminating metaphor if correctly interpreted. It captures nicely the *positive* task of Wittgenstein's philosophy.

Now the *point* of arranging the 'grammatical facts' in a readily surveyable form – like a map of the conceptual terrain – is to dissolve philosophical problems and destroy philosophical illusions. Now this *negative* aspect of Wittgenstein's endeavours is commonly given a metaphorical *therapeutic* characterization. The philosopher, he wrote, is the man who has to cure himself of many sicknesses of the understanding before he can arrive at the notions of a sound (healthy) human understanding (RFM 302). What a mathematician is inclined to say about the objectivity and reality of mathematical facts is not a philosophy of mathematics, but something for philosophical treatment. The philosopher treats a question – *like an illness* (PI §§254f.). There is not *a* philosophical method, though there are indeed *methods*, like different *therapies* (PI §133). In philosophizing we may not *terminate* a disease of thought. It must run its natural course, and a *slow* cure is all important (Z §382).

The analogy is a good one, although one must not forget that it is *only an analogy*. Philosophical confusions are not caused by infection but by forms of misunderstanding. They are 'cured', so to speak, not causally by medicine, but rationally by arguments. Philosophical analysis reminds us how we use words, shows that the bounds of sense were transgressed, offers us analogies and points out disanalogies, or juxtaposes the case in hand with imaginary language games designed to highlight grammatical features we overlooked. In this way, we attain an overview, which produces not health but *understanding*.

Int. Indeed, it is a good analogy. But I thought he used a psychoanalytic analogy too, which has been taken up by other philosophers such as John Wisdom, and was argued to be the key to the interpretation of Wittgenstein's later philosophy by your late colleague Gordon Baker.

PMSH. Yes, that's right. Let me first clarify what Wittgenstein said. He held that the philosopher transforms latent nonsense into patent nonsense, just as the psychoanalyst transforms latent emotions into patent ones – for only when they are thus exposed can they be confronted. A primary activity of philosophers is to warn against wrong comparisons, wrong similes that are rooted in our forms of expression, without our being altogether conscious of this. Wittgenstein's method here resembles the analyst's: by making us aware of what was unconscious, he tries to render it harmless (MS. 109, 174). Like the analyst, Wittgenstein encourages us to release repressed qualms (PG 381f.).

Int. That's great! What else did he say about this?

PMSH. He drew attention to further similarities between his methods of philosophical analysis and psychoanalysis. This analogy was to cause a great deal of trouble, and perhaps it was, in a sense, ill-advised. What he said was this: just as a criterion for correct psychoanalysis is the patient's acknowledgement of the proposed analysis, so too:

> One of the most important tasks is to express all false trains of thought so characteristically that the reader says 'Yes, that's exactly what I meant'. – To trace the physiognomy of every error.
> Indeed we can only convict someone else of a mistake if he acknowledges this expression of [what he is inclined to say].
> For only if he acknowledges it as such, is it the correct expression. (BT 410)

Again, just as the psychoanalyst expects resistance from his patient, so too in philosophy one of the difficulties is

> the contrast between the understanding of the subject and what most people *want* to see. Because of this, the very things that are most obvious can become the most difficult to understand. What has to be overcome is not a difficulty of the intellect, but of the will. (BT 406)

And just as in neurotic disorders there are obsessions, so too in philosophical confusions there is an obsession with certain words, turns of phrase, pictures and an obsessive insistence that things *must* be thus-and-so (AWL 98f.). And just as jokes are psychoanalytically revealing, so too jokes are grammatically revealing – indeed one could write a philosophy book that consisted of nothing but jokes. One might think here of Lewis Carroll's *Alice through the Looking Glass*, which is full of philosophical jokes.

Int. But the analogy seems a jolly good one. Why do you object to it?

PMSH. I don't actually object to it at all. The analogy *is* a good one, but it is important to realize that it is but an analogy. What I object to is making too much of it and forgetting that it's just an analogy, which must not be pushed too far.

Int. What do you mean 'too far'?

PMSH. What I mean is that the analogy must not be pushed to the point of obscuring the *differences* between Freud's psychoanalytic techniques and Wittgenstein's conception of philosophy and philosophical method.

Int. What *are* the differences that you have in mind? People who make much of this analogy – indeed who even deny that it *is* a mere analogy – don't talk about differences.

PMSH. That's right. But they should. And it's not too difficult to see the differences. Let me spell some of the more important ones out for you – so that you aren't made a victim of an analogy that has got out of hand.

- First, psychoanalysis involves a complex theory or hypothesis about the workings of the human psyche – by contrast, Wittgenstein's philosophy rests on no *theory or hypothesis* whatsoever.
- Second, psychoanalytic problems are produced, according to Freud, by *childhood traumas;* philosophical problems are produced by *features of our language*, by *our intellectual dispositions* and by our misguidedly imitating or pretending to imitate *the model of the natural sciences*.
- Third, psychoanalytic therapy treats *patients* who *cannot function optimally in the stream of life* – the Wittgensteinian philosopher treats *questions* (PI §255). Philosophers – even those who are in the grip of philosophical, conceptual illusions – still function perfectly optimally in the course of their lives, barring the eccentricities of academia.
- Fourth, the resolution of the problems of philosophy purports to possess *a rational validity* which, unlike the resolution of a psychoanalytic illness, is *not patient-dependent*. So, the exercise has a generality absent from psychoanalytic treatment, precisely *because* the philosopher treats *questions*.

Int. Hold it a moment. You said, indeed you quoted Wittgenstein as saying, that he had to trace the physiognomy of every mistake, that one can't convict anyone of a mistake until one had got him to admit that that was exactly what he meant – which is exactly analogous to the patient undergoing psychoanalysis. Because the criterion for the success of the analysis is the patient's acknowledgement.

PMSH. Yes, that's correct. But remember that there is a certain amount of rhetoric here. After all, when Wittgenstein criticizes Plato, Augustine, Frege or Russell – all of whom he explicitly criticizes – he doesn't fault his own criticisms on the ground that unfortunately these chaps aren't around to agree with the way he puts their views. No, no. What he means is surely that for really good philosophical criticism and for the disentangling of really deep philosophical confusion, one must dig right down to the roots of the error. The deep mistakes that he exposes are, as we have seen again and again, ubiquitous mistakes, made, often in somewhat different ways, by numerous great thinkers throughout the history of philosophical thought.

Int. So you mean that what he is really trying to do is to find the roots of the confusion and to describe the sources of the error in such a way that anyone reading what he writes will say: 'Oh *that's* why he thought such-and-such', as well as 'Yes, that's exactly why I thought such-and-such'.

PMSH. Exactly. Now, there are further important disanalogies between Wittgenstein's methods and psychoanalysis. I have mentioned four. Now the fifth is this:

- In so far as there are *arguments* in psychoanalysis, they do not show that *forms of words* that seem to make sense are nonsense; on the contrary, forms of words (especially in dreams) that *seem to be nonsense* are shown on analysis to *make sense*. There could not be a more vivid and striking difference. Philosophical analysis, as Wittgenstein conducts it, transforms latent nonsense into patent nonsense. But Freud tried to transform, for example, the latent nonsense of a dream into patent sense.
- A sixth difference is that the psychoanalyst is concerned with the causes of *a particular person's malady*. Wittgenstein, by contrast, is concerned with misleading features of *the common, shared grammar of our language*. It is partly because European languages, at any rate, present pains, or subjective experiences in general, in the *representational form* of possessions that we all get tied in knots when we think about the question of whether you can have my pain.

Now, can you see the limits of the psychoanalytic analogy?

Int. Yes. You've made it very clear, and also very striking. I see that although there are analogies, one mustn't let them get out of hand.

PMSH. That's right. It is noteworthy that Wittgenstein got exceedingly angry when John Wisdom and A. J. Ayer exaggerated the psychoanalytic analogy and attributed it, thus exaggerated, to him (MS. 138, 17a). The two techniques, he said to his pupil Norman Malcolm, are completely different.

Philosophy, Truth and Knowledge

Philosophy, as we have seen, is not a cognitive discipline. Unlike the empirical sciences, its goal is not to discover *new truths*. And in the sense in which there are distinctive propositions of physics and distinctive propositions of chemistry, *there are no distinctive philosophical propositions.*

> **Int.** Oh, I'm glad you've brought that up again. I've been thinking about it since our last discussion of the matter, and it seems to me that what Wittgenstein says can't be right. I mean, are there *really* no philosophical propositions? What about 'There can be no private language?' – is that not a true philosophical proposition? Or 'The meaning of a word is its use in the language'? Or 'The meaning of a word is not the object it stands for'? Or 'solipsism and idealism are misconceived metaphysical theories'?
>
> **PMSH.** This is a very good question.
>
> **Int.** [*excitedly*] You bet! And they ramify. I mean, these surely are philosophical propositions? And surely, if Wittgenstein is right, they are *true* to boot! So *there are philosophical truths*! Now, before my discussions with you and before I heard you talk on these themes, I didn't know any of these truths. Now, dammit, haven't I *learnt* something new? And if I've learnt something new, then I have achieved philosophical *knowledge*. So Wittgenstein *must be wrong* in claiming that philosophy is *not* a cognitive discipline. It *is* a cognitive discipline!
>
> **PMSH.** [*slightly amused*] Calm down, my dear fellow! I know it's very exciting when one thinks one has found a gaping breach in the walls, but you must take things slowly.
>
> Let's start with a trivial proposition – 'Bachelors are unmarried'. This is not an empirical generalization – it is a *grammatical* proposition. That is, it is *a rule* for the use of the word 'bachelor' (or for any synonym of 'bachelor' in other languages), dressed up in the guise of an empirical proposition – after all, it looks just like 'Bachelors are unhappy'. There is nothing philosophical about it, and it is not the task of philosophy to discover or advance such propositions. Of course, *it is true* that bachelors are unmarried – just as it is true that the chess king moves one square at a time. But it is not that the *rule* is true; *there is no such thing as a true or false rule*, only true or false statements *of a rule*. And to be sure, the assertion: the chess king moves one square at a time *is* a true statement of a rule of chess. It states the content of a chess rule.
>
> **Int.** Yes, we've been over that already, and I have conceded that to you. I don't see what this has to do with it!

PMSH. Well, now what about the proposition 'pain is a sensation'? Obviously, it too is a grammatical proposition. It is the expression of a rule for the use of the word 'pain'.

Int. What sort of rule?

PMSH. Well, it is a simple inference rule: it entitles one to infer from the fact that someone has a pain in his arm that he has a sensation in his arm. Similarly, 'pain has a bodily location' is a grammatical proposition. And the rule *it* expresses amounts to this: it always *makes sense* to ask of a pain: 'Where, in the body, is it?' or 'Where does it hurt?'.

Int. All right – I can go along with that.

PMSH. What then of the following proposition: 'The location of pain is where the sufferer sincerely points when asked where it hurts'? Isn't that a grammatical proposition too?

Int. Yes, it surely is. It gives us the logical criterion for the application of the phrase 'location of pain'. So it explains an aspect of the meaning of the phrase 'the location of pain' by specifying a criterion for pain location.

PMSH. Quite so. So there is no difference in principle between a grammatical rule such as 'Bachelors are unmarried' and 'The location of a pain is where the sufferer sincerely points'.

Int. Well, I don't know about that. After all, you can find 'bachelor = df. unmarried man' in the dictionary. But you won't find 'the location of a pain is where the sufferer from the pain sincerely points when he is asked where it hurts' in any dictionary I have ever come across.

PMSH. Well, yes. But that does not make it any less a grammatical proposition. It is merely a rule for the use of a phrase that is further removed from the interests of lexicographers and grammarians than 'Bachelors are unmarried men'. The grammarian will tell you that the sentence form 'I have a pain in my ...' has to be completed by a noun. A philosopher will remind you that it must be completed by an expression signifying part of the subject's body.

So far, so good?

Int. Yes. But surely the proposition: 'There can't be a private language' is not a rule of grammar. Surely this *is* a philosophical proposition!

PMSH. Let's not be too hasty. 'There can't be a private language' is akin to 'One can't trisect an arbitrary angle with a compass and rule' or 'One can't square a circle'. Such sentences are, of course, misleading. For they do not say that squaring a circle or trisecting an angle are too difficult for us poor mortals – as if God might succeed where we fail. No, what they say is *that there is no such thing*. There is no such thing in Euclidean plane geometry as trisecting an arbitrary angle with a compass and ruler and equally no such thing as squaring a circle – just as there is no such thing as checkmate in draughts. Will you go along with that?

Int. [*slightly hesitantly*] Hmmm ... let's see. I'm not sure where you're taking me.

PMSH. [*cheerfully*] Well, I promise not to take you anywhere you won't voluntarily go!

All right. There is no such thing as checkmate in draughts, and no such thing as squaring a circle. Equally, *there is no such thing as a private ostensive definition*. That too is a grammatical proposition – it is an *exclusionary rule*. And what it excludes is not an impossible possibility, but *a form of words*, namely 'private ostensive definition'. This is a form of words that has no application in our language. What Wittgenstein did in the *Private Language Arguments* was to draw our attention to features of the grammar of the word 'sample' and of the phrase 'ostensive definition'. In so doing, he reminded us that an ostensive definition is a rule for the use of a word. He then reminded us of some of the grammatical features of the word 'rule' and of the phrase 'following a rule'. Then he exhibited some confusions associated with the idea of privacy here. And he showed that, *given* these rules for the use of these words and phrases, then the intelligibility of a private analogue of a public ostensive definition is ruled out. All this was a sequence of movements *within grammar* – and the upshot was not a philosophical proposition akin to propositions of physics and chemistry, but *another true grammatical proposition*. Now, of course, it is not the kind of proposition that a grammarian is likely to come up with, nor is it the kind of proposition that anyone is likely to allocate to ordinary conventional grammar. Above all, of course, it is not a proposition that is special to a particular language such as English, but rather it applies to *any* language with appropriately similar structure and concepts. One might indeed say that what it expresses is a *conceptual truth*.

Int. [*slightly dazed*] Gosh! ... I hadn't thought any of that. That's really fantastic! So that's what is really meant by the phrase 'conceptual truth'.

PMSH. Exactly. The grammatical propositions that are the concern of philosophy can be said to be *conceptual truths*. They describe or state what does and what does not *make sense*. And so they elucidate and delimit the bounds of sense. That gives them a generality that is not typically associated with local grammars of natural languages such as French or German. They apply at a higher level of abstraction – to equivalences across similar languages. But this does not make them any less *grammatical* – that is, any less *rules for the use of words*. And they are no more *philosophical propositions* concerning a uniquely *philosophical subject matter* than such propositions as 'bachelors are unmarried'. To repeat: they are rules for the use of words.

Int. Well, I can see what you're driving at. And I can see that it fits what Wittgenstein says. But you have not answered the point I made about learning something new. I mean, before Wittgenstein *no one knew* that there could be no such thing as a private ostensive definition; it never occurred to anyone. And surely, *I* now know something that I didn't know before. Before I listened to you, it never crossed my mind that there is no such thing as a private ostensive definition.

PMSH. That is true. As indeed it is true that before I pointed out to you that the difference between 'nearly' and 'almost' is that they behave differently under negation, this had never occurred to you either. Mastery of the use of a word, as I have stressed before, does *not* imply *mastery of its comparative use*. In *this* sense, and *in this sense alone*, one might say that philosophy *does* add to human knowledge. But note two crucial points that make this concession very minor.

- First, that what is added is knowledge *that takes the form of realization*, not the form of *discovery*.
- Second, the realization is not of *features of the world* that we describe by means of language but *features of language* that we use to describe features of the world. And it is not of *facts* concerning the world, it is of *rules concerned with describing the world and stating facts*. To put matters metaphorically, what you have learnt belongs to knowledge of the net, not to knowledge of the fish. You have realized something important about the means of representation, not about what is represented.

So, with this minor qualification, I suggest that it *is* appropriate to characterize philosophy as a quest for *a form of understanding*, not for the enlargement of knowledge.

Misunderstandings

Informing philosophers that they had misunderstood the nature of their investigations for the past two and a half thousand years was never likely to win their immediate approval. Telling them that their subject was not even a cognitive discipline and that philosophers did not add to the sum of human knowledge about the world around them was sure to enrage them. And so indeed it did. From the 1970s, philosophers craved theories: theories of meaning for natural languages. Since the 1980s, they have been in pursuit of theories of mind and brain, on the one hand, and metaphysical theories, on the other. By the 1990s, they were craving entry to the community of cognitive scientists. By the turn of the century, metaphysics was all the rage.

Although it seemed none too clear what metaphysics was, at any rate it gave the appearance of being a subject matter that philosophers could safely claim for themselves. It bred its own jargon: 'possible worlds', 'trans-world identity', 'rigid designation', and it invoked all the complex formal apparatus of modal logic, which ensured that outsiders could not penetrate. It demanded a long apprenticeship from graduate students who wished to join the enterprise. So it engendered a protective hermeticism. Cognitive science offered the illusion of a joint enterprise with scientists, and hence the promise of the glory associated with science. Cognitive neuroscience in turn led to the development of what was called 'neurophilosophy'.

This reversion to metaphysics, on the one hand, and blatant scientism, on the other, obviously flew in the face of everything Wittgenstein had taught. The new wave of philosophers knew little about Wittgenstein. But they did inchoately grasp that if what he had taught was true, then it would show their own endeavours to be worthless. Hence, they missed few opportunities to castigate and caricature Wittgenstein. The result was that the next generation of philosophers and students of philosophy laboured under grievous misunderstandings of Wittgenstein. I should like to draw your attention to some of the more egregious criticisms that became and remain common – and also to show you why they are wrong. Here is a selection:

- Wittgenstein is said to have denied that there are any real philosophical problems – to have held that the so-called problems of philosophy are *mere pseudo-problems*.
- Some critics thought that Wittgenstein had *trivialized* a profound subject – reducing it to mere scrutiny of language.
- Some seized upon Wittgenstein's remark that philosophy leaves everything as it is and accused him of being a *quietist* – of holding that philosophy is no more than an idle activity like doing crossword puzzles, an activity that has no serious consequences.
- Others could not understand why a philosopher, any more than a scientist, should have the least concern with the *ordinary* use of words. For surely, both philosophers and scientists should be allowed to use words as they please, and to introduce new, non-ordinary technical uses of words as they wish.
- Even if critics grant, for the sake of argument, that philosophy is concerned with the use of words, *whose* use concerns it? Should Wittgensteinian philosophers not engage in social surveys of linguistic usage? Actually, such critics announce in contempt that all Wittgensteinians do is to try to impose *their* uses of language on others, pretending to be linguistic policemen.

So, let's examine these allegations.

(i) The first accusation was that Wittgenstein argued that philosophy consists of no more than *pseudo-problems*. But this is untrue. Wittgenstein, in his later philosophy, never characterized the problems of philosophy as pseudo-problems. They are perfectly *genuine problems* (puzzling questions, matters for inquiry, difficulties) – only not empirical, scientific or theoretical ones. They are problems that, for the most part, need to be dissolved or resolved by description, not by theory. They are, indeed, deep – but not deep problems about a *special subject matter* (such as the 'logical structure of the world'). They are deep problems precisely because, as he wrote: 'their roots are as deep in us as the forms of our language' (PI §111).

(ii) The second accusation was that Wittgenstein *trivialized philosophy*. It is true that he remarked that 'What we *find out* in philosophy is trivial; it does not teach us new facts, only science does that' (LWL 26). But we have now seen what he was driving at: philosophy does not teach us new facts about the world. We don't find anything out about the metaphysical structure of the world or any other features of the world. Philosophy does not even teach us new rules for the use of words. Rather, it draws our attention to perfectly familiar rules for the use of words and points to certain comparative features of those rules which we may not have realized. This is *a method* – not its *result*. The results of doing philosophy in the new way are anything but trivial. They are the resolution of problems and the elimination of conceptual illusion and confusion. They are the attainment of an overview of a problematic segment of our conceptual scheme, hence an understanding of how the concepts fit together. Philosophy has indeed 'lost its nimbus'. But it has lost neither its depth nor its importance. The depth lies in the confusions which it is the task of philosophy to eradicate, and the importance lies in their significance in philosophy, in science and in daily life.

(iii) The third allegation was that Wittgenstein's philosophy advocates *quietism* and holds philosophy to be *impotent* or *inconsequential*. But this too is false. The idea that philosophy is *inconsequential*, a mere idle amusement, was far removed from Wittgenstein's mind and diametrically opposed to his conception of philosophy. The remark in *Investigations* §124 that philosophy 'leaves everything as it is' was misinterpreted. In context, it says that philosophy leaves everything *in language and grammar* as it is. This has nothing to do with being inconsequential or quietist. What it says is that it is not the task of philosophy to *reform language*, to produce *an ideal language*, as Frege and Russell had supposed. For our philosophical problems are confusions and unclarities arising out of our *current conceptual forms*. These confusions can be understood and dispelled only by examining how they arise in our existing language and grammar, and then disentangling the knots we have tied in our understanding. Substituting a different array of conceptual forms – as Frege and Russell proposed – would do no more than sweep the problems under the carpet – not solve or resolve them. Moreover, the new forms, for example, of the invented language of the predicate calculus, themselves give rise to their own array of confusions with which philosophers have been struggling ever since Frege and Russell introduced their new logic.

In a profound sense, Wittgenstein was the first to give philosophy a *warrant* to interfere *in the sciences*. For it is just because, as Wittgenstein wrote: 'the philosopher is not a citizen of any community of ideas' (Z §455) that the philosopher has *the right* to criticize members of communities of ideas when they transgress the bounds of sense. Although philosophy can no longer aspire to be the Queen of the Sciences, she remains *The Tribunal of Sense* – that is, the systematic critic of conceptual confusion. It is not the task of the philosopher to interfere with the proofs of mathematicians; but what mathematicians *say* about their proofs is grist for philosophical mills. Far from leaving mathematics as it is, a good philosophy of mathematics, Wittgenstein remarked 'will have the same effect on the growth of mathematics as sunlight has on the growth of potato shoots (in a dark cellar they grow yards long)' (PG 381). This is anything but quietism. Similarly, 'in psychology there are experimental methods and *conceptual confusion*' (PPF §371) and the eradication of such confusions is a task of Wittgenstein's philosophy of psychology. We have occasionally mentioned theses in psychology, in cognitive science and in cognitive neuroscience that exemplify the kinds of conceptual confusions that it is the task of philosophy to reveal and eradicate. The consequences of such conceptual criticism are anything but trivial – it may overturn empirical theories, not by falsifying them, but by showing their questions to be incoherent. And it may show that experiments do not prove what they were thought to prove.

Of course, this engenders angry opposition. On the one hand, critics complain that Wittgenstein held philosophy to be impotent – inconsequential. That, in their view, derogates from the dignity of philosophy and puts Wittgenstein beyond the pale. On the other hand, when Wittgenstein engages in potent criticisms of mathematicians' remarks on the nature of their subject and Wittgensteinian philosophers submit the natural sciences, such as cosmology, psychology or cognitive neuroscience to conceptual criticism, they are accused of unwarranted interference in subjects that are not their own. This incoherence displays incomprehension of the nature of philosophy and of its field of operations, coupled with a deficient grasp of what a conceptual confusion is.

(iv) A fourth common criticism is that Wittgenstein held that philosophy is *about* language, that he was arguing that philosophy is a branch of linguistics, or is 'merely' about words, or that it canonizes the ordinary use of words. This too is misconceived. For philosophy is no *more* about words than it is *about concepts* or *about essential natures*. Since the rules for the use of words delimit what it makes sense to say; they also determine the nature or essence of things. For they determine the features of things that warrant subsuming them under a given concept. Wittgenstein expressed the point nicely in the *Investigations*:

> One ought to ask, not what images are or what goes on when one imagines something, but how the word 'imagination' is used. But that does not mean that I want to talk only about words. For the question of what imagination essentially is, is as much about the word 'imagination' as my question. And I am only saying that this question is not to be clarified – neither for the person who does the imagining, nor for anyone else – by pointing; nor yet by a description of some process. The first question also asks for the clarification of a word; but it makes us expect a wrong kind of answer. (PI §370)

Philosophy is no less about the nature of things than it has been hitherto. But with this difference, now we should realize that the nature of things – their essential nature – is determined by the grammar of our language. For grammar lays down the conditions under which something is to be *called*, for example, a colour, a number, a sensation, a perception, true or false and so forth. And in determining this, it determines what we *call* a colour, a number, a sensation and so on. And in doing so, it determines *the nature* of a colour, a number, a sensation and so forth. Investigating the use of a word, examining the grammatical rules for its correct use, is at the same time examining the concept it expresses. And to examine the concept of colour, of number, of sensation or perception and so forth *is* to examine the nature of colour, number, sensation or perception – *in so far as they can be said to have* a nature or essence. But, contrary to the venerable tradition and to currently prevailing orthodoxy, it is language and its use that are in the driving seat! For, as Wittgenstein wrote: 'Grammar tells us what kind of object anything is' (PI §373) – it tells us what is *to count* as a so-and-so.

(v) A fifth common criticism is that Wittgenstein did not merely hold philosophy to be *about* language and its use, but also that he held it to be about *mere* language and its use – 'it's *just* about language!' critics say contemptuously. This is meant to show again that philosophy according to Wittgenstein is about something trivial. This criticism is misplaced. For even if it were true that, according to Wittgenstein, philosophy is *just* about language and its use, that would not show that it is trivial. *There is nothing trivial about language*, or about the confusions into which we are led through our failure to have an overview of a problematic domain of grammar. We are the kinds of creatures we are because we possess a language. Our distinctive capacities – our rationality, our knowledge of good and evil, our possession of a conscience, our self-consciousness, our capacity for apprehension of necessary truths – *are all functions of the fact that we are language-using creatures.* So note:

a. There is no 'merely' about the grammatical problems that concern philosophy.
b. Conceptual confusions, far from being inconsequential, wreak havoc with scientific and social scientific research programmes – the history of science is littered not only with *mistaken* theories, but also with the wreckage of *misconceived* theories rooted in conceptual incoherences.
c. Nor are conceptual confusions merely *innocent* excrescences on the thought of Everyman in his home-baked reflections on morality, law and politics. For common-or-garden debate about justice, liberty, rights, democracy, about capital punishment or abortion, about education and culture are riddled with such confusions.

Philosophy, in Wittgenstein's hands, may have lost its nimbus, but it has found a vocation. It may no longer aspire to reveal the logical or metaphysical structure of the world or the foundations of human knowledge or the limits of human understanding, but its role is to confront conceptual puzzlement, to describe the bounds of sense and to show when they are transgressed.

(vi) Wittgenstein was concerned with resolving philosophical problems. And he held that a primary method for so doing was to examine *the ordinary use of words*. A sixth accusation against him is that he *abased himself* before 'ordinary use' – the ways in which the man on the Clapham omnibus speaks. But that, it was objected, is ridiculous – since there is no reason why scientists and philosophers should be constrained by the usage of the ill-educated or non-specialists.

It is true that Wittgenstein wrote: 'What we do is to bring words back from their metaphysical to their everyday use' (PI §116). That does not mean that his concern was solely with the *everyday* words. He was speaking, *in that context*, of such words as 'knowledge', 'exists', 'object', 'I', 'sentence' and 'name' – and these are indeed *everyday* words with everyday *uses*. But, of course, Wittgenstein was concerned with ordinary, everyday language only to the extent that the problems he was dealing with arise in respect of matters expressed in everyday language. But when he discussed transfinite arithmetic, Cantorian set theory or Hilbert's metamathematics, his concern was not with ordinary, everyday language but with the technical language of mathematicians and *its* use.

Did he hold that one may not introduce technical terminology into philosophy? He certainly did not think that there was any deep need for it. But he placed no prohibition on introduction of new terms and did indeed introduce a few himself (e.g. 'family-resemblance concepts', 'language games', 'genuine duration').

What Wittgenstein *did* object to was the common manoeuvre of philosophers to dismiss the ordinary use of a word, say 'knowledge' and replace it by a so-called *special philosophical use*, allegedly justified on the grounds that this philosophical use will shed more light on some philosophical problem. This Wittgenstein thought was chicanery. The philosophical problems about knowledge arise in connection with our common-or-garden concept, the very concept that is expressed by the use of the ordinary noun 'knowledge' and its cognates. To replace this by a new use with different rules is not to solve a problem but to conceal it. It is as if we were puzzled about *how birds fly* and went to our teacher with our puzzlement, and he presented us with a *blueprint of an aeroplane*. Problems about the nature of knowledge can be solved or resolved only by examining *our concept* of knowledge. This we can do only by examining *our use* of the word 'knowledge'.

So, insofar as the main problems that he dealt with concern concepts that occur in ordinary non-technical language, Wittgenstein did hold that we must scrutinize ordinary use. But, his critics objected, unlike the Norwegian philosopher Arne Naess, he never did any *socio-linguistic surveys*! He never actually *asked* any men or women on the Clapham omnibus how they use words. He relied exclusively on his own use of words or on that of Cambridge dons of his day – and is that not methodologically disreputable? – The objection displays deep confusion.

A philosopher who is a competent speaker of his language has no more need to consult others about the use of a word than a mathematician needs to consult others whether 2 + 2 = 4, or a chess master needs to consult other chess players on how the chess king moves. A competent speaker of the language *by definition* knows the correct uses of the ordinary, non-technical terms of his language. That is what it is to be a competent speaker. Of course, that does not mean that he may not forget some aspect of use, or that he may not give a defective description of use – but then he can be corrected and will recognize his slip when it is pointed out to him.

But what if his interlocutor uses a given word differently? That does not matter in the least, for the astute philosopher will simply accept this proposed use for the sake of argument, and show that it is, in one way or another, incoherent, or that it does not have the dramatic consequences claimed for it, or show that this new use is inadvertently crossed with the old – and that inferences are being drawn from it that can licitly be drawn only from the old use. It is important to realize that Wittgenstein *did not object to deviations from ordinary usage as such*. His objection was to the idea that a new use can resolve a conceptual difficulty that arises from the received use of a term. *One cannot untie a knot in a piece of string by taking a new piece of string.* Wittgenstein did not act as a linguistic policeman; *he did not prohibit anything*. He merely pointed out when people were unwittingly talking nonsense.

(vii) Wittgenstein has been accused of a philistine defence of *common sense*. This is wrong. He insisted that there is no common sense answer to philosophical problems. The common sense answer to Zeno's puzzlement 'How can Achilles possibly overtake the tortoise?' is 'By putting one foot down after the other' – and that will help no one. Such answers, if offered by a philosopher, merely make fun of the questions (TS. 220, §126). What needs to be done is to find the sources of the confusions that lead intelligent people to be baffled by Zeno's Paradox, or to become bewildered, as Augustine was, about how we can possibly do something we all do constantly, namely measure time, or to think that objects *cannot* exist unperceived, or that we can never *really* know what someone else is thinking or feeling, or that the mind *must* be identical with the brain. It is here, in the entanglements in the web of language, that the real philosophical problems lie. Disentangling them has nothing to do with 'common sense', even in those cases where the final answer is one which comes within the ambit of common sense and with which common sense would agree (BB 48, 59; AWL 108f.).

(viii) Finally, it has been said that Wittgenstein was not a *systematic philosopher*, even that his conception of philosophy precludes the idea of *systematic philosophy*. This is misleading, at least if it suggests that Wittgenstein gives us no more than collections of scintillating *aphorisms*. It is true that he does not offer us a systematic theory of anything; he does not offer us an unsystematic theory either, since he denied the intelligibility of theories in the domains of philosophy. However, his remarks are anything but haphazard and unsystematic collections of insights. Not only are they arranged with meticulous care, with a particular argumentative goal in mind, they also explore, in a thoroughly systematic fashion, the sources of error and illusion. If being systematic, with respect to philosophical problems, consists in thoroughness, in exploring a great range of conceptual connections, in examining analogies and disanalogies with related concepts, in investigating the numerous pitfalls that might lead one astray, then Wittgenstein *was* systematic. He travelled 'over a wide field of thought, criss-cross in every direction' (PI, Preface), sketching the landscape from numerous different directions. The resultant sketches conjunctively give us an idea of the landscape

– as a photo-album does. On the other hand, it is also true that he does *not* give us, or on the whole *try to give us*, paintings. He does not supply systematic surveys of the subjects he deals with, in the sense of presenting chapters on understanding, thinking, imagining, the meaning of a word, the meaning of a sentence and so forth. But he often supplies, in his multitudinous scattered remarks, the materials for such synopses. It is also true that he rarely spells out his arguments in detail. The batteries of questions that he bombards us with are often designed to get *us* to think our way through to the conclusion. He often shoots an arrow at his target, leaving it to the reader to see why *that* was the target and that the arrow *has* hit it. This gives his writing formidable evocative power and richness – but also great potential for misunderstanding and misinterpretation.

Conclusion

I noted in a previous lecture that in 1930/31 Wittgenstein remarked that what he was doing was the *heir* to what used to be called philosophy. He also observed that now there could no longer be great philosophers, but only skilful ones. We need finally to clarify this.

Did he hold that his new philosophy is the *only* heir to what was traditionally called 'philosophy'? In a trivial sense, clearly not. For among the things investigated by what used to be called 'philosophy' were the natural sciences (long denominated 'natural philosophy'), empirical psychology (which attained independence only at the end of the nineteenth century) and mathematical logic (now being assimilated into mathematics). But the interesting question is whether there are other *philosophical* heirs? Did Wittgenstein advance his conception of philosophy and philosophical method as one among others? Was it his view that there are other, intellectually respectable, ways of handling the questions he dealt with? – I can see no sign of any such tolerance. The only point I would wish to make here is to stress that Wittgenstein's conception of philosophy is tailored to philosophy of logic and language, epistemology and philosophy of psychology, and the philosophies of the various sciences. When it comes to practical philosophy, such as moral, political and legal philosophy, then new factors come into play. For there one is dealing not only with conceptual clarification, but also with what human beings ought to do and how they ought to be.

Why did the new method imply that there could now be skilful philosophers, but no great ones? Why could there not have been skilful philosophers in the past? Because as long as philosophers laboured under the illusion that their quest was for the essence of the world, the foundations of knowledge, the ultimate principles of human understanding and so forth, there could be no *skills* in producing what was sought, only skills in articulating the vision. To have a great vision is not the exercise of a skill. Descartes was a *great* philosopher, but there can be no skilful neo-Cartesians who carry on the work of uncovering the indubitable foundations of all human knowledge – since there are none. Hume was a *great* philosopher, but there can be no skilful neo-Humeans, who carry on the work of investigating the patterns of association of ideas that determine the scope and limits of human knowledge – for there are no such patterns that do any such thing. In the past, there could be *great* philosophers, gripped by a *metaphysical vision*. But with Wittgenstein's new conception of what philosophy now is and of what it can and cannot do, that vision has faded into thin air. There is *a new method* – indeed, a multiplicity of methods. The philosophically relevant description of the grammar of words, the disclosing of misleading analogies and disanalogies between uses of words, the arrangement of the grammatical data to exhibit the precise character of the philosophical illusion that grips us, the noting of the circumstances of use, the detection of misleading pictures in language and so on – all these are matters of skill. The exercise of such skills produces *results* – clarifications, apprehension of conceptual affinities and differences, ordering of concepts – that are permanent achievements and can, as Wittgenstein put it, 'be put in the archives' (BB 44).

Does this mean that at last philosophy is achieving philosophical knowledge – that this can be put in the archives? No, not at all. It is *conceptual clarifications* that can be put in the archives. Conceptual confusions can be laid to rest. But does that mean that philosophy will in due course come to an end? No, not at all, any more than medicine will come to an end. Philosophy has a task to perform as long as human beings continue to become conceptually confused, continue to tie knots in their understanding that need to be unravelled by patient ordering of grammatical forms. To the extent that conceptual confusion has no end, to that extent the task of philosophy and the need for philosophy has no end either.

One might perhaps say that with Wittgenstein *philosophy came to maturity* – casting aside illusions of grandeur. Past philosophers went in quest of a map of Treasure Island, hoping that by means of this map they would be able to discover great and wonderful treasures – about the ultimate nature of things, the metaphysical structure of the world, the existence of God and the immortality of the soul. It is only with Wittgenstein that we are brought to our senses, that we come to realize that the treasure *is the map*. There are no *other* treasures to be discovered. But the map will enable us to find our way around the labyrinths of language without getting lost – and that is surely treasure enough.

ABBREVIATIONS

Wittgenstein's Published Works

The following abbreviations, listed in alphabetical order, are used to refer to Wittgenstein's published works.

BB   *The Blue and Brown Books* (Blackwell, Oxford, 1958).
BT   *The Big Typescript*, ed. and tr. C. G. Luckhardt and M. A. E. Aue (Blackwell, Oxford, 2005).
LPE   'Wittgenstein's Notes for Lectures on "Private Experience" and "Sense Data"', ed. R. Rhees, repr. in *Ludwig Wittgenstein: Philosophical Occasions 1912–1951*, ed. J. Klagge and A. Nordmann (Hackett, Indianapolis and Cambridge, 1993), pp. 202–88.
LW I   *Last Writings on the Philosophy of Psychology*, vol. I, ed. G. H. von Wright and H. Nyman, tr. C. G. Luckhardt and M. A. E. Aue (Blackwell, Oxford, 1982).
PG   *Philosophical Grammar*, ed. R. Rhees, tr. A. J. P. Kenny (Blackwell, Oxford, 1974).
PI   *Philosophical Investigations*, ed. P. M. S. Hacker and Joachim Schulte, tr. G. E. M. Anscombe, P. M. S. Hacker and Joachim Schulte, revised 4th edn (Wiley-Blackwell, Oxford, 2009).
PPF   *Philosophy of Psychology – A Fragment* (previously known as *Philosophical Investigations*, Part II), published in *Philosophical Investigations*, revised 4th edition ed. P. M. S. Hacker and Joachim Schulte, tr. G. E. M. Anscombe, P. M. S. Hacker and Joachim Schulte (Wiley-Blackwell, Oxford, 2009).
PR   *Philosophical Remarks*, ed. R. Rhees, tr. R. Hargreaves and R. White (Blackwell, Oxford, 1975).
RFM   *Remarks on the Foundations of Mathematics*, ed. G. H. von Wright, R. Rhees and G. E. M. Anscombe, rev. edn (Blackwell, Oxford, 1978).
RLF   'Some Remarks on Logical Form', *Proceedings of the Aristotelian Society*, suppl. vol. 9 (1929), pp. 162–71.

RPP I   *Remarks on the Philosophy of Psychology*, vol. I, ed. G. E. M. Anscombe and G. H. von Wright, tr. G. E. M. Anscombe (Blackwell, Oxford, 1980).
TLP   *Tractatus Logico-Philosophicus*, tr. D. F. Pears and B. F. McGuinness (Routledge and Kegan Paul, London, 1961).
Z   *Zettel*, ed. G. E. M. Anscombe and G. H. von Wright, tr. G. E, M, Anscombe (Blackwell, Oxford, 1967).

Reference style: all references to *Philosophical Investigations* are to sections (e.g. PI §1), references to *Philosophy of Psychology – A Fragment* are to numbered remarks in PI, 4th ed, references to other printed works are either to numbered remarks (TLP) or to sections signified '§' (Z. RPP, LW); in all other cases references are to pages (e.g. LFM 21 = LFM, page 21).

DerivativePrimary Sources

AWL   *Wittgenstein's Lectures, Cambridge 1932–35, from the Notes of Alice Ambrose and Margaret MacDonald*, ed. Alice Ambrose (Blackwell, Oxford, 1979).
LFM   *Wittgenstein's Lectures on the Foundations of Mathematics, Cambridge 1939*, ed. C. Diamond (Harvester Press, Hassocks, Sussex, 1976).
LWL   *Wittgenstein's Lectures, Cambridge 1930–32, from the Notes of John King and Desmond Lee*, ed. Desmond Lee (Blackwell, Oxford, 1980).
M   G. E. Moore's notes entitled 'Wittgenstein's Lectures in 1930–33', repr. in *Ludwig Wittgenstein: Philosophical Occasions 1912–1951*, ed. J. Klagge and A. Nordmann (Hackett, Indianapolis and Cambridge, 1993), pp. 46–114.
VoW   *The Voices of Wittgenstein*, transcribed and edited by Gordon Baker, tr. Gordon Baker, Michael Mackert, John Connolly and Vasilis Politis (Routledge, London, 2003).

Nachlass

All references to other material cited in the von Wright catalogue (G. H. von Wright, *Wittgenstein* (Blackwell, Oxford, 1982), pp. 35ff.) are by MS or TS number followed by page number ('r' indicating recto, 'v' indicating verso) or section number '§', as it appears in the Bergen electronic edition of *Wittgenstein's Nachlass*.

FURTHER READING

There is, of course, no substitute for reading the *Philosophical Investigations*. Of Wittgenstein's other writings, *The Blue Book* (published in *The Blue and Brown Books*) is the most readily comprehensible, although it presents only a phase in Wittgenstein's philosophical development. For a lucid presentation of Wittgenstein's thought in the mid-1930s on philosophy of logic and language, F. Waismann's *The Principles of Linguistic Philosophy* is undoubtedly the most accessible. It was written to a large extent under Wittgenstein's supervision.

An engaging short intellectual biography is E. Kanterian, *Wittgenstein* (London, 2007) published by Reaktion Books in their series of Critical Lives. There are two full-scale biographies of Wittgenstein, Brian McGuinness, *Young Ludwig:Wittgenstein's Life 1889–1921* (Duckworth, London, 1988), which covers only the first half of Wittgenstein's life, and Ray Monk, *Ludwig Wittgenstein: The Duty of Genius* (Jonathan Cape, London, 1990). A wonderful personal memoir of Wittgenstein is Norman Malcolm, *Ludwig Wittgenstein: A Memoir, with a Biographical Sketch by G. H. von Wright*, 2nd edn (Oxford University Press, Oxford, 1984).

For further Wittgenstein-inspired dialogues that play with his ideas, see P. M. S. Hacker, *Intellectual Entertainments: Eight Dialogues on Mind, Consciousness and Thought* (Anthem Press paperback, London 2020).

INDEX

access: *see* private access
animal thought 115–17, 166–67, 237–38
Aristotle 238–39
Augustine's picture of language 21–34, 111–12
Augustinian conception of language 22–34, 36–42

beetle in a box 193–94
behaviour 141, 221–24; causes of 226–28
behaviourism 228–32
body 240–41
brain 242–51
brain in a vat 250–60

calculating machines 236–37
certainty 162–63, 267–68
chess 40–41
Chomsky, Noam 64–65, 135, 240, 266–67
Cogito ergo sum 202
computers' thinking 236–37, 245
concepts 114–17
conceptual claims/truths/propositions 11–15
connecting language with reality 80–85
consciousness of pain: *see* pain, consciousness of
criteria for ascription of experience 203–6; of understanding 61–62
criterion 210–13

depth grammar 8
description 49–51
diary of sensations 182–83

epistemic privacy: *see* private knowledge of experience
experience, avowal of 175–76

fact 94–96

family resemblance 86–89, 96
fly-bottle 133
Frege, Gottlob 2, 47, 62–63, 92, 97–98, 144–45, 161–62
Freud, S. 294–95

games 87–89
grammar 48, 58–60, 103–9, 263–71, 297–99
groundless self-ascription of experience 206–10, 218–19

having 151–57

I (first person pronoun) 59–60
identity, numerical and qualitative 138, 143–44, 147–57
imagination, talking in one's 119–22, 166
impossibility, logical, conceptual 58, 99–102, 234–35
inalienability of experience 145–47
indefinables 81–83
inner/outer 224–28
interpreting 72–73
introspection 129, 161–68, 202

James, W. 165

knowing one is in pain: *see* pain, knowing one is in
knowing the meaning of a word: *see* understanding

Lewes, G. H. 233
Locke, John 26, 30, 32, 113, 133–35, 178, 185
logical geography 285–86
Łukasiewicz, J. 92

mathematical propositions 91–99

meaning and use 53–61, 71–72, 75–80; explanation of 43–49
meaning of a word 17–34, 42–49, 53–61
meaning something 69–72
mental state 62–66
mereological fallacy 242–51
metaphysics 12, 31–32, 66–67, 94–108, 259–61, 307–8
metre rule 84–85
Mill, J. S. 29, 224
mind 239
mind's eye 165–66
Moore, G. E. 4, 156
Mozart 12–13

names 24–28, 35–43
naming a sensation 182–83
necessary truths 93–109
neuroscience 243–51

ostensive definition, teaching, training 26–28, 80–85, 111–12
other minds 140–41, 197–206, 216–21; analogical argument for 216–19; theory-theory of 219–21
overview 283–86, 291
ownership 149–50

pain: behaviour 180, 233–34, 241; consciousness of 168–70; criterion of identity for 147–57, 218–19; identification of 218; knowing one is in 170–75; location of 146–49; referring to 128–42
parrot 32, 134
philosophy: as a cognitive discipline 254–59, 299; explanations in 277–79; leaves everything as it is 301–2; methods in 286–89; nimbus of 260–61, 301; and ordinary language 302–6; problems in 261–67, 301; and psycho-analysis 293–95; theory in 275–79; as therapy 292–93
private (privileged) access 129, 175–76, 203
private knowledge of experience 129–30, 140, 159–76

private language 127–42
private ostensive definition 136–37, 177–95
private ownership of experience 129–30, 139, 143–57
psuchē 239
psychological attributes, bearer of 234–40

referential conception of language/linguistic meaning 17–34, 37–42
rule for use of a word 57–61
rules and truth 103–4, 296–97
Russell, Bertrand 1–2, 6, 26, 31, 82, 161
Ryle, Gilbert 5, 291–92

samples in ostensive explanations/definitions 83–85, 137, 184–85, 189–90
samples, mental 139, 183–92
Schlick, Moritz 3
science as source of metaphysics 272–73
scientism 273–79
secondary qualities 130–33
secondary uses of words 235, 237
sentence-meaning 20–21, 29–30, 49–51
Siamese twins 149
solidity 108
speaker's meaning: *see* meaning something
Strawson, Peter 4–5, 146, 285

table/dictionary/in the imagination 187–89
theory of mind 199–203
thought 113–25; and language 117–23; limits of 117; location of 124–25; organ of 123–25
Tractatus Logico-philosophicus 2–3, 6–7, 9–10, 82
truth 268–69
Turing, Alan 236–37

understanding 30–34, 61–68; and ability 65–69; new sentences 68
use: *see* meaning and use

Watson, J. 229
word meaning: *see* meaning of a word

www.ingramcontent.com/pod-product-compliance
Lightning Source LLC
Chambersburg PA
CBHW020331240426
43665CB00043B/217